Heresy and Authority in Medieval Europe

EDWARD PETERS

HERESY
AND
AUTHORITY
IN
MEDIEVAL
EUROPE

THE MIDDLE AGES

A SERIES EDITED BY EDWARD PETERS

Henry C. Lea Associate Professor of Medieval History
University of Pennsylvania

HERESY
AND
AUTHORITY
IN
MEDIEVAL
EUROPE

DOCUMENTS IN TRANSLATION

Edited,
with an Introduction, by
EDWARD PETERS

University of Pennsylvania Press
Philadelphia, 1980

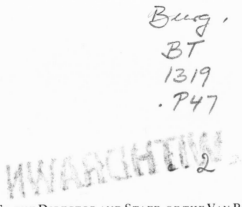

To the Director and Staff of the Van Pelt Library
University of Pennsylvania

. . . nullus enim in saltubus venatus iucundior . . .
(Erasmus, *Ep.* 182)

Copyright © 1980 by Edward Peters
All rights reserved
Printed in the United States of America

Library of Congress Cataloging in Publication Data
Peters, Edward, 1936-
    Heresy and authority in medieval Europe.

(The Middle Ages)
    Bibliography: p. 309
    1.   Heresies and heretics—Middle Ages, 600-1500.
2.   Sects, Medieval.   I.   Title.   II.   Series: Middle Ages.
BT1319.P47   273′.6   79-5262
ISBN 0-8122-7779-1
ISBN 0-8122-1103-0 (pbk.)

CONTENTS

[v]

INTRODUCTION:
HERESY AND AUTHORITY
IN MEDIEVAL EUROPE

The debates about the nature of Christian belief and the sources of legitimate authority in the Christian community that began to trouble the peace of the early churches two thousand years ago had both immediate and longer-lasting effects. From the epistles of St. Paul to the great age of church councils in the fifth and sixth centuries, the twin concepts of orthodoxy and heterodoxy were constituted as the third of the divisions that defined a true Christian, following the distinctions between Christianity and paganism on the one hand, and Christianity and Judaism on the other. The substance of Christian belief was articulated in apostolic and patristic literature, based upon an increasingly homogeneous scriptural canon and selected traditions, circulated widely, and finally, from the fourth century on, given juridical form by councils and prelates. Those against whom the early Fathers wrote and the early councils legislated were first described (as they are in the epistles of St. Paul) as factious, sectarian, and schismatic; that is, they were regarded as attempting to divide the indivisible community of the Church. From the second century on, they were increasingly described as heretics—that is, as people who *chose* (from the Greek word *hairesein*) a belief that the representatives of orthodox Christian communities defined as heterodox and therefore untenable by a true Christian.

St. Paul had written his letters to particular communities of Christians in the cities of the central and eastern Mediterranean world of the Roman Empire. Some of the earliest treatises against heterodoxy were written by individual laymen and clerics and supported by their personal authority as respected Christians. Sometimes, particular communities themselves were held up as models of Christian orthodoxy, as in the case of the community at Rome long before the bishop of Rome was acknowledged as an arbiter of orthodoxy both as an individual and as successor to St. Peter. From the fourth century on, however, the institutional and sociological circumstances of heterodoxy and orthodoxy changed. Christianity became the favored, and by the end of the century the only legal religion of the Roman Empire. Religious affairs acquired a civil, juridical dimension which they did not begin to lose in Europe until the seventeenth and eighteenth centuries. Thus, the experience of heterodox and orthodox beliefs created structures of authority and dissent that affected both spiritual and temporal life in all spheres of activity through the first thirteen centuries of European history. After the fourth century the heretic was at odds, not merely with a part of one of the Christian communities within the Roman Empire, but with the empire itself, conceived and self-proclaimed as a Christian community. An organized, articulated, hierarchical Church now defined orthodoxy in conciliar canons and papal decrees which were read and recognized throughout the Roman-Christian world. Civil sanctions were added to individual and institutional condemnations of particular heretics and heretical and schismatic movements. Even with the passing of the power of the Roman Empire in western Europe and the Mediterranean, the new Germanic kingdoms which succeeded it defined themselves as no less thoroughly Christian and regarded the societies they organized and ruled as bound by the same conceptions of heterodoxy and orthodoxy as had been those of the late empire. The Roman laws against heretics and schismatics were among the first Roman laws to be adopted by later European societies. The concepts of orthodoxy and heterodoxy constituted one of the many links between Mediterranean antiquity and the early medieval world that followed it.

If the problem of dissent and heresy initially preoccupied only the small, individual Church communities of the first and second centuries, after the fourth century it constituted a social problem on a wide scale. The later history of heresy, too, touches upon far more aspects of life than the question of theological affirmation or dissent. Although it is a part of religious history, heresy is a part of social history as well, for the Christian community, like other communities, lives in time. The very concepts of consensus, authority, tradition, and heterodoxy that were hammered out by heretics and churchmen from the first century on continued to influence ecclesiastical, social, and civil thought long after individual heretics and heretical movements had disappeared, the last heretics been reduced to ashes, and the doors of the Inquisitions finally locked or broken. Throughout the Middle Ages and early modern European history, theological uniformity was synonymous with social cohesion in societies that regarded themselves as bound together at their most fundamental levels by a religion. To maintain any belief in opposition to authoritative orthodoxy was not merely to set oneself in opposition to theologians and ecclesiastical officials and lawyers, as it might be in the pluralistic societies of the nineteenth or twentieth centuries, but in opposition to a whole culture in all of its manifestations.

It is no accident of historiography that successful dissenting movements—first during the Reformation of the sixteenth century, and later, in civil communities, during the struggles for toleration and political liberty in the seventeenth and eighteenth centuries—looked back to the heretics of the early Church and medieval Europe as the precursors of later ideas of freedom of conscience and civil liberty. Nor is it an accident of historical temperament that the history of heresy has only in the twentieth century managed to free itself from the confessional and ideological debates of the centuries until the nineteenth and claimed for itself a place with other kinds of study as a legitimate part of the history of both theology and society as a whole. The pathbreaking studies of Henry Charles Lea and Paul Fridéricq in the second half of the nineteenth century have found eloquent and profound successors in our own century. If the history of heresy is no longer a particularly nasty weapon in confessional or ideological conflict, it is something much more useful—a legitimate and disciplined means of understanding the behavior and beliefs of human beings in time, or at least some of the most important and widest-ranging aspects of behavior and belief, and some of the most complex and interesting of those human beings.

From the seventh to the eleventh centuries in western Europe, the structure of society and the primarily monastic character of religious culture did not foster widespread dissenting beliefs with a popular, lay base, nor did it allow for the range of intellectual inquiry that later led to the growth of intellectual, philosophical heresy. From the eleventh century to the fifteenth, however, dissenting movements appeared with greater frequency, attracted more followers, acquired philosophical as well as theological dimensions, and occupied more and more the time and the mind of ecclesiastical and civil authority. In the perception of dissent during this period, in the steps taken to deal with it, in the sources of dissenting beliefs, and in the culture of dissenters and orthodox alike lies the history of medieval heresy and the force it exerted on religious, social, and political communities long after the Middle Ages.

The history of medieval heresy and its place in early European society and culture is still being written, and this book is not the place to sum it up or add to it. The running bibliography in the introductions to chapters and the notes on individual texts will provide clear indications to most of it. Nor does this book present much argument for or against any of the contending theories that the historical literature has produced. Medieval heresies differed one from another in different periods and places, and any focus, in as general and purely pedagogical a book as this, must be upon the concept of heresy as orthodox authority defined it and acted upon it. As Christine Thouzellier, one of the best modern historians of heresy, has said:

> For the medieval period . . . in western Europe, the definition of a heretic may only be posed in terms of its function in Christianity and in revelation, according to the formula of Isidore [of Seville, below, no. 7]: "Heretics [are] those who have withdrawn from the Church." One is a heretic who criticizes or refuses to accept Christian dogmas and rejects the teaching authority of the Roman Church, which one had recognized before. This is the definition of medieval heresiologists, for whom the Jew and the Moslem are not heretics. The heretic is neither abnormal nor neurotic: he is rather a man seeking after the truth, and whom, always in the view of Christianity, the dogmas of revealed truths no longer satisfy. He may be led to his condition by personal considerations of a metaphysical order, or by social signs which lead him to perceive, in a society constituted as Christian, certain anomalies and deviations which no longer correspond to its initial purpose.

This general categorization indeed fits the broadest definition given by a medieval heresiologist, in this case Robert Grosseteste, chancellor of Oxford University and bishop of Lincoln, who stated early in the thirteenth century: "Heresy is an opinion chosen by human faculties, contrary to holy Scripture, openly taught, and pertinaciously defended. *Haeresis* in Greek, *electio* [choice] in Latin."

By Grosseteste's day, Christian Europe had witnessed two centuries of new forms of dissenting beliefs and had drawn heavily upon the experience of the early Church to conceptualize and define them. The variety of dissenting opinions and the specific contents of heretical beliefs mattered less than the fact that they *were* heresies. How these various forms of dissent were as-similated to a concept of heresy is one of the themes in medieval history and one of the primary themes of this book.

In offering a series of original source materials in translation, a process which may be in itself, if not carefully controlled, a way of making historical judgments, I have been guided by Grosseteste's and Thouzellier's broad definitions. Working on the principle that one legitimate focus of the study of heresy is the point of view of church authorities, I have been able to include scholarly, or "intellectual," heresies, as well as heretical movements with a largely popular following, and movements within the relatively restricted confines of individual religious orders, such as the Spiritual Franciscans (below, nos. 50-54). There are, to be sure, other ways of looking at the history of heresy, but this approach has the advantage of permitting the widest range of documents that nevertheless have a connecting theme—Grosseteste's defini-tion.

The organization of the book clearly indicates that its focus is the period between the tenth and the fifteenth centuries in western Europe. Although during that period a new European society faced the problem of religious dissent differently from the way early churchmen had, its representatives drew heavily upon apostolic and patristic literature in describing the dissidents of their own day; thus some knowledge of the early history of heresy and Christianity is essential for understanding the approach of the later period. The first chapter, therefore, attempts to show how the terms *schism, heresy, heterodoxy,* and *orthodoxy* took shape in the Christian vocabulary and how they came to be applied in religious controversies. Further, certain early heresies seemed to later churchmen so similar to the dissent they themselves faced that they borrowed the early names to label contemporaries. Of these, Manichaeism and Arianism were clearly the most popular. One of the most distinctive features of historical Christianity is its juridical character; the problem of coercion entered ecclesiastical society in the fourth century, when the Roman Empire became officially Christian. St. Isidore of Seville was the author of perhaps the most widely used reference book of the early and central Middle Ages, and Isidore's definition of heresy was widely quoted and was perhaps as familiar to later churchmen as any other. In the monastic atmos-phere of the early Middle Ages, the movement of Adoptionism seemed to be a useful example of the shift from the early to the later Church. These have been the guiding principles for the highly selective first chapter.

The second chapter deals with the wide variety of forms of dissent that emerged in the century and a half between 1000 and 1145. This period has received the greatest attention from recent scholars, and the reactions it inspired in churchmen played an important role in the twelfth-century Church's concept and definition of heresy. The chapter concludes with St. Bernard's Sermon on *The Song of Songs* of 1144, the most comprehensive statement on the rise of heterodox opinion by the most influential churchman of the early twelfth century.

The most prominent ecclesiastical response to dissent in this period was to assume that the heretics of the twelfth century were descendants of what St. Bernard and others called "the heretics of old," that is, the makers and holders of unorthodox opinions who vexed the Church in the period between the first and sixth centuries. In the earlier period, the energies and writings of many churchmen had been devoted to defining and condemning heterodoxy and, in the process, shaping orthodox dogma. This large literature of heresiology was known to later churchmen, such as St. Bernard, and from it he and others drew their ammunition against the new heretics.

Several scholars, notably Jeffrey Russell, have warned that popular heretical movements may have started as early as the ninth century and that we must not be misled by the scarcity of sources into making fundamental judgments about the appearance of popular heresies in the eleventh century. Russell's words are backed by the extensive character of his learning and the sharpness of his judgment. Faced with a choice, however, I have decided to begin the book's focus with the eleventh century, because from it can be traced the progressive awareness on the part of churchmen of religious dissent, which peaks first in St. Bernard's Sermon on *The Song of Songs* of 1144 (below, no. 16), then in the encounter with Catharism and Waldensianism (below, chaps. III and IV), and finally in the institutionalizing of means of detecting and dealing with heresy (below, chaps. V and VI).

The third chapter deals with the greatest heresy of the twelfth and thirteenth centuries, Cathar dualism, which St. Bernard encountered toward the end of his life, and which was left to others to investigate more thoroughly. Twelfth- and thirteenth-century churchmen recognized the wide divergence of Cathar doctrine from orthodox Christianity, and they also shaped characteristic forms of dealing with it (and with all heresies).

Chapter IV deals with the Waldensian movement, one whose theology was far closer to orthodox Christianity than that of the Cathars, but whose anti-ecclesiastical fervor and durability made it a threat to orthodox belief long after Catharism had disappeared. Catharism and Waldensianism may be considered the archetypal heretical movements of the Middle Ages.

The Church followed two roads in dealing with heterodoxy. The first may be called the way of *caritas*, which urged penitence, reform, preaching, exhortation, propaganda, and instruction in converting heretics and maintaining the faithful in their faith. Chapter V gives some exemplary texts on the way of *caritas*. Chapter VI deals with the way of *potestas*, the use of legal coercion against the heretics and their supporters. Although the best-known manifestations of ecclesiastical *potestas* are the Albigensian Crusade of 1208-29 and the Inquisition, there were manifestations in temporal law codes as well, and these are illustrated by documents from Sicily, France, and England.

Chapter VII deals with the growth of intellectual heterodoxy among the learned classes of thirteenth- and fourteenth-century Europe, and chapters VIII, IX, and X deal with various movements of popular and learned reform spirituality that ran afoul of ecclesiastical authority in the fourteenth and fifteenth centuries.

In any book of this scope and size, covering, as this one does, nearly fifteen hundred years of complex history and doctrine, there are bound to be omissions of individual texts and whole movements that bring the reader's interests into conflict with the editor's. Those who find their own favorite heresies or texts omitted may take some consolation in the fact that the editor has had to leave out many of his own. In some cases I have deliberately left out whole movements, partly because adequate materials already exist in translation, and partly because to include anything from them would necessitate including a great deal, and therefore omitting other texts. The treatment of the early Christian Church and the Byzantine Church is obviously not comprehensive, but selective. So is the material on Adoptionism from the late eighth century, which could have been added to by including materials on Iconoclasm, the eucharistic controversy, and the works of Gottschalk and John the Scot. The rather greater selectivity of the first chapter was necessitated by the focus of the book on the period between 1000 and 1415.

From the eleventh century on, the problem of the number and variety of sources becomes much greater than it had been for the period between the sixth and eleventh centuries. There are many more texts for the eleventh and twelfth centuries that I might have included, but I have striven for economy of focus as well as space, and the movements cited are illustrative, if not comprehensive. Other sources in translation may be found in the works cited in the bibliography at the end of this introduction and in the bibliographic notes within the chapters themselves. For the Cathars and Waldensians, the problem is similar, and so is the solution. I have given disproportionately more space to the Church's opposition to heresy outside of legal and physical coercion than many books do, but it is my impression that this aspect is probably the least often considered by historians, who are often all too eager to get on to the Inquisition, the fagot, and the stake. There is, conversely, somewhat less material here on the coercive steps taken against heresy in the thirteenth, fourteenth, and fifteenth centuries, although the major steps in the process are adequately illustrated.

By the fourteenth and fifteenth centuries, the literature becomes overwhelming, and I have been most selective here. The topics of the Spiritual Franciscans, the popular rural heresies of southern France, Wyclif, the Lollards, and the case of John Hus are both the minimum and the maximum such a book allows. Their selection does, however, maintain the themes of representation and the general concept and definition of heresy that guide the rest of the book. Finally, there is much more to intellectual dissent and to ecclesiology than the space given to intellectual errors, on the one hand, and to John of Brevicoxa, on the other, indicates.

The locations of all the texts in this book are listed in numbered sequence in the Sources and Acknowledgments at the end. When no translation is acknowledged, the translation is the work of the editor.

I have made this book, as I have made others, so that students, teachers, and general readers may have a convenient, if not comprehensive, collection of representative, well-translated original documents with which to work, arranged coherently and deliberately, but not ideologically, argumentatively, or least of all confessionally. In making it I have been greatly helped by the staff of the University of Pennsylvania Press, especially Robert Erwin and John McGuigan, who have read intelligently through two other, much longer, versions of this book. I have also been greatly assisted by the Van Pelt Library of the University of Pennsylvania, to the director and staff of which, particularly on the sixth floor, this book, routine as it may be, is dedicated. From the outset of my work I have had the encouragement and advice of Professor Charles T. Davis of Tulane University, and in its later stages that of Professor Jeffrey B. Russell of the University of California, Santa Barbara. Their advice has been immensely helpful, even when I may not have been able to follow it as much as I—and they—might have liked. I gratefully acknowledge the generosity of Mr. Burton Van Name Edwards and Mr. Steven Sargent of the University of Pennsylvania for permission to print their translations of, respectively, Alcuin on Adoptionism and the material from the Register of Jacques Fournier. Professor Erika Laquer Wood of the College of Wooster has given much good advice and sharp comment. Professor James M. Muldoon of Rutgers University, Camden, has very generously read most of my translations from Latin and corrected them. None of these scholars, however, shares with me the responsibility for any lapses of scholarship or language that survive after their scrutiny. I also happily acknowledge the help of Dr. Joseph and Professor Nancy Ruane.

EDWARD PETERS
Philadelphia, 1980

Bibliography of Sources in Translation

SERIES

The Ante-Nicene Christian Library. Edinburgh, 1868-70.
A Select Library of Nicene and Post-Nicene Fathers. New York, 1886-90.
The Fathers of the Church. New York, 1947-73.
The Library of Christian Classics. Philadelphia, 1953-66.

INDIVIDUAL COLLECTIONS: THE EARLY CHURCH

B.J. Kidd. *Documents Illustrative of the History of the Church, to 461 A.D.* 2 vols. London, 1920, 1923.
J. Stevenson. *A New Eusebius.* London, 1957.
E. Giles. *Documents Illustrating Papal Authority, A.D. 96-454.* London, 1952.
P. R. Coleman-Norton. *Roman State and Christian Church.* 3 vols. London, 1966.
Colman J. Barry. *Readings in Church History,* vol. 1. Westminster, Md., 1966.
Henry Bettenson. *Documents of the Christian Church.* Oxford, 1963.

INDIVIDUAL COLLECTIONS: THE EARLY MIDDLE AGES

Cyril Mango. *The Art of the Byzantine Empire, 312-1453*. Englewood Cliffs, N.J., 1972.

J. N. Hillgarth. *The Conversion of Western Europe, 350-750*. Englewood Cliffs, N.J., 1969.

E. Peters. *Monks, Bishops, and Pagans*. Philadelphia, 1975.

Charles Brand. *Icon and Minaret*. Englewood Cliffs, N.J., 1969.

Stewart C. Easton and Helène Wieruszowski. *The Era of Charlemagne*. Princeton, N.J., 1961.

George E. McCracken and Allen Cabaniss. *Early Medieval Theology*. Library of Christian Classics, vol. 9. Philadelphia, 1957. Cited here because of its importance for a very badly documented period.

A. Bryer. and J. Herrin eds. *Iconoclasm*. Birmingham, 1977.

INDIVIDUAL COLLECTIONS: THE HIGH MIDDLE AGES

R. I. Moore. *The Birth of Popular Heresy*. New York, 1976.

Jeffrey Burton Russell. *Religious Dissent in the Middle Ages*. New York, 1971.

Walter Wakefield and Austin P. Evans. *Heresies of the High Middle Ages*. New York, 1969.

Ailbe J. Luddy. *The Case of Peter Abelard*. Dublin, 1947.

INDIVIDUAL COLLECTIONS: THE LATE MIDDLE AGES

C. M. D. Crowder. *Unity, Heresy and Reform, 1378-1460*. New York, 1977.

A. R. Myers. *English Historical Documents, 1327-1485*. London, 1969.

Matthew Spinka. *Advocates of Reform: From Wyclif to Erasmus*. The Library of Christian Classics, vol. 14: Philadelphia, 1953.

Matthew Spinka. *John Hus at the Council of Constance*. New York, 1965.

Heiko Augustinus Oberman. *Forerunners of the Reformation: The Shape of Late Medieval Thought*. New York, 1966.

L. R. Loomis; J. H. Mundy; and K. M. Woody. *The Council of Constance: The Unification of the Church*. New York, 1961.

GENERAL COLLECTIONS WITH SOME DOCUMENTS ON HERESY

Brian Pullan. *Sources for the History of Medieval Europe*. New York, 1966.

James Bruce, Ross and Mary Martin McLaughlin. *The Portable Medieval Reader*. New York, 1949.

Henry J. Schroeder. *The Disciplinary Decrees of the General Councils*. St. Louis, 1937.

G. G. Coulton. *Life in the Middle Ages.* vols. 1 and 2. Cambridge, 1967.

Marshall W. Baldwin. *Christianity Through the Thirteenth Century.* New York, 1970.

Roland H. Bainton. *The Medieval Church.* Princeton, 1962.

MEDIEVAL SOURCE MATERIALS IN TRANSLATION

C. P. Farrar. and Austin P. Evans. *Bibliography of English Translations from Medieval Sources.* New York, 1946. Brought up to 1968 by the following work:

M. A. Ferguson. *Bibliography of English Translations from Medieval Sources, 1944-1968.* New York, 1973.

SCHOLARLY STUDIES INDICATED BY SHORTENED TITLES IN THE TEXT

R. I. Moore. *The Origins of European Dissent.* New York, 1977.

Malcolm Lambert. *Medieval Heresy.* New York, 1977.

Jeffrey Burton Russell. *Dissent and Reform in the Early Middle Ages.* Berkeley and Los Angeles, 1965.

James Fearns. *Ketzer und Ketzerbekämpfung im Hochmittelalter.* Göttingen, 1968. A very useful collection of Latin texts on the history of heresy in the central Middle Ages.

I

"THE HERETICS OF OLD": THE DEFINITION OF ORTHODOXY AND HERESY IN LATE ANTIQUITY AND THE EARLY MIDDLE AGES

The first Christian communities grew up in the Jewish and pagan worlds of the first century. By the second century they had defined themselves as spiritually separate from both. But the process of separation was never as complete as the Christians thought; many conscious and unconscious bonds still tied them to the thought world of late antiquity, as the presence and character of conflicting beliefs within the Christian communities clearly demonstrated. From the letters of St. Paul to the formal heresiological treatises of the second and third centuries, Christian writers claiming the authority of orthodoxy—"right" teaching or belief—warned their fellow Christians that there existed right and wrong beliefs concerning Christ and his teachings. Many of them argued at first that the wrong beliefs had come from an imperfect separation from Judaism on the one hand, or exposure to the influence of pagan philosophy on the other. To St. Paul, for example, the Corinthians faced the danger of accepting "another Jesus," another spirit, a different gospel (2 Cor. 11:4); he warned the Galatians against different, distorted gospels (Gal. 1:6). The lively spiritual world of the first century, as reflected in Paul's Epistles and the Acts of the Apostles, offered many opportunities for the distortion or displacement of what Paul considered the single authentic message of Christ. St. Paul's argument for a single Christian truth gave the character of heterodoxy ("erroneous" teaching) to all other competing beliefs. On the basis of his experience with competing beliefs within different Christian communities, St. Paul coined the terms in which all such later conflicts were to be understood and acted upon.

Heresy did and does not exist in and of itself, but only in relation to orthodoxy. Orthodoxy cannot exist in turn without authority, and it is the quality of authority in orthodoxy that defines and denounces heresy. In a narrower and specifically historical sense, the heresies dealt with in this book are any beliefs concerning the nature of Christian truth or the character of the Church that churchmen, in the name of orthodoxy, authoritatively condemned. From its first appearance in the New Testament, the term *hairesis* and its cognate term *schisma*, schism, illustrate the Christian use of terminology familiar to the pagan world, but given a new meaning in a wholly new context. The Greek word *hairesein* originally meant simply "to take," but its frequent occurrence in discussions of competing philosophical schools in a pluralisic intellectual culture soon gave it the more specific meaning of "choice," and later the still narrower meaning of a "choice" among different schools and movements of philosophy. In these senses, there was nothing pejorative about the word, particularly since there existed no philosophical school that made universal claims to a monopoly of truth. The plurality of social bonds in the ancient world easily accommodated a diversity of intellectual groups, just as it accommodated different ethnic, linguistic, and religious groups.

Jewish writers in the Greek-speaking Hellenistic world used the substantive *hairesis* in much the same way as the pagan Greeks did. The plural form *haireseis* designated different groups, or sects, within the Jewish community. In the Latin of Cicero and other Roman writers the Greek *hairesis* became the Latin *haeresis*, and it retained its meaning of "choice" among different philosophical movements.

Hairesis/haeresis, then, was a perfectly commonplace term used in a nonpejorative sense by Greeks, Jews, and Romans alike; in some pagan circles it continued to be used in this sense until after the first century A.D. Among Jews and Christians, however, the term began to acquire an exclusively pejorative sense, perhaps via the changing meaning of its Hebrew cognates, surely by the powerful Judaeo-Christian conviction that in the realm of certain beliefs there *was* no option for plurality of opinion, that Judaism and Christianity were *not* simply competing philosophical-religious movements like Epicureanism or Stoicism, that those who held beliefs that the community or its leaders found objectionable were not exercising permissible free choice in an intellectually or spiritually pluralistic society, but attacking God and dividing the indivisible community of believers.

Whatever caused the diversity of beliefs in the Jewish and Christian communities that are recorded in the Acts of the Apostles and the Epistles of St. Paul, it is clear that to the writers of these books it was a serious matter. Indeed, in one of the best-known Pauline texts dealing with the diversity of sects and beliefs in the early Church (1 Cor. 11:18-19) St. Paul says: "For I hear that when you meet in church there are divisions [*schismata*] among you, and in part I believe it. For there must be factions [*haireseis*] so that those who are approved may be made known among you." The Epistle to Titus is somewhat harsher: "The factious man [*hereticum hominem* in the Latin Vulgate] after the first and second correction, avoid, knowing that he is perverted and sinful and condemned by his own judgment" (Titus 3:10-11). It seems safe to say that for St. Paul, *hairesis* and *schisma* had the meaning of "discordant," rather than "theologically deviant." The concord of the communities of the early Church was always a major theme in Acts and Epistles, and schism and heresy probably were denounced because they were divisive rather than, in the modern sense, subversive.

To a certain extent, the discord that Paul perceived in the early churches derived from his general view of human nature, as expressed in Gal. 5:20:

> Anyone can see that kind of conduct that belongs to the lower nature of humans: fornications, impurity, and indecency; idolatry and sorcery; quarrels, contentious temper, envy, fits of rage, selfish ambitions, dissensions, sectarianism, and jealousies; drinking bouts, orgies, and the like. I warn you, as I have warned you before, that those who behave in such a manner will never inherit the kingdom of God.

This view, held by Paul and others, of the natural propensity of fallen human nature was supported by their vision of human history; the linking of contemporary sectarians with false prophets in Hebrew history in 2 Pet. 2:1-9 is an example:

> But Israel had false prophets as well as true; and you likewise will have false teachers among you. They will import disastrous heresies, disowning the very Master who bought them and bringing swift disaster upon their own heads. They will gain many adherents to

their dissolute practices, through whom the true way will be brought into disrepute. In their greed for money they will trade on your credulity with sheer fabrications. But the judgment long decreed for them has not been idle; perdition awaits them with unsleeping eyes.

Discordant teaching had thus existed in the past as it does in the present, and indeed, as Paul reiterates, as it will in the future. It is the product of debilitated, not searching, minds, a sign of decadence, not creativity:

This is what you are to teach and preach. If anyone is teaching otherwise and will not give his mind to wholesome precepts—I mean those of our Lord Jesus Christ—and to good religious teaching, I call him a pompous ignoramus. He is morbidly fascinated with mere verbal questions and quibbles, which give rise to jealousy, wrangling, slander, base suspicions, and endless quarreling. All these are typical of men who have let their reasoning powers become atrophied and have lost their grip of truth. [1 Tim. 6:3-5]

The attraction exerted by new and initially exciting teachings is a constant theme of Pauline Christianity, based no doubt on Paul's own experiences of new communities' fascination with holy men possessing ostensibly legitimate credentials and a dynamic manner of teaching:

For the time will come when they will not stand wholesome teaching, but will follow their own fancy and gather a crowd of teachers to tickle their ears. They will stop their ears to the truth and turn to mythology. But you yourself must keep calm and sane always; face hardship, work to spread the gospel, and do all the duties of your calling. [2 Tim. 4:3-4]

The letters to Titus and Timothy, written to men who were expected to lead local churches, are particularly revealing, then, because these disciples are warned of what to expect in the way of human nature and the insidious attractiveness of discordant teachings. Thus, in the earliest documents of Christian history, discord, the conflicts generated by fallen human nature, and the unceasing expectation of false prophets and teachers combine to create the earliest semantic framework of orthodoxy and dissent.

The earliest Christian communities placed great emphasis upon their internal solidarity and, by extension, upon the uniformity of practice and solidarity of belief among all Christians scattered in communities throughout the Greco-Roman world. As Henry Chadwick has described it: "The unity of the scattered Christian communities depended upon two things—on a common faith and on a common way of ordering their life and worship. They called each other 'brother' or 'sister.' Whatever differences there might be of race, class, or education, they felt bound to each other by their focus of loyalty to the person and teaching of Jesus." Chadwick's use of the word "loyalty" is appropriate because it was loyalty rather than a well-defined body of specific beliefs that marked out the early Christians' attitudes to each other and to the person and teaching of Jesus. But loyalty alone was hard put to withstand the persuasive and varied intellectual and spiritual world of late antiquity. Even the words of the Greek and Latin scriptures could be—and were—terms with a long spiritual and intellectual history behind them. More terms than *hairesis* traced their history deep into the controversies and philosophical vocabularies of pagan antiquity. As Chadwick goes on to say: "The missionaries to the Gentile world were not speaking in a vacuum to people without existing prejudices and expectations. The moment they passed outside the ambit of the synagogues of the Jewish dispersion and their loosely attached Gentile adherents, the missionaries were in a twilight world of pagan syncretism, magic, and astrology." Even in a "twilight world" such as that of late antiquity, as Peter Brown and others have shown, there were powerful influences at work, and many of even the best-intentioned Christians found themselves in the grip of powerful forces. And to some of these, St. Paul wrote his letters: the Corinthians, the Colossians, the Galatians, Titus and Timothy.

Later writers hint at a new meaning of *haeresis*. *Schisma* appears to have retained its old meaning of division, party, or faction without specific doctrinal basis for the break. *Haeresis*, however, gradually acquired the meaning of a specific doctrine that was counter to Christian truth; that is, from the second century at least, *haeresis* began its modern career.

Upon what was Christian truth based? First, as the writings of St. Paul and other Church Fathers make clear, it was based upon scripture. Scripture contained God's communication to humanity, a divinely inspired account of sacred history, and the whole corpus of belief and law that molded the Christian life and regulated the Christian community. Before the fourth century, however, there was no universally accepted canonical body of scripture, and a wide variety of different sorts of texts might claim to be authentic. Both orthodox and heterodox thinkers cited scripture to prove their points, but not, as in post-fourth-century disputes, always the same body of scripture. The canon of scripture and then the interpretation of this canon were matters of great importance to Christian thinkers at all points on the spectrum of religious opinion.

In the fifth century, St. Vincent of Lerins emphasized the scriptural basis of both orthodox and heterodox uses of scripture:

> Do the heretics also make use of the testimonies of holy scripture? Indeed they do, and to a great degree. They go through each and every book of the Bible: Moses and the Books of Kings, the Psalms, the Apostles, the Gospels, the Prophets. They utter almost nothing of their own that they do not try to support with passages from the scripture—whether they are among their own disciples or among strangers, in private or in public, whether in sermons or in writings, in private meetings or in forums.

Heretics, too, claimed to bear the authentic message of Christianity, and, like orthodox churchmen, they necessarily turned to scripture in order to justify their own beliefs and condemn the beliefs of the orthodox.

Scripture itself, therefore, very early became prominent in the definition of orthodoxy and heterodoxy. Before the establishment of the orthodox canon of the Old and New Testaments at the Council of Carthage in 397, many texts after that date regarded as apocryphal were cited with the same authority as the later canonical books. In addition to an uncertain scriptural canon, there emerged a number of different ways of interpreting scripture. Not only did early Christian thinkers have to take into account the literal meaning of the texts, but they had to deal with a group of figurative means of interpreting scripture which derived from Hellenistic techniques of literary and philosophical analysis, especially as these had been applied to scripture by Philo of Alexandria, the great Jewish biblicist of the first century A.D. and developed in the Alexandrian Christian community by Origen (185-254), the most profound and widest-ranging of the early Christian biblical scholars. Thus, for the churchmen of late antiquity and the Middle Ages, scripture was a vast storehouse of information and instruction, and even changing styles of biblical interpretation did not reduce that store. In order to understand both heretics and their opponents, it is necessary to recognize that both parties continually resorted to scripture, and that the power of scripture extended down through the sixteenth century and beyond.

After scripture itself, the most authoritative element in the early Church was tradition—in Greek, *paradosis*. As the small Christian communities of the Near East began to grow, and as Christian communities emerged in other parts of the Roman Empire, scripture and tradition together slowly identified a common set of beliefs which came to be regarded as binding on the individual Christian and the community. Some elements of tradition had been transmitted orally, although with many variations, from the earliest days of Christianity. As R. P. C. Hanson has said, "Nobody who has read the literature of the Christian Church in the first two centuries can avoid the conclusion that eminent Christian writers, whose minds were certainly not formed in the critical mold which has shaped the minds of modern scholars, very readily attributed to apostolic tradition any custom or rite or tradition which they could not find directly referred to in the Bible and which they thought to be older than living memory." Other elements may be traced in the texts of the earliest Christian creeds, or statements of belief, some of which grew out of controversies within the Christian community and others of which developed out of such routine occasions as catechetical teaching, the baptismal ceremony, preaching and letter-writing, certain parts of the liturgy, the disputes with heretics and pagans, and the rite of exorcism. In addition to the various forms of the early creed, the rule of faith (*regula fidei*), which varied from writer to writer but everywhere shows general similarities, contained accounts of the Church's teaching. Finally, the continuity of customs and rites and the establishment of the scriptural canon at the Council of Carthage in 397 further contributed to the creation of a set of orthodox beliefs, assent to which was essential for membership in the Christian community.

During the course of the fourth and fifth centuries, individual creeds and rules of faith began to give way to creeds established by ecclesiastical leaders for the whole Christian community, promulgated in ecumenical church councils and often used as proof-texts for determining the orthodoxy of any individual's Christian beliefs. St. Irenaeus (130-200) and St. Cyprian (d. 258) were among the most influential writers who dealt with the necessary universality of belief and fundamental unity of the whole Church. By the middle of the fifth century, St. Vincent of Lerins (d. 450) produced in his *Commonitorium* one of the most influential definitions of true tradition that the Church ever witnessed. The "Vincentian Canon" defined true Christian belief as "that which has been believed everywhere, always, and by everyone." With the writing of Vincent's *Commonitorium*, the great fifth-century church councils, and the influential pontificates of such fifth-century churchmen as Pope Leo I (d. 461), scripture, tradition, and ecclesiastical authority had shaped a body of Christian doctrine and necessary beliefs that may be said to have constituted the foundations of orthodoxy until the Reformation of the sixteenth century and, in many instances, even beyond the sixteenth century. Against this orthodoxy could be tested any beliefs, and any beliefs that failed such a test could readily and universally be branded as heretical, or at least heterodox. To understand the course and development of heterodox beliefs, the nature of orthodoxy itself must be understood first.

Among the hundreds of scriptural citations upon which early Christians based their ideas of ecclesiastical unity, order, and authority, none is more direct than the text in John 10:17: "There will be one flock and one shepherd." Two other texts, both from the Gospel of St. Matthew, articulate the command of Christian unity in terms of apostolic authority:

> Jesus asked the apostles, "And you, who do you say that I am?" Simon Peter answered, "You are the Messiah, the Son of the Living God." Jesus said: "Simon, son of Jonah, you are indeed blessed, for flesh and blood have not revealed this to you, but my Father. And I say to you that you are Peter, and upon this rock I will build my church, and the powers of hell will not conquer it. I will give you the keys of the Kingdom of Heaven. And whatever you bind on earth will be bound in heaven, and whatever you shall loose on earth shall be loosed in heaven." [Matt. 16:15-19]

> The eleven disciples went to Galilee, to the mountain where Jesus had told them to meet him. When they saw him, they fell prostrate before him, although some still doubted. Jesus then came up to them and spoke to them. He said: "Full authority in heaven and on earth has been committed to me. Go forth therefore, and make disciples of all nations, baptizing them in the name of the Father, the Son, and the Holy Spirit, and teach them to observe all that I have commanded you. And know that I am with you all days, even to the end of the world." [Matt. 28:16-20]

In the eyes of early Christians, therefore, besides the loyalty to Jesus' person and teachings, there was an implicit recognition, dating from the earliest scriptures themselves, that authority in the Christian community was given by Jesus to the apostles, especially, according to some, to Sts. Peter and Paul. The teachings of the apostles, whether in works that were later admitted to the scriptural canon or those declared apocryphal, thus were cited as establishing tradition and justifying ecclesiastical opinions.

Besides the canonization of scriptural books and the insistence upon apostolic authority, writers after the mid-second century produced "Rules of Faith," statements of belief that later evolved into formal creeds. Especially in the fourth and fifth centuries, credal statements were designed specifically to refute one or another heretical opinion. Scripture, apostolic tradition, and statements of the content of faith were thus the earliest, and among the strongest, weapons forged against heresy. By the fourth and fifth centuries, heresy loomed as far more dangerous than simple dissension within local communities, and these principles were invoked again and again to counter the spread of deviant belief. They became the foundations of the Church's *magisterium*, its authority to define orthodox belief and to condemn deviations from it.

By the second century, tradition and authority required a certain kind of life from the believer. This life was to be guided by a rule, a *kanon*. The term *kanon* derived from the Greek word for a carpenter's rule or straight-edge. The *kanon* of the Christian life came to be considered as the determinant of attitudes toward religion and belief, while the more familiar creed, which probably grew out of the rules of faith, is a guide to the specific content of beliefs. Although there were a variety of creeds produced during the fourth and the fifth centuries, some have survived more popularly than others. One of the most influential, for example, is the creed promulgated by the Council of Nicaea in 325 and repromulgated with some modifications at the Council of Constantinople in 381, the "Nicene" Creed (no. 5). One of the earliest creeds is that of Rufinus of Aquileia, written about 404 A.D.:

> I believe in God the Father almighty
> and in Jesus Christ, His only son, our Lord,
> who was born of the Holy Spirit and Mary the Virgin
> who was crucified under Pontius Pilate and buried,
> and on the third day rose again from the dead,
> and ascended into the heavens,
> and sits at the right hand of the Father,
> from whence He will come to judge the living and dead;
> and [I believe] in the Holy Spirit,
> the holy Church,
> the remission of sins,
> and the resurrection of the flesh.

This creed, an early form of the "Apostles' Creed," as well as the Creed of Nicaea-Constantinople and the "Athanasian" Creed, reflects older Christian traditions as well as addressing some of the troublesome questions raised by dissenters in the fourth century.

The sense of unity and the indivisibility of orthodox belief was contrasted by St. Vincent of Lerins in the fifth century with the heretic's isolation, pride, restlessness, fickleness, and intellectual dependence upon uncanonical sources. In the second-century writings of Tertullian, St. Irenaeus, and others, a psychology of the heretic began to emerge: the heretic was a certain *kind* of person, not merely an honest, if misled, dissenter. Against the *consensus ecclesiae*, the common opinion of the Church, the heretic proudly posited a personal vision which threatened ecclesiastical unity, wholly ignoring scripture, tradition, and creed.

The individual heretic was at first answered by individuals—St. Paul, Tertullian, St. Irenaeus, St. Cyprian, and Hippolytus—but by individuals whose personal prestige permitted them to speak informally for the whole Christian community. But the age of individual dissent and individual response on behalf of orthodoxy ended in the fourth century. Henri Marrou has spoken most succinctly of the "new religiosity,"

> a spiritual revolution of which the Mediterranean world had been the center during the first centuries of our era (and which we may consider as having been fully accomplished by the end of the fourth century); once again—as in the period of the ancient city and primitive paganism, and in opposition to the relatively profaning character of the hellenistic period—religion, the problem of the relationship between man and the divinity, appeared as a central preoccupation, a *raison d'etre*, the axis of human life. At the same time . . . the notion of "religion" was itself transformed. It now defined itself as a collection of beliefs consisting of the idea that one has of God and of the cult which one must render to God, which introduces the essential notion of *the Church:* the community of believers assembled in a *consensus* confessing the same orthodox faith.
>
> This type of community appeared to the people of this period as the highest, the most normal form of human community. It resulted in an intimate interpenetration, a fusion of the religious and the national or the social community, to speak briefly, a fusion of the Church and the Nation or the State. And with good reason: if one places the religious problem at the center of existence, from the moment when people are in accord with one another over essential beliefs it is the community that is welded together. On the other hand, if the heretic rejects orthodoxy, how could he possibly later make peace with those whose communion he has once rejected?
>
> The tendency to base all political and social unity upon religious unity characterizes all the societies of late antiquity and the early Middle Ages.

Four statements between the second and the sixth centuries illustrate the developing concept of ecclesiastical authority and unity based both on scripture and on the historical experience of the Christian communities. These expressions of the ideal by St. Irenaeus, Tertullian (no. 1), St. Cyprian of Carthage, and St. Vincent of Lerins suggest the direction of early patristic thought and the sources of early Christian thinkers' ideas of tradition and authority.

The growth of a specific concept of ecclesiastical authority to represent the *consensus ecclesiae* paralleled the development of a number of particular spiritual movements which caused great concern on the part of communities and community spokesmen alike. The earliest of these heresies was Gnosticism, elements of which probably antedated Christianity, but which took on its fullest form by applying a series of theosophical tenets to Christian cosmology. Gnosticism took on many forms and shared many aspects of other heretical movements, and it manifested itself differently in the work of different leaders. It elicited the first great work of Christian theology, St. Irenaeus's *Against All Heresies*, which depicts Gnostic cosmology and also portrays one of the archetypal figures in the history of heresy, that of the heresiarch, the great individual leader of a heretical movement, in this case the infamous Simon Magus.

Other heretical beliefs focused upon the person of Jesus and the relationship between the Father and the Son. Thus, for example, Docetism taught that the human body of Christ was merely an illusion and that the passion and resurrection were illusory as well. Veering in the opposite direction, Sabellianism (or Patripassianism, as it was known in the West), identified the Father and Son so closely that it claimed that the Father suffered the passion. Other movements emphasized still other aspects of the relationship. Related to Sabellianism, Dynamic Monarchianism held that Jesus was a superior human being "adopted" by the preexistent Christ and infused with divine powers. Dynamic, or Adoptionist, Monarchianism was also related to certain sects of Jewish Christians known as Ebionites, and it formed a kind of prototype for later heresies that had an Adoptionist tendency, notably Nestorianism, the eighth-century Spanish Adoptionist movement (no. 8), and the slightly earlier Armenian-Byzantine Paulician movement. Modal Monarchians, on the other hand, argued that the difference between the Father and Jesus lay primarily in the "modes" or manifestations in which the divine spirit operated.

In the second century also, Montanism opened the question of continuing revelation. Montanus of Phrygia began to prophesy that the Holy Spirit was about to descend upon the faithful and that the heavenly Jerusalem would descend to earth soon. Montanus and his followers lived an ascetic life, and withdrew to Phrygia to await the second coming, claiming to be the only true Christian Church. A common element in Gnosticism and Montanism, at least, was the exclusivity of their adherents' idea of the Church. Each group argued that theirs was the only Church and that others were mere idolaters or worse. The claim of membership in a "true" Church, guided by secret revelation, appears to have become one theme of many heresies, one of the recurring themes of Christian history.

There are other themes as well that emerge from the second century on and seem to recur in one form or another throughout Christian history, thereby helping to explain some, at least, of the reasons why later churchmen considered later heresies to be old heresies revived. But similarity of structure does not necessarily entail continuity in history. Thus, Manichaeism (no. 2) posited two gods, one good and the other evil, the former the ruler of the spirit, the latter the creator of the material world and the imprisoner of souls in it. Manichaeism has been compared to later dualist heresies, such as Bogomilism (below, no. 17) and Catharism (below, chapt. III). The existence of a variety of sects among Christians by the third century led pagans to attack Christianity on the grounds of its internal diversity. Origen, the great Christian biblical scholar, undertook to answer these charges in his famous reply to the pagan Celsus, the *Contra Celsum.*

From the first to the fourth centuries, orthodox doctrines and attacks on heresy had come from individual writers whose authority lay in their personal prestige and their informal acceptance by the majority of Christian communities. After the christianization of the Roman Empire in the fourth century, however, the Church acquired an articulated organization, and ecclesiastical officials, bishops, popes, and church councils could speak with an official voice. A number of heretical or schismatic movements, such as Donatism, found in the fourth century that dissent was conceived and treated very differently from the way it had been only a generation or two earlier. Donatists argued that clergy who had given over Christian sacred books to save themselves from pagan Roman persecution had become unworthy of their priestly character, and the sacraments they administered were therefore invalid. A century of imperial and ecclesiastical opposition and persecution destroyed historical Donatism by the beginning of the fifth century, but the Donatists had raised another question that later revived after the eleventh century: do immoral clergy act as vehicles for divine grace when they administer the sacraments? Orthodox opinion answered in the affirmative, yet the question was raised again in the Gregorian Reform movement in the eleventh and twelfth centuries and yet again in the Reformation of the sixteenth century.

The most influential of all christological heresies, however, was that of Arianism (nos. 3-5), which preoccupied churchmen in the fourth and fifth centuries and left so strong a legacy of fear that it became in the twelfth century the prototype of all heresies. Arian doctrine subordinated the Son to the Father, and its long life and political consequences made it the only ancient heresy that troubled both the Roman and the Germanic worlds between the fourth and the sixth centuries. In the late fourth century, the doctrines of Pelagius, a British Christian, aroused the intellectual and aristocratic worlds of Rome, North Africa, and Palestine. Pelagius's doctrine of grace and the autonomy of the individual Christian aroused the opposition of St. Augustine, the greatest theologian of the Latin Church, and led to the beginnings of the long Christian debate about predestination. Augustine's debate with Pelagius was one of the last widespread debates on theological heresy in the Latin West before the coming of the Germanic kingdoms and the disappearance of Roman imperial authority. In the East, however, a number of christological and trinitarian heresies occupied the work of Fathers and councils through the sixth century. Of these movements, Monophysitism was probably the most important, although we are unable to consider it here.

A final legacy of western Christianity from the Roman Empire was the practice of coercing heretics back to the orthodox faith. Although, in principle, membership in the Christian community had to be purely voluntary, from the fourth century on coercion became one of the possibilities in Christian life, backed by the civil authority of the Roman Empire. The first heretic to be executed was the Spaniard Priscillian in 383, and the appearance of the *Theodosian Code* in 438 (no. 6) enshrined coercive measures in Roman law, thereby laying the groundwork for later civil and ecclesiastical institutions and theories of coercion (below, chapt. VI).

Early in the seventh century, after the ancient world that had already defined many occasions of difference between orthodoxy and heterodoxy had passed, St. Isidore of Seville compiled a vast encyclopedia of what he thought was the knowledge of the ancient Christian world, called *The Twenty Books of Etymologies, or Origins*. In Books VII and VIII of the *Etymologies* (below, no. 7), Isidore defined the Church and the Synagogue, orthodoxy, heresy, and schism, summing up as best he could the history of ecclesiastical debate that had raged from first-century Corinth to seventh-century Constantinople. Much of later writers' information about "the heresies of old" came from Isidore, as well as from St. Augustine, and Isidore's text is an important link in the chain that connects early heresy with its later medieval counterpart. From Isidore's time on, Latin Christianity, at least, was faced with the newer task of converting the Germanic and Slavic inhabitants of Europe to a drastically simplified Christianity. In the West, with few exceptions, the question of widespread doctrinal popular heresy was adjourned until the eleventh century.

LITERATURE

The best discussion of the circumstances of dissenting opinion in the early Church may be found in the English translation of Walter Bauer's great work *Orthodoxy and Heresy in Earliest Christianity*, edited and translated by Robert A. Kraft et al. (Philadelphia, 1971). Bauer's original thesis has been eloquently criticized by H. E. W. Turner, *The Pattern of Christian Truth* (London, 1954). Turner has been partly answered in Robert Kraft's appendix to his translation of Bauer, *Orthodoxy and Heresy*, pp. 286-316, and a comparison of the two .arguments, with Kraft's commentary, is probably the most illuminating introduction to the subject.

The best short introduction to Church history is Henry Chadwick, *The Early Church* (Baltimore, 1967). Also useful is Jean Danielou and H.-I. Marrou, *The First Six Hundred Years*, The Christian Centuries, vol. 1 (New York, 1964). Longer, more detailed, and with an immense bibliography is Karl Baus, *From the Apostolic Community to Constantine* (London, 1965). Shorter and more sophisticated is Leonhard Goppelt, *Apostolic and Post-Apostolic Times* (London, 1970).

There are excellent discussions of the terminology of heresy and orthodoxy in Goppelt, *Apostolic and Post-Apostolic Times*, pp. 165-77; S. L. Greenslade, *Schism in the Early Church* (New York, 1962), pp. 17-34; Liguori G. Müller, *The 'De Haeresibus' of Saint Augustine* (Washington, D.C., 1956), pp. 37-52.

On St. Bernard's conception of heresy and medieval connections to patristic literature, see Jean Leclercq, "L'Hérésie d'après les écrits de S. Bernard de Clairvaux," in *The Concept of Heresy in the Middle Ages*, pp. 12-26 (below, p. 64). For medieval and patristic typology, see H. Grundmann, "*Opportet et haereses esse*: Das Problem der Ketzerei im Spiegel der mittelalterlichen Bibelexegese," *Archiv für Kulturgeschichte* 45 (1963): 129-64; idem, "Der Typus des Ketzers in mittelalterlicher Anschauung," in *Kultur und Universalgeschichte: Festschrift für Walter Goetz* (Leipzig and Berlin, 1927), pp. 91-107; Yves M.-J. Congar, "*Arriana haeresis* comme désignation du néomanichéisme au XIIe siècle: Contribution à l'histoire d'une typification de l'hérésie au moyen age," *Revue des sciences philosophiques et théologiques* 43 (1959): 449-61. See also Moore, *Origins of European Dissent*, pp. 26-28.

On the separation from Judaism, besides the general histories cited above, see also A. F. J. Klijn and G. J. Reinink, *Patristic Evidence for Jewish-Christian Sects* (Leiden, 1973). On the importance of scripture, see *The Cambridge History of the Bible*, vol. 2 (Cambridge, 1969), and, for doctrine generally, J. N. D. Kelly, *Early Christian Doctrines*, rev. ed. (New York, 1978). For tradition, see R. P. C. Hanson, *Tradition in the Early Church* (London, 1962) and H. von Campenhausen, *The Formation of the Christian Bible* (London, 1972). On techniques of exegesis, see R. P. C. Hanson, *Allegory and Event* (London, 1959). For the creed, see J. N. D. Kelly, *Early Christian Creeds* (London, 1972).

There are excellent guides to bibliographical studies of the early Fathers in the general histories cited above, particularly that of Henry Chadwick. On Gnosticism, see Hans Jonas, *The Gnostic Religion* (Boston, 1963); Robert M. Grant, *Gnosticism and Early Christianity* (New York, 1966). Translations of Gnostic sources may be found in R. M. Grant, *Gnosticism: A Source Book of Heretical Writings from the Early Christian Period* (New York, 1961); Robert Haardt, *Gnosis: Character and Testimony*, translated by F. J. Hendry (Leiden, 1971); Werner Foerster, *Gnosis: A Selection of Gnostic Texts*, translated by R. McL. Wilson, 2 vols. (Oxford, 1972, 1974). On the shaping of ecclesiastical authority in dealing with Gnosis and later heresies, see Hans von Campenhausen, *Ecclesiastical Authority and Spiritual Power in the Church of the First Three Centuries*, translated by J. A. Baker (London, 1969). See also Elaine Pagels, *The Gnostic Gospels* (New York, 1979).

Besides the work of Bauer, Turner, and Greenslade cited above, and the general histories of the early Church, I have found the following books helpful, both as a student and as a teacher: G. L. Prestige, *Fathers and Heretics* (London, 1938); Arthur Darby Nock, *Conversion* (Oxford, 1933); E. R. Dodds, *Pagan and Christian in an Age of Anxiety* (New York, 1965); Arnaldo Momigliano, ed., *The Conflict between Paganism and Christianity in the Fourth Century* (Oxford, 1963); Henry Chadwick, *Early Christian Thought and the Classical Tradition* (Cambridge, 1966); Robert A. Markus, *Christianity in the Roman World* (London, 1974); Peter Brown, *Religion and Society in the Age of St. Augustine* (New York, 1972). These works very competently provide essential background material on several of the writers represented here, notably Irenaeus and Tertullian. For Origen, see C. Bigg, *The Christian Platonists of Alexandria* (Oxford, 1913), and for St. Augustine, Müller's translation of the *De Haeresibus* and Peter Brown, *Augustine of Hippo* (Berkeley and Los Angeles, 1969). On Donatism, see W. C. Frend, *The Donatist Church* (Oxford, 1952). For Arianism, see H. M. Gwatkin, *Studies of Arianism* (Oxford, 1900), and for Monophysitism, W. H. C. Frend, *Martyrdom and Persecution in the Early Church* (Oxford, 1965), and idem, *The Rise of the Monophysite Movement* (Cambridge, 1972). For Pelagius, see John Ferguson, *Pelagius: A Historical and Theological Study* (Cambridge, 1956), and Robert F. Evans, *Pelagius: Inquiries and Reappraisals* (London, 1968). For Priscillian, see Henry Chadwick, *Priscillian of Avila* (Oxford, 1976).

Norman Cohn, *The Pursuit of the Millennium*, rev. ed. (New York, 1970), is a brilliant study of the apocalyptic millenarianism of the second through the seventeenth centuries. It also treats some of the questions of continuing revelation, particularly through social movements from late antiquity into early modern Europe. There is extremely important material on the emerging role of the popes in doctrinal struggles in E. Giles, *Documents Illustrating Papal Authority, A.D. 96-454* (London, 1952).

The best short introduction to Byzantine religious life may be found in Hans-Georg Beck et al., *The Church in the Age of Feudalism*, translated by Anselm Biggs, The Handbook of Church History, vol. 3, edited by Hubert Jedin and John Dolan (New York, 1969), pp. 26-53, 174-94, 404-26. This volume also has an extensive bibliography. For Paulicianism, see Nina G. Garsoian, *The Paulician Heresy* (The Hague and Paris, 1967); for Bogomilism, Dimitri Obolensky, *The Bogomils* (Cambridge, 1948); for Iconoclasm, see A. Bryer and J. Herrin, eds., *Iconoclasm* (Birmingham, 1977). The best account of the events leading up to the schism of 866-67 is F. Dvornik, *The Photian Schism* (Cambridge, 1948). The best account of dissenting movements in the West in this period is Jeffrey B. Russell, *Dissent and Reform in the Early Middle Ages* (Berkeley and Los Angeles, 1965). Cyril Mango, *The Art of the Byzantine Empire* (Englewood Cliffs, N.J., 1972) is an excellent collection of wide-ranging texts. For Iconoclasm, see especially pp. 16-20, 41-54, 149-80. There is a brief comparison of eastern and western Iconoclasm in Edward J. Martin, *A History of the Iconoclastic Controversy* (London, 1952), and a fine study by David Freedberg, "The Structure of Byzantine and European Iconoclasm," in Bryer and Herrin, *Iconoclasm*, 165-77. On the *Libri Carolini*, most of the scholarly debate is summed up in Liutpold Wallach, *Diplomatic Studies in Latin and Greek Documents from the Carolingian Age* (Ithaca,

N.Y., 1977). The full text of Claudius of Turin (along with other sources illustrating Carolingian theological disputes) may be read in G. McCracken and A. Cabaniss, *Early Medieval Theology*, Library of Christian Classics, vol. 9 (Philadelphia, 1957).

1   Tertullian: An Injunction against Heretics

Besides scripture, tradition, and the rules of faith and creed, early Christianity soon found gifted writers to express its beliefs and defend them against heterodox attacks. One of the earliest and greatest of these was Quintus Septimius Florens Tertullianus, Tertullian of Carthage, who lived from about 160 to 200 A.D. Tertullian was a convert to Christianity, and his literary eloquence became immensely influential in shaping literary defenses of Christian belief. Tertullian skillfully drew upon pagan learning, but he savagely attacked the morals and culture of pagan Rome. His tract *De praescriptione haereticorum*, ranks with that of St. Irenaeus as the most formidable early statement of authority and tradition, cast ingeniously in the form of a literal legal indictment against the heretics. The importance of this text is its reliance upon authority and tradition and its skillful use of scriptural citations to authenticate every statement.

Of Tertullian's many works dealing with heresy, particularly important is the *Adversus Marcionem*, recently reedited and translated by Ernest Evans, *Tertullian: Adversus Marcionem*, 2 vols. (Oxford, 1972).

The Lord teaches that many ravening wolves will come in sheep's clothing. What is sheep's clothing, but the outward appearance of the name of Christian? What are these ravening wolves, but those thoughts and treacherous spirits which hide within [the name of Christian] to infest the flock of Christ? Who are false prophets but false preachers? Who are false apostles but fraudulent evangelists? Who are Antichrists but rebels against Christ? Today there are heresies attacking the Church through perversity of doctrines, and those attacks are no less intense than the persecutions Antichrist will employ in later days. The only difference is that persecution makes martyrs, and heresy makes apostates only. And therefore there was need that heresies should exist, so that those who were approved might be made manifest; just as those who had been steadfast in persecutions were they who did not fly to heresies....

Moreover, if he [St. Paul] criticizes dissensions and divisions, which clearly are evils, he immediately adds heresies also. That which he has associated with evils he certainly indicates is an evil, and indeed, the worse, since he says that he *believed* as touching divisions and dissensions for this reason—that he *knew* there must be heresies also. For he shows that in seeing .a more grievous evil, he easily believed that lighter ones also exist.... Finally, if the sense [of St. Paul's epistle to the Corinthians] points to the keeping of unity, and the limitation of divisions, and if heresies keep men from unity just as much as divisions and dissensions do, then he places heresies in the same category in which he places divisions and dissensions....

This is the same Paul who elsewhere numbers heresies among the wicked works of the flesh and who advises Titus that a man who remains a heretic after the first rebuke must be rejected since he is perverted and sins, being condemned by himself. But in nearly every epistle where he urges them to avoid false doctrines he reproves heresies, which themselves are false doctrines. They are called by the Greek word *haireseis* in the sense of choice which a man exercises either to establish them or to adopt them. Therefore he has called the heretic condemned by himself because he has chosen for himself something for which he is condemned. For us it is not lawful to introduce any doctrine of our own choosing, neither may we choose some doctrine which someone else has introduced by his own choice. We have for our authority the Apostles of the Lord, who did not choose of themselves to introduce anything by their own will, but faithfully gave to the nations and peoples the religion which they had received from Christ. Wherefore, "though an angel from heaven should preach any other gospel," he would be cursed by us....

These are the doctrines of men and demons, created for itching ears eager for the spirit of this world, which the Lord called foolishness. The foolish things of this world confound even philosophy itself. For the things of this world are such that its wisdom makes the interpreter rash in explaining the nature of God and the order He established. Finally, heresies themselves are tricked out by philosophy. Hence the Aeons, and who knows what "finite forms" and "the trinity of man" according to Valentinus. He belonged to the school of Plato. The god of Marcion, more excellent because of his indolence, came from the Stoics. The doctrine that the soul dies is taken over from the Epicureans. The denial of the resurrection of the body is taken from the combined schools of all the philosophers. When matter is made equal with God it is the work of Zeno. Where anything is alleged about a god made of fire, the doctrine comes from Heraclitus. The same things are turned and twisted by heretics and philosophers. The same questions are involved. Where does evil come from? And how? And where does man come from? And how? And, as Valentinus has lately asked, where does God come from? And he answers: from an exercise of the mind and an abortive birth. Wretched Aristotle! Who taught him the art of dialectic, skillful and cunning in building up and pulling down, using changes in sentences, making extreme guesses at truth, tough in argumentation, active in raising objections, contrary against itself, dealing backwards and forwards with everything, so that he really deals with nothing. From this come those fables and genealogies, unprofitable questions, and words that spread like a cancer, from which the Apostle Paul restrains us, telling us that philosophy should be avoided, writing to the Colossians, "Beware lest anyone beguile you through philosophy and vain deceit after the ways of men" beside the help of the Holy Spirit. Paul had been at Athens, and had, through arguments there, learned about that wisdom of humans which pretends to the Truth but actually corrupts it, itself also being divided into many parts by the variety of sects opposing each other.

What then has Athens to do with Jerusalem? What does the Academy [of Plato] have to do with the Church? What do heretics have to do with Christians? Our school is the porch of Solomon [rather than the porch of the Stoics] who himself has told us that we must seek the Lord in simplicity of heart. Away with those who have introduced a Stoic, a Platonic, a dialectical Christianity!

We do not need this kind of curiosity now that we have Jesus, nor do we need inquiry now that we have the gospel. If we believe this, we need believe nothing besides. For we believe first that we ought to believe nothing more. I come to that point which even our own brothers offered as a reason for curious inquiry into other things, and which heretics use to justify curious doubt. It is written, they say, "Seek and ye shall find." But we should remember when the Lord said this: at the beginning of his teaching, when people doubted "whether He was the Christ." Not even Peter had said that He was the son of God. Even John the Baptist was not sure of Him. He said, "Seek and you shall find," with good reason, because men had not yet sought Him nor acknowledged Him.

2   St. Augustine: On Manichaeism

Gnosticism and Manichaeism, both religions that originated outside Christianity, brought into it the problem of dualism, that is, the question of rival gods. Manichaeism was named after its founder, the Persian Mani (216-76), who blended Gnosticism and Zoroastrianism into a powerful dualistic faith, featuring an ascetic morality and different grades of adherents. Mani's program outraged both the Zoroastrian priests of Persia and the Christians of the Mediterranean, although it attracted many followers, including the young Augustine in the third quarter of the fourth century. Mani explained the problem of evil in the universe by positing that the god of darkness had stolen sparks of divine light and imprisoned them in human material bodies. The purpose of human life according to Mani was to release those sparks of divinity by rigorously suppressing bodily pleasures. The attractive character of Manichaeism in the fourth and fifth centuries generated a large literature opposing it, and the question of its survival into Armenian Paulicianism and Byzantine Bogomilism (below, no. 17) and later Latin Catharism was long answered in the affirmative by scholars who regarded later dualism as a continuation of earlier dualism. Recent scholars, however, have questioned the continuity of Manichaeism in favor of the theory that dualism is a possible tenet of several varieties of Christian thought. In spite of the tendency of scholars not to see continuity, the name "Manichee," like that of "Arian," was widely used by later medieval writers to describe the heresies of their own day.

The sources for many of the earliest heresies are to be found in the writings of orthodox churchmen, and hence we see the heretics through the eyes of their enemies. Infrequently, some direct heretical source materials are discovered, as was the case with the discovery of many Gnostic materials at Nag-Hammadi in Egypt in 1945. Other heretical materials are sometimes found quoted in treatises that purport to refute them. Heresiology, however, soon became a recognized branch of orthodox Christian literature, and many writers wrote to record the variety of heresies as well as to combat specific ones. The first major ecclesiastical writer to develop this genre was St. Irenaeus (130-200), Bishop of Lyon in Gaul, whose great work *Adversus omnes haereses* (*Against All Heresies*) is cited above and became enormously influential among later writers on heresy. St. Hippolytus (170-236) wrote an extensive work entitled *Refutation of All Heresies,* in which he attempted to show that all heresies derived from one form or another of pagan philosophy. St. Epiphanius (315-403) compiled his *Panarion* in an attempt to list all heresies, and in the *Ecclesiastical History* of Eusebius of Caesarea (260-340) there is much material on the development of early heresies. Other writers as well provided catalogues of heresies, one of the best-known being the *De haeresibus* of St. Augustine (354-430). Thus, although many direct heretical sources have been lost, there is much material surviving, and the development of heresiology as a literary genre preserved much more.

The source given here is chapter forty-six of St. Augustine's *Concerning Heresies.* It is a particularly appropriate text to use for Manichaeism, since Augustine had been a Manichaean adherent in his younger years and knew the cult very well.

The Manichaeans sprang from a certain Persian called Manes, but when they began to publish his mad doctrine in Greece, his disciples chose to call him Manichaeus to avoid the word for "madness." For the same reason some of them, somewhat more learned and therefore more deceitful, called him Mannicheus, doubling the letter *n,* as if he were one who pours out manna.

He invented two principles, different from and opposed to each other, both eternal and coeternal; that is, he imagined they have always been. Following other ancient heretics, he also believed that there were two natures and substances, that is, one good and one evil. Proclaiming, on the basis of their teachings, a mutual strife and commingling of the two natures, purgation of good from evil, and eternal damnation, along with the evil, of the good which cannot be purged, these heretics devise many myths. It would be too tiresome to treat all their doctrines in this work.

As a consequence of these ridiculous and unholy fables, they are forced to say that both God and the good souls, which they believe have to be freed from their admixture with the contrary nature of the evil souls, are of one and the same nature.

Then they declare that the world has been made by the nature of the good, that is, by the nature of God, but yet that it was formed of a mixture of good and evil which resulted when these two natures fought among themselves.

From Ligouri G. Müller, *The "De Haeresibus" of St. Augustine* (Washington, D.C.: The Catholic University of America Press, 1956), pp. 85-97. Reprinted with the permission of the author and publisher.

However, they claim that not only do the powers of God effect this purgation and liberation of good and evil throughout the whole universe and of all its elements, but also that their own Elect achieve the same results by means of the food of which they partake. And they state that the divine substance is intermingled with this food just as it is with the whole universe, and imagine that it is purified in their Elect by the mode of life which the Manichaean Elect live, as if their mode of life were holier and more excellent than that of their Auditors. For they would have their church consist of those two classes, Elect and Auditors.

Moreover, they believe that this portion of the good and divine substance which is held mixed and imprisoned in food and drink is more strongly and foully bound in the rest of men, even their own Auditors, but particularly in those who propagate offspring. Now whenever any portion of the light is completely purified, it returns to the kingdom of God, to its own proper abode, as it were, on certain vessels, which are, according to them, the moon and the sun. In addition, they maintain that these vessels are likewise fashioned from the pure substance of God.

They also state that this physical light, which lies before the gaze of mortal eyes, not only in those vessels where they believe it to exist in its purest state, but also in certain other bright objects where they consider it held in admixture and needing purification, is the divine nature. For they ascribe five elements which have generated their own princes to the people of darkness and give to these elements the names: smoke, darkness, fire, water, and wind. Two-footed animals were generated in smoke, and from this source they believe men to take their beginnings; serpents were generated in darkness; quadrupeds in fire; swimming creatures in the waters; flying creatures in the wind. Five other elements have been sent from the kingdom and substance of God to conquer the five evil elements, and in that struggle air has become mixed with fire, light with darkness, good fire with bad fire, good water with bad water, good wind with bad wind. They make this distinction between the two vessels, that is, the two lights of heaven, saying that the moon has been made of good water, and the sun has been made of good fire.

Moreover, on those vessels there are holy powers, which at one time change themselves into males to attract females of the opposing faction, and at another into females to attract males of that same opposite faction. The purpose of this is to enable the light which they have intermingled in their members to escape when their passions are aroused by this attraction, and to allow it to be taken up by the angels of light for purification, and when purified to be placed aboard those vessels to be carried back to their proper realm.

In this circumstance, or rather because of some demand of their detestable superstition, their Elect are forced to consume a sort of eucharist sprinkled with human seed in order that the divine substance may be freed even from that, just as it is from other foods of which they partake. However, they deny that they do this, claiming that some others do it, using the name of the Manichaeans. But they were exposed in the church at Carthage, as you know, for you were a deacon there at the time when, under the prosecution of Ursus the tribune, who was then prefect of the palace, some of them were brought to trial. At this time a girl by the name of Margaret gave evidence of their obscene practices and claimed, though she was not yet twelve years old, that she had been violated in the performance of this criminal rite. Then with difficulty he compelled Eusebia, some kind of Manichaean nun, to admit that she had undergone the same treatment in this regard, though at first, she maintained that she was a virgin and insisted on being examined by a midwife. When she was examined and when her true condition was discovered, she likewise gave information on that whole loathsome business at which flour is sprinkled beneath a couple in sexual intercourse to receive and commingle with their seed. This she had not heard when Margaret gave her testimony, for she had not been present. Even in recent times some of them have been exposed and brought before ecclesiastical authority, as the "Episcopal Acts" which you have sent us show. Under careful examination, they admitted that this is no sacrament, but a sacrilege.

One of them, whose name is Viator, claimed that those who commit such acts are properly called Catharists. Nevertheless, though he asserted that there are other groups of the Manichaean sect divided into Mattarii and especially Manichaeans, he could not deny that all of these three forms were propagated by the same founder and that all of them are, generally speaking, Manichaeans. Surely the Manichaean books are unquestionably common to all of them, and in these books are described these dreadful things relating to the transformation of males into females, and of females into males to attract and to loosen through concupiscence the princes of darkness of both sexes so that the divine substance which is imprisoned in them may be set free and escape. This is the source of the obscene practices which some of the Manichaeans refuse to admit pertain to them. For they imagine that they are imitating divine powers to the highest degree and so they attempt to purge a part of their god, which they really believe is held befouled just as much in human seed as it is in all celestial and terrestrial bodies, and in the seeds of all things. And for this reason, it follows that they are just as much obliged to purge it from human seed by eating, as they are in reference to other seed which they consume in their food. This is the reason they are also called Catharists, that is, Purifiers, for they are so attentive to purifying this part that they do not refrain even from such horrifying food as this.

Yet they do not eat meat either, on the grounds that the divine substance has fled from the dead or slain bodies, and what little remains there is of such quality and quantity that it does not merit being purified in the stomachs of the Elect. They do not even eat eggs, claiming that they too die when they are broken, and it is not fitting to feed on any dead bodies; only that portion of flesh can live which is picked up by flour to prevent its death. Moreover, they do not use milk for food although it is drawn or milked from the live body of an animal, not with the conviction that there is nothing of the divine substance intermingled with it, but because error itself is inconsistent. For they do not drink wine either, claiming that bitterness is a property of the princes of darkness, though they do eat grapes. They do not even drink must, even the most freshly pressed.

They believe that the souls of the Auditors are returned to the Elect, or by a happier short-cut to the food of their Elect so that, already purged, they would then not have to transmigrate into other bodies. On the other hand, they believe that other souls pass into cattle and into everything that is rooted in and supported on the earth. For they are convinced that plants and trees possess sentient life and can feel pain when injured, and therefore that no one can pull or pluck them without torturing them. Therefore, they consider it wrong to clear a field even of thorns. Hence, in their madness they make agriculture, the most innocent of occupations, guilty of multiple murder. On the other hand, they believe that these crimes are forgiven their Auditors because the latter offer food of this sort to their Elect in order that the divine substance, on being purged in their stomachs, may obtain pardon for those through whose offering it is given to be purged. And so the Elect themselves perform no labors in the field, pluck no fruit, pick not even a leaf, but expect all these things to be brought for their use by their Auditors, living all the while, according to their own foolish thinking, on innumerable and horrible murders committed by others. They caution their same Auditors, furthermore, when they eat meat, not to kill the animals, to avoid offending the princes of darkness who are bound in the celestials. From them, they claim, all flesh has its origin.

And if they make use of marriage, they should, however, avoid conception and birth to prevent the divine substance, which has entered into them through food, from being bound by chains of flesh in their offspring. For this is the way, indeed, they believe that souls come into all flesh, that is, through food and drink. Hence, without doubt, they condemn marriage and forbid it as much as is in their power, since they forbid the propagation of offspring, the reason for marriage.

They assert that Adam and Eve had as their parents princes of Smoke, since their father, whose name was Saclas, had devoured the children of all his associates and in lying with his wife had, as if with the strongest of chains, bound in the flesh of his offspring whatever he had received mixed with the divine substance.

They maintain that the serpent of whom our scriptures speak was Christ, and they say that our first parents were illuminated by the latter so that they might open the eyes of knowledge, and discern good and evil; further, that this Christ came in recent times to set souls free, not bodies; and that he did not come in real flesh, but presented the simulated appearance of flesh to deceive human perception, and therein he feigned not only death, but resurrection as well. They assert that the god who gave the Law through Moses, and who spoke in the Hebrew prophets, is not the true God, but one of the princes of darkness. Even in the New Testament they, claiming falsification, choose among the various books, and thus they accept what they like from it and reject what they do not like. They prefer certain apocryphal writings to the scriptures, as if they contained the whole truth.

They claim that the promise of the Lord Jesus Christ regarding the Paraclete, the Holy Spirit, was fulfilled in their heresiarch Manichaeus. For this reason, in his writings he calls himself the apostle of Jesus Christ, in that Christ had promised to send him and had sent the Holy Spirit in him.

For the same reason Manichaeus also had twelve disciples in imitation of the twelve apostles. The Manichaeans keep this number even today. For they have twelve of their Elect whom they call Masters, and a thirteenth who is their chief, seventy-two bishops who receive their orders from the Masters, and priests who are ordained by the bishops. The bishops also have deacons. The rest are called merely the Elect. But even any of their members who seem suitable are sent to strengthen and support this error where it exists, or to plant it where it does not.

They allege that baptism in water grants no salvation to anyone, and do not believe that they have to baptize any of those whom they deceive.

In the daytime they offer their prayers toward the sun, wherever it goes in its orbit; at night, they offer them toward the moon, if it appears; if it does not, they direct them toward the North, by which the sun, when it has set, returns to the East. They stand while praying.

They ascribe the origin of sin not to a free choice of the will, but to the nature of the opposing element, which they hold is intermingled in man. For they assert that all flesh is the work, not of God, but of an evil mind, which emanating from the opposite principle, is coeternal with God. As they will have it, carnal concupiscence, by which the flesh lusts against the spirit, is not an infirmity engendered in us by the corruption of our nature in the first man, but a contrary substance which clings to us in such a way that if we are freed and purged, it can be removed from us, and can live, even alone, immortally in its own nature. These two souls, or two minds, the one good, the other evil, are in conflict with one another in man, when the flesh lusts against the spirit, and the spirit against the flesh. This defect in our nature has not been healed, as we say it has, nor will it ever be healed. But that substance of evil, after being disjoined and separated from us, even at the end of this world, upon the conflagration of the universe, will live in a kind of globe, as if in an eternal prison. They claim that a sort of envelope or covering, composed of souls which are good by nature, but which, nevertheless, have not been able to be purged from the contagion of the evil nature, will continually come and cling to this globe.

3   Theodoret: The Rise of Arianism

Arianism began, as many schismatical and heretical movements did, in a local controversy, this time between the presbyter Arius of Alexandria and his bishop, Alexander. The question between them was the nature of the relationship between Christ and God the Father. Arius denied the coeternity and equality of Christ, insisting upon Christ's inferiority. The lively intellectual climate of Alexandria and the Greek East generally led to a widening of the argument until both sides had made it the major issue in the Greek-speaking Christian Church. Powerful churchmen in their own right and churchmen who had the ear of the Emperor Constantine brought the question to imperial attention, and Constantine called a church council together in Nicaea, near Constantinople, in 325. There more than two hundred bishops argued out the philosophical and theological language that became the terminology of official Orthodox Christianity. Nicaea was something new in the Christian world, and it has been regarded as the first of the Ecumenical Councils and one of the most important events in European history. The council raised the question, not only of theological language and hard dogmatic definition of spiritual reality, but of the relative authority of individuals and offices, independent bishops and an assembly of bishops, the council and the emperor, and the council and the pope. Thus, the problem of the authority to define orthodoxy and heresy was associated at the outset with the problem of where authority lay in the Christian community. The long controversy over Arianism contributed greatly to developing the technical theological language of orthodox belief and in strengthening the hands of imperial churchmen in the face of heterodoxy. The Nicene Creed (no. 5) was one result of the controversy, which lingered on into the fifth century and formed the backdrop for the entry of the Christian Roman emperor onto the scene of religious disputes.

There is a very great amount of source material for the Arian movement, not only its early fourth-century stages, but its fourth- and fifth-century career, and its later career among the Germanic invaders of the Roman Empire. Another striking difference between fourth-century heretical movements and earlier movements is the available source material for the former. When a movement was able to focus the attention of the whole Church, either in council or in the activity of ecclesiastical leaders, holy men, and emperors, it kept many pens busy. Thus, fourth-century and later heresy entered more frequently into the routine life of the Church than it had earlier, and the specialty of heresiology, as well as the question of ecclesiastical authority, became a prominent aspect of ecclesiastical life.

The texts printed here illustrate some of the aspects of Arianism that led to its being considered later the symbol of all heresies: the character of Arius as a heresiarch, the suffering of holy men persecuted by wicked emperors, the decision of the Church in council, and the intricacies of credal formation.

Number 3 is taken from Theodoret's *Ecclesiastical History*, book 1, the best early description of Alexandria and the beginnings of Arianism; Number 4, also from book 1 of Theodoret's *History*, illustrates the drawing into the controversy in Alexandria of powerful and learned eastern prelates, in this case Eusebius, bishop of the imperial residence of Nicomedia; number 5 is the text of the creed adopted at Nicaea and readopted with some modifications at the Council of Constantinople in 381. It became the most widely used of all Christian creeds.

Alexandria is an immense and populous city, charged with the leadership not only of Egypt, but also of the adjacent countries, the Thebaid and Libya. After Peter, the victorious champion of the faith, had, during the sway of the aforesaid impious tyrants, obtained the crown of martyrdom, the church in Alexandria was ruled for a short time by Achillas. He was succeeded by Alexander, who proved himself a noble defender of the doctrines of the gospel. At that time, Arius, who had been enrolled in the list of the presbytery, and entrusted with the exposition of the holy scriptures, fell a prey to the assaults of jealousy, when he saw that the helm of the high priesthood was committed to Alexander. Stung by this passion, he sought opportunities for dispute and contention; and, although he perceived that Alexander's irreproachable conduct forbade his bringing any charges against him, envy would not allow him to rest. In him the enemy of the truth found an instrument whereby to stir and agitate the angry waters of the Church, and persuaded him to oppose the apostolical doctrine of Alexander. While the patriarch, in obedience to the holy scriptures, taught that the Son is of equal dignity with the Father, and of the same substance with God who begat him, Arius, in direct opposition to the truth, affirmed that the Son of God is merely a creature or created being, adding the famous dictum, "There once was a time when He was not," with other opinions which may be learned from his own writings. He taught these false doctrines perseveringly, not only in the church, but also in general meetings and assemblies; and he even went from house to house, endeavoring to make men the slaves of his error. Alexander, who was strongly attached to the doctrines of the apostles, at first tried by exhortations and counsels to convince him of his error; but when he saw him playing the madman and making public declaration of his impiety, he deposed him from the order of the presbytery for he heard the law of God loudly declaring, "*If thy right eye offend thee, pluck it out, and cast it from thee.*"

4 Theodoret: Arius's Letter to Eusebius of Nicomedia

The bishop greatly wastes and persecutes us, and leaves no stone unturned against us. He has driven us out of the city as atheists, because we do not concur in what he publicly preaches, namely, God always, the Son always; as the Father so the Son; the Son coexists unbegotten with God; he is everlasting; neither by thought nor by any interval does God precede the Son; always God, always Son; he is begotten of the unbegotten; the Son is of God himself. Eusebius, your brother bishop of Caesarea, Theodotus, Paulinus, Athanasius, Gregorius, Aetius, and all the bishops of the East have been condemned because they say that God had an existence prior to that of his Son, except Philogonius, Hellanicus and Macarius, who are unlearned men, and who have embraced heretical opinions. Some of them say that the Son is an eructation, others that he is a production, others that he is also unbegotten. These are impieties to which we cannot listen, even though the heretics threaten us with a thousand deaths. But we say and believe and have taught, and do teach, that the Son is not unbegotten, nor in any way part of the unbegotten; and that he does not derive his subsistence from any matter; but that by his own will and counsel he has subsisted before time and before ages as perfect God, only begotten and unchangeable, and that before he was begotten, or created, or purposed, or established, he was not. For he was not unbegotten. We are persecuted, because we say that the Son has a beginning, but that God is without beginning.

5 The Creed of Nicaea (325) and Constantinople (381)

We believe in God, the Father almighty, maker of heaven and earth, and of all things visible and invisible;
And in one Lord Jesus Christ, the only begotten Son of God,

begotten of the Father before all ages,
Light of Light, true God of true God, begotten, not made,
of one substance with the Father, through whom all things were made;
who for us men and for our salvation came down from the heavens,
and was made flesh of the Holy Spirit and the Virgin Mary,
and became man and was crucified for us under Pontius Pilate
and suffered and was buried, and rose again on the third day
according to scriptures, and ascended into the heavens
and sits on the right hand of the Father,
and comes again in glory to judge living and dead,
and of whose kingdom there shall be no end;
And in the Holy Spirit, the Lord and the Life-Giver,
that proceeds from the Father, who with the Father and Son
is worshiped together and glorified together, who spoke
through the prophets;
In one holy Catholic and Apostolic Church;
We acknowledge one baptism for the remission of sins;
We look for a resurrection of the dead, and the life of the age to come.

6   *Compelle Intrare*: The Coercion of Heretics in the *Theodosian Code*, 438

By the last decade of the fourth century, the now-christianized Roman Empire began to attack religious dissidents as it treated political dissidents and criminals, with legal means. The involvement of fourth-century emperors in church councils, in establishing dogma, and in supporting the imperial Church all prepared for this step, but several other elements played important parts as well. First, the experience of the Church in North Africa of living in close proximity to the Donatist Church had engendered bitter feelings, and from 399 on the Church urged the emperors to enforce harsher and harsher laws against their heterodox rivals. The bitterness engendered by personal experience of heresy, and the growth of heretical movements in the fifth century—which tied up church property, generating conflicting claims to episcopal and other offices, and often raised the threat of scandal—gave the problem of heresy several new dimensions. Finally, the idea of salutary discipline, which had always been a part of Christian communal thought, came to be extended to enemies of the faith as well as to penitents. St. Augustine, with his progressively bleaker view of human nature and human institutions, illustrates this last point well:

> No one is indeed to be compelled to embrace the faith against his will; but by the severity, or one might rather say, by the mercy of God, it is common for treachery to be chastised by the scourge of tribulation . . . for no one can do well unless he has deliberately chosen, and unless he has loved what is in free will; but the fear of punishment keeps the evil desire from escaping beyond the bounds of thought.

In other words, only through the exercise of free choice might one acquire spiritual merit, although the use of coercive force is appropriate, both to punish sinners and to make the world safer for good Christians. Augustine's words carried conviction. It is from his view of human nature and its weakness, illustrated in his doctrines against Pelagius, and not from expediency, that he enunciated the legitimation of coercive civil force against heretics. "Let the kings of the earth serve Christ," Augustine later wrote, "by making laws for him and for his cause." The view of the use of coercion within Christian communities and its extension into a new rationale for civil authority in general, has been called "political Augustinianism," and it played a conspicuous role in shaping the political theories of the Middle Ages and the early modern periods.

Once again, Augustine found scriptural justification for his approach, this time in the parable in Luke 14:21-24 which tells of the man who prepared a great feast and sent his messenger out to summon the guests when it was ready. One by one, the guests sent their regrets, and the master ordered the messenger to go out and bring in the poor, the halt, and the lame. When this was done, the messenger told the master that there still was room at his table:

> And the lord said unto the servant, "Go out unto the highways and the hedges, and compel them to come in [compelle intrare, in the Latin Vulgate] that my house may be filled. For I say unto you, that none of those men which were bidden shall taste of my banquet."

Patristic and medieval exegetes made much of this passage. For example, the excuse of the man originally invited that he had just bought five yoke of oxen and had to see how good they were was interpreted as the human preoccupations with the five senses and material pleasures. For Augustine, the original guests were the Jews, the cripples from the city are the Gentiles converted to

Christianity, and those who were compelled to come in at the last are those who return to the faith from heresy and schism. This tradition of scriptural interpretation passed down to the Middle Ages and beyond, and laid the groundwork for the coercive apparatus in late imperial and medieval society.

Around 380 Priscillian in Spain gathered an ascetic group of followers around him and appears to have taught a Manichaean-Gnostic doctrine characterized by fierce asceticism and a great interest in magic and astrology. Priscillian aroused considerable opposition, however, and in 383 he was executed by imperial order, the first Christian to be executed for heresy by a Christian power.

Even more formidable than the actions of a single emperor, however, was the incorporation of antiheretical positions in Roman law, beginning with the *Theodosian Code* of 438, and extending into the great collection of Justinian, the *Corpus Iuris Civilis*, of the sixth century. Antiheretical laws in the Roman lawbooks had a great influence on late medieval theories on dealing with heretics.

An acute and sensitive study of the general background of religious coercion in the late empire is Peter Brown, "St. Augustine's Attitude to Religious Coercion," *Journal of Roman Studies* 54 (1964): 107-16, reprinted in Peter Brown, *Religion and Society in the Age of Saint Augustine* (New York, 1972), pp. 260-78. See also R. A. Markus, *Saeculum: History and Society in the Theology of St. Augustine* (Cambridge, 1970), Chap. 6, "*Coge intrare*: The Church and Political Power," pp. 133-53.

BOOK XVI

I, 2. It is Our will that all the peoples who are ruled by the administration of Our Clemency shall practice that religion which the divine Peter the Apostle transmitted to the Romans, as the religion which he introduced makes clear even unto this day. It is evident that this is the religion that is followed by pontiff Damasus and by Peter, bishop of Alexandria, a man of apostolic sanctity; that is, according to the apostolic discipline and the evangelic doctrine, we shall believe in the single Deity of the Father, the Son, and the Holy Spirit, under the concept of equal majesty and of the Holy Trinity.

Excerpts from Clyde Pharr, *The Theodosian Code and Novels and the Sirmondian Constitutions* (copyright 1952 by Clyde Pharr), pp. 440-57. Reprinted with the permission of Princeton University Press.

We command that those persons who follow this rule shall embrace the name of Catholic Christians. The rest, however, whom We adjudge demented and insane, shall sustain the infamy of heretical dogmas, their meeting places shall not receive the name of churches, and they shall be smitten first by divine vengeance and secondly by the retribution of Our own initiative, which We shall assume in accordance with the divine judgment (28 February 380).

II, 1. We have learned that clerics of the Catholic Church are being so harassed by a faction of heretics that they are being burdened by nomination and by service as tax receivers, as public custom demands, contrary to the privileges granted them. It is Our pleasure, therefore, that if Your Gravity should find any person thus harassed, another person shall be chosen as a substitute for him and that henceforward men of the aforesaid religion shall be protected from such outrages (31 October 313). . . .

IV, 2. There shall be no opportunity for any man to go out to the public and to argue about religion or to discuss it or to give any counsel. If any person hereafter, with flagrant and damnable audacity, should suppose that he may contravene any law of this kind or if he should dare to persist in his action of ruinous obstinacy, he shall be restrained with a due penalty and proper punishment (16 June 388). . . .

V, 1. The privileges that have been granted in consideration of religion must benefit only the adherents of the Catholic faith. It is Our will, moreover, that heretics and schismatics shall not only be alien from these privileges but shall also be bound and subjected to various compulsory public services (1 September 326). . . .

V, 5. All heresies are forbidden by both divine and imperial laws and shall forever cease. If any profane man by his punishable teachings should weaken the concept of God, he shall have the right to know such noxious doctrines only for himself but shall not reveal them to others to their hurt. If any person by a renewed death should corrupt bodies that have been redeemed by the venerable baptismal font, by taking away the effect of that ceremony which he repeats, he shall know such doctrines for himself alone, and he shall not ruin others by his nefarious teaching. All teachers and ministers alike of this perverse superstition shall abstain from the gathering places of a doctrine already condemned, whether they defame the name of bishop by the assumption of such priestly office, or, that which is almost the same, they belie religion with the appellation of priests, or also if they call themselves deacons, although they may not even be considered Christians. Finally, the rescript that was recently issued at Sirmium shall be annulled, and there shall remain only those enactments pertaining to Catholic doctrine which were decreed by our father of eternal memory and which We ourselves commanded by an equally manifold order,which will survive forever (20 August 379).

V, 11. All persons whatsoever who are tossed about by the false doctrine of diverse heresies, namely, the Eunomians, the Arians, the Macedonians, the Pneumatomachi, the Manichaeans, the Encratites, the Apotactites, the Saccophori, and the Hydroparastatae, shall not assemble in any groups, shall not collect any multitude, shall not attract any people to themselves, shall not show any walls of private houses after the likeness of churches, and shall practice nothing publicly or privately which may be detrimental to Catholic sanctity. Furthermore, if there should exist any person who transgresses what has been so evidently forbidden, he shall be expelled by the common agreement of all good men, and the opportunity to expel him shall be granted to all who delight in the cult and the beauty of the correct observance of religion (25 July 383). . . .

V, 41. Although it is customary for crimes to be expiated by punishment, it is Our will, nevertheless, to correct the depraved desires of men by an admonition to repentance. Therefore, if any heretics, whether they are Donatists or Manichaeans or of any other depraved belief and sect who have congregated for profane rites, should embrace, by a simple confession, the Catholic faith and rites, which We wish to be observed by all men, even though such heretics have nourished a deep-rooted evil by long and continued meditation, to such an extent that they also seem to be subject to the laws formerly issued, nevertheless, as soon as they have confessed God by a simple expression of belief, We decree that they shall be absolved from all guilt. Thus for every criminal offense, whether it was committed before or should be committed afterward, a thing which We regret, although punishment seems to be especially urgent for the guilty, it shall suffice for annulment that they should condemn their false doctrine by their own judgment and should embrace the name of Almighty God, which they may call upon even in the midst of their perils, for when the succor of religion has been invoked, it must nowhere be absent in afflictions. Therefore, just as We order that the previous laws which We have issued for the destruction of sacrilegious minds shall be forcefully pressed to the full effect of their execution, in like manner We decree that those persons who have preferred the faith of pure religion, even though by late confession, shall not be bound by the laws which have been issued. We sanction the foregoing regulations in order that all persons may know that the infliction of punishment on the profane desires of men shall not be lacking, and that it redounds to the advantage of true worship that the support of the laws should also be present (15 November 407).

7   St. Isidore of Seville: On the Church and the Sects

Isidore of Seville (ca. 570-636) was bishop of that city and one of the most influential writers of late antiquity. He was the author of theological and devotional works, histories, and the immense, encyclopedic *Etymologies*, a compendium of human knowledge in twenty books. Isidore preserved many important opinions of earlier Christian writers˙and some interesting pieces of pagan lore. But the great importance of the *Etymologies* lay in its immense popularity. It was the most generally used and cited reference book down to the twelfth century, and later medieval encyclopedic compilations followed in its wake. Thus, Isidore's remarks on heresy and schism played an important and familiar part in later approaches to heresy.

This text is from the last part of book VII and the first part of book VIII of Isidore's *Etymologies*.

BOOK VII, 14: ON THE FAITHFUL

The name "Christian," as far as the interpretation shows, derives from anointing, or else from the name of the founder [of this religion] and creator. From Christ, Christians are named, just as Jews are named from Judah. From the master, the name is given to the sectaries. Christians, however, were once called Nazarenes by the Jews, almost as a term of scorn, because Our Lord and Savior came from a certain neighborhood in Galilee and was called Nazareus. But those who have only the name and not the thing should not glory in the title of Christians. Since the title should follow from the deed, most certainly he is a Christian who by his deeds shows that he is a Christian, behaving as he behaved who first bore the name.

The name "Catholic" may be interpreted as universal or general. For in Greek, universal is designated by *katholikon*. The name "Orthodox" means right-believing and, as he believes, in right living. *Orthos* is right in Greek, and *doxa* means glory: that is, a man of right glory. No one may be called by this name unless he lives as he believes. . . .

BOOK VIII: ON THE CHURCH AND THE SECTS

1. On the church and the synagogue

Ecclesia is a Greek word, which in Latin means convocation, because all are called to it. Catholic, universal, *apo tou kath olon*, that is, according to a wholeness. The conventicles of the heretics are not like this, but are drawn together tightly in each region, not scattered and diffused throughout the whole world. About the Church the Apostle [Paul] said to the Romans, "Thanks be to my God for all of you, who proclaim your faith throughout the whole world" [Rom. 1:8]. Universal is so called from one, for it is gathered together in one. As the Lord said in the gospel, "He who is not with me is against me" [Luke 11:23]. . . . The Church began at the place where the Holy Spirit came from heaven and filled those who were gathered there. Because of its journey through time, the Church is called Sion, because from the length and distance of its journey it contemplates the promise of heavenly things. Therefore, it takes the name Sion, that is, speculative. Moreover, in the sense of the future [state of the Church], it is called Jerusalem, for Jerusalem means vision of peace. There, all adversities resolved in peace, which is Christ, the Church will exist in contemplation.

Synagoga is the Greek word for congregation, which is the appropriate name for the people of the Jews to have. Their synagogue may appropriately be called a synagogue, although it is also called an *ecclesia*. But the apostles never called our Church a synagogue, but always a church, whether discerning the cause, or whether between a congregation, that is, a synagogue, and a convocation, that is, a church, something particular is intended. For sheep are accustomed to congregate, whence we call them flocks; a convocation, however, uses more of reason, that is, it is more human. . . .

3. On heresy and schism

Haeresis is called in Greek from choice, because each one chooses that which seems to him to be the best, as in the case of the Peripatetic [Aristotelian] philosophers, the Academics [Platonists], and the Epicureans and Stoics, or as others do, who, contemplating their perverse dogma, recede from the Church of their own will. And so heresy is named from the Greek from the meaning of choice, since each [heretic] decides by his own will whatever he wants to teach or believe. But it is not permitted to us to believe anything on the basis of our own will, nor to choose to believe what someone else has believed of his own will. We have the authority of the apostles, who did not choose anything out of their own will to believe, but faithfully transmitted to the nations the teaching they received from Christ. Even if an angel from heaven should teach otherwise, it would be called anathema. Sects are so called from following and holding [*sequendo et tenendo*]. Now sects are a habit of spirits, and are formed around a discipline or a proposal, holding to which they follow along, holding to different opinions from others in the cult of religion. Schism comes from the word for cutting. Schismatics believe in the same rite and the same cult as others, but they delight in separating from the congregation. Men make schisms when they say, "We [alone] are the just," "we only are holy," and so forth. Superstition is so called from what is superfluous, or innovative observances. . . .

5. On the heresies of the Christians

They are heretics who depart from the Church, calling themselves by the name of their author. . . . Arians are so called from Arius the presbyter of Alexandria, who did not recognize the Son as coeternal with the Father and asserted different substances in the Trinity, against which the Lord said "I and the Father are One"[John 10:30]. . . . Priscillianists are so called after Priscillian, who in Spain composed a teaching which combined the errors of the Gnostics and the Manichees. . . . Pelagians are called after the monk Pelagius. These place free will ahead of divine grace, claiming that will is all that is needed to fulfill the divine commands. Nestorians are called after Nestorius, bishop of Constantinople, who claimed that the Virgin Mary was the mother, not of God, but of man, so that one person was made of the flesh, another of the divinity, and did not believe in One Christ in the word of God and in the flesh. . . . There are other heresies without founders and without names. Some of them believe that God has three forms, and others that the divinity of Christ can suffer. Others mark a point in time when Christ was born of the Father. Others do not believe that by the descent of Christ the freeing of all in the lower regions was accomplished. Others deny that the soul is the image of God. Others think that souls are changed into demons and animals of every kind. Others hold different opinions on the condition of the universe. Others think that there are many worlds. Others think that water has existed as long as God has. Others walk about with unshod feet, while still others will share a meal with no one.

These heresies have risen against the Catholic faith and have been condemned by the apostles, the holy Fathers, or the councils. And while they are not in agreement with one another, being divided by many errors, it is with one name that they conspire against the Church of God. But whoever understands scripture in any sense other than that which the Holy Spirit, by whom it was written, requires, even though he may not withdraw from the Church, may nevertheless be called a heretic.

8   Alcuin: Against the Adoptionist Heresy of Felix

The great watershed of the sixth and seventh centuries marks not only the end of antiquity but the beginning of a new division of the Mediterranean world and its adjoining lands. From 640 on, Islam spread westwards from Arabia through Roman Africa and into Spain; it spread eastwards into Syria and beyond Persia. From the invasion of the Lombards into Italy in 568, and the migration of Slavic, Turco-Tartar, and Magyar peoples into south central and southeast Europe at about the same time, the Greek- and Latin-speaking parts of the old Roman world became even more separated. Communication among these three worlds became less regular, and each part developed a distinctive culture. Although the Islamic and the East

Roman, or Byzantine, influences upon Latin Europe are not properly within the scope of such a book as this, several texts dealing with dissenting and heretical movements, especially in Byzantium and Latin Europe, are important and ought to be known in the context of later western European heretical movements.

One of the most important differences between the worlds of Byzantium and Latin Europe was the preservation in the former (and the virtual absence in the latter) of a highly speculative, philosophically alert, subtle, and numerous group of churchmen and laypeople who preserved a tradition of intellectual Christianity that had produced heresies and orthodoxies since the third century and continued to produce them until the fourteenth. To a certain extent the heretical movements of Byzantium after the sixth century are not very different from the kinds of heresies that abounded in the fourth and fifth centuries. Even though many centers of heresy had been lost to Byzantium during the Moslem invasions of Africa and the Near East, old heretical texts survived to inform new generations about Gnosticism, Arianism, and the various christological heresies, especially Monophysitism, that had been ruthlessly suppressed only a century or so earlier by diligent emperors and muscular church councils and patriarchs. In Byzantium old heresies had a great capacity for survival and new ones a great capacity for growth in a fertile religious culture that had a large proportion of literate and educated clerics and laypeople, a proportion that would not be reached in the Latin West until the twelfth century.

Among Byzantine movements that played enduring roles in the East and exerted some influence on the West, Paulicianism, Iconoclasm, and Bogomilism are particularly important. The Paulicians originated in Armenia, deriving their name from the third-century heretic Paul of Samosata, and circulated throughout the Byzantine Empire, although their greatest strength lay in their powerful military state on the Euphrates which flourished briefly in the third quarter of the ninth century. At the same time, Paulicianism slowly changed from an Adoptionist heresy into a dualist one. The durability and flexibility of Paulicianism contributed to its survival.

Iconoclasm attacked the practice of representing the divinity pictorially, criticized religious images generally, and asserted that to attribute material dimensions to such spiritual beings as God the Father, Christ, and the Virgin Mary was to limit them by denying their spiritual essence. Iconoclasm appealed historically to a variety of eastern Mediterranean peoples, including Jews and Moslems, and it appealed later to western religious thinkers as well.

During the greatest period of Iconoclastic dominance in Byzantine history, from 720 to 843, the movement generated a large and pugnacious literature and widespread social and spiritual unrest. It provided a further occasion for disagreement between Byzantine East and Latin West, and it laid down many of the principles of pictorial representation that later influenced eastern and western religious art.

The fertility and diversity of Byzantine religious life, however, was not matched in the Latin West. There, the battle was much more against the residual paganism of the Germanic, Celtic, and Slavic peoples than against old or new heresies. Most of the effort of Latin Christian churchmen was aimed at conversion and against backsliding movements toward paganism; its monuments are the heroic missionary and monastic achievements of the period between the fourth and the ninth centuries.

Carolingian Christianity allowed little room for doctrinal inventiveness and contained no potentially popular followings for dissident teachers. Most of the heterodoxy of the Carolingian world was that of the cloister or that discussed among prelates. The few local movements that did acquire popular followings, based upon their moral criticism of the existing Church, such as that of Aldebert, have been studied most extensively by Jeffrey Russell. Although several monastic and prelatal religious ideas caused widespread concern, the Spanish movement known as Adoptionism, illustrated in this chapter, perhaps attracted the most attention.

The movement that became the heresy of Adoptionism was related to earlier Nestorianism and argued that Jesus Christ was the adopted son of God. It appears to have begun in Spain in the second half of the eighth century and to have been promulgated by Elipandus, bishop of Toledo. A letter from Pope Hadrian I of 785 gives a brief picture of its impression:

> From your country another dismal thing has come to us, saying that certain bishops living there, namely Elipandus and Ascaricus with others agreeing with them, do not blush to confess the Son of God adopted, although no heretical leader, however great, has dared to utter such blasphemy, except that perfidious Nestorius who has declared that the Son of God is pure mortal.

Elipandus's doctrines were circulated more widely by Felix, bishop of Urgel, a respected churchman. Elipandus's and Felix's doctrines were condemned at the Council of Regensburg in 792 and in another letter of Hadrian I to the bishops of Gaul and Spain in 793:

Oh, you impious men, you who are ungrateful for so many benefits, do you not fear to whisper with a poisonous mouth that he, our liberator, is an adopted son, as it were, a mere man subject to human misfortune, and what a disgrace to say that he is a servant ... for although in the imperfect representation of the prophet he was called servant because of the condition of servile form which he assumed from the Virgin ... this was said only allegorically of Christ.

Adoptionism was condemned again at the Council of Frankfurt in 794 and by Pope Leo III in 796, as well as in Carolingian capitulary legislation. The most articulate attack upon Adoptionism, however, came from Alcuin of York, the most influential theological adviser of Charlemagne. In 797 Alcuin wrote his treatise *Adversus Felicis heresin* (no. 8), and in 798 he wrote a longer work on the same subject. Although Adoptionism has been called an affair of prelates, having no popular following, it is noteworthy because of its impact on the highest circles of Carolingian government and as evidence of the sociology of eighth-century doctrinal deviance. The last protagonist of the controversy, Felix of Urgel, was finally condemned at Aachen in 800 and sentenced to perpetual confinement at Lyons, where he died in 818.

LITERATURE

Much of the literature is discussed in Liutpold Wallach, *Alcuin and Charlemagne: Studies in Carolingian History and Literature* (Ithaca, N.Y., 1959; emended ed. New York, 1968) and in M. L. W. Laistner, *Thought and Letters in Western Europe A.D. 500-900* (London, 1957), pp. 286-314. The texts above are from H. Denziger, *Enchridion Symbolorum*, 30th ed. (Freiburg, 1950), pp. 151-52. The texts from Alcuin's *Liber Adversus Felicis heresin* have been translated for his volume by Mr. Burton Van Name Edwards of the University of Pennsylvania. The Latin originals may be found in *Patrologia Latina*, vol. 101, cols. 87, 92, 99, 102, 120.

1. We read among the stories of secular letters that certain men skilled in the medical arts, when they heard that some cities were infected with the calamity of pestilence, because of love of their citizens, devised some kind of medicine in a preventive solicitude by which they might protect their citizens from the infestation of the approaching disease, lest the attacking danger unexpectedly destroy part of the kindred multitude. It seems to us that this same thing must

be undertaken in devotion against the pestilence of heretical perverseness, whose doctrine creeps in like a cancer, spreads like a virus, kills like the venom injected by the teeth of a serpent into whom he wounds. Nor should the concern for the integrity of souls in the truth of the Catholic faith be of less account to us than the concern for bodily health is shown to have been for the ancients.

2. Behold a certain part of the world is infected by the poison of heretical perverseness, asserting that Christ Jesus is not the true son of God the Father, not his own Son, but adopted; and the Nestorian heresy, returning to life after a long time from the East, where it was condemned by the authority of two hundred Fathers in a synod, secretly fled to the West so that where the visible sun hides itself from human eyes, there the sun of justice is withdrawn from the hearts of the unfaithful. Nestorius by an impious assertion denies that the most blessed Virgin Mary is the mother of God, but only of a man; similarly these people, deceived by the same perverseness, deny that she is truly the mother of the Son of God, but rather is the mother of the adopted son of someone; meaning that Christ-God is adopted with us, through whom we are made adopted sons by God the Father.

o   o   o

13. Therefore, if the Lord Christ was the adopted Son according to the flesh, just as some with a weak faith chatter, in no way is there one Son, since in no way can his own Son and the adopted Son be one Son, since one is recognized as the true Son, the other as the untrue. Why do we employ our depraved rashness to constrain the omnipotence of God? He is not bound by the law of our mortality: "For whatever he wishes, God does in heaven and earth" [Ps. 113:3]. However, if he wished to create his own Son for himself from a virgin's womb, who has dared to say that he could not? "For who can resist His will?" [Rom. 9:19] Why would anyone dare to investigate the secrets of his will or power? Or why shouldn't we believe his testimony about his Son, whom he has named so many times in his gospel, and not another? This same Son also often called him his father.... That person demonstrated the unity of the human and divine persons in order that that man, who was seen, might be believed to be truly the Son of God.

o   o   o

30. Behold how this venerable Father resists the recently introduced name of adoption! How can there not be four persons if there is the Father, the Holy Spirit, the true Son and the adopted Son? For just as

we have often said, all who soundly know understand his own Son and adopted Son to be two, just as true and untrue are two. And how impious it is to say that there are two sons, the one his own, the other adopted!

o   o   o

37. Remove, I beg you, from your heart the name of adoption from Christ-God so that you will be in the true Son of God and will have eternal life in him. Alas blind perverseness! While it strives to seem wise, it is shown to be stupid, and while it presumes to examine the high mysteries of the divinity with a presumptious audacity—according to the words of the scripture "You shall not seek higher things" [Sirach 3:22]—and precipitately falls into the deep pit of error. For the same man is Son of the Virgin, conceived by the Holy Spirit, conceived a true God from the beginning of his conception, and born the true God at the proper time. Behold God the Father wished the True God to be born, so that there would be one person of God and man, and the Son of God would be one, God and man. How could he not want him to be the true Son, whom he wished to be God? Or could he do that and could not do this? Now where is the omnipotence of God, whose will no one resists? If he could and didn't want to, why did he begrudge him the truth of the Son, to whom he did not begrudge the truth of the deity? And what is it that the paternal voice says: "This is my beloved Son in whom I am well pleased"? And again on the mountain: "This is my beloved Son, in whom I am well pleased; believe Him." The devil doubts if the Son of God is whom he sees, and therefore in his temptation, he always requires this, so that he might know if he is the Son of God. These asserters of adoption, however, with a greater presumption than the devil, publicly deny that he is the true Son of God, but they do not fear to affirm a sharing of our adoption.

o   o   o

3. There is no heretic except from contention. Wish not to contend in vain, for the evangelical doctrine shines through the whole world; we hold this unanimously and preach it faithfully. How could we mere men, at the end of the world, with the charity of many cooling, invent anything better than to follow apostolic and evangelical doctrine with the entire intention of the soul and with all firmness and truth of faith, not creating new names, not professing something unusual, not singing empty praises in our name because of the novelty of some doctrine, lest we be found reprehensible where we would want to be praisewor-

thy? Turn in hope to the most holy mercy of the Lord your God and pray to him day and night that you might change in the last days of your life toward the way of truth and the peace of the Catholic faith, lest, if the holiness of the universal Church rejects you here, there it will shut you off from having eternal peace....

4. Behold, the schismatic error breaks a part off from her [the Church] and stains the unity of charity. Therefore, the Church remains in us or in you. For there are two parts and there is not the concord of unity. We cry out with the whole world as a witness that Christ is the true Son of God.... Why do you hesitate after such a thundering, representing his birth by the new name of adoption, which is not found in the entire length of the Old and New Testament? Realize, brothers, that it is a small thing to Christ-God not to have more elect in this world than you few; not to have a church broader than the one located within your narrow borders.... Is this power taken from him [Peter] and given to you at the end of the world so that a new church may be erected over you at the end of time in a corner of the world, and not according to apostolic traditions? Take care diligently, venerable brother, that this edifice of yours not be built on the sand and that your labor will not be in the home of another.... All evangelical authority shouts out, all sayings of the apostles bear witness, the breadth of the world believes, the Roman Church preaches that the Christ Jesus is the true and proper Son of God. Why do you wish to impose the name of adopted? What is an adopted son, except a false son? And if Christ Jesus is the false son of God the Father, and (which is impious to say) if it is wrong that he is God, the entire dispensation of our salvation is false, since if the Son is adopted in respect to humanity, that God-Man who was born of the Virgin is adopted....

5. Many just and true things are found in your writings. Beware, lest you differ from the opinions of the holy Fathers only in this name of adoption; you should not be a lover of your opinion with a few, but an asserter of the truth with many.

II

THE PROBLEM OF REFORM, DISSENT, AND HERESY IN THE ELEVENTH AND TWELFTH CENTURIES

The eleventh and twelfth centuries have been regarded by most modern historians as marking a new beginning in European history. With the ending of Viking, Magyar, and Arab invasions and the growth of population and agricultural productivity, European society developed rapidly through the eleventh, twelfth, and thirteenth centuries. Scholars have traced the consequences of this change in books as diverse as Marc Bloch's *Feudal Society*, Charles Homer Haskins's *The Renaissance of the Twelfth Century*, R. W. Southern's *The Making of the Middle Ages*, and Georges Duby's *Rural Economy and Country Life in the Medieval West*. Robert Lopez has written of the *Commercial Revolution of the Middle Ages*, and Philippe Wolff of *The Awakening of Europe*. In the long view, the links between eleventh-century and eighteenth-century European society seem stronger than ever, and the difference between this period and the Carolingian period which preceded it, as well as the age of political and industrial revolution which followed it, seems sharper.

Thus, the growth and variety of forms of religious dissent that the sources reveal suddenly around the year 1000 is an important facet of the European experience during a period of profound change and social and cultural transformation. Although no historian would consider the changes in religious temper simply a function of change in other areas of life, no historian can ignore change in all such areas if the history of the whole life of European society is to be understood. The religious sensibility of the eleventh and twelfth centuries is a manifestation of the deepest strata of European culture. It, too, was transformed in the eleventh and twelfth centuries, partly by what it perceived as a sudden growth of religious dissent. The shock of dissent and the nature of churchmen's and laypeople's reaction to it led to a new interest in the history of heresy and shaped the place of heresy in the mentality of the later twelfth, thirteenth, and fourteenth centuries, in institutional life, in social structures, and in the creation of persuasive or coercive forces called into existence, or resurrected, to deal with it.

Historians of heresy, and theologians, have long debated whether the wave of heretical movements which swept over Europe after the year 1000 originated in the tenth and eleventh centuries or earlier. One cause of their debate is the theologians', and some historians' tendency to regard orthodox belief as a norm, stated early in the life of a religion, and maintained by an ecclesiastical establishment against which dissent periodically raises its voice, becoming schism or heresy as it grows in intensity and alienation from the core belief. A second cause is in the pattern and frequency of surviving source materials for the history of religious dissent, especially for the period between the eighth and the twelfth centuries. Except for a few dissenting movements in the eighth and ninth centuries that appear to have involved chiefly a few monastic churchmen and prelates, religious dissent among the laity that shows some evidence of popular interest and support appears in a few sources between the period between 1000 and 1050, virtually none between 1050 and 1100, and then reappears in a great number and variety of manifestations from 1100 on. At the same time, a vast movement for religious reform, first in the monasteries and finally led by the papacy itself after 1049, called a great many cultural traditions and institutions into question. Several recent historians of popular heresy have seen strong connections between movements for ecclesiastical reform and religious dissent in the eleventh and twelfth centuries.

One way of considering the cultural history of the eleventh and twelfth centuries is to ask how different thinkers in this period posed—and answered— the question "How must a Christian live in the world?" The answers constitute not a history of dissent and heresy alone, but of devotional life and religious sensibility on the part of all Europeans. The question "How must a Christian live in the world?" was answered differently by both dissenters and reformers, from the way it would have been answered between the seventh and the eleventh centuries. Then, moralists would have answered (as many did) that

the world was a fallen setting for fallen human nature—treacherous, full of
temptation, violent—and the human beings in it were too weak to do much
about it. Ideally, the best thing a Christian could do about living in the world
was to leave it, withdrawing to the spiritual shelter of the monastic life, the
dominant form of religious life before the twelfth century. Those who could
not leave the world fought, in effect, a rearguard action. They had to stand
fast, in recognized social ranks, against potential chaos. Laborers were to labor
for the rest of society. If they did this diligently, right order would be
established, and the prayers would pray from their monastic enclosures for
those who could not pray for themselves. This right order of a tripartite society
was a gift of God, and God had given it so that humans might use it to defend
themselves from fallen nature. Liturgy, ritual, the power of saints and relics,
alms and penitence, these were the human spiritual weapons against the world.
"It is," the historian Janet Nelson has remarked,

> a religion of emphasis on shame rather than sin, atonement rather
> than repentance, orthopraxy rather than orthodoxy, of locally based
> cults, each rural community equipped with the relics of its patron
> saint, each individual striking his own bargain with invisible protec-
> tors.... The confident manipulation of recognized symbols by ritual
> specialists is believed to restore equilibrium between the natural and
> supernatural worlds; the divinity is appeased or swayed by correctly
> performed sacrifice or the penance by proxy of monks. Humbler folk
> use Christian or pagan magic for self-protection.

Such institutions as kingship and the relation of spiritual to temporal authority
in this period may also be understood in terms of this world-view.

From the tenth century on, the question began to be answered differently.
On the one hand, changes in material culture transformed the small, scattered
rural centers of Carolingian civilization into the complex network of urban and
rural societies that stands out sharply by the mid-twelfth century. Most of the
elements of stability that had sufficed until the eleventh century sufficed no
longer; physical and social mobility produced social friction, competition
eroded the preserves of a tripartite society, and political authority was no
longer vested in anointed, priestly kings, but in ambitious, princely state
builders and their rivals. Power was no longer given by God so that human
society might be preserved from its own baser instincts (a view in which the
Carolingians may be said to have anticipated the later theories of Thomas
Hobbes); it was, rather, a tool to be used in changing the world. For the reform

monks and popes, as for the territorial princes, power became an offensive weapon to make a new world. In that world the question "How must a Christian live?" found new and very different answers.

Janet Nelson has persuasively suggested some of the most striking:

> The first [phase] is a resolution of the theodicy in terms of a heavy reinvestment of religious capital in received religious belief and practice; there is a blossoming of devotional piety, manifested in pilgrimages, in the Peace Movement, in the Crusades, in church building, in the heyday of patronage for the Cluniacs. At the belief level, there is adaptation through redefinition of doctrines, a reaffirmation of the efficacy of eucharistic ritual expressed in the doctrine of the Real Presence ... and a holding out of hope to sinners through indulgences and the doctrine of Purgatory. Renewed emphasis on ritual efficacy presupposes the ritual cleanliness of the practitioners; there is a demand for clerical conformity to the norms of purity already exemplified in the monastic life, with a primary insistence upon chastity, and a secondary onslaught on simony. At the same time, the laity set for themselves new standards of purity; moral values are increasingly internalized, sin and guilt replacing shame, repentance replacing ritual atonement. Perhaps most significant of all, there is renewed emphasis on institutional unity, and the common religious heritage of Christendom as a whole; the trend is centripetal, towards increased conformity.

Nelson goes on to suggest that although this massive, creative, and highly dynamic effort offered satisfaction to many, it created even greater dissatisfaction in others. All Christians, according to the great theologian M.-D. Chenu, stood in the twelfth century "at the crossroads of the apostolic life," and some examples of the search for the apostolic life may illustrate the devotional climate described by Nelson and the setting for the first documentary evidence of the growth of popular heresy.

The reform of tenth-century monastic life that began at Cluny in Burgundy and a few other centers swelled to a great tide in the eleventh century. At the end of the eleventh century, new monastic orders, such as the Cistercians, and new orders of canons regular, such as the Premonstratensians, infused the religious life with even greater rigor. The twelfth century became the golden age of the regular religious life, and the spokesmen of that life, particularly St. Bernard (1090-1153), became the most influential churchmen of their age. Yet attractive as the revived monasticism of the eleventh and twelfth centuries was for many, it failed to attract others. Hermits, wandering preachers, individual spiritual leaders like Robert of Arbrissel, and others appear in greater numbers in the eleventh century.

These figures could, with considerable effort, judiciousness, tact, and prudence, be held to ecclesiastical obedience and kept within the broadening mainstream of religious life, and indeed, the versatility of the Church, driven in part by the relentless force of the Gregorian Reform movement, is one of the most striking features of twelfth-century European culture. Yet beyond these new figures there were others, many of whom had begun as reformers, who were outraged both at the insufficiency of reform and at what they claimed to be the loss of an older way of religious life. Still others appeared as spiritual eccentrics, seeking an individual religious life apart from existing institutions. Some of them attracted large personal followings, and they attacked not only clerical abuses, but more and more the basis of clerical status itself. Frequently they based the legitimacy of their teachings on scripture alone and the vision of the apostolic life they derived from it. Few of them were theologians, as that term came to have a technical meaning in the twelfth century, and few of them were learned. Indeed, the lack of systematic heretical "doctrine" and the absence of learned men from these circles has led historians to distinguish sharply between popular and learned heresy throughout later medieval history. Learned or not, they, too, had their own answers to the question "How should a Christian live in the world?"

What we know about them, we know largely from the records left by their enemies, who sought to emphasize the fact and consequences of their deviance, not accurately report them. Their enemies were usually literate monks, well-read in patristic sources and the literature of older heretical movements, and they were inclined to depict contemporary movements as if they were old heresies reborn, or resurfaced. Adhémar of Chabannes, for example, a monk who wrote his chronicle in Angoulême around 1030, notes briefly under the entry for the year 1018 that "Manichaeans appeared in Aquitaine, leading the people astray. They denied baptism, the cross, and all sound doctrine. They did not eat meat, as though they were monks, and pretended to be celibate, but among themselves they enjoyed every kind of indulgence. They were messengers of Antichrist, and caused many to wander from the faith." Adhémar's brief description offers a good example, both of the kinds of sources in which we find the earliest notices of popular heresy, and of the world-view of the person recording them. He obtained the name of "Manichaeans" from patristic sources (see above, no. 2), taking perhaps a name that seemed to describe kinds of beliefs similar to those he had heard about in Aquitaine. Whether Adhémar's "Manichaeans" were dualist in faith is open to question. The "Manichaeans" led a life of ritual asceticism, an inversion in Adhémar's eyes of the asceticism of the monk, for the chronicler goes on to state that asceticism was merely a mask for their licentiousness (a standard monastic commonplace in dealing with heterodox ascetic movements). In denying (probably infant) baptism, the veneration of the cross and "all sound doctrine," the "Manichaeans" probably represent a group with conservative points of view on these topics, for the insistence on infant baptism and the active veneration of the cross were relatively new movements within the Church. From the tenth century on, the legend of Antichrist loomed large in European culture, and Adhémar was being timely in attributing to him the errors of the heretics. Thus, although Adhémar is describing a group of real Christian dissenters, he depicts them by a method whose character has to be properly understood in order for the historian to see through to a fact via the monk's perception. The first three sections in this chapter (nos. 9-11) offer sources which present similar problems.

Numbers 12 through 16 offer more clearly delineated portraits and more systematically recognizable forms of dissent. Across the period between the early eleventh century and the early twelfth lies the great watershed of the Gregorian Reform movement with its impact on every form of religious life (and hence on every form of social bond) known to western Europeans. From the figure of Ramihrdus, lynched at Cambrai in 1076, to Peter Abelard, who died peacefully in a Cluniac monastery in 1142, we deal with figures who, in one way or another, were produced by the reform movement. Some of them may have been reformers only (as Ramihrdus was likely to have been), but others were critics of the reform movement and established themselves as the only true guides toward life in this world and salvation in the next. Such were Tanchelm, Peter of Bruys, and Henry of Le Mans (no. 11). Arnold of Brescia led a political revolt to free the city of Rome from papal control (no. 12) based on his view that the clergy should own no property. Finally, the new schools of the twelfth century produced severe intellectual quarrels, and of these the case of Peter Abelard (nos. 13-14) is probably the best-known. By the middle of the twelfth century, St. Bernard, the most influential churchman in the West and the man with the widest experience of the varieties of twelfth-century dissent, delivered his great sermon on the Song of Songs, perhaps the most revealing extant commentary from an unimpeachably orthodox source of the collective impression that two centuries of dissent had produced in the Church (no. 16).

The dissenting figures described here and in other collections of source materials for the eleventh and early twelfth centuries have no common doctrine and even no common set of criticisms of orthodox belief. The origins of their dissent and its nature have been, and still are, matters of scholarly debate. Except for the cases of Ramihrdus and Abelard, however, they may be considered collectively as offering new kinds of association, new bonds of the spirit for people who, for whatever reasons, were becoming increasingly dissatisfied with the old, and remained unimpressed with, even hostile to, the reforms of the late eleventh century. They were met by representatives of the Church who, faced with the shock of dissent on a large scale and in a great variety of opinions, turned to the writings of the Church Fathers, to St. Augustine, Irenaeus, Tertullian, and Gregory the Great, thinking they saw in the heretics of old the prototypes of contemporary dissenters. This encounter, whatever its various causes, laid the groundwork for the definition of medieval heresy.

At the conclusion of his Sermon on the *Song of Songs*, St. Bernard reminded his listeners of the antiquity of the heretics' teachings, if not of their style: "For I do not recall having heard anything new or strange in all their mouthings, numerous as they are, but that which is worn by use and long agitated by the heretics of old, and which has been well threshed and winnowed by our theologians." Bernard's view of the antiquity of heretical doctrines is a commonplace of twelfth-century theology and is based upon a particular theory of ecclesiastical history. Bernard considered heresy as the second of the four great temptations that the Church would face in its history. The first of these had been the series of bloody persecutions at the hands of pagan authorities before the christianization of the Roman Empire. Heresy, which Bernard called a "bloodless persecution," was the second. The third was the growth of ambition among the clergy, and the fourth was to be the appearance of Antichrist. Of these four temptations, according to Bernard, three had already occurred; in his anticipation of the coming of Antichrist, Bernard joined a current of apocalyptic thought that had been revived in the tenth century and came into its full importance in the movement associated with Joachim of Fiore in the thirteenth century. Indeed, prophecy played an important role in both camps for several centuries after Bernard wrote. For Bernard, heresy had been introduced in the time of the persecutions, and therefore the doctrines of twelfth-century dissenters could only be the old doctrines of Mani and Arius revived. Although heresy was not Bernard's major concern (he was much more concerned with what he considered the third temptation, the growing ambition of the clergy), nevertheless he threw his full energy and the full weight of his prestige behind the view that twelfth-century heresies were old heresies reborn, thereby justifying the Church's approach to the diverse forms of twelfth-century heterodoxy through the antiheretical writings of the Church Fathers of the second through the sixth centuries.

As will be seen below in chapters V and VI, the immense prestige of St. Bernard and the recovery of patristic antiheretical writings in the popular textbooks of Gratian and Peter Lombard in the middle of the twelfth century combined to give the Church both a theory of heresy and the legal means of dealing with it.

LITERATURE

The best general introduction to the historiography of heresy is Jeffrey Burton Russell's long article, "Interpretations of the Origins of Medieval Heresy," *Medieval Studies* 25 (1963): 26-53, a masterful and essential bibliographical study. The most extensive scholarly bibliography of studies on heresy written in this century is Herbert Grundmann, "Bibliographie des études récentes (aprés 1900) sur les hérésies médiévales," in Jacques Le Goff, ed., *Hérésies et Sociétés dans l'Europe pré-industrielle, 11e-18e siècles* (Paris-La Haye, 1968), pp. 407-67, which lists 761 books and articles through 1965. A slightly fuller version was published separately as *Bibliographie zur Ketzergeschichte des Mittelalters, 1900-1966* (Rome, 1967). For work since the end of Grundmann's bibliography, several collections of studies have conveniently brought recent scholarly production up to date in their apparatus. The Le Goff volume itself is essential, since its range and the quality of its articles represent the best ongoing European scholarship on the subject. In addition, see especially Derek Baker, ed., *Schism, Heresy, and Religious Protest*, Studies in Church History, vol. 9 (Cambridge, 1972), and W. Lourdaux and D. Verhelst, eds., *The Concept of Heresy in the Middle Ages, 11th-13th Centuries* (The Hague, 1976). For a bibliographical survey that will bring the work of Grundmann up to date, see the forthcoming work of Jeffrey B. Russell and Carl Berkout, *A Bibliography of Medieval Heresies* (Toronto: Pontifical Institute of Medieval Studies, 1981). A number of historical and theological journals regularly publish articles dealing with the history of heresy. Among these, the *Cahiers de Fanjeaux* is especially good.

Several full-length studies have also appeared since Russell's and Grundmann's work. Prominent among them are Russell's own *Dissent and Reform in the Early Middle Ages* (Berkeley and Los Angeles, 1965), R. I. Moore, *The*

Origins of European Dissent (New York, 1977), and Malcolm Lambert, *Medieval Heresy* (New York, 1977).

Excellent collections of original source materials in translation for this period are Walter Wakefield and Austin P. Evans, *Heresies of the High Middle Ages* (New York, 1969), superbly selected, annotated, translated, and documented, and R. I. Moore, *The Birth of Popular Heresy* (New York, 1976). Rosalind B. Brooke, *The Coming of the Friars* (New York, 1975) contains several important texts for the history of eleventh- and twelfth-century heresy.

Among very recent studies, these deserve particularly close attention: Giorgio Cracco, "Riforma ed eresia in momenti della cultura Europea tra X e XI secolo," *Rivista de Storia e Letteratura Religiosa* 7 (1971): 412-77, a fine study of the religious temper of the tenth and eleventh centuries; idem, "Pataria: *Opus e Nomen*," *Rivista di Storia della Chiesa in Italia* 28 (1974): 357-87, the best account of the circumstances of the Patarine movement in late eleventh-century Italy. In addition to Cracco's fine studies, see also Jean Musy, "Mouvements populaires et hérésies au XIe siècle en France," *Revue Histo-rique* 253 (1975): 33-76. Lester K. Little, *Religious Poverty and the Profit Economy in Medieval Europe* (Ithaca, N.Y., 1978), offers a distinctive and important view of many eleventh- and twelfth-century religious movements in the context of new spiritualities generated by the economic and social change of the period.

Other studies dealing with the problem include: R. I. Moore, "The Origins of Medieval Heresy," *History*, n.s. 55 (1970): 21-36; idem, "Some Heretical Attitudes to the Renewal of the Church," *Studies in Church History* 14 (1977): 87-93; Christopher Brooke, "Heresy and Religious Sentiment, 1000-1250," in Brooke, *Medieval Church and Society* (New York, 1972), pp. 139-61. By far the greatest monograph on the religious temper of the eleventh through the thirteenth centuries is Herbert Grundmann, *Religiöse Bewegungen im Mitte-lalter*, 2d ed. (Hildesheim, 1961). Grundmann's later work on religious movements has been collected in Herbert Grundmann, *Ausgewählte Aufsätze*, Teil 1, *Religiöse Bewegungen* (Stuttgart, 1976). Grundmann was probably the single greatest authority on medieval religious movements in this century, and his work is indispensable to the serious student. Two recent anthologies of scholarly studies in Italian are Ovidio Capitani, ed., *L'eresia medievale* (Bologna, 1971), and idem, *Medievo eretico* (Bologna, 1978).

On the intellectual background of some leaders of the reform movement, see Lester K. Little, "Intellectual Training and Attitudes Toward Reform, 1075-1150," in *Pierre Abélard: Pierre le Vénérable*, Colloques internationaux du CNRS, no. 546 (Paris, 1975), pp. 235-54.

9   Paul of St. Père de Chartres: Heretics at Orléans, 1022

Several sources, all in substantial agreement, tell the story of the knight Aréfast and his discovery of and triumph over a band of heretical teachers in Orléans in the year 1022. This episode is quite different from most other contemporary episodes of dissent in several respects. For one thing, it is attested to by more than one source; and the text translated here, that of Paul of St. Père de Chartres, probably derived in part from Aréfast's eyewitness account. For another, it is the first extensively described encounter between orthodox believers and learned heretics, although the character of the heretics' beliefs cannot be clearly identified with other heterodox movements of the eleventh and twelfth centuries. The composition of the heretics' group is also significant, since it included laypeople as well as clerics. In its insistence upon secret knowledge reserved for the initiated, the demonological characteristics attributed to it, and the high social standing of most of its members, the group at Orléans is quite different from most other briefly described eleventh-century episodes.

LITERATURE

Wakefield and Evans, *Heresies of the High Middle Ages*, pp. 74-81; Russell, *Dissent and Reform*, pp. 27-35; Moore, *Origins of European Dissent*, pp. 24-31; Lambert, *Medieval Heresy*, pp. 24-39. Latin text in Fearns, *Ketzer und Ketzerbekämpfung*, pp. 10-12.

THE SYNOD OF ORLÉANS, 1022

I think it worthwhile to record for posterity how Aréfast, with the help of God, and his own admirable native cunning, detected a wicked heresy which was active in the city of Orléans and was spreading its vicious and deadly poison through the provinces of Gaul, and had it thoroughly crushed. Aréfast was a relation of the counts of Normandy,

From R. I. Moore, *The Birth of Popular Heresy* (New York: St. Martin's Press, 1975; London: Edward Arnold, 1975). Reprinted with the permission of the publishers.

polished in speech, cautious in counsel and sound in morals, and therefore highly regarded as an emissary both to the king of France and to other nobles. In his household he had a clerk named Heribert who went to study in the city of Orléans. Though his visit should have been adequately occupied in discovering true authors, he fell blindly into the pit of heresy. In the city there lived two clerks, Stephen and Lisois, who were widely famed for their wisdom, outstanding in holiness and generous with alms. Heribert sought them out and in a short time had become their docile disciple; intoxicated by them with a deadly draught of evil disguised by the sweetness of the holy scriptures, he was demented, ensnared by a diabolical heresy, and believed that he was skilled in divinity and had ascended the citadel of wisdom.

When he returned home, he was anxious to convert his lord, whom he loved dearly, to the path of error. He approached him gradually, with subtle phrases and said that Orléans shone more brightly than other cities with the light of wisdom and the torch of holiness. His words revealed to Aréfast that he had strayed from the path of righteousness. He immediately informed Count Richard and asked him to write to King Robert to tell him of the disease that was lurking in his kingdom before it should spread any further, and to ask the king not to deny Aréfast himself whatever help he needed to root it out. Thunderstruck by this news, the king instructed Aréfast to go to Orléans at once with his clerk, and promised him every assistance.

When he set out at the royal command, Aréfast went first to Chartres, to consult with the venerable Bishop Fulbert, but as it chanced he was away on a mission to Rome. He unfolded the plan of his journey to a wise clerk named Everard, sacristan of the church of Chartres and asked for his advice on the project—where he should draw the lines of battle, and with what weapons he should provide himself against such a range of devilish and deceitful arts. Everard wisely advised him to seek the help of the Almighty every morning, to go to church, devote himself to prayer, and fortify himself with the holy communion of the body and blood of Christ. Thus protected by the sign of the cross, he should proceed to listen to the wickedness of the heretics, contradicting nothing that he should hear them say, and pretending that he wished to become their disciple, while he quietly stored everything away in his heart.

Aréfast followed this advice, and when he reached Orléans, took communion every day and, fortified by prayer, went to the house of the heretics as though he were a simple disciple coming to hear their teaching. At first they taught him by citing texts from the holy scriptures, and by employing certain figures of speech. When they saw that he listened carefully, as a perfect pupil should, they put to him, among other metaphors, the image of a tree in a wood: "We regard you," they said, "as a tree in a wood, which is transplanted to a garden, and watered regularly, until it takes root in the earth. Then it is stripped of thorns and other excess matter, and pruned down to the ground with a hoe, so that a better branch can be inserted into it, which will later bear sweet fruit. In the same way you will be carried out of this evil world into our holy company. You will soak in the waters of wisdom until you have taken shape, and armed with the sword of the Lord, are able to avoid the thorns of vice. Foolish teachings will be shut out from your heart and you will be able with a pure mind, to receive our teaching, which is handed down from the Holy Spirit."

He received everything they told him with exclamation of thanks to God, until they thought that they had converted him to their heresy. Then, feeling secure, they revealed the depths of their wickedness to him, disguised in the words of the holy scriptures. They said, "Christ was not born of the Virgin Mary, he did not suffer for men, he was not really buried in the sepulchre and did not rise from the dead," to which they added, "there is no cleansing of sin in baptism, nor in the sacrament of the body and blood of Christ administered by a priest. Nothing is to be gained from praying to the holy martyrs and confessors."

When these doomed and wretched men had spewed forth these and other abominable sentiments from their festering bellies, Aréfast replied, "If these things which you have spoken of offer no chance of salvation to men, as they hope, I must press you urgently to tell me what does offer hope. Otherwise my soul, which you have brought to doubt, will soon fall into the ruin of despair."

"There is no doubt, brother," they answered, "that until now you have lain with the ignorant in the Charybdis of false belief. Now you have been raised to the summit of all truths. With unimpeded mind you may begin to open your eyes to the light of the true faith. We will open the door of salvation to you. Through the laying of our hands upon you, you will be cleansed of every spot of sin. You will be replenished with the gift of the Holy Spirit, which will teach you unreservedly the underlying meaning of the scriptures, and true righteousness. When you have fed on the heavenly food and have achieved inner satisfaction you will often see angelic visions with us, and sustained by that solace you will be able to go where you will without let or hindrance, whenever you want to. You will want for nothing, for God, in whom are all the treasures of wealth and wisdom, will never fail to be your companion in all things."

Meanwhile the king and Queen Constance had come to Orléans, as Aréfast had asked, with a number of bishops, and on the following day, at his suggestion, the whole wicked gang was arrested by royal officials at the house where they met, and brought before the king and queen and an assembly of clerks and bishops at the church of Ste. Croix.

Before we come to the disputation, I must tell you those who have not heard how these people confected the meal which they call heavenly. They met on certain nights in the house which I have mentioned, each holding a light in his hand, and called a roll of the names of demons, like a litany, until suddenly they saw the devil appear among them in the guise of some wild beast. Then, as soon as they saw that sight, the lights were put out and each of them grabbed whatever woman came to hand, and seized her to be put to ill use. Without regard to sin, whether it were a mother, or a sister, or a nun, they regarded that intercourse as a holy and religious work. On the eighth day they lit a great fire among them, and the child who was born of this foul union was put to the test of the flames after the manner of the ancient pagans, and burned. The ashes were collected and kept with as much reverence as the Christian religion accords to the body of Christ, to be given as a last sacrament to the sick when they are about to depart this life. There was such power of diabolic evil in this ash that anyone who had succumbed to the heresy and tasted only a small quantity of it was afterwards scarcely ever able to direct his mind away from heresy and back to the truth. It is enough to speak of this only briefly, so that Christians should beware of this nefarious device, and will be sure not to imitate it. But I have digressed; I will return to the burden of my story, and if the barbarity of these infidels is treated hastily it is because a fuller discussion of it might disgust a sensitive reader.

When they were brought before the king and the assembly of bishops Aréfast addressed the king first:

"My lord, I am a knight of your faithful vassal Richard, count of Normandy, and do not deserve to be held bound and chained before you."

"Tell us at once," the king replied, "how you come to be here, so that we may know whether you should be kept in chains as a criminal or released as an innocent man."

"I heard of the learning and piety of those who stand before you with me in chains," answered Aréfast, "and came to this city in the hope of profiting from the example of their good works and teaching. That is why I left my own country and came here. Let the bishops who sit with you decide and judge whether I committed any crime in that."

To this the bishops replied, "If you tell us the nature of the wisdom and piety which you have learnt from these men, we will have no difficulty in reaching a conclusion."

"Your majesty," said Aréfast, "order them to repeat before you what they taught me. When you have heard it you may decide whether they are worthy of praise or should be condemned to death."

When the king and the bishops ordered the heretics to explain the principles of their faith these enemies of all truth spoke for one another, but would not open a path into the foulness of their heresy. Just as the more a snake shrinks in the hand, the more easily it can escape, so the harder they were pressed the more elusively they seemed to evade the truth. Then Aréfast, seeing that they were playing for time, and trying to cloud over their views with a shield of words, turned to them and said:

"I thought that you were teachers of truth, not of falsehood, so long as I saw that you taught me your doctrine, which, you claimed, brings salvation steadfastly, and promised that you would never deny it, even if it meant sustaining punishment, or enduring death itself. Now I see that your promises are forgotten. Through fear of death, you want to be dissociated from your doctrines, and you count it little to leave me, your former disciple, in danger of death. The royal command should be obeyed, and the authority of so many bishops respected, so that I may know whether any of the things of which I have learnt from you are contrary to the Christian religion, and which of them, in their judgment, should be followed, and which rejected. You taught me that nothing in baptism merits forgiveness of sin; that Christ was not born of the Virgin, did not suffer for men, was not truly buried, and did not rise from the dead; that the bread and wine which seem to become a sacrament on the altar in the hands of priests through the operation of the Holy Spirit cannot be turned into the body and blood of Christ."

When Aréfast had finished speaking, Bishop Guarin of Beauvais questioned Stephen and Lisois, who seemed to be leaders in the heresy, whether they held and believed these things as Aréfast had reported them. They had prepared themselves a dwelling with the devil in hell, and replied that he had remembered accurately, and they did hold and believe in those things. The bishop said that he believed that Christ was born of the Virgin—which is possible—and that he suffered in human form for us, and then defeated death and rose again on the third day, and in his Godhead, to teach us that we too might be reformed and rise again.

They replied with the tongues of snakes, "We were not there, so we cannot believe that these things are true."

"Do you believe that you yourselves had human parents, or not?" asked the bishop. When they replied that they did he continued, "If you believe that you were procreated by your parents when you did not exist before, why do you refuse to believe that God was born of God without a mother before time, and born of the Virgin, by the shadow of the Holy Spirit within the limits of time?"

"What nature denies is always out of harmony with creation."

"Before anything was done by nature, do you not believe that God the Father through the Son made everything from nothing?"

To this these aliens from the faith replied, "You may tell all this to those who are learned in earthly things, who believe the fabrications which men have written on the skins of animals. We believe in the law written within us by the Holy Spirit, and hold everything else, except what we have learnt from God, the maker of all things, empty, unnecessary, and remote from divinity. Therefore bring an end to your speeches and do with us what you will. Now we see our king reigning in heaven. He will raise us to his right hand in triumph and give us eternal joy."

From the first until the ninth hour of that day everyone put forward various arguments to make them renounce their errors, and they resisted with the obstinacy of iron. Then they were all commanded to put on the holy vestment of their order, and immediately stripped of them again with full ceremony by the bishops. At the king's command, Queen Constance stood before the doors of the Church, to prevent the common people from killing them inside the Church, and they were expelled from the bosom of the Church. As they were being driven out, the queen struck out the eye of Stephen, who had once been her confessor, with the staff which she carried in her hand. They were taken outside the walls of the city, a large fire was lit in a certain cottage, and they were all burned, with the evil dust of which I have spoken above, except for one clerk and a nun, who had repented by the will of God.

10.   Guibert of Nogent: Heretics at Soissons, 1114

Guibert of Nogent (ca. 1064-ca. 1126) wrote his *Memoirs*, one of the most distinctive and interesting works of the twelfth century, in imitation of St. Augustine's *Confessions*, thus playing an important role in the history of Christian autobiography. His work casts considerable light on one eleventh-century boyhood and monastic career. Guibert was a monk, however, and by late eleventh-century standards a learned man. His account of the "Manichees" at Soissons borrows heavily from earlier ecclesiastical descriptions of heretical beliefs and behavior.

LITERATURE

Wakefield and Evans, *Heresies of the High Middle Ages*, pp. 101-4; Russell, *Dissent and Reform*, pp. 46-47; Moore, *Birth of Popular Heresy*, pp. 67-69. This excerpt is from John F. Benton, ed. and trans., *Self and Society in Medieval France: The Memoirs of Abbot Guibert of Nogent* (New York: Harper and Row, 1970), second printing, with corrections based on Durham Cathedral Library MS. B. III. 7, fol. 364-64v. The editor has graciously supplied me with an additional correction based on the manuscript, the justification for which he is publishing elsewhere. The text is on pp. 212-14.

Since we have in mind the heretics whom this abominable man loved, a certain peasant named Clement lived with his brother Evrard at Bucy, a village near Soissons. As was commonly reported, he was one of the leaders of the heresy. That foul count used to say of him that he had found no one wiser. This heresy is not one that openly defends its faith, but, condemned to everlasting whispers, it spreads secretly. The following is said to be the sum of it.

They declare that the divine dispensation of the Virgin's Son is a delusion.

From John F. Benton, *Self and Society in Medieval France* (New York: Harper and Row, 1970), pp. 212-14. Reprinted with the permission of the publisher.

They consider void the baptism of young children not yet of an age of understanding under any sort of godfathers and godmothers.

They call upon God's own Word, which comes into being by some long rigmarole of talk.

They so abominate the mystery which is enacted on our altar that they call the mouths of all priests the mouth of hell.

If they ever receive our sacrament to hide their heresy, they arrange their meals so as to eat nothing more that day.

They do not separate their cemeteries from other land as being sacred in comparison.

They condemn marriage and propagation by intercourse.

Clearly, although there are few of them in the Latin world, you may see men living with women without the name of husband and wife in such fashion that one man does not stay with one woman, each to each, but men are known to lie with men and women with women, for with them it is impious for men to lust after women.

They abstain from all food which is produced by sexual generation.

They have their meetings in underground vaults or unfrequented cellars, without distinction of sex. After they have lighted candles, some loose woman lies down for all to watch, and, so it is said, uncovers her buttocks, and they present their candles at her from behind; and as soon as the candles are put out, they shout "Chaos" from all sides, and everyone fornicates with whatever woman comes first to hand.

If a woman becomes pregnant there, after the delivery the infant is taken back to the place. They light a great fire and those sitting around it toss the child from hand to hand through the flames until it is dead. Then it is reduced to ashes and the ashes made into bread. To each person a portion is given as a sacrament, and once it has been received, hardly anyone recovers from that heresy.

If you review the heresies described by Augustine, you will find this like none of them so much as that of the Manicheans. This heresy, which first originated among the more learned people, filtered down to the country population. These people, who pride themselves on keeping up the apostolic life, esteem only the reading of the Acts of the Apostles.

The two heretics named before were brought for examination to Lisiard, the illustrious lord bishop of Soissons. When they were charged by the bishop with holding meetings outside the church and were said to be heretics by their neighbors, Clement replied, "Haven't you read in the Gospels, master, where it says, 'Beati eritis'?" Since he knew no Latin, he thought this meant, "Blessed are the heretics." He also believed that they were called "heretics" as if they were "heritors," doubtless not those of God. When they were examined about their belief, they gave most Christian answers, yet did not deny their meetings. But since such people deny charges and always draw away the hearts of the dull-witted in secret, they were assigned to the ordeal of exorcised water. As it was being prepared, the bishop asked me to extract their opinions from them privately. When I proposed to them the subject of infant baptism, they said, "He that believeth and is baptized shall be saved." And when I perceived that with them a good saying covers much wickedness, I asked what they thought of those who are baptized in the faith of others. They replied, "In God's name do not expect us to search so deeply. When you add to that single verse, we believe everything you say." I then remembered that line to which the Priscillianists formerly agreed; that is, "swear, perjure yourself, but do not reveal the secret." I said to the bishop, "Since the witnesses who heard them professing such beliefs are not present, sentence them to the ordeal prepared for them." There was in fact a certain lady whose mind Clement had addled for a year, and there was also a deacon who had heard other wicked statements from the man's own mouth.

The bishop celebrated mass, and from his hand they received the sacrament with these words: "Let the body and blood of the Lord try you this day." After this, the pious bishop and Archdeacon Pierre, a man of great honesty who had scorned the promises they had made to escape the ordeal, proceeded to the water. With many tears the bishop recited the litany and then pronounced the exorcism. After that they took an oath that they had never believed or taught anything contrary to our faith. Clement was then thrown into the vat and floated like a stick. At this sight, the whole church was filled with unbounded joy. Their notoriety had brought together such an assembly of both sexes that no one present could remember seeing one like it before. The other confessed his error, but, being impenitent, was thrown into prison with his convicted brother. Two other established heretics from the village of Dormans had come to look on and were held with them.

We then went on to the Council of Beauvais to consult with the bishops about what ought to be done. But in the interval the faithful people, fearing weakness on the part of the clergy, ran to the prison, seized them, placed them in a fire outside the city, and burned them to ashes. To prevent the spreading of the cancer, God's people showed a righteous zeal against them.

11   William the Monk: The Debate with Henry of Le Mans

The late eleventh and early twelfth centuries witnessed the appearance of significant numbers of *Wanderprediger*, wandering preachers of repentance and salvation who belonged to no religious order and were often laymen. Some of these, such as Peter the Hermit, preacher of the first Crusade, Robert of Arbrissel, founder of the community at Fontevrault, and Bernard of Tiron, founder of the order of Savigny, occupy prominent places in the devotional life of the orthodox Church of the period. Others, however, preached with equal vehemence, but directed their energies against both clerical abuses and the clergy itself. Of these, Henry of Le Mans was probably the most successful and striking. St. Bernard states that Henry had originally been a monk, but when Henry first appears in history, at Bishop Hildebert's city of Le Mans in 1116, he is no longer a monk, but a preacher of penitence who turned the city population against the clergy, attacked new ecclesiological developments such as marriage laws, and controlled the city for several weeks. Henry next appears at the Council of Pisa in 1135, where he was condemned, and it may have been in 1135 or 1136 when he engaged in debates with the monk William, whose account of these arguments is the first systematic record of heretical beliefs in the twelfth century. Henry continued his preaching after the condemnation at Pisa, drawing after him the wrath of St. Bernard, and he disappears from history around 1140, after having preached in northern and southern *Francia*, come under the influence of Petrobrusianism, and successfully raised up the spectre of the arch-heretic, a figure which survives in most later antiheretical literature.

Literature

Wakefield and Evans, *Heresies of the High Middle Ages*, pp. 107-18, 122-26; Moore, *Origins*, pp. 82-114; Lambert, *Medieval Heresy*, pp. 39-52. Latin texts in Fearns, *Ketzer und Ketzerbekämpfung*, pp. 21-24.

After parting from Your Worthy Presence, I came to a place where I had a bitter controversy with the heresiarch Henry. I have taken pains to describe to Your Prudence the course of the argument, so that if the beast, by any chance, comes into your vicinity you may be forewarned that by many arguments and proofs he has been clearly shown to be a heretic and you may firmly keep him away from the limits of your church.

Thereupon, I addressed the fellow in these words: "I ask you who propose such wicked tenets, so hurtful to our faith: in obedience to whom do you preach? Who commissioned you to this function? What scriptures do you accept?" And he [replied]: "To answer your question about obedience: I confess that I obey God rather than man, for obedience is owed to God rather than to men. To answer your question about my mission: He sent me who said, 'Go, teach ye all nations.' He who imposed the duty was the same as He who said, 'Thou shalt love thy neighbor as thyself.' Furthermore, I accept the scriptures of the New Testament, by which I verify and corroborate the aforesaid statements. But in case you seek to draw arguments against me from Jerome, Augustine, and other doctors of the Church, I admit giving their words due regard but not as vital to salvation."

Concerning children who die before the age of understanding.

You [Henry] argue that children attain salvation if they die before the age of understanding and by this you destroy the doctrine of original sin; thus you fall into the Pelagian heresy. For you say: "It is a wicked thing to condemn a man for another person's sin, in accordance with the text, 'The soul that sinneth, the same shall die,' and likewise, 'The son shall not bear the iniquity of the father. Everyone shall bear his own burden.' "

That baptism should not be given with chrism and oil.

Now we pass on to another point. You say: "There is no Gospel command to baptize with chrism and oil."

That the body of Christ cannot be consecrated by unworthy ministers

Now we come to a third article. "The body of Christ," so you say, "cannot be consecrated by an unworthy minister." In this I see your wickedness explicitly, for you wish to make this a means of weakening

From Walter Wakefield and A. P. Evans, *Heresies of the High Middle Ages* (New York: Columbia University Press, 1969), pp. 115-17. Reprinted with the permission of the publisher.

the basis of a great sacrament and of depriving the Church of that by which the body of man is strengthened and the spirit sustained. For you say, "Mass may be sung and Christ's body consecrated, provided anyone can be found worthy to do so"; thus enjoining us to discover an imaginary person who never can be found, because no one is without sin, not even a day-old child. "For all have sinned and do need the glory of God." You ask the impossible, seeking to shatter the ordinances of our faith. You, together with the Arians and other heretics, never cease to rend the robe of Christ.

Merely the agreement of the persons concerned constitutes a marriage

Give attention, if you can, and let us go on to the sacrament of matrimony, on which you are in error. "Merely the agreement of the persons concerned, without any rite or ecclesiastical ceremony, constitutes a marriage," you say, "and what is so contracted cannot be dissolved save on grounds of fornication." In this your error is disgraceful.

Priests of the present day do not have the power to bind or loose

But since you do not know what things constitute, or are impediments to, or dissolve marriages, I forbear to discuss them with you. Let us now turn to the subject of priests and prelates of the Church, against whom you rave. "Priests of today," you represent, "have not the power to bind or loose, for they are stripped of this power by having criminally sinned."

There is no gospel command to go to a priest for penance

Now let us pass on to another point, which concerns penance. You say: "There is no Gospel command to go to a priest for penance, for the apostle James says, 'Confess your sins one to another,' and so on. He did not say, 'Confess to priests,' but 'Confess one to another.'"

Bishops and priests ought not to have wealth or benefices

Now you say, "Bishops and priests ought not to have benefices or wealth." In this you do not abate your frenzy against priests.

That churches of wood or stone should not be constructed

Of churches, which you have discussed in your first chapter, you say that they ought not to be built of wood or stone. . . . Yet you seek to subvert and trouble the house of God and its beauty, and the whole condition of the Church. What follows—"No good work helps the dead, for as soon as men die they either are utterly damned or are saved"—is openly heretical.

12   Otto of Freising: Arnold of Brescia in Rome, 1148-55

Arnold, probably a descendant of the minor nobility around the city of Brescia in northern Italy, was born around 1100 and may have studied at Paris under Peter Abelard before 1120. He became a canon regular in his native city, where he apparently became convinced of the evils of clerical wealth and participated in the revolt against Bishop Manfred of Brescia between 1135 and 1138. Arnold was expelled from Italy by Pope Innocent II in 1139, attended the Council of Sens in 1140, and went again to Paris in the same year. Arnold excited the hostility of St. Bernard and King Louis VII of France. Expelled from Paris, he went to Zurich, and then to Rome, where he was temporarily reconciled to Pope Eugenius III around 1146. The turmoil in Rome in these years, however, presented a comunal movement to oppose papal government, and Arnold emerged at the head of that movement after 1148, remaining so until his death in 1155. A number of sources exist for his life and beliefs, among the most impressive and hostile the account of Otto, bishop of Freising and uncle of the Emperor Frederick Barbarossa, printed here.

LITERATURE

G. W. Greenaway, *Arnold of Brescia* (Cambridge, 1931); Moore, *Origins of European Dissent*, pp. 115-38, Wakefield and Evans, *Heresies of the High Middle Ages*, pp. 146-51.

Now on his way to the City the king encamped near Viterbo. Thither came the Roman pope Hadrian, with his cardinals, and was received with the honor due to his office. He was given a deferential hearing as he uttered bitter complaints against his people. For the aforesaid people, since their endeavor to reinstate the order of senators, in their rash daring did not shrink from inflicting many outrages on their popes. There was this additional aggravation of their seditious conduct, that a certain Arnold of Brescia, of whom mention has been made above, under guise of religion and—to use the words of the gospel—acting as a wolf in sheep's clothing, entered the city, inflamed to violence the minds of the simple people by his exceedingly seductive doctrines, and induced—nay, rather, seduced—a countless throng to espouse that cause.

That Arnold, a native of Italy from the city of Brescia, a cleric ordained only as a lector of the church there, had once had Peter Abelard as his teacher. He was a man not indeed dull of intellect, yet abounding rather in profusion of words than in the weight of his ideas; a lover of originality and eager for novelty. The minds of such men are inclined to devise heresies and the tumult of schisms. Returning from his studies in France to Italy, he assumed the religious habit that he might deceive the more, assailing all things, carping at everything, sparing no one—a disparager of the clergy and of bishops, a persecutor of monks, a flatterer only of the laity. For he used to say that neither clerics that owned property, nor bishops that had regalia, nor monks with possessions could in any wise be saved. All these things belong to the prince, and should be bestowed of his beneficience for the use of the laity only. Besides this, he is said to have held unreasonable views with regard to the sacrament of the altar and infant baptism. While he was keeping the church of Brescia in uproar in these and other ways, which it would take too long to enumerate, and was maliciously defaming ecclesiastical personalities to the laity of that land, who have itching ears as regards the clergy, he was accused by the bishop and pious men of that city at the great council held at Rome under Innocent. Therefore the Roman pontiff decided that silence should be imposed upon the man, that his pernicious teaching might not spread to more people. And thus it was done.

So that man, fleeing from Italy, betook himself to the lands beyond the Alps, and there assuming the role of teacher in Zurich, a town of Swabia, he sowed his pernicious doctrine for some time. But when he learned of the death of Innocent he entered the city, near the

From C. C. Mierow, *The Deeds of Frederick Barbarossa by Otto of Freising* (New York: Columbia University Press, 1953), pp. 61-63, 142-44. Reprinted with the permission of the publisher.

beginning of the pontificate of Eugenius. As he found it aroused to rebellion against its pope, he incited it all the more to revolt, not following the counsel of the wise man who says of a situation of this kind, "Heap not wood upon his fire." He set forth the examples of the ancient Romans, who by virtue of the ripened judgment of the senate and the disciplined integrity of the valiant spirit of youth made the whole world their own. Wherefore he advocated that the Capitol should be rebuilt, the senatorial dignity restored, and the equestrian order reinstituted. Nothing in the administration of the city was the concern of the Roman pontiff; the ecclesiastical courts should be enough for him. Moreover, the menace of this baneful doctrine began to grow so strong that not only were the houses and splendid palaces of Roman nobles and cardinals being destroyed, but even the reverend persons of some of the cardinals were shamefully treated by the infuriated populace, and several were wounded. Although he incessantly and irreverently perpetrated these things and others like them for many days (that is, from the death of Celestine until this time) and despised the judgment of the pastors, justly and canonically pronounced against him, as though in his opinion they were void of all authority, at last he fell into the hands of certain men and was taken captive within the limits of Tuscany. He was held for trial by the prince and finally was brought to the pyre by the prefect of the city. After his corpse had been reduced to ashes in the fire, it was scattered on the Tiber, lest his body be held in veneration by the mad populace.

13   Peter Abelard at the Council of Soissons, 1121: The *Historia Calamitatum*

The texts printed here so far represent the anticlerical and antiecclesiological aspects of eleventh- and twelfth-century religious dissent. They reflect popular movements with substantial followings, but with little doctrinal or theological sophistication. They deeply troubled the ecclesiastical authorities who had to deal with them and the ecclesiastical writers who described them. The eleventh and twelfth centuries, however, also witnessed an educational revolution and the creation of a new learned class of clerics, whose rhetorical and logical skills made them extremely popular and influential. Their schools, led by independent masters, attracted many students, and their application of the study of logic to theology created the groundwork for early scholasticism. Their theological methods, however, displeased many churchmen, chiefly because, as their enemies claimed, they tended to reduce theology to an intellectual discipline and apply critical methods to the understanding of dogma. The most spectacular success among these teachers was Peter Abelard (1079-1142), whose long and troubled career has made him the best-known twelfth-century thinker and writer. St. Bernard's denunciation of Abelard's "errors" in 1140 illustrates the growing influence of St. Bernard as a spokesman for the Church as well as the growing concern with heterodoxy that led Bernard and others to their condemnation of Abelard. Although later medieval schools afforded considerable protection and latitude to their members, the case of Abelard illustrates the widening of concern over heretical belief and teaching that marks the early twelfth century and echoes something of the general resistance to early scholasticism that the century witnessed. Thus, along with the revival of learning there developed a hostility to some of the distinctive features of that learning as well as to some of its social consequences.

Perhaps the first case in which the new learning encountered hostility over theological matters was that of Berengar, *scholasticus* (master) in the episcopal city of Tours. Berengar (1000-1088) had studied logic intensively and applied Aristotelian categories somewhat bluntly to the problem of the Real Presence of Christ in the Eucharist, which he eventually denied. Although Berengar was defeated in literary disputes with Archbishop Lanfranc of Canterbury and Guitmund of Aversa, condemned by a number of popes and councils, and forced to issue statements of belief that repudiated his former positions, he attracted no great following and died in peace. Roscellinus of Compiègne (d. 1020), following a slightly different approach to theology, argued against the prevailing Platonic theology of the late eleventh century, stating that the only real things were not the universal categories of neo-Platonism, but individual objects and their names (hence the name Nominalism given to Roscellinus's method). Such a view led Roscellinus to heterodox opinions on the Trinity and other subjects, but again, his is a case of unintentional error generated in the rarefied atmosphere of the lecture hall. A final instance in which learning might appear to be heretical is the frequency after the eleventh century of accusations of magical practices against learned figures, the first of whom was Gerbert of Aurillac, Pope Sylvester II (ca. 945-1003).

Peter Abelard (1079-1142) was born at Le Pallet in Brittany, the son of a minor Breton noble. He took to letters early in life, and moved farther and farther from home as he used up the abilities of local teachers. Abelard studied dialectic at Paris and quickly became a leading teacher himself. He attracted many pupils, contended with the leading contemporary logicians, fell in love with and then married Heloise, and entered monastic life. Abelard had written a treatise *On the Unity and Trinity of God* around 1120, a work which marked his entry into theological literature, and his book aroused the anger of a number of rivals and theologians who resented logicians' intrusion into their specialized field. Abelard's work was condemned at the Council of Soissons in 1121. After a troubled life in and out of several monasteries, however, Abelard returned to Paris around 1135 and resumed teaching—and controversy. In 1139 William of St.-Thierry wrote to St. Bernard, warning him that "Peter Abelard is again teaching and writing novelties. His books cross the seas and leap over the Alps. His novel statements on the faith, his new dogmas, are being broadcast over provinces and kingdoms, preached with solemnity and defended with impunity to such a point that they are said to enjoy authority in the Roman Curia." William's letter also listed several of the theological errors he thought he had found in Abelard's work. St. Bernard replied in an offhand manner, but, after a personal meeting with Abelard, the saint began actively to press for Abelard's condemnation. Abelard recounted some of his early trials with opponents in his remarkable autobiography, the *Historia Calamitatum*, which gives a good portrait of the controversialist and his opinions of his enemies. St. Bernard's correspondents included Pope Innocent II, to whom Bernard wrote Letter 189 (no. 14), describing Abelard's second condemnation, this time at the Council of Sens in 1140. St. Bernard's hostility elicited from Pope Innocent II a papal condemnation of Abelard in 1140:

> We, who though unworthily, are observed to sit in the chair of St. Peter, to whom it has been said by the Lord, "And thou, being once converted, convert thy brethren"; and after having taken counsel with our own brethren, the principal bishops, have condemned by the authority of the sacred canons the chapters you sent us by your discretion and all the teachings of this Peter Abelard, with their author. And we have imposed perpetual silence upon him as a heretic. We declare also that the followers and defenders of his error must be separated from the faithful and must be bound by the chain of excommunication.

Abelard was planning to go to Rome to plead his case personally before the pope when he died in 1142, while residing at the monastery of Cluny.

The case of Abelard is interesting for many things besides the history of heresy, and indeed it has been argued that Abelard was not a heretic at all, certainly not in the sense that some of the reformers and dissenters considered above were. But Abelard's career occurred precisely at the moment when the new "masters of the theological science" seemed to be taking over the teaching of theology, and were, in fact, laying the groundwork for the scholastic thought of the late twelfth and thirteenth centuries. Resistance to this movement was considerable, and in the light of the careers of Berengar and Roscellinus and the widespread popularity of logical method, in addition to Abelard's own abrasive personality and methods, it is possible to regard his condemnation as part of a widespread fear that theology was being taken over not by holy, but by clever men whose cleverness threatened to destroy its higher spiritual content. The association made by St. Bernard between Abelard and Arnold of Brescia, although it is in part fraudulent, suggests that Bernard regarded both thinkers as part of a larger fabric of heterodoxy which was currently threatening Christian society.

LITERATURE

A fine introduction to the period and its movements is Philippe Wolff, *The Awakening of Europe* (Baltimore, 1968), as is R. W. Southern, *The Making of the Middle Ages* (New Haven, 1953). On Carolingian theological disputes, see M. L. W. Laistner, *Thought and Letters in Western Europe A.D. 500-900* (reprint ed., London, 1957), pp. 286-314. For Berengar, see M. Gibson, "The Case of Berengar of Tours," *Studies in Church History* 7 (1971): 61-68; idem, *Lanfranc of Bec* (Oxford, 1978), pp. 63-97. For Roscellinus, see F. Überweg, *A History of Philosophy*, translated by G. S. Morris (London, 1880), pp. 365-77. There is an immense literature on Abelard. See J. G. Sikes, *Peter Abailard* (Cambridge, 1932), and for his influence, see D. E. Luscombe, *The School of Abelard* (Cambridge, 1969).

Texts of the dispute will be found translated in the following: Ailbe J. Luddy, *The Case of Peter Abelard* (Dublin, 1947); Peter Abelard, *The Story of Abelard's Adversities*, translated by J. T. Muckle (Toronto, 1964); B. S. James, *The Letters of Saint Bernard of Clairvaux* (Chicago, 1965); Samuel J. Eales, trans., *The Life and Works of St. Bernard* (London, 1896).

On the last day of the council, before the session convened, the legate and the archbishop deliberated with my rivals and sundry

others as to what should be done about me and my book, this being the
chief reason for their having come together. And since they had
discovered nothing either in my speech or in what I had hitherto
written which would give them a case against me, they were all
reduced to silence, or at the most to maligning me in whispers. Then
Geoffroi, bishop of Chartres, who excelled the other bishops alike in
the sincerity of his religion and in the importance of his see, spoke
thus:

"You know, my lords, all who are gathered here, the doctrine of this
man, what it is, and his ability, which has brought him many followers
in every field to which he has devoted himself. You know how greatly
he has lessened the renown of other teachers, both his masters and our
own, and how he has spread as it were the offshoots of his vine from
sea to sea. Now, if you impose a lightly considered judgment on him,
as I cannot believe you will, you will know that even if mayhap you are
in the right there are many who will be angered thereby, and that he
will have no lack of defenders. Remember above all that we have
found nothing in this book of his that lies before us whereon any open
accusation can be based. Indeed it is true, as Jerome says: 'Fortitude
openly displayed always creates rivals, and the lightning strikes the
highest peaks.' Have a care, then, lest by violent action you only
increase his fame, and lest we do more hurt to ourselves through envy
than to him through justice. A false report, as that same wise man
reminds us, is easily crushed, and a man's later life gives testimony as
to his earlier deeds. If, then, you are disposed to take canonical action
against him, his doctrine or his writings must be brought forward as
evidence, and he must have free opportunity to answer his questioners.
In that case, if he is found guilty or if he confesses his error, his lips can
be wholly sealed. Consider the words of the blessed Nicodemus, who,
desiring to free Our Lord Himself, said: 'Doth our law judge any man
before it hear him and know what he doeth?' " [John, 7:51].

When my rivals heard this they cried out in protest, saying: "This is
wise counsel, forsooth, that we should strive against the wordiness of
this man, whose arguments, or rather, sophistries, the whole world
cannot resist!" And yet, methinks, it was far more difficult to strive
against Christ himself, for whom, nevertheless, Nicodemus demanded
a hearing in accordance with the dictates of the law. When the bishop
could not win their assent to his proposals, he tried in another way to
curb their hatred, saying that for the discussion of such an important
case the few who were present were not enough, and that this matter
required a more thorough examination. His further suggestion was that

my abbot, who was there present, should take me back with him to our abbey, in other words to the monastery of St. Denis, and that there a large convocation of learned men should determine, on the basis of a careful investigation, what ought to be done. To this last proposal the legate consented, as did all the others.

Then the legate arose to celebrate mass before entering the council, and through the bishop sent me the permission which had been determined on, authorizing me to return to my monastery and there await such action as might be finally taken. But my rivals, perceiving that they would accomplish nothing if the trial were to be held outside of their own diocese, and in a place where they could have little influence on the verdict, and in truth having small wish that justice should be done, persuaded the archbishop that it would be a grave insult to him to transfer this case to another court, and that it would be dangerous for him if by chance I should thus be acquitted. They likewise went to the legate, and succeeded in so changing his opinion that finally they induced him to frame a new sentence, whereby he agreed to condemn my book without any further inquiry, to burn it forthwith in the sight of all, and to confine me for a year in another monastery. The argument they used was that it sufficed for the condemnation of my book that I had presumed to read it in public without the approval either of the Roman pontiff or of the Church, and that, furthermore, I had given it to many to be transcribed. Methinks it would be a notable blessing to the Christian faith if there were more who displayed a like presumption. The legate, however, being less skilled in law than he should have been, relied chiefly on the advice of the archbishop, and he, in turn, on that of my rivals. When the Bishop of Chartres got wind of this, he reported the whole conspiracy to me, and strongly urged me to endure meekly the manifest violence of their enmity. He bade me not to doubt that this violence would in the end react upon them and prove a blessing to me, and counseled me to have no fear of the confinement in a monastery, knowing that within a few days the legate himself, who was now acting under compulsion, would after his departure set me free. And thus he consoled me as best he might, mingling his tears with mine.

Straightway upon my summons I went to the council, and there, without further examination or debate, did they compel me with my own hand to cast that memorable book of mine into the flames. Although my enemies appeared to have nothing to say while the book was burning, one of them muttered something about having seen it written therein that God the Father was alone omnipotent. This reached the ears of the legate, who replied in astonishment that he could not believe that even a child would make so absurd a blunder. "Our common faith," he said, "holds and sets forth that the Three are alike omnipotent." A certain Tirric, a schoolmaster, hearing this, sarcastically added the Athanasian phrase, "And yet there are not three omnipotent Persons, but only One."

This man's bishop forthwith began to censure him, bidding him desist from such treasonable talk, but he boldly stood his ground, and said, as if quoting the words of Daniel: " 'Are ye such fools, ye sons of Israel, that without examination or knowledge of the truth ye have condemned a daughter of Israel? Return again to the place of judgment' [Daniel, 13:48—The History of Susanna], and there give judgment on the judge himself. You have set up this judge, forsooth, for the instruction of faith and the correction of error, and yet, when he ought to give judgment, he condemns himself out of his own mouth. Set free today, with the help of God's mercy, one who is manifestly innocent, even as Susanna was freed of old from her false accusers."

Thereupon the archbishop arose and confirmed the legate's statement, but changed the wording thereof, as indeed was most fitting. "It is God's truth," he said, "that the Father is omnipotent, the Son is omnipotent, the Holy Spirit is omnipotent. And whosoever dissents from this is openly in error, and must not be listened to. Nevertheless, if it be your pleasure, it would be well that this our brother should publicly state before us all the faith that is in him, to the end that, according to its deserts, it may either be approved or else condemned and corrected."

When, however, I fain would have arisen to profess and set forth my faith, in order that I might express in my own words that which was in my heart, my enemies declared that it was not needful for me to do more than recite the Athanasian Symbol, a thing which any boy might do as well as I. And lest I should allege ignorance, pretending that I did not know the words by heart, they had a copy of it set before me to read. And read it I did as best I could for my groans and sighs and tears. Thereupon, as if I had been a convicted criminal, I was handed over to the Abbot of St. Médard, who was there present, and led to his monastery as to a prison. And with this the council was immediately dissolved.

The abbot and the monks of the aforesaid monastery, thinking that I would remain long with them, received me with great exultation, and diligently sought to console me, but all in vain. O God, who dost judge justice itself, in what venom of the spirit, in what bitterness of mind, did I blame even Thee for my shame, accusing Thee in my madness! Full often did I repeat the lament of St. Anthony: "Kindly Jesus, where wert Thou?" The sorrow that tortured me, the shame that overwhelmed me, the desperation that wracked my mind, all these I could then feel, but even now I can find no words to express them. Comparing these new sufferings of my soul with those I had formerly endured in my body, it seemed that I was in very truth the most miserable among men. Indeed that earlier betrayal had become a little thing in comparison with this later evil, and I lamented the hurt to my fair name far more than the one to my body. The latter, indeed, I had brought upon myself through my own wrongdoing, but this other violence had come upon me solely by reason of the honesty of my purpose and my love of our faith, which had compelled me to write that which I believed.

14   St. Bernard to Pope Innocent II: Against Abelard, 1140

1. It is necessary that offenses come. It is necessary but not pleasant. And therefore the prophet says, "O that I had wings like a dove, for then would I flee away and be at rest" [Ps. 55:6]. And the apostle wishes to be dissolved and to be with Christ. And so another of the saints: "It is enough, O Lord, take away my life, for I am not better than my fathers" [1 Kings 19:4]. I have now something in common with the saints, at least in wish if not in desert. For I could wish myself now taken from the midst of this world, overcome, I confess, by the fearfulness of my spirit and by the troubles of the time. I fear lest I be found better disposed than prepared. I am weary of life, and whether it is expedient to die I know not; and so perhaps even in my prayers I differ from the saints, because they are provoked by the desire of better things, while I am compelled to depart by scandals and anxieties. He says in fact, "To be dissolved and to be with Christ is far better" [Phil. 1:23]. Therefore in the saint desire prevails, and in me sense; and in this unhappy life neither is he able to have the good he desires, nor I not to have the trouble which I suffer. And for this reason

we both desire indeed to depart, with the same wish, but not from the same cause.

2. I was but just now foolishly promising myself some rest, when the schism of Leo was healed, and peace restored to the Church. But lo! that is at rest, but I am not. I knew not that I was in a vale of tears, or I had forgotten that I dwell in a land of forgetfulness. I paid no attention to the fact that the earth in which I dwell brings forth for me thorns and thistles, that when they are cut down others succeed, and when these are destroyed others grow ceaselessly, and spring up without intermission. I had heard these things indeed, but, as I now find out, vexation itself gives better understanding to the hearing. My grief has been renewed, not destroyed, my tears have overwhelmed me, because evil has strengthened, and when they had endured the frost, the snow fell upon them. Who hath power to resist this frost? By it charity freezes, that iniquity may abound. We have escaped the lion, Leo, to fall on the dragon [i.e., Peter Abelard] who perhaps may do us not less injury by lurking in ambush than the former by raging on high. Although I would that his poisonous pages were still lying hid in bookcases and not read at the crossroads. His books fly abroad; and they who hate the light because they are evil have dashed themselves against the light, thinking light darkness. Over cities and castles is darkness cast instead of light; instead of honey, or rather in honey, his poison is on all sides eagerly drunk in. His books have passed from nation to nation, and from one kingdom to another people. A new gospel is being fashioned for peoples and nations, a new faith propounded, another foundation laid than that which is laid. Virtues and vices are discussed immorally, the sacraments of the Church unfaithfully, the mystery of the Holy Trinity craftily and extravagantly; but everything is given in a perverse spirit, in an unprecedented manner, and beyond what we have received.

3. Goliath advances, tall in stature, clad in his armor of war, preceded by his armor-bearer, Arnold of Brescia. Scale overlaps scale, and there is no point left unguarded. Indeed, the bee which was in France has sent his murmuring to the Italian bee, and they have come together against the Lord and against his anointed. They have bent their bow, they have made ready their arrows within the quiver, that they may privily shoot at them which are true of heart. In their life and habits they have the form of godliness, but they deny its power, and they thereby deceive many, for they transform themselves into angels of light, when they are Satan's. Goliath standing with his armor-bearer between the two lines, shouts against the armies of Israel, and curses

the ranks of the saints, and that the more boldly because he knows that no David is present. In short, he puts forward philosophers with great praise and so affronts the .teachers of the Church, and prefers their imaginations and novelties to the doctrine and faith of the Catholic Fathers; and when all fly from his face he challenges me, the weakest of all, to single combat.

4. The archbishop of Sens, at his solicitation, writes to me fixing a day for the encounter, on which he in person, and with his brother bishops, should determine, if possible, on his [Abelard's] false opinions, against which I had ventured to lift my voice. I refused, not only because I am but a youth and he a man of war from his youth, but also because I thought it unfitting that the grounds of the faith should be handed over to human reasonings for discussion, when, as is agreed, it rests on such a sure and firm foundation. I said that his writings were enough for his condemnation, and that it was not my business, but that of the bishops, whose office it is to decide on matters of faith. He nonetheless, nay, rather the more on this account, lifted his voice, called upon many, assembled his accomplices. What he wrote about me to his disciples I do not care to say. He spread everywhere the report that on a fixed day he would answer me at Sens. The report reached everyone, and I could not but hear of it. At first I held back, nor was I much moved by the popular rumor. At length I yielded to the advice of my friends (although much against my will, and with tears), who saw how all were getting ready as if for a show, and they feared lest from my absence cause of offense should be given to the people and the horn of the adversary be exalted; and, since the error was likely to be strengthened if there were no one to answer or contradict it, I betook myself to the place appointed and at the time, unprepared, indeed, and unarmed, except that I revolved in my mind those words, "Take no thought how ye shall answer, for it shall be given you in that hour what ye shall say" [Matt. 10:19]; and, again, "The Lord is my helper, I will not fear what man may do unto me" [Ps. 118:6]. There had assembled, besides bishops and abbots, very many religious men, masters of the schools from different states, and many learned clergy; and the king, too, was present. And so in the presence of all, my adversary standing opposite, I produced certain articles taken from his books. And when I began to read them he departed, unwilling to listen, and appealed from the judges that he had himself chosen, a course I do not think allowable. Further, the articles having been examined were found, in the judgment of all, opposed to the faith, contrary to the truth. I have written this on my

own behalf, lest I should be thought to have shown levity, or at all events rashness, in so important a matter.

5. But thou, O successor of Peter, wilt determine whether he, who assails the faith of Peter, ought to have shelter at the See of Peter. Thou, I say, the friend of the bridegroom, wilt provide measures to free his bride from lying lips and from a deceitful tongue. But that I may speak a little more boldly with my Lord, do thou, most loving Father, take heed to thyself, and to the grace of God which is in thee. Did he not, when thou wast small in thine own eyes, place thee over nations and kingdoms? For what, but that thou shouldst pull down, and destroy, and build, and plant? See what great things he, who took thee from thy father's house, and anointed thee with the oil of his mercy, has since done for thy soul: what great things for his Church, by your means, in his vineyard, heaven and earth being witness, have been, as powerfully as wholesomely, uprooted and destroyed; what great things, again, have been well built, planted, and sown. God raised up the madness of schismatics in your time, that by your efforts they might be crushed. I have seen the fool in great prosperity, and immediately his beauty was cursed; I saw, I say, I saw the impious highly exalted and lifted up above the cedars of Lebanon, and I passed by, and lo he was gone. It is necessary, St. Paul says, "that there be heresies and schisms, that they that are approved may be made manifest" [1 Cor. 11:19]. And, indeed, in schism, as I have just said, the Lord has proved and known you. But that nothing be wanting to your crown, lo! heresies have sprung up. And so, for the perfection of your virtues, and that you may be found to have done nothing less than the great bishops, your predecessors, take away from us, most loving Father, the foxes which are laying waste the vineyard of the Lord while they are little ones; lest if they increase and multiply, our children despair of destroying what was not exterminated by you. Although they are not even now small or few, but imposing and humerous, and will not be exterminated save by you, and by a strong hand. Iacinctus has threatened me with many evils; but he has not done, nor could he do, what he wished. But I thought that I ought to bear patiently concerning myself what he has spared neither to your person nor to the Curia; but this my friend Nicholas, as he is also yours, will better tell in person.

15   Everinus of Steinfeld:
Letter to St. Bernard, 1143

From the late tenth century to Abelard, the rising tide of dissent of all kinds appeared to some mid-twelfth-century churchmen as stemming from a single source, an assault by the devil upon Christian society. The technical term *heresy*, although not appropriate to many of the cases considered in the texts so far, came to be used of all forms of dissent, from the personal to the political. St. Bernard knew of many of these, and he had personally encountered Henry of Le Mans, Abelard, and Arnold of Brescia, when a letter from his disciple Everinus of Steinfeld informed him of yet newer heresies that had sprung up in the Rhineland. Everinus's letter introduces heterodox beliefs quite different from those described by Paul of St. Père de Chartres and Guibert of Nogent, and his concern was taken up by St. Bernard in 1144, in his sixty-fifth sermon on the *Song of Songs*, the text following this one.

There have been lately some heretics discovered amongst us, near Cologne, whereof some with satisfaction returned again to the Church: two of these, viz. one that was a bishop amongst them, and his companions, openly opposed us in the assembly of the clergy and laity, the lord archbishop himself being present, with many of the nobility, maintaining their heresy from the words of Christ and the apostles. But when they saw they could go no further, they desired that a day might be appointed for them, upon which they might bring along with them men skillful in their belief, promising to return to the Church provided they should find their masters defective in answering what was opposed to them; but that otherwise they would rather die than depart from their judgment. Upon this their declaration, after that for three days together they had been admonished and found unwilling to repent, they were seized by the people, being incited by overmuch zeal, and put into the fire and burnt; and (what is most wonderful) they entered to the stake, and bare the torment of the fire, not only with patience, but with joy and gladness. In this case, O Holy Father, were I present with you, I should be glad to have your answer, how these members of the devil could with such courage and constancy persist in their heresy, as is scarcely to be found in the most religious in the faith of Christ.

Their heresy is this: they say that the Church is only amongst them, because they alone follow the steps of Christ, and continue in the imitation of the true apostolic life, not seeking the things of this world, possessing neither house, lands, nor anything in propriety, according as Christ did, who neither possessed any himself, nor gave leave to his disciples to possess anything. "Whereas ye (say they to us) join house to house, and field to field, seeking the things of this world; so that even they also, who are looked upon as most perfect amongst you, such as are your monks and regular canons, though they do not possess these things as proper, but as common, yet do they possess all these things." And of themselves they say, "We the poor of Christ, who have no certain abode, fleeing from one city to another, like sheep in the midst of wolves, do endure persecution with the apostles and martyrs; notwithstanding that we lead a holy and strict life in fasting and abstinence, persevering day and night in prayers and labors, and seeking only from thence what is necessary to support our lives, we maintain ourselves thereby, because we are not of the world. But as for you lovers of the world, ye have peace with the world, because ye are of the world. False apostles, who adulterate the word of Christ, seeking their own, have misled you and your forefathers; whereas we and our fathers, being born apostles, have continued in the grace of Christ, and shall continue so to the end of the world. To distinguish us from one another, Christ saith, 'By their fruits ye shall know them': our fruits are the footsteps of Christ." In their diet they forbid all manner of milk, and whatsoever is made of it, and all that is procreated by copulation. This is that which they oppose to us concerning their conversation. As to the sacraments, they conceal themselves; yet did they openly confess to us that daily at their tables, when they take their meals, they, according to the form of Christ and his apostles, do consecrate their meat and drink into the body and blood of Christ, by the Lord's Prayer, to nourish themselves therewith, as being the members and body of Christ. But as for us, they say we hold not the truth in the sacraments, but only a kind of shadow, and tradition of men. They also openly confess, that besides water, they baptized also with fire and the Holy Ghost, and had been so baptized themselves; alleging to this purpose the testimony of St. John the Baptist, baptizing with water, and saying concerning Christ, "He shall baptize you with the Holy Ghost and with fire": and in another place, "I indeed baptize you with water, but there stands one in the midst of you, whom you know not,

who shall baptize you with another baptism besides that of water."
And that this other baptism was to be performed by the imposition of
hands they endeavoured to make out by the testimony of St.
Luke, who, in the Acts of the Apostles, describing Paul's baptism which he
received from Ananias at the command of Christ, makes no mention of
water, but only the laying on of hands; and whatsoever else we find,
whether in the Acts of the Apostles or in St. Paul's Epistles, they apply
to this baptism; and they say that every elect (for so they call all those
that are baptized amongst them) hath power to baptize others whom
they find worthy, and to consecrate the body and blood of Christ at
their meals. For first, by their laying on of hands, they receive some of
their auditors into the number of believers, and then they have leave
to be present at their prayers, until that, after having had sufficient
trial of them, they make them elect. They condemn our baptism,
condemn marriage; but the reason why, I could not get out of them,
either because they durst not own it, or rather because they knew none.

There are also some other heretics in our country, who are altogether
different from these, by whose mutual discord and contests they were
both of them discovered to us. These deny that the body of Christ is
made on the altar, because all the priests of the Church are not
consecrated. For the apostolical dignity say they, is corrupted, by
engaging itself in secular affairs, and the sitting in the chair of Peter;
yet because it does not wage God's warfare as Peter did, it has deprived
itself of the power of consecrating, which was so great in Peter; and
what it has not itself, the archbishops and bishops, who live like men of
the world, cannot receive from it, viz. the power of consecrating others:
to this purpose alleging these words of Christ: "The Scribes and
Pharisees sit in Moses's chair; what therefore they bid you do, that
do." As if such as these had only the power of preaching and
commanding, but nothing more. Thus they make void the priesthood
of the Church, and condemn the sacraments besides baptism only; and
this only in those who are come to age, who, they say, are baptized by
Christ himself, whosoever be the minister of the sacraments. They do
not believe in infant baptism; alleging that place of the gospel,
"Whosoever shall believe, and be baptized, shall be saved." All
marriage they call fornication, besides that which is between two
virgins, male and female; quoting for this the words of our Savior,
wherewith he answers the Pharisees, "What God hath joined let no
man separate"; as if God did only join such together, as he did our first
parents: as likewise those words of our Saviour, which he speaks to the
Jews, in answer to what they objected to him about the bill of divorce,

"From the beginning it was not so"; and the following words, "Whosoever marrieth her that is divorced, commits adultery"; and that of the Apostle, "Let marriage be honorable to all, and the bed undefiled."

They put no confidence in the intercession of the saints; they maintain that fasting, and other afflictions which are undertaken for sin, are not necessary to the just, nor to sinners; because at what time soever the sinner repents of his sin, they are all forgiven to him; and all other things observed in the Church, which have not been established by Christ himself or his apostles, they call superstitions. They do not admit of any purgatory fire after death; but that the souls, as soon as they depart out of the bodies, do enter into rest or punishment; proving it from that place of Solomon, "Which way soever the tree falls, whether to the south or to the north, there it lies": by which means they make void all the prayers and oblations of believers for the deceased.

We therefore desire you, Holy Father, to employ your care and watchfulness against these manifold mischiefs, and that you would be pleased to direct your pen against these wild beasts of the reeds; not thinking it sufficient to answer us, that the tower of David, to which we may take our refuge, is sufficiently fortified with bulwarks, that a thousand bucklers hang on the walls of it, all shields of mighty men. For we desire, Father, that for the sake of us simple ones, and that are slow of understanding, you would be pleased by your study to gather all these arms in one place, that they may be the more ready to be found, and more powerful to resist these monsters. I let you know also, that those of them who have returned to our Church, told us that they had great numbers of their persuasion scattered almost everywhere; and that amongst them were many of our clergy and monks. And as for those who were burnt, they, in the defense they made for themselves, told us that this, their heresy, had been concealed from the time of the martyrs until these times; and that it had been preserved in Greece, and some other countries. These are those heretics who call themselves Apostles, having a pope of their own; whereas the other despise our pope, and yet own themselves to have no other besides him. These Apostles of Satan have amongst them continent women (as they call them) widows, virgins, their wives, some of which are amongst the number of their elect, others of their believers, as in imitation of the apostles, who had power to lead about women with them. Farewell in the Lord.

16   St. Bernard: Sermon 65 on *The Song of Songs*, 1144

I have already delivered to you two sermons upon one verse; I propose to deliver a third, if it will not weary you to listen. And I think it even necessary to do so; for though, as far as relates to our domestic vine, which is no other than yourselves, my brethren, I have, I think, sufficiently forearmed you in the two preceding sermons against the crafty advances of three kinds of foxes; namely, flatterers, calumniators, and certain seducing spirits who are skilled and experienced in presenting evil under the guise of good; yet that is not the case with the dominical, that is, the Lord's vine. I speak of that vine which has filled the earth, and of which we also are a part; a vine great and spreading, planted by the hand of the Lord, redeemed by his blood, watered by his word, propagated by his grace, and rendered fruitful by his spirit. The more carefully I have dealt with that which was of private and personal concern, the less valuable were my remarks with regard to that which was common and public. But it troubles me greatly, on behalf of that vine, to behold the multitude of its assailants, the fewness of its defenders, and the difficulty of the defense. The hidden and furtive character of the attack is the cause of this difficulty. For from the beginning the Church has had foxes; but they have been soon found out and taken. A heretic combated openly (indeed, that was the principal reason why the name was given, because the desire of the heretic was to gain an open victory), and was manifestly overcome. Those foxes, therefore, were easily taken. But what if a heretic, when the truth was set clear in the light before him, remained in the shadow of his obstinacy, and, bound (as it were) hand and foot in the outer darkness, withered away in solitude? Even then the fox was deemed to be "taken" when his impiety was condemned, and the impious one cast out, thenceforth to live in a mere show of life without fruitfulness. From this to such a one, according to the prophet, comes a sterile womb and dry breasts [Hos. 9:14]: because an error, publicly confuted, does not soon shoot up again, and an evident falsehood does not take root.

2. What shall we do to take those foxes, the most malignant and dangerous of all, who prefer the inflicting of severe injury to the enjoyment of open victory, and who crawl to, and steal upon, their purpose in order not to be seen? With all heretics the one intention has always been to obtain praise for themselves by the remarkable extent of their knowledge. But there is a heresy which alone is more malignant and more artful than others, since it feeds upon the losses of others, and neglects its own glory. It is instructed, I believe, by the examples of those ancient heresies which, when betrayed, were by no means suffered to escape, but were forthwith captured; and so is careful to actuate secretly, by a new method of mischief, this mystery of iniquity, and that with the greater freedom the less it is suspected. Furthermore, its promoters have met together, as it is said, at places appointed in secret, and concerted together their nefarious discourses. "Take oaths, if needful; take them even falsely," they said the one to the other, "rather than betray the secret." But at another time they do not consider it right by any means to swear, not even in the smallest degree, because of those words in the Gospel: "*Swear not at all; neither by heaven . . . nor by the earth*" [Matt. 5:34-35], etc. O foolish and hard of heart, filled with the spirit of the Pharisees, ye, too, strain at a gnat and swallow a camel [Matt. 23:24]. To swear is not permitted, but to swear falsely, that is permissible, as if the allowance to do the latter did not carry with it the former also! In what passage of the gospel, of which you do not, as you falsely boast, pass over one iota, do you find that exception? It is clear that you, both by superstition, forbid the taking of an oath, and, at the same time, wickedly presume to authorize a perjury. O strange perversity! That which is given only as a counsel of perfection—namely, "*Swear not*"— that they observe as rigidly and contentiously as if it were a positive command; while that which is laid down as an unchangeable law— namely, never to be guilty of perjury—they dispense with at their own will as a thing indifferent. No, say they; but let us not make known our secret. As if it were not to the glory of God to make known teaching [that is to edification] [Dan. 2:28-29]! Do they envy the glory of God? But I rather believe that they are ashamed to have their secret known, being conscious that it does not redound to their glory; for they are said to practice in secret things obscene and abominable, even as the hinder parts of foxes are offensive.

3. But I do not wish to speak of that which they deny; let them answer only to those which are known and manifest. Are they careful, according to the gospel precept, not to give that which is holy unto the

dogs, or to cast pearls before swine [Matt. 7:6]? But do not they who regard all who belong to the Church as dogs and swine, plainly confess that they are not of the Church themselves? For they consider that their secret, whatever it is, should be kept wholly from the knowledge of all, without exception, who are not of their sect. What their doctrine is they do not avow, and they adopt every means to avoid its becoming known; but yet they do not succeed. Reply to me, O man, who art wise above that which is meet, and yet more foolish than can be expressed in words. Is the secret which you are concealing of God, or is it not? If it is, why do you not make it known to his glory? For it is to the glory of God to reveal that which comes from him. But if it is not, why do you put faith in that which is not of God, unless because you are a heretic? Either, then, let them proclaim the secret as coming from God to the glory of God, or let them confess that the secret is not of God, and thereby allow that they are heretics; or, at least, let them allow that they are manifestly enemies of the glory of God, since they are unwilling to make manifest a thing which would be conducive to that glory. For it is stated with preciseness in scripture: It is the glory of kings to conceal a matter, but it is the glory of God to reveal discourse. Are you not willing to reveal it? Then you do not desire to glorify God. But perhaps you do not receive this scripture. Doubtless this is the case, for [sectaries] profess that they are followers of the gospel, and the only ones. Let them, then, reply to the gospel. "What I tell you in darkness," saith the Lord, "that speak ye in light: and what ye hear in the ear, that preach ye upon the housetops" [Matt. 10:27]. Now it is not permitted to you to be silent. How long is that kept under the veil of secrecy which God declares is to be made known? How long is your gospel to be hidden? I suspect that your gospel is not that of St. Paul, for he declares that his gospel is not hidden, or rather he says this: "If our gospel be hid, it is hid to them that are lost" [2 Cor. 4:3]. Does not this apply to you who have among you a gospel that is hidden? What is more plain than that you are in the way of being lost? Or perhaps you do not receive even the Epistles of St. Paul. I have heard that it is so with certain persons among you. For, although you all agree in differing from us, you do not all agree in all respects among yourselves.

4. But, at all events, you all receive, without exception, if I do not mistake, the words, the writings, and the traditions of those who were personally with the Savior, as of equal authority with the gospel. Now, did they keep their gospel secret? Did they hide the weakness of the flesh in the Divine Son, the terrible circumstances of his death, or the ignominy of his cross? Did not their words, indeed, go forth into

the whole world [Ps. 9:4]? Where, then, is there in you that following of the apostolic life and conduct of which you boast? They cry aloud, you whisper in secret; they teach in public, you in a corner; they "fly as a cloud" [Is. 60:8], while as for you, you conceal yourselves in the darkness and in the cellars of your houses. What likeness to them do you display? Is it in that you do not indeed take women as traveling companions, but as inmates? Who could suspect those who raised the dead to life of anything unbecoming? Do you do likewise, and whatever be the circumstances in which you were found, I will be far from suspecting you. Otherwise you are rashly usurping to yourself the privilege of those whose sanctity you do not possess. To expose yourselves always to temptation and never to fall by it, is not that a greater miracle than to raise the dead? You are not able to do that which is less, and do you wish me to believe that you do that which is greater? You wish to be thought irreproachable. Let it be granted that you are so; yet suspicion is not wanting. You are to me a subject of scandal; take away the occasion of the scandal, that you may show yourself what it is your boast to be, a true follower of the gospel. Does not the gospel condemn that man who offends [scandalizaverit] even one member of the Church? And you are a scandal to the whole Church. You are a fox that spoils the vines. Help me, my friends, to take him, or rather do ye, O holy angels, take him for us. He is crafty in the extreme; he is enveloped in his iniquity and impiety. Evidently he is so small and so subtle that he may easily elude the notice of men. But shall he elude yours also? It is to you, therefore, as the companions of the Bridegroom, that those words are addressed: "Take us the little foxes." Do, then, that which you are commanded: take for us this little fox so skilled in dissimulation that we have so long been in pursuit of him in vain. Teach us and suggest to us in what manner his guile may be discovered. For this is to take the fox, because as a pretended Catholic he does much more injury than when made manifest as really a heretic. For it is not in the power of man to discover what is in the heart of another man, unless indeed he is either enlightened to this end by the Spirit of God, or instructed by the care of the angels. What sign will you give to make open and manifest to all this pernicious heresy which knows so well how to disguise itself, not only by words, but also by actions?

5. And, indeed, the recent spoiling of a vine shows clearly that the fox has been there. But I know not by what art that most crafty animal so conceals his footsteps, that it is by no means easy to be discovered where either his ingress or his egress was made. Though the mischief

done is evident, the doer of it is not visible, and he hides his presence by the very destruction he has done. In fact, if you interrogate him as to his faith, nothing is more christianlike; or as to his conduct, nothing more unblamable; and he seems to justify his discourse by his actions. Such a man is seen, in order to give testimony of his faith, to frequent the church, to honor the clergy [presbyteros], to offer his gifts, to make confession, to participate in the sacraments. What can be more orthodox? Then as relates to character and conduct, he deceives no one, he exalts himself over no one, nor does violence to any. Furthermore, his cheeks are pale with fasts; nor does he eat the bread of idleness, but labors with his hands for his maintenance. Where, then, is the fox? We held him fast just now. How has he escaped from our hands? In what manner has he so suddenly disappeared? Let us pursue him, let us seek him; we shall recognize him by his fruits. Assuredly the spoiling of the vines is a proof that the fox has been there. Women have quitted their husbands, men have deserted their wives, to join themselves to these people. Clerks and priests, as well young as old [intonsi et barbati], often abandon their flocks and their churches, and are found in the throng, among weavers male and female. Is not that a terrible spoiling indeed? Are not these the doings of foxes?

6. But perhaps they do not all perform actions so unmistakable, and if they do there is no proof of the fact. How, then, shall we take these? Let us return to the former accusation, for there is no one among them but is involved in that. I ask, then, of some one of those people: "My good man, who is that woman with you, and what is her relation to you? Is she your wife?" "No," he replies; "I have taken a vow which does not allow me to marry." "Is she your daughter?" "No." "What, then, is she your sister, or your niece, or, at least, a relation or family connection of yours?" "No, she is not related to me in any way." "How, then, can you live safely thus? It is not permitted to you to act in this way. If you are not aware of it, let me remind you that the Church forbids it. If you do not wish to give scandal to the Church, obey the command. If you do not do so, then, from that one fact, others will be, without doubt, inferred as probable, though they be not open and manifest."

7. "But" (he says to me) "in what place of the gospel do you find any proof that this is forbidden?" Very well, you have appealed to the gospel; to the gospel you shall go. If, then, you obey the gospel, you will not give occasion for scandal, for this is a thing which the gospel plainly forbids. And this scandal is just what you do give, in not conforming to the regulation of the Church. You had been previously

under suspicion of despising the gospel, and being an enemy of the Church, but now you are manifestly convicted of it. What think you of it, my brethren? If he remains obstinate, and will neither obey the gospel, nor show any respect unto the Church, what room is there for hesitation? Does it not seem to you that the fraud is discovered, that the fox is taken? If he suffers a scandal to remain which he has it in his power to put an end to, he is convicted of disobedience to the gospel. What ought the Church to do but to expel a person who is unwilling to take away scandal, so that she may not share his disobedience? For she has a commandment in the gospel as to this, and it bids her not spare her own eye, or hand, or foot, if it be a cause of scandal, but to pluck out the one and cut off the other, and cast it away. "If he neglect to hear the Church," it is said, "let him be unto thee as an heathen man and a publican" [Matt. 18:6-9, 17].

8. Have we reached any result? I think we have; we have taken the fox, since we have discovered his deception. Those pretended Catholics who were really destroyers of the Church have been made manifest. Even while you were taking with me sweet [and heavenly] food, I mean the body and blood of Christ, while we walked in the House of God as friends, a place for persuasion, or, rather, an opportunity for perversion, was found, according to the saying of scripture: "A hypocrite with his mouth destroyeth his neighbor" [Prov. 9:9]. But now I easily, according to the wise admonition of St. Paul, avoid "a man that is a heretic after the first and second admonition, knowing that he that is such is subverted, and sinneth, being condemned of himself" [Titus 3:10-11], and that it behooves me to be on my guard, lest he cause my subversion also. It is, then, something gained, according to the word of the wise, that transgressors should be taken in their own naughtiness [Prov. 9:6], and especially those transgressors the weapons of whose warfare are deceit and snares. Open attack and defense they do not venture upon, for they are a despicable and rustic race, devoid of education, and wholly destitute of generous courage. In short, they are foxes, and little foxes. Even their errors are not defensible, not clever and able, nor even plausible, except only to country women and ignorant persons, such as are all those of their sect whom I have as yet seen. For I do not recall, among all their assertions which I have heard (and they are many), anything novel or extraordinary, but only commonplaces long since broached among the heretics of old, and by our divines confuted and crushed. Yet it ought to be shown, and I will endeavour to show, what absurdities these are, being partly such as they have fallen into through incautiously taking one

side or the other in questions disputed between Catholics, partly such as they have exposed themselves to by their dissensions with each other, and partly such as some of them who have returned to the Church have discovered to us, and this I will do, not that I may reply to them all (for that is unnecessary), but in order that they may be known. But that will be a task for another sermon, to the praise and glory of the name of him who is the bridegroom of the Church, Jesus Christ our Lord, who is above all, God blessed for ever. Amen.

III
THE CATHARS

The widely diverse forms of religious dissent that troubled Christian Europe between 1000 and 1145 are difficult to catalogue and systematize. They appear to have sprung from different sources and to have manifested themselves differently, although most of them can be related to the religious temper of the age and the movement for reform that touched all aspects of religious life from 1050 on. Churchmen who noticed them developed a means of describing them that was more homogeneous than the forms of dissent themselves. Summed up in St. Bernard's sermon on the *Song of Songs*, churchmen's views linked religious dissent with the heresies described in patristic literature and understood them in terms of a series of historical "temptations" of the Church. From the mid-twelfth century on, however, two movements in particular became especially prominent in terms of dissent. Dualists in the Netherlands, the Rhine Valley, eastern France, and in Languedoc and Italy, professing beliefs roughly similar to those of Guibert of Nogent's "Manichees" at Soissons in 1114, argued for the existence of two gods, one good and the other evil, one the creator and sustainer of the spirit, the other the lord of material creation and darkness. Like Guibert, some historians have called these different manifestations of dualism "medieval Manichaeism." But the problem of the continuity of Manichaeism, whether independently in the West, or via Bogomilism from Bulgaria, has also led scholars to argue that twelfth-century European dualism was a native—and recent—development, independent of ongoing influence from anywhere and a consequence of the religious experience of the eleventh and early twelfth centuries.

Bogomilism grew up in Bulgaria, a center of tension between Byzantine and Bulgar powers throughout the late ninth and tenth centuries. By the early tenth century, Byzantine churchmen noted a strong presence of dualism among the converted Bulgars, some of them attributing this movement to a revival of "Manichaeism," while others attributed it to the influence of the now-dualist Paulicians. Whatever the origins of Bogomilism among the Bulgars, around the middle of the tenth century a village priest in Bulgaria assumed the name Bogomil (which means "worthy of the pity of God") and began to preach a consistently dualist religion. It attracted large followings throughout southeastern Europe in the tenth and eleventh centuries and may have influenced the Latin West (the problem is still a matter of considerable scholarly debate) before its traditionally assigned appearance around 1140. One of the most important documents in Bogomil history is the treatise of Cosmas the Priest against the sect, written around 970 and printed below (no. 17). Cosmas's treatise is the best early source on most Bogomil beliefs.

Although the recent work of Malcolm Lambert has indicated the possibility of a Bogomil influence in western Europe much earlier than most scholars had previously thought, there is still no unanimous agreement on the question. What is clear is that dualist beliefs, too sketchily described in the sources to make their precise identification possible, began to spread widely after the beginning of the twelfth century; one form of dualism or another clearly preoccupied churchmen, and won more converts than any other kind of heresy, until the end of the twelfth century. Under a number of different names— Patarines, Publicans, Manichees—dualist sects sprang up, as the sources below indicate, in the Rhineland, Languedoc, and Italy, and they attracted progressively more attention as the century went on. In Languedoc, the heretics took the name of Cathari, "The Pure Ones," from the Greek term *katharos*, "pure." As Cathars, they were known to the Church and prosecuted with increasing vigor after the middle of the twelfth century.

The letter from Everinus of Steinfeld to St. Bernard in 1143 (above, no. 15) brought to the saint, as we have seen, news of yet another heresy on top of those the Cistercian leader had seen already. The dualist heretics described by Everinus at Cologne are far from being individual eccentrics or small, isolated coteries like those of Orléans a century earlier. They engaged successfully in debate with orthodox churchmen, and when they were seized by the local populace, they met their deaths steadfastly, raising profound questions in Everinus's mind about the source of their courage and consistency. Everinus describes two groups of rival heretics, whose differences are as great as their similarities. A few decades later, Walter Map echoes the commonplace of old heresies revived in his description of "Patarines and Manichees" and the equally old commonplace of attributing to the heretics orgiastic, secret rites. The first exposition of Catharist beliefs, however, comes from the remarkable description written by Eckbert of Schönau in 1165. By that date, heretics with similar beliefs had been noticed at Liège in 1145, Périgueux around 1160, Arras in 1162-63, and, briefly and abruptly, in England in 1163. They are noted at Vézelay in 1167 and at Rheims in 1176-80. By the period 1163-67, when Eckbert delivered his sermons, the tenets of the dualist sects had become well enough known for a full-fledged exposition.

Although dualist beliefs flourished in many parts of Europe, it was in Languedoc and Italy that they became most prominent and hardest to eradicate. Much has been written about Languedocian propensities to heresy, and Peter of Bruys had found fertile ground there before dualism became prominent. In the sixties of the twelfth century, however, it became clear that neither Peter the Venerable's tract against Petrobrusianism, nor St. Bernard's mission of preaching in Languedoc in 1145, had dampened heretical enthusiasm. Evidence of the spread of dualist heresy is found in the account of the assembly held at Lombers in 1165 (no. 18), from which it is clear that eastern, Bogomil or Paulician, influences had been at work, and that a bishop like Jocelin of Lodève had his hands full in dealing with openly professed, articulate, and passionately devoted heretics. The South continued to be a bed of heresy, and the doomed comital house of Toulouse was losing the first of its many battles with both the heretics and the Church. The visit to the South of Henry, abbot of Clairvaux, repeated that of St. Bernard in 1145, and found his apprehensions to have been fully justified—although Henry had no more success than his predecessor St. Bernard in quelling the heresy, and no more than his successor Armand Amaury would have at Montpellier in 1206. Henry's letter suggests that the ecclesiastical policy of Cistercian preaching missions to the South was not working, although it paved the way for the later and more successful preaching missions of the Dominicans in the thirteenth century. Henry's letter also helped prepare the ground for the formidable denunciation of heresy issued by Pope Alexander III at the Third Lateran Council in the next year, 1179 (below, no. 28).

By the second decade of the thirteenth century, Pierre des Vaux de Cernay, a young monk from the neighborhood of Paris who had accompanied the Albigensian crusaders led by Simon de Montfort in 1212, wrote an important and generally well-informed description of Cathar beliefs in his *Historia Albigensis*, which was completed in 1218 (no. 20). After the Albigensian Crusade and the establishment of the Inquisition (below, chaps. V and VI), the

Inquisition kept extensive records of its interrogations, developed a much more accurate description of heretical beliefs, and devised many ways to ferret heresy out. The description of Cathar beliefs in Languedoc and northern Italy by one inquisitor, Rainier Sacconi, in 1254 (no. 21) reflects the thoroughness of the Inquisition's work and provides a valuable source for Cathar ideas.

One crucial event in Cathar history was the rivalry between "absolute" and "mitigated" dualism, the former arguing that good and evil were eternal principles, independent of one another, and the latter that the spirit of evil had been produced by the good god and was ultimately subordinated to him. Most scholars agree that the initial dualist faiths of mid-twelfth century Europe were of the mitigated variety, and that the absolute dualism of some late twelfth and early thirteenth century Cathars came from a renewed influence of Bulgarian Bogomils, exemplified in the Cathar "Council" of Saint Félix de Caraman in 1167 (no. 19). The differences between absolute and mitigated dualists were one source of friction within the heretical community. Their rivalry is described in a document published by Fr. Antoine Dondaine in 1939 (no. 22). The labors of Fr. Dondaine since the 1930s have been extensive, and they have resulted in the publication of many Catharist texts which were not available to earlier historians of heresy. The texts themselves round out the picture of Catharism.

The question of the sources of Cathar beliefs is only one perplexing aspect of the history of medieval heresy. Another question, just as complex, is that of Cathar recruitment and support, from converts to sympathizers. The presence of large numbers of sympathizers in Languedoc and Italy greatly vexed the Church, and its preaching missions, first under the Cistercians, then under the Dominicans, were probably aimed primarily at these rather than at converts. It should also be noted that although the Cistercian preaching missions of the second half of the twelfth century bore little fruit, those of the first half of the thirteenth century certainly had considerable results (below, chapt. V); it is hard to gauge the impact of these preachers, especially on those whose sympathy with heresy was unknown and may have been further weakened by their sermons. One incident that particularly reveals the nature of Cathar support is found in an account of a disputation held at Pamiers in southern France in 1207. There, when the Cathars were defended by the sister of Bernard Roger, count of Foix, she was harshly told by one of the clerics: "Go, my lady, and return to spinning your yarn. Don't put yourself into the middle of this kind of dispute." The prominent role of women in Cathar ritual and practice suggests one source of such female support for their doctrines. Later in the dispute, a cleric demanded of a knight, Pons Adhémar of Rodelia, whether he knew any of the Waldensian heretics there: "We know them well," he responded. "Why then," asked the bishop, "do you not expel these people and shun them?" And the knight answered, "We cannot do that, for we were raised with them, and we have relatives among them, and we see that they lead honest and decent lives." "Thus," says the chronicler William of Puy Laurens, "does falsity in the appearance of a good life lead people away from the truth." The close relationships among families may have prevented Catholic family members, like Pons, from being too hostile to relatives and close friends who were Cathars or Waldensians. Other historians have discussed other reasons for the support received by heretics, from the corruption of the Languedocian and northern Italian clergy to economic and social reasons. However many and complex the causes of such sympathy, there is no question that it existed, and that it bothered the Church as much as heresy itself. The geography of heresy and the nature of the societies in which it did or did not take root, is the subject of a large and far from unanimous literature.

The problem of the decline of Cathar beliefs and the well-organized Cathar church is also of considerable interest, and it, too, has generated many explanations. On the one hand, some historians argue that the response of the Church—instituting new preaching methods, new and more comprehensive forms of penance, using persuasion, and moving in a direction of religious sensibility that undercut the Cathar beliefs in a bleak, dualistic universe— ultimately shriveled the bases of Cathar belief. Another school, prominent in the nineteenth century and recently revived strongly in the work of Malcolm Lambert, argues that force—the Crusade and the Inquisition—destroyed Catharism. Whether one, or a combination of both sets of causes was at work, by the fourteenth century Catharism was virtually ended.

LITERATURE

Wakefield and Evans, *Heresies of the High Middle Ages*, pp. 159-200, 235-43, 289-345, 351-630; Moore, *Birth of Popular Heresy*, pp. 74-100; Moore, *Origins of European Dissent*, pp. 139-242; Lambert, *Medieval Heresy*, pp. 49-67, 95-150; Latin texts in Fearns, *Ketzer und Ketzerbekämpfung*, pp. 24-37. See also Brooke, *The Coming of the Friars*, pp. 71-88, 153-60; B. Hamilton, "The Cathar Council of St.-Félix," appendix to Moore, *Origins of European Dissent*, pp. 285-89. There is an extensive bibliography in Walter L. Wakefield, *Heresy, Crusade and Inquisition in Southern France* (Berkeley and Los Angeles, 1974), and in Jonathan Sumption, *The Albigensian Crusade* (Boston, 1978). There is a fine discussion of the place of Catharism in the new social attitudes of the twelfth century in Lester K. Little, *Religious Poverty and the Profit Economy in Medieval Europe* (Ithaca, N.Y., 1978), pp. 113-45, and another in John H. Mundy, *Europe in the High Middle Ages* (New York, 1973), pp. 515-61. The standard work on Catharism is that of Arno Borst, *Die Katharer* (Stuttgart, 1953). References to eastern dualism are given above, chapt. I, page 28.

Two recent studies continue work on the problem of eastern relations and the Council of Saint-Félix: R. Manselli, "Les 'chrétiens' de Bosnie: le catharisme en Europe orientale," *Revue d'histoire ecclésiastique* 72 (1977): 600-613; Bernard Hamilton, "The Cathar Council of Saint-Félix Reconsidered," *Archivum Fratum Praedicatorum* 48 (1978): 23-53.

17 The Sermon of Cosmas the Priest against Bogomilism

The dualism of the Gnostics and Manichaeans ceased generally to be a problem in eastern and western Christendom after the fifth century. As noted above, however, Armenian Paulicianism turned dualistic in the eighth century, and in Bulgaria there arose the movement known as Bogomilism, which was vigorously dualist in theology. One school of historians, perhaps best represented in English by Steven Runciman's *The Medieval Manichee* (reprint ed., New York, 1961), holds that a continuous dualistic tradition existed from earliest Manichaeism and that this tradition infected the West in the twelfth century or even earlier. Although most scholars have rejected the idea of continuous dualist traditions and eastern Bogomil influence before 1140-65 (see below, chapt. IV), the best recent comprehensive survey of medieval heresy, Malcom Lambert *Medieval Heresy* (New York, 1977), has emphasized it again, chiefly upon the evidence of recent eastern European and German scholarship, although less categorically than have others.

The text printed here is a treatise of Cosmas the Priest, written around 970. It is the first modern statement of Bogomil beliefs and an important document in the consideration of the later western Cathars.

LITERATURE

Lambert, *Medieval Heresy*, pp. 7-23; M. Loos, *The Dualist Heresy in the Middle Ages* (Prague, 1974); H. C. Puech and A. Vaillant, *Le Traité contre les Bogomils de Cosmas le Prêtre* (Paris, 1945).

It came to pass that in the reign of the orthodox Tsar Peter of Bulgaria, there appeared a priest by the name of "Bogomil" ("Beloved of God"), but in reality "Bogunemil" ("not beloved of God"). He was the first who began to preach in Bulgaria a heresy, of which I shall relate below. As I commence to condemn the teachings and the deeds of the Bogomils, it seems to me that the air is polluted by their deeds and preachings. But for the sake of the pious I shall expose the deceitful teachings of these in order that no one, after knowing them, shall fall into their snares, but keep afar from them, because, as God says, "Each tree is known by its own fruit."

The heretics in appearance are lamb-like, gentle, modest and quiet, and their pallor is to show their hypocritical fastings. They do not talk idly, nor laugh loudly, nor do they manifest any curiosity. They keep themselves away from immodest sights, and outwardly they do everything so as not to be distinguished from the Orthodox Christians, but inwardly they are ravening wolves. The people, on seeing their great humility think that they are orthodox, and able to show them the path of salvation; they approach and ask them how to save their souls. Like a wolf that wants to seize a lamb, they pretend at first to sigh; they speak with humility, preach, and act as if they were themselves in heaven. Whenever they meet any ignorant and uneducated man, they preach to him the tares of their teachings, blaspheming the traditions and orders of the Holy Church.

But what do the heretics say?—"We pray to God more than you do; we watch and pray and do not live a lazy life as you do." Alas! This is similar to the words of that proud Pharisee who, when he prayed, said, "God, I thank thee that I am not as other men are, extortioners, unjust, adulterers, or even as this publican" [Luke, 18:11].

The demons are afraid of the cross of Christ, but the heretics cut it and make of it their tools. The demons are afraid of the image of the Lord God, painted on a board; the heretics do not reverence icons, but call them idols. The demons fear the relics of the saints and dare not to approach the reliquary caskets in which lie the precious treasures that are given to the Christians to free them from misfortune; the heretics on seeing us revering these objects, mock them and laugh at us.

About the cross of God they say, "How can we bow to the cross? Is it not the tree on which the Jews crucified the Son of God? The cross is detestable to God." That is why they instruct their followers to hate the cross and not to reverence it, saying, "If some one murders the son of the king with a piece of wood, is it possible that this piece of wood should be dear to the king? This is the case with the cross."

Why do you heretics inveigh against the sacred orders that are given us by the holy apostles and holy fathers, the liturgy, and the rest of the services which are carried on by good Christians? You say that the apostles established neither the liturgy, nor the holy sacrament, but it was John Chrysostom who instituted them. Do you know that from the incarnation of Christ to John Chrysostom it was more than three hundred years? Were the churches of God without any liturgy or holy sacraments during that time? Did not the Apostle Peter establish the liturgy which the Romans preserve till the present day? James, the brother of the Lord God, who was appointed bishop of Jerusalem by Jesus himself, composed a liturgy which we hear sung at the sepulchre up to the present day. Later on, Basil the Great from Cappadocia, having been inspired by God, gave us the liturgy and arranged the holy sacrament, dividing it into three parts according to the commandment of the Holy Ghost. Why, then, do you say that the holy sacrament and the ecclesiastical orders are not given by God, and why do you abuse the Church and the priests, calling them "Blind Pharisees"? And why do you constantly bark at them like dogs after a horseman? You, being blind in your spiritual eyes, cannot understand the epithets of Saint Paul, who appointed bishops, priests, and others of the clerical order over all the world. But according to what is written, "For they being ignorant of God's righteousness, and going about to establish their own righteousness have not submitted themselves to the righteousness of God" [Rom. 10:3].

Although the Orthodox priests live a lazy life as you say, blaming them, they do not, however, blaspheme God as you do and they would not commit any secret wickedness. Listen to what the apostle says, "Who art thou that judgest another man's servant" [Rom. 14:4]. "But in a great house there are not only vessels of gold and of silver, but also of wood and of earth; and some to honor, and some to dishonor. If a man therefore purge himself from these he shall be a vessel unto honor, sanctified, and meet for the master's use, and prepared unto every good work" [2 Tim. 2:20-21]. You, heretics, do not believe that the orders of the clergy are always sanctified by God; listen to what the great apostle writes to the Philippians: "Paul and Timotheus the servants of Jesus Christ, to all the saints in Christ Jesus which are in Philippi, with the bishops and deacons: grace be unto you and peace from God our Father, and from the Lord Jesus Christ" [Phil. 1:1-2]. And to Titus he writes, "For this cause left I thee in Crete that thou shouldst set in order the things that were wanting, and ordain elders in every city, as I had appointed thee, which was given thee by prophecy, with the laying on of the hands of the presbytery" [1 Tim. 4:14]; and again, "Let the elders that rule well be counted worthy of double honor, especially those who labor in the word and in teaching" [1 Tim. 5:17].

The heretics on hearing these words reply: "If you were sanctified, as you say, why do you not carry out your life according to the law and to the words of Paul? 'A bishop then must be blameless, the husband of one wife, vigilant, sober, orderly, of good behavior, given to hospitality, apt to teach, not given to wine, no striker, not greedy of filthy lucre, not a brawler, not covetous; one that ruleth well his own house, having his children in subjection with all gravity. Likewise, the deacons must be grave, not double-tongued, not given to much wine, not greedy of filthy lucre; holding the mystery of the faith in a pure conscience. And let these also first be proved; then let them use the office of being a deacon, being found blameless.' [1 Tim. 3:2-4, 8-10]. The priests do just the reverse of this. They are given to drink, rob and secretly commit sin and there is nobody to prevent them. For the apostle Paul says, 'Them that sin rebuke before all, that the others may fear' [1 Tim. 5:20]. The bishops, who are not able to contain themselves, cannot stop the priests from doing wrong." We shall answer them, "Read what Jesus Lord says to the apostles" [Matt. 23:2-3].

What falsehood have you found in the prophets and why do you blaspheme them and not recognize the books written by them? Why do you pretend to love Christ, and reject the prophecies of the holy prophets about him? The prophets did not speak their own words, but they proclaimed what the Holy Ghost had ordered them to speak.

The heretics dishonor John the Baptist, the Forerunner, the dawn of the Great Sun: they call him the forerunner of Antichrist, although God declared him to be the greatest of all the prophets, saying, "Verily I say unto you, among them that are born of women there hath not risen a greater than John the Baptist" [Matt. 11:11]. Even He bent his divine head down and was baptized of him.

The heretics do not venerate the Holy Mother of Our Lord Jesus

Christ, but talk nonsense of her; their words and insolences are so bad that they must not be written in this book.

They read Saint Paul who says about idols, "For as much then as we are the offspring of God, we ought not to think that the Godhead is like unto gold or silver, or stone, graven by art and man's device" [Acts 1:29]; and, finding justification in this, they think that it is spoken about the icons, and for this reason they seek in these words ground for not reverencing icons in private. But, being afraid of the people, they attend the church and kiss the crucifix and icons. We have learned this from those who returned again to our Orthodox faith. They say, "We do all this because of the people, and not from sincerity. We hold to our faith secretly."

"We reject David and the prophets. We admit only the gospel; we do not carry out our lives according to the law of Moses, but according to the law given through the apostles."

Hear what Jesus Christ says: "Think not that I am come to destroy the law, or the prophets: I am not come to destroy, but to fulfill" [Matt. 5:17]; and again, "If they hear not Moses and the prophets, neither will they be persuaded, though one rise from the dead" [Luke 16:31]; and again, "But if ye believe not his writings, how shall ye believe my words?" [John 5:47].

What falsehood and evil did you see in the law and the prophets, and why do you blaspheme them and reject the scriptures? Here is what the Lord God says of the pious men who had lived according to the first law, "There shall be weeping and gnashing of teeth when ye shall see Abraham, and Isaac, and Jacob, and all the prophets in the Kindgom of God, and yourselves cast forth without" [Luke 13:28]. Why do you say that the prophets were not holy and had not prophesied through the Holy Ghost? Can you not read in Matt. 22:42-45, what David through the Holy Ghost predicted? Who can explain this matter better than Peter, the great apostle, who says, "For the prophecy came not in old time by the will of man but holy men of God spoke as they were moved by the Holy Ghost" [2 Pet. 1:21; 2:1,2].

The wretched ones think that they know the depth of the scriptures and, being willing to comment upon them, they give a wrong meaning to them. But all this they do for their own destruction, as Peter says [2 Pet. 3:15-17].

Since we know the heretics well, let us drive them away, because they are the enemies of the holy cross. Blaspheming all the ordinances given to the holy church, they count their teaching to be sacred, babbling certain fables, which their father, the devil, teaches them.

Although it is unbecoming, as I said, everything under the sky is defiled by them, nevertheless I have already related to you a little. The rest I will not tell you, because as the apostle says, "For it is a shame even to speak of those things which are done by them in secret" [Eph. 5:12].

Many people do not know what their heresy is, and think that they suffer for the sake of righteousness, and will be rewarded by God for their chains and imprisonment. Let such persons hear what Paul says, "And if a man also strives for masteries, yet is he not crowned, except he strive lawfully" [2 Tim. 2:5]. How can they arouse anybody's sympathy for their great suffering if they call the devil the creator of man and of all God's creatures; and because of their extreme ignorance, some of them call the devil a fallen angel, and the others account him an unjust steward? These words of theirs are only ridiculous for those who possess intelligence, because these words, like a rotten garment, cannot be tied together. And they worship the devil to such an extent that they call him the creator of the divine words and ascribe the divine glory to him. They have forgotten what God said through the prophet, "I am the Lord: that is my name: and my glory I will not give to another, neither my praise to graven images" [Isa. 42:8].

Having read that the deceitful devil said to Jesus: "All these things will I give thee, if thou wilt fall down and worship me" [Matt. 4:9], the heretics trust the devil and take him as a sovereign of the creatures of God. And again having read, "Now is the Judgment of this world: now shall the prince of this world be cast out" [John 12:31], and, "I will not talk much with you: for the prince of this world cometh" [John 14:30], they call the devil the ruler and the prince of God's creatures.

Because the heretics have alienated themselves from the cross of Christ and rejected it, the devil leads them easily according to his will. As those who fish with a fishhook cannot fish unless they use worms as bait, so the heretics conceal their poison with their hypocritical humility and fasting; and also carrying the gospel with them, and putting a wrong construction upon it, they are able to seduce the people. They do this to their own perdition; and they purpose to destroy all love and Christian faith. But in vain do they try to do this, and in vain are their prayers. Paul says, "Whether therefore ye eat, or drink, or whatsoever you do, do all to the glory of God" [1 Cor. 10:31].

And to what meaning of the scriptures do they not give a wrong sense? What do they not blaspheme in this world, which was established by God? They blaspheme not only the earth but also the heaven, saying that everything exists by the will of the devil: the sky, sun, stars, air, earth, man, churches, crosses: everything which emanates from God they ascribe to the devil; in general, they consider everything on the earth, animate and inanimate as devilish. Having read in the gospel what our Lord says in the parable of the two sons, they claim that Christ is the older, and the devil, who has deceived his father, is the younger. They give the name of the latter as Mammon and admit that he is the creator and author of the earthly things. They say that he has ordered the people to marry, to eat meat and to drink wine. In general, in blaspheming all our things, they think themselves to be inhabitants of the heavens, and call those who marry and live in this world the servants of Mammon. And, feeling aversion for all these things, they do not admit them, not for the sake of temperance as we do, but because we consider them to be pure. Here is what the Holy Ghost, through the mouth of Paul, says: "Forbidding to marry and commanding to abstain from meats, which God created to be received with thanksgiving of them which believe and know the truth. For every creature of God is good, and nothing is to be refused if it be received with thanksgiving" [1 Tim. 4:3-4]. Do ye hear, heretics, these words of the Holy Ghost who says that legal marriage is pure before God and moderate eating and drinking never destroy a man [1 Cor. 10:31; cf. also Titus 1:15]?

Do you see, brothers, how thoroughly damned they are, rejecting holy baptism and feeling an aversion to baptized children? If it happens to them by chance to see a child they shrink from it as from a bad smell. Being themselves a bad smell for angels and people, they turn away, spit, and cover their faces. Although they want to tell a lie according to their habit, saying that they are Christians, you must not believe them, because they are deceivers like their father, the devil. How can they call themselves Christians, as they do not make the sign of the cross, do not write down the prayers of the priests, and do not honor ministers. They hate children, about whom the Lord Jesus says, "Except ye be converted, and become as little children, ye shall not enter into the Kingdom of Heaven" [Matt. 18:3], and again, "Suffer little children, and forbid them not to come unto me, for of such is the Kingdom of Heaven" [Matt. 19:14]; and they call them little mammons, little devils, and little wealthy men, thinking that riches are from Mammon.

The heretics try to destroy also that which the holy apostles have built up, and what they have taught with much effort. What David says about them [Ps. 36:20] is right. How can they not be counted as enemies of God and of man, if they reject the miracles of God? Because they call the devil the creator, they deny that Christ has performed miracles. On reading the evangelists who write about miracles, they put a wrong construction on the words, to their own ruin, saying, "Christ neither gave sight to the blind, nor healed the lame, nor raised the dead, but these are only legends and delusions which the uneducated evangelists understood wrongly." They do not believe that the multitude in the desert was fed with five loaves of bread; they say, "It was not loaves of bread, but the four Gospels and the Acts of the Apostles."

The prayers of their flattery are a thousand. Shutting themselves up in their huts, they pray four times a night and four times a day, and they open the five doors, which are to be closed. Bowing, they recite, "Our Father," but for this they must be condemned, because only in words do they call the creator of the heaven and earth, father; elsewhere they ascribe his creation to the devil. When they worship, they do not make the sign of the cross. We ask them, saying: "Who ordered you to fast on Sunday, the day of the Resurrection, to bow and to work?" They answer that this is not written in the gospel, but it is arranged by men, and therefore they reject all holy days, and do not revere the memory of saints, and martyrs, and fathers.

They try to conceal themselves by the words of the gospel in which our Lord says, "When thou prayest, thou shalt not be as the hypocrites are, for they love to pray standing in the synagogues and in the corners of the streets, that they may be seen of men" [Matt. 6:5]. They disfigure their faces in order that they may appear unto men to fast. On reading the words of Jesus, "When thou prayest, enter into thy closet, and when thou hast shut the door, pray to thy Father which is in secret; and thy Father which seeth in secret shall reward you openly. But when ye pray, use not vain repetitions as the heathen do" [Matt. 6:6-7]; they give them a wrong meaning and consider "the corners of the streets" to be churches, and the liturgies and other ceremonies to be babbling.

And hear their other words, through which they seduce the souls of uneducated people, saying as follows, "It is unbecoming for a man to labor and to do earthly work, as the Lord God says, 'Therefore take no thought, saying, what shall we eat, or what shall we drink, or wherewithal shall we be clothed (For after all these things do the Gentiles seek) for your heavenly Father knoweth that ye have need of all these things' " [Matt. 6:31-33]. That is why some of them do not want to do anything with their hands, wander from house to house and devour the property of the people deceived by them. But according to the words of the Lord God, they shall receive greater condemnation. Let us hear what Paul, who never received his bread as a gift says: "Ye yourselves know that these hands ministered unto my necessities, and to them that were with me" [Acts 20:34]. And about the lazy people he writes, "If any would not work, neither should he eat" [2 Thess. 3:10].

The heretics are condemned to a double condemnation, because, spreading a different teaching as new apostles and forerunners of the Antichrist, they prepare people for admiring the Son of Perdition. They teach their own people not to obey their masters; they blaspheme the wealthy, hate the tsar, ridicule the elders, reproach the nobles, regard as vile in the sight of God those who serve the tsar, and forbid servants to obey their masters.

I wish to tell you another heretical story, with which the devil, who despises human beings, catches them. When they read the words of James, the brother of Jesus, who says, "Confess your faults one to another, and pray one for another, that ye may be healed" [James 5:16], they do not understand that this is said to priests. Furthermore, "Is any among you sick? Let him call for the elders of the Church; and let them pray over him, anointing him with oil in the name of the Lord: and the prayer of faith shall save the sick, and the Lord shall raise him up; and if he has committed sins, they shall be forgiven him" [James 5:14-15]. The heretics confess and give absolution one to another, for their sins, although they themselves are bound with the chains of the devil, and this is done not only by men but also by women, which action is worthy of condemnation. The apostle says, "Let the woman learn in silence with all subjection. But I suffer not a woman to teach nor to usurp authority over the man, but to be in silence" [1 Tim. 2:11-12], and James says to the men, "Be not many masters, my brethren, knowing that we shall receive the greater condemnation" [James 3:1].

[Then there follow the anathemas, which are important as throwing light on the Bogomilian teaching.]

He who does not love our Lord Jesus Christ, cursed be he!

He who does not believe in the Holy Inseparable Trinity, cursed be he!

He who does not admit the Holy Communion and the blood of Christ, cursed be he!

He who does not pray with hope to the Virgin Mary, cursed be he!

He who does not kiss the icons of our Lord, of the Holy Virgin, and of all the Saints with veneration and love, cursed be he!

He who does not honor the words of the Gospel and Apostles, cursed be he!

He who believes that the Holy Prophets have not spoken through the Holy Ghost, but have prophesied of their own initiative, cursed be he!

He who does not honor all the Saints and does not revere their relics with love, cursed be he!

He who blasphemes the Holy Liturgy and all prayers given to the Christians by the Apostles and the Holy Fathers, cursed be he!

He who does not believe that all visible and invisible creatures are created by God, cursed be he!

He who puts a wrong construction upon the Gospel and the words of the Apostles, and does not read them as the holy men have interpreted them, cursed be he!

He who does not carry out the commandments of Moses as given by God, and talks evil, cursed be he!

He who does not believe that the Ecclesiastical Orders are established by God and the Apostles, cursed be he!

He who blasphemes lawful marriage and the rich who wear wedding garments with respect, cursed be he!

He who reproaches those that eat meat and drink wine according to the law, and who thinks that they are not worthy to enter into the Kingdom of God, cursed be he!

18 A Standoff at Lombers, 1165

The bishop of Lodève, by command of the bishop of Albi, and of his assessors, asked those who caused themselves to be called "good men":

1. If they received the law of Moses, and the Prophets, or the Psalms, and the Old Testament, and the doctors of the New Testament. They answered before all the multitude, that they did not receive the law of Moses, nor the Prophets, nor the Psalms, nor the Old Testament; but only the Gospels, the Epistles of Paul, and the seven canonical Epistles, the Acts of the Apostles, and the Apocalypse.

2. He asked them of their faith, that they might set it forth. They answered that they would not say unless they were compelled.

3. He interrogated them concerning the baptism of children, and if they will be saved by baptism? They said, that they should say nothing; but would answer out of the Epistles and Gospels.

4. He questioned them as to the body and blood of Christ; where it was consecrated, or by whom, and who received it, and if it was more, or better consecrated by a good than by a bad person? They answered that those who received worthily were saved; and those who received unworthily, procured to themselves damnation; and they said that it was consecrated by every good man, whether an ecclesiastic or a layman; and they answered nothing else, because they would not be compelled to answer concerning their faith.

5. He asked them what they thought of matrimony; and if a man and a woman who were so joined together could be saved? They would not answer, except this only—namely, that man and woman were united to avoid luxury and fornication, as St. Paul has said in his Epistle.

6. He asked them concerning repentance—whether when it took place at the time of death it availed to salvation; or if soldiers who were mortally wounded could be saved if they repented at the point of death; or if every person ought to confess his sins to the priests and ministers of the Church or to any layman; or of whom it was that St. James spoke when he said, "Confess your sins one to another"? They said in reply, that it was sufficient for sick persons to confess to whomsoever they pleased; but of soldiers they would not speak, because St. James says nothing except of sick persons.

He asked also of them whether the contrition of the heart and the confession of the mouth alone were necessary to repentance? Or if it was necessary that after repentance they should make satisfaction by fastings, mortifications, and alms, bewailing their sins, if they had the means? They answered, and said that James had said only that they should confess and so be saved; and they did not wish to be better than the Apostle, and to add any thing of their own, as the bishops do.

They said also, many things without being asked. That it is altogether unlawful to swear any oath, as Jesus said in the gospel, and James in his epistle.

They said also, that Paul stated in his epistle what sort of persons were to be ordained in the Church as bishops and presbyters; and that if such persons were not ordained as St. Paul directed they were not bishops nor priests, but ravening wolves and hypocrites and seducers, loving salutations in the marketplaces, the chief seats and highest places in feasts, desiring to be called Rabbi and Master contrary to the commands of Christ, dressed in albs and white garments, and wearing on their fingers gold rings with gems, which their master Jesus had not commanded; and pouring forth many other reproaches. And therefore since they were not bishops and priests (except as those were priests who had betrayed Christ) they ought not to obey them, because they were evil men; not good teachers, but hirelings.

In answer to what they said, many authorities of the New Testament were produced by the Lord Pontius, archbishop of Narbonne, and by Arnold, bishop of Nismes, and Peter, abbot of Sendres, and the abbot of Fontfroid.

The allegations and the authorities of the New Testament having been heard on both sides (for they would not receive judgment except by the New Testament) the bishop of Lodeve, after silence had been made, by command of the bishop of Albi and the assessors above-named, gave the following sentence, according to law, and from the New Testament, in the presence of all the persons aforesaid:

"I, Jocelin, bishop of Lodève, by command of the bishop of Albi, and his assessors, adjudge those who call themselves 'Boni homines' to be heretics, and I condemn the sect of Oliverius, and of his companions, and those who hold the sect of the heretics of Lombers wheresoever they may be; and this we judge by authority of the New Testament, that is, the Gospels, and Epistles, and Psalms, and Acts of the Apostles and the Apocalypse."

The heretics answered, that the bishop who had given sentence was a heretic and not they; and that he was their enemy, and was a ravening wolf, and a hypocrite, and an enemy of God, and had not judged rightly; and they would not answer concerning their faith, because they were aware of him, as the Lord had commanded them in the Gospels. "Beware of false prophets who come unto you in sheep's clothing, but inwardly they are ravening wolves"; and that he was a fraudulent persecutor of them; and they were prepared to show by the Gospels and Epistles that he was not a good shepherd, neither he nor the other bishops, and priests, but rather hirelings.

The bishop answered that the sentence had been given against them agreeably to law; and that he was prepared to prove, in the court of the Lord Alexander, the Catholic Pope, and in the court or Louis, king of France, and in the court of Raymond, count of Toulouse, or of his wife, who was present, or in the court of Trencavel, then present, that the cause had been rightly judged; and that they were manifestly and notoriously heretics; and he promised that he would accuse them of heresy, in every Catholic court, and would submit to the decision of a trial.

Seeing themselves however to be convicted, and confounded, they turned themselves to all the people saying, "Hear, O good men, our faith, which we confess—we now confess out of love to you, and for your sakes." The aforesaid bishop replied, "You do not say that you will speak for the Lord's sake; but for the sake of the people'; and they said, 'We believe in one living and true God, trine and one, Father, Son, and Holy Spirit—that the Son of God took flesh, was baptized in Jordan, fasted in the desert, preached our salvation, suffered, died, and was buried, descended into hell, rose the third day, ascended into heaven, sent the Spirit, the Paraclete, on his disciples on the day of Pentecost, will come at the day of judgment to judge the quick and the dead, and that all will rise. We acknowledge also that what we believe with the heart, we ought to confess with the mouth. We believe that he is not saved who does not eat the body of Christ, and that it is not consecrated except in the church, and also not except by a priest, and that it is not better done by a good than by a bad priest. We believe also, that no one is saved except by baptism; and that children are saved by baptism. We believe also that man and wife are saved, though carnally united; and that every one ought to receive penance in the heart and with the mouth, and to be baptized by a priest and in the church." And, indeed, if any thing more in the Church could be shown by the Gospels or Epistles, they would believe and confess it.

The aforesaid bishop also asked them if they would swear that they held and believed that faith; and if there was anything else which they ought to confess that they had improperly believed or taught or not. In reply, they said that they would not in anywise swear; because they should do contrary to the Gospels and Epistles. Authorities of the New Testament were however brought against them by the aforesaid Catholic persons; and thus the authorities on both sides having been heard, the aforesaid bishop rising up gave judgment in the following manner:

"I, Jocelin, bishop of Lodève, by authority and mandate of the bishop of Albi and of his assessors, judge and give sentence that these heretics are in error as to the matter of oaths; and ought to swear if they will repent, and that an oath is to be tendered where the faith is in question; and since they are of evil report and accused of heresy, they ought to clear themselves from the charge; and returning to the unity of the Church, they ought to affirm their faith by an oath, as the Catholic Church holds and believes, lest the weak who are in the Church should be corrupted, and lest sickly sheep should infect the whole flock."

19   The Cathar Council at Saint-Félix-de-Caraman, 1167

In the year 1167 of the Incarnation of Our Lord, in the month of May, the church of Toulouse was guided by Pope Niquinta in the castle of Saint-Félix, where a great many men and women of the church of Toulouse and of neighboring churches were gathered to receive the *consolamentum*, which Pope Niquinta proceeded to give. After this, Robert of Epernon, bishop of the church of the "French," arrived with his advisors; likewise, Mark arrived with the council of Lombardy. Later Sicard the Cellarer, bishop of the church of Albi, arrived with his council; finally, Bernard Catalan arrived with the council of the church of Carcasonne. The council of the church of Aran was also there. Thus assembled in an innumerable number, the men of the church of Toulouse wished to have a bishop, and they elected Bernard Raimond. At the same time, in like manner, Bernard Catalan and the council of the church of Carcasonne, delegated and instructed by the church of Toulouse, and with the will and approval of Sicard the Cellarer, elected Guiraud Mercier, and the men of Aran elected Raimund of Casals. After this, Robert of Epernon received the *consolamentum* and episcopal orders from Lord Pope Niquinta to become the bishop of the church of the "French." Likewise, Sicard the Cellarer received the *consolamentum* and episcopal orders to be the bishop of the church of Albi; likewise Mark received the *consolamentum* and episcopal orders to be the bishop of the church of Lombardy; likewise, Bernard Raimund received the *consolamentum* and episcopal orders to be the bishop of the church of Toulouse; Guiraud Mercier also received the *consolamentum* and episcopal orders to be the bishop of the church of Carcasonne; likewise Raimund de Casals received the *consolamen-*

tum and episcopal orders to be the bishop of Aran. Afterwards, Pope Niquinta said to the church of Toulouse: "You have asked me to tell you whether the observances of the primitive church were moderated or rigid; I tell you that the seven churches of Asia were distinct and separate, and that not one of them did anything in any way contradictory to another. Now, the churches of Romania, Dragovitza, Melenguia, Bulgaria, and Dalmatia are distinct and separate, and not one of them did anything contradictory to another. Therefore, they are at peace among themselves. You do likewise."

The church of Toulouse elected Bernard Raimund, William Garsias, Ermengaud de Foret, Raymond de Baimiac, Guilabert de Bonvilar, Bernard William Contor, Bernard William Bonneville, and Bertrand d'Avignonet to define its territory. The church of Carcasonne chose Guiraud Mercier, Bernard Catalan, Gregory and Peter Warmhands, Raymond Pons, Bertrand de Molino, Martin of Ipsa Sala, and Raymond Guibert as divisers of the church of Carcasonne. After having met in council, they decided that the church of Toulouse and the church of Carcasonne ought to be divided as are the [Catholic] bishoprics, thus: the bishopric of Toulouse and the archbishopric of Narbonne are separated in two places, and with the bishopric of Carcasonne at Saint-Pons where the mountain comes along between the castle of Cabardès and the castle of Hautpoul to the boundary between Saissac and Verdun and passes between Montréal and Fanjeaux, and as the other bishoprics, similarly, are divided at the boundary of Razès as far as Lérida where it touches Toulouse, the church of Toulouse will have in its control and under its authority all that touches upon Toulouse. Likewise, the church of Carcasonne will have under its authority and administration the whole bishopric of Carcasonne and the archbishopric of Narbonne and all other lands descending towards the sea up to Lérida, as it has been divided and said. That the churches thus marked out in their boundaries, as it has been said, may have peace and concord among themselves, and none of them should injure or be in disagreement with another.

These are the witnesses and guarantors of this deed: Bernard Raimond, William Garsias, Ermengaud de Foret, Raymond de Baimiac, Guilabert de Bonvilar, Bernard William Contor, Bernard William Bonneville, Bertrand d'Avignonet, and of the church of Carcasonne, Guiraud Mercier, Bernard Catalan, Gregory and Peter Warmhands, Raymond Pons, Bertrand de Molino, Martin de Ipsa Sala, and Raimond Guibert. And all of these charged Ermengaud de Foret and demanded that he draw up and engross a charter for the church of Toulouse; and likewise they requested Pierre Bernard to draw up and engross a charter for the church of Carcasonne. And this was done. The lord Pierre Isarn had a copy of the old charter drawn up from the authority of this committee which divided the churches as it is written above, on Monday, August 14, [1167]. In the year 1232 of the Incarnation of Our Lord, Peter Pollanus made a copy of this as requested and ordered.

20 Pierre des Vaux de Cernay: The *Historia Albigensis*

First it is to be known that the heretics held that there are two creators: viz. one of invisible things, whom they called the benevolent god, and another of visible things, whom they named the malevolent god. The New Testament they attributed to the benevolent god, but the Old Testament to the malevolent god, and rejected it altogether, except certain authorities which are inserted in the New Testament from the Old, which, out of reverence to the New Testament, they esteemed worthy of reception. They charged the author of the Old Testament with falsehood, because the Creator said, "In the day that ye eat of the tree of the knowledge of good and evil ye shall die"; nor (as they say) after eating did they die, when, in fact, after the eating the forbidden fruit they were subjected to the misery of death. They also call him a homicide, as well, because he burned up Sodom and Gomorrah and destroyed the world by the waters of the deluge, as because he overwhelmed Pharaoh and the Egyptians in the sea. They affirmed also that all the fathers of the Old Testament were damned, that John the Baptist was one of the greater demons. They said also, in their secret doctrine, [*in secreto suo*] that that Christ who was born in the visible and terrestrial Bethlehem and crucified in Jerusalem was a bad man, and that Mary Magdalene was his concubine; and that she was the woman taken in adultery, of whom we read in the gospel. For the good Christ, as they said, never ate, nor drank, nor took upon him true flesh, nor ever was in this world, except spiritually in the body of Paul. I say in the terrestrial and visible Bethlehem, because the heretics feigned that there was another new and invisible country, and in that country, according to some, the good Christ was born and crucified.

Also the heretics said that the good god had two wives, Collant and Colibant, and from them begat sons and daughters. There were other heretics who said that there is one Creator but that he had for sons Christ and the devil. These, also, said that all creatures were good, but that by the daughters of whom we read in the Apocalypse [*marg.* Genesis], all things had been corrupted.

They said that almost all the Church of Rome was a den of thieves, and that it was the harlot of which we read in the Apocalypse. They so far annulled the sacraments of the Church, as publicly to teach that the water of holy baptism was just the same as river water, and that the Host of the most holy body of Christ did not differ from common bread, instilling into the ears of the simple this blasphemy, that the body of Christ, even though it had been as great as the Alps, would have been long ago consumed and annihilated by those who had eaten of it. Confirmation and confession they considered as altogether vain and frivolous. They preached that holy matrimony was meretricious, and that none could be saved in it if they should beget children. Denying also the resurrection of the flesh, they invented some unheard-of notions, saying that our souls are those of angelic spirits who, being cast down from heaven by the apostacy of pride, left their glorified bodies in the air; and that these souls themselves, after successively inhabiting seven terrene bodies of one sort or another, having at length fulfilled their penance, return to those deserted bodies.

It is also to be known that some among the heretics were called "perfect" or "good men"; others "believers" of the heretics. Those who were called perfect wore a black dress, falsely pretended to chastity, abhorred the eating of flesh, eggs and cheese, wished to appear not liars when they were continually telling lies, chiefly respecting God. They also said that they ought not on any account to swear.

Those were called "believers" of the heretics, who lived after the manner of the world, and who though they did not attain so far as to imitate the life of the perfect, nevertheless hoped to be saved in their faith; and though they differed as to their mode of life, they were one with them in belief and unbelief. Those who were called believers of the heretics were given to usury, rapine, homicide, lust, perjury, and every vice; and they, in fact, sinned with more security and less restraint, because they believed that without restitution, without confession and penance, they should be saved, if only, when on the point of death, they could say a Pater Noster, and receive imposition of hands from the teachers.

As to the "perfect" heretics, however, they had a magistracy whom they called deacons and bishops, without the imposition of whose hands, at the time of his death, none of the believers thought he could be saved; but if they laid their hands upon any dying man, however wicked, if he could only say a Pater Noster, they considered him to be so saved that without any satisfaction and without any other aid, he immediately took wing to heaven.

21   Rainier Sacconi: A Thirteenth-Century Inquisitor on Catharism

The sect of the Cathari is divided into three parts, or principal divisions [sectas principales]; of which the first are called Albanenses, the second Concorezenses, the third Bagnolenses, and these are all in Lombardy. The other Cathari, however, whether in Tuscany, the Marquisate [of Trevisano], or in Provence, do not differ in their opinions from the said Cathari, or some of them. For all these Cathari have some common opinions in which they agree, and there are some peculiar opinions in which they disagree. The common opinions of all the Cathari are these—namely, that the devil made the world, and all things in it. Also, that all the sacraments of the church—namely, the sacrament of baptism of material water, and the other sacraments, are not profitable to salvation, and that they are not the true sacraments of Christ, and of his Church; but delusive, and diabolical, and of the church of the malignants. Also, it is a common opinion of all the Cathari that carnal marriage is always a mortal sin, and that the future punishment of adultery and incest will not be greater than that of lawful matrimony; nor would any among them be more severely punished. Also, all the Cathari deny that there will be a resurrection of the flesh. Also, they believe, that it is a mortal sin to eat flesh, or eggs, or cheese, even in case of urgent necessity. Also, that the secular powers sin mortally in punishing malefactors or heretics. Also, that no one can be saved but by them. Also, that all children, even unbaptized, will be eternally punished with no less severity than homicides and thieves. The Albanenses, however, differ on this point, saying that no creature of the good god will perish. Also, they all deny purgatory.

Also, it is a common opinion of all the Cathari that whosoever kills a bird, from the least to the greatest, or quadrupeds, from the weasel to the elephant, commits a great sin; but they do not extend this to other animals.

The Cathari (like apes who try to imitate the actions of men) have four sacraments, but such as are false, nugatory, unlawful, and sacrilegious, which are the imposition of hands, the benediction of bread, penance, and orders. Of each of these we shall speak in course.

Imposition of Hands is called by them "consolamentum," and "Spiritual Baptism," and "Baptism of the Holy Spirit," without which, according to them, no mortal sin is remitted, nor is the Holy Spirit given to anyone; but by it (only however as performed by them) both are granted. On this point the Albanenses differ a little from them; for they say that the hands are of no efficacy in the matter because they hold them to have been created by the devil (as will be hereafter stated), but only the Lord's Prayer, which they repeat at that time; and that each is necessary, namely, the imposition of hands and the Lord's Prayer. It is also a common opinion of all the Cathari, that by that imposition of hands and Lord's Prayer, there is no remission of sins, if they who perform the imposition of hands are, at that time, in any mortal sin. This imposition of hands is performed by two at least; and not only by their bishops [prælatis], but also by the inferiors [subditis], and, in cases of necessity, even by the female members of the sect [a Catharibus].

The Benediction of the Bread of the Cathari, is a certain breaking of bread, which they daily perform at dinner and supper. This breaking of bread is performed in the following manner—when the members of the sect, male and female, go to the table, they all stand and say the Lord's Prayer. In the meantime, he who is first in rank or in orders, holding a loaf (or more than one if the number present requires it) and saying, "The grace of our Lord Jesus Christ be with us all," breaks the bread in pieces, and distributes it to all who are at the table, not only to the Cathari, but also to their believers, adulterers, thieves, and homicides. The Albanenses, however, say that that material bread is not blessed, nor capable of receiving any benediction, because, according to them, it is in itself a creature of the devil; and in this they differ from all the others, who say that the bread is actually blessed. None of them, however, believe that from that bread the body of Christ is made.

The Penance of all the Cathari is, beyond all doubt, false, vain, delusive, and noxious, as will be shown in what follows. For, in order to constitute true and fruitful penance, three things are required—namely, the contrition of the heart, the confession of the mouth, and the satisfaction of works. But I, Brother Rinherus, once a heresiarch, now, by the grace of God, a priest of the order of the Preaching Friars, though unworthy, do unhesitatingly say, and testify before God that I lie not, that there is nothing of those three things among the Cathari, or in their penance. For the poison of error, which they have drunk from the mouth of the old serpent, does not allow of their having any sorrow for their sins. This error, however, is fourfold—first, that eternal glory is not diminished for any sin—secondly, that the punishment of hell is not increased to the impenitent—thirdly, that there is no purgatory for anybody—fourthly, that, by the imposition of hands, guilt and punishment is entirely remitted by God; for that a child of one day old will not be less punished than Judas the traitor, but all are (according to their belief) equal, both in glory and punishment—except, however, the Albanenses; who say that every one will be restored to his former state, but not for his own deserts, and that in each kingdom (that is, of God and of the devil), some are greater than others. I say also, that many of them, who are infected with the before-mentioned errors, often grieve when they recollect that they did not give full license to their appetites before they made profession of the heresy of the Cathari; and this is the reason why many of the believers, both men and women, think no more of incest than of lawful union. Some of them, however, are, perhaps, restrained from sin of this kind by its horrible nature and by instinctive shame.

Another proof that they do not grieve for the sins which they committed before their profession of heresy, is this—that they make no restitution of what they have acquired by usury, theft, or rapine; nay, they keep it, or rather leave it to their children and grandchildren, who are living in the world; because they say that usury is no sin. Moreover, I say that in the seventeen years during which, alas! I was in their society, I never saw any one of them engaged in private prayer apart from others, or manifest sorrow for his sins, or weep, or smite upon the breast, and say, "God be merciful to me a sinner"; or anything of the kind which could denote contrition. Nor do they ever implore the patronage of angels or saints, or of the blessed Virgin Mary, nor fortify themselves with the sign of the cross.

We come next to the confession of the Cathari—what it is, and when, and to whom they make it. Their confession is this—"I am before God and you to make confession, and to accuse myself of all my sins which are in me in any way, and to receive from you all pardon from God and from yourselves." This confession is made publicly, before all who are assembled, where there are often a hundred and more Cathari, male and female, and their believers. And every one makes this confession when he receives the said imposition of hands, and he makes it especially to their prelate, holding the book of the Gospels, or of the whole New Testament on his breast; who, having given absolution, places the said book upon his head, and the other Cathari who are present. . . his right hand, immediately beginning the prayers.

Whenever any one who has received the said imposition of hands falls into any sin of the flesh, or any which is in their opinion mortal, he is required to confess that sin only and not any others; and again, privately, to receive imposition of hands from his prelate, and from one other at least with him. All bowing down to the ground, before the prelate, holding the book on his breast, one (speaking for all) says with a loud voice, "We come before God, and you, confessing our sins, because we have greatly sinned in word, and deed, in sight, and thought," and the like. Whence it evidently appears that all the Cathari die in their sins, without confession. And in this way they confess only once in the month, if they conveniently can.

The satisfaction of the Cathari comes next—wherein it may be inquired whether the Cathari perform their works for the satisfaction of those sins which they had committed before they had joined the sect? To which I briefly answer, no—although it may appear strange to the ignorant. For they frequently pray, and fast, and at all times abstain from meat, eggs, and cheese; all which have the appearance of being works of satisfaction for their sins, and of which they often vainly boast. There is, however, a threefold error in them, which prevents their having the nature of satisfaction. The first is that all guilt and punishment of this kind is remitted by their imposition of hands and prayer, or by prayer only, according to the Albanenses, as has been already stated. The second error is that God does not inflict the punishment of purgatory (which they altogether deny) on any one, or any temporal punishment in this life, which they consider as inflicted by the devil. This is also the reason why they do not enjoin the penance of abstinence on any one, either as penance or for the remission of their sins. The third error is that every man is necessarily bound to perform those works, as being commanded by God. Thus even a child of ten years old, who had never committed any mortal sin before he became a Cathari, is punished in the same way as an old man who during a long period had never ceased from sin. For any Catharist among them would not be more severely punished for having drunk poison, intending to destroy himself, than for having eaten a fowl to save his life, either in the way of medicine or in any other case of necessity, nor will, according to them, be more severely punished hereafter. They say also the same with regard to marriage, as has been already stated. Also they give little or no alms to strangers, except, perhaps, to avoid scandal among their neighbors, and that they may get credit for them. They give also very little to their own poor, and the cause is twofold—the first is, that they do not hope to obtain by it an increase of future glory or the pardon of their sins; the second is that almost all of them are very close and avaricious.

Next follows the prayers of the Cathari—this they consider as absolutely necessary when they take food or drink. Many of them, on this account, have directed those who waited upon them in sickness not to put any food or drink into their mouths if they (the sick person) could not at least say a Pater Noster; whence it is very probable that many of them kill themselves by these means, or are killed by their heretical brethren [cohæreticis].

From what has been said, it most clearly appears that the Cathari do not, in fact, perform any penance—especially as they have not contrition for their sins, nor confess them, nor make satisfaction for them, although they afflict themselves much, and are most grievously punished for their errors and sins.

Orders, the fourth sacrament of the Cathari, comes next—concerning which observe five things. First, that they have orders. Secondly, their names. Thirdly, the office of each order. Fourthly, how, and by whom, they are conferred. Lastly, how many churches of the Cathari there are, and where they are situated.

In the first place, then, observe that the orders of the Cathari are four. He who is in the first and chief order is called Bishop [Episcopus]. He who is in the second, the Elder Son [Filius Major]. He who is in the third, the Younger Son [Filius Minor]. He who is in the fourth and last, Deacon [Diaconus]. The others among those who are not in any order, are called Christians [Christiani et Christianæ].

Secondly, observe that it is the office of the bishop always to take the lead in whatever they do—namely, in the imposition of hands, in the breaking of bread, and the beginning of prayer; which things are in his absence performed by the elder son, or if he is not present, by the younger son. Moreover, those two sons go about either singly or together to visit all the Cathari who are under the bishop and all are bound to obey them. The same in all respects is done by the deacons, and each one with regard to those who are under him, in the absence of the bishop and his sons. And observe, that the bishop and his sons have deacons of their own in every city where they reside. Also, observe, that it is the office of the deacons to hear confessions of venial sins, which are made once in a month, as has been already stated, and to give absolution to those under their care, enjoining on them three days of fasting, or a hundred bows with bended knees [*inclinationes flexis genibus*] and that office is called, if I may so speak, *caregare servitium*.

The orders aforesaid are conferred by the bishop, and also, with the bishop's license, by his sons. The ordination of a bishop used to be performed in this manner. On the death of a bishop, the younger son ordained the elder son bishop; and he, afterwards, ordained the younger son an elder son. After that, a younger son was elected by all the bishops and inferiors, who were convened for this purpose by the bishop, and was ordained a younger son; and this mode of ordaining a younger son has not been altered among them. That, however, which has been mentioned with reference to the bishop has been changed by all the Cathari who dwell in the neighborhood of the sea; saying that by such an ordination the son seemed to appoint the father, which had a very incongruous appearance; and therefore is now done differently, in this manner—the bishop, before his death, ordains the elder son as bishop; and, if he dies, the son becomes bishop, and the younger son becomes an elder son the same day. Thus almost all the Cathari have, at all times, two bishops. Wherefore John of Lyons, who is one of those who are thus ordained, styles himself in his epistles "John of Lyons, by the grace of God, elder son and ordained bishop," etc. Each ordination is, however, manifestly reprehensible—for neither does a natural son appoint his father, nor do we ever read of one, and the same church having two of its sons bishops at the same time, any more than of a woman having two lawful husbands. All the aforesaid orders are conferred by imposition of hands, and this honor, namely, of conferring the above-mentioned orders and of giving the Holy Spirit, is attributed to the bishop alone, or, to him who is the chief and principal person, in holding the book of the New Testament on the head of him on whom hands are laid.

Observe, moreover—that the Cathari are in a state of great uncertainty and peril of their souls—for instance, if their prelate (especially a bishop) has secretly committed any mortal sin (and many cases have occurred among them) all those on whom he has laid hands are deceived, and, if they die in that state, perish. For the sake, therefore, of avoiding this danger, all the churches of the Cathari (except one or two) receive the *consolamentum* (that is, the imposition of hands, which is their baptism, as I have already said) twice, and some thrice; and what I have here stated is matter of public notoriety among them.

The Churches, however, of the Cathari amount to sixteen; and blame me not, O Reader! that I use the word churches, but rather those who have assumed the title. Their names are these—the church of the Albanenses, or of Sansano; the church of Concorezzo; the church of the Bagnolenses, or of Bagnolo; the church of Vicenza, or of the Marquisate [of Trevisano]; the church of Florence; the church of the Valley of Spoleto; the church of France, the church of Toulouse; the church of Cahors [Carthaensis, *marg.* Cadurcensis]; the church of Albi; the church of Sclavonia; the church of the Latins at Constantinople; the church of the Greeks, at the same place; the church of Philadelphia of Romaniola; the church of Bulgaria; the church of Dugranicia; and they all derive their origin from the two last.

The first of these, namely the Albanenses, live at Verona, and in many cities of Lombardy and are in number about five hundred, of both sexes. Those of Concorezzo are almost all over Lombardy, and are full fifteen hundred, or even more. The Bagnolenses live in Mantua, Brescia, Bergamo, and the Duchy of Milan (but few only) and in Romaniola, and are about two hundred. The church of the Marquisate [of Trevisano] has nothing at Verona, but they are about a hundred and fifty. The church of Toulouse, and of Albi, and of Cahors [Charchagensis, *marg.* Cadurcensis] with some which formerly existed, as the church of Auch [Auzinensis, *marg.* Ausciensis] which is almost destroyed, are about three hundred. The church of the Latins in Constantinople consists of about fifty. Also, the churches of Sclavonia, of the Greeks, of Philadelphia, of Bulgaria, and of Dugranicia, are composed of all nations. O Reader! you may safely say, that there are not four thousand Cathari, of both sexes, in all the world, but believers innumerable, and this computation has often been made among them.

We come next, to the peculiar opinions among the Cathari, and first, as to the church of the Albanenses (which is otherwise called of Senzano) because they err on more points than the rest of the Cathari. In the first place, then, it is to be especially observed, that these Albanenses are divided into two parties, holding different, and contrary opinions. The head of one party is Getesmanza, their bishop of Verona, and most of the elder, and a few of the younger belong to his sect. The head of the other party is John of Lyons, their elder son and ordained bishop of Bergamo, and, on the other hand, the younger ones, and very few of the elder, follow him. And this party is considerably greater than the other. The first party hold all the old opinions, which the older Cathari held in the year of our Lord 1233.

The opinions of these, beside the common ones already mentioned, are the following—that there are two principles from God, namely, of good and of evil. Also, that the Trinity, namely, the Father, the Son, and the Holy Ghost, is not one God, but that the Father is greater than the Son, and the Holy Ghost. Also, that each principle, or each god, created his own angels and his own world; and that this world and all that is in it was created, made, and formed by the evil god. Also, that the devil and his angels ascended into heaven, and having there fought with the Archangel Michael, an angel of the good god, he withdrew from thence a part of the creatures of God, and infuses them daily into the bodies of men and brutes, and even from one body to another, until the said creatures are restored to heaven. These creatures of god are called, according to them, "the people of God," and "souls and sheep of the house of Israel," and by other names. Also, that the Son of God did not really assume human nature of the Virgin Mary, but one like him, whom they state to have been an angel; and that he did not truly eat and drink, nor truly suffer, nor was dead and buried, nor was his resurrection true, but only supposed, as we read of himself, "being, as was supposed, the Son of Joseph." In like manner of all the miracles which Christ wrought. Also, that Abraham, Isaac, and Jacob, Moses and many others of the ancient fathers, and St. John the Baptist, were enemies of God, and servants to the devil. Also, that the devil was author of the whole of the Old Testament, except these books— namely, Job, the Psalms, the books of Solomon, of Wisdom, Ecclesiasticus, Isaiah, Jeremiah, Ezekiel, Daniel, and the twelve Prophets; of which some were written in heaven, namely those which were written before the destruction of Jerusalem, which they believe to be the heavenly. Also, that this world will never have an end. Also, that the Judgment is already past, and that there will be no further Judgment. Also, that hell and eternal fire, or eternal punishment are in this world and not elsewhere. Thus, indeed, all the Albanenses in general held the above-mentioned opinions at the period referred to, except the more simple, to whom some of these things were not revealed.

22 Chroniclers and Cathars on Catharism: The Heretics of Lombardy

A

At the time when the heresy of the Catharists in Lombardy was beginning to spread for the first time, they had a bishop by the name of Mark . . . whose episcopal orders derived from Bulgaria. A certain priest, Nicheta, came from Constantinople into Lombardy and began to question Mark's orders. Therefore Bishop Mark with his followers, dubious of their own position, left the Bulgarian order and received from Nicheta the order of Drugonthia. [There now follows a discussion of a schism within the Catharist Church in Lombardy between factions, each claiming that it represented the legitimate Catharist hierarchy.]

The beliefs of one of the groups of Catharists, those who follow the order of Drugonthia now follows: They believe and preach that there are two gods or lords without beginning and without end, one of them good and the other deeply evil; and they say that each god created angels, the good god the good angels and the bad god the bad angels, and that the good god is omnipotent in heaven, while the evil god has lordship over all of this world. And they say that Lucifer is the Son of the God of darkness, as it says in the Gospel of Saint John: "You are from your father the devil . . . ." And they say that this Lucifer rose from his kingdom and ascended into heaven . . . . And there he transformed himself into an angel of light. The other angels, admiring his beauty, interceded for him before the Lord, and he was taken up into heaven where he was made the overseer of the angels . . . . With this authority he seduced the other angels into evil. And then they say that there was a great battle in heaven, and that "that ancient serpent was cast down from heaven" with the angels that he had led astray . . . . And they say that the life of human bodies partly derives from the evil spirits that the devil has created and partly from the spirits that have fallen from heaven. The souls of the fallen do penance in the body. If they cannot obtain salvation in one body, their soul enters into

From Jeffrey Burton Russell, *Religious Dissent in the Middle Ages* (New York: John Wiley & Sons, 1971), pp. 71-76. Reprinted with the permission of the publisher.

another body and does penance there. And when their penance has finally been done, their bodies and spirits go to heaven and remain there.

The teachings of the other group of Catharists are as follows. They say that Lucifer and his companions sinned in heaven, but they are unsure what was the origin of this sin. Some of them say—this is difficult to understand—that it was the fault of a certain evil spirit having four faces, one of a man, one of a bird, one of a fish, and one of an animal. This evil spirit had no beginning and dwelt in the primeval chaos, having no power of creating. And they say that Lucifer (who had been good until then) descended from heaven and, seeing the face of this evil spirit, admired it. After having conversed with this evil spirit and having been influenced by him, Lucifer was led astray. He returned to heaven where he led others astray, and finally he and his followers were cast out of heaven. They did not, however, lose their natural powers as angels. And these heretics say that Lucifer and the other evil spirit wanted to create a material universe but were unable to do so. But they won over to their side one of the angels who was a chief assistant of God, and with the help of this good angel and the permission of God, they created the material universe. The heretics say that this Lucifer made Adam out of mud and in the form of Adam choked the good angel to death .... And he made Eve and caused Adam to sin through her. And they say that what was meant by the eating of the forbidden fruit was fornication.

The common opinion of all the Catharists is that all the things that are spoken of in the book of Genesis about the flood, about the sparing of Noah, about God's covenant with Abraham, and about the destruction of Sodom and Gomorrah—all these things were deeds done by the devil, who is called "god" in the Old Testament. And this god led the people out of Egypt and gave them the Law in the desert and led them into the Promised Land and sent them prophets—all for the purpose of being worshiped as god, causing the Jewish people at the instigation of the prophets to offer him blood sacrifice. And if the Jewish prophets at any time predicted anything about the Christ who was to come, it was not through their free will but rather through the action of the Holy Spirit. And they claim that Almighty God did all these deeds not through himself but through the devil acting for him as his minister. Thus they claim that whatever the devil did was done with the authority and the strength and the power that God delegated to him and that he did all of these things with the permission of God. It was the devil's plan in all this to rule the world, though the true God had of course another intention, that of achieving goodness and the salvation of souls through their penitence . . . .

They say that Christ did not really take on the flesh, that he did not eat or drink, nor was he crucified nor did he die, nor was he buried, and all things that he did according to human nature were not truly done but only in appearance . . . .

They say that John the Baptist was sent by the devil, and that baptism was established in order to hinder the teaching of Christ . . . .

All of the Catharists condemn marriage and deny the resurrection of the body. They all say that baptism with water is of no use whatsoever to salvation . . . .

B

On the principle of evil.

It is to be firmly believed by the wise that there is another principle of evil, powerful in iniquity, from whom Satan and all the other evil powers who oppose the true God derive their strength . . . . For otherwise the wise would have to believe that the true divine power is struggling and fighting with itself . . . .

On the alien god and the many gods.

If anyone should doubt what we have said, let him grasp the fact that there is another god and lord aside from the true God and Lord . . . . There are many gods and lords and powers opposed to the true God and his son Jesus Christ, as the scriptures themselves testify . . . .

That the creator of the universe is not the true God but the other god.

It is perfectly clear from scriptures that the god and lord who is the creator of the world is different from him to whom the blessed commend their spirits . . . . Our opponents [i.e., the Catholics] say that according to Genesis the Lord is the creator of the visible things of this world: the heaven and the earth, the sea, men and beasts, birds and reptiles . . . . But I say that the creator of the visible things of this world is not the true God. And I prove this from the evil of his words and deeds, and the changeableness of his words and deeds as described in the Old Testament . . . . [There follows a discussion of the morally questionable actions of God as described in the Old Testament. The Catharists, it will be observed, were offering one answer to the old

problem of reconciling the existence of God with the existence of evil:
evil was to be attributed to the evil god, not to the true God.] It is
evident enough to the wise that the true God could not be this creator
who mercilessly tempts men and women to destruction . . . .

C

Then the officiant shall take the book from the hands of the
believer and say: "John (if that indeed is his name), do you wish to
receive this holy baptism of Jesus Christ . . . and to keep it your whole
life long in purity of heart and mind; and not to fall in any manner into
sin?" And John shall reply: "Yes, I do. Call upon the good God for me
that he may give me his grace." And the officiant shall say: "May the
true Lord God grant you the grace to receive this gift to his honor and
to your own welfare." Then the believer shall stand reverently before
the officiant and say, along with the acolyte: "I have come before you
and before God and before the Church and before your holy order for
the purpose of receiving pardon and forgiveness for all my sins from
the beginning until now. Pray that God may grant me this. Bless us;
have mercy on us." Then shall the officiant reply: "May you receive
pardon and mercy for all your sins from God, from the Church, from
God's sacred order, from his precepts and his disciples, and may the
Lord God of mercy forgive you and receive you into life everlasting."
And the believer shall say: "Amen, may it be done unto us, O Lord,
according to your will." Then shall the believer rise and in front of the
officiant place his hands upon the gospels. And the officiant shall then
place the book upon the believer's head, and all the other elect and
other Christians who shall be there shall place their right hands upon
his head. And the officiant shall say: "In the name of the Father and
the Son and the Holy Spirit." And he who is receiving the *consolamentum* shall say: "Amen." And all the others shall say clearly: "Amen."
Then shall the officiant say: "Bless you and keep you. Amen. Let it be
done unto us, Lord, according to your will. May the Father and the
Son and the Holy Spirit send you away in peace, having forgiven your
sins. Let us worship the Father and the Son and the Holy Spirit [three
times]: Holy Father, the true, the just, and the merciful, now send
away your servant in peace and receive him into your justice. Our
Father [the Lord's prayer follows] . . . ." And he shall say aloud five
prayers and then the "Let us worship" three times. And then he shall
say one prayer and then again the "Let us worship" three times. Then
he shall read the beginning of the Gospel according to John: "In the

beginning was the Word," and so on. When the gospel has been read, he shall again say three times the "Let us worship," and then another prayer. And then again three times the "Let us worship," and he shall offer a benediction. And the Christian [i.e., he who is receiving the *consolamentum*] shall kiss the book and then bow three times, saying: "Bless, bless, bless, spare us; may God grant you a good reward for the good that you have done me for the love of God." Then shall the elect, the Christian men, and the Christian women receive the *servicium* [the general Catharist service of confession and absolution] according to the custom of the Church.

May all good Christians pray to God for him who has written these rules. Amen. Thanks be to God.

IV

THE WALDENSIANS

Historians have sometimes argued that Catharism was not really a heresy at all, but an entirely different religion from Christianity, and in spite of its popularity, its organization, and its selective reliance upon scripture, it stands in stark contrast to many of the dissenting and heretical movements seen so far. However, movements which praised apostolic poverty criticized the laxity of the clergy, read scripture in vernacular versions, claimed the right of preaching sppiritual reform, encouraged private devotion, and emphasized the spiritual needs of laypeople were much more common—whether these movements were, as was that of Henry of Le Mans, generally conservative in outlook, or, as was that of the Waldensians, much more radical. It is with these movements that the thread of continuity between the early eleventh and the late twelfth centuries is much more visible. They can be understood as religious movements within Christianity, linked with the late eleventh-century reforms, and identified with what M.D. Chenu has called "the search for the apostolic life." Both Chenu and Rosalind Brooke have emphasized the devotion and energy that new forms of religious life pursued in the eleventh century, and the careers of hermits, wandering preachers, founders of new religious orders, individual holy men, and those who sympathized with them play a prominent role in the history of eleventh- and twelfth-century culture, as well as in the history of heresy in particular.

Many of these movements were begun, as Moore and Lambert have made clear, by people who wanted to push some of the reform doctrines of the Gregorian movement, especially those dealing with lay and clerical status, to conclusions that lay beyond the point to which the twelfth-century Church was willing to go. Indeed, the passionate religious temper of the twelfth and thirteenth centuries is one of the few elements that link these movements, particularly the Waldensians, with Catharism; to focus one's concern upon the questions of religious sentiment, rather than upon heresy or orthodoxy specifically, is a very useful approach to understanding the psychological and emotional context of heretical movements.

Waldensianism, named after the twelfth-century merchant Valdès, was the most prominent of these evangelical movements, although those of the Humiliati, the Speronisti, and the Poor of Lombardy also played prominent roles in the late twelfth and thirteenth centuries, as did the Beguines and Beghards. Nor did any of these movements begin as heresies. The story of Valdès's conversion is typical of many spiritual experiences in the late twelfth century. In 1173, Valdès, a wealthy merchant of Lyons (the forename Peter that has been assigned to him has no basis in the sources and may have been attributed to him to link him to St. Peter), whose conscience appeared to have been bothering him because of the money he had made as a usurer, heard a *jongleur* tell the story of St. Alexis. The old French *Vie de Saint Alexis*, popular in the twelfth century, told the story of the heir of a wealthy family who ran away on his wedding night, lived a life of harsh asceticism, returned to his family home unrecognized, and lived out the rest of his life as a hermit in his own parents' house. Stirred by this and repeated hearings of the story, Valdès consulted the local clergy, one of whom quoted to him the lines from the gospel of Matt. 19:21, Jesus' advice for salvation: "Go, sell all your possessions, give the proceeds to the poor, and you will have riches in heaven. Then come and follow me." This text, along with other scriptural texts (cf. Matt. 6:19; 6:25-34; 10:9-42), inspired Valdès to separate from his wife, place his daughters in the convent at Fontevrault, dispose of his property, and begin to beg for his own food. Gradually, Valdès assembled a group of sympathetic followers into a kind of penitential order, sworn to apostolic poverty and preaching spiritual reform. Valdès had the Bible translated for the benefit of himself and his group (no. 23), thus raising the question of unauthorized translations from scripture, and he continued to preach without ecclesiastical authority. In 1179 Valdès was questioned by Pope Alexander III at the Third Lateran Council, and praised by the pope for opposing Catharism and living a life of voluntary poverty, but forbidden to preach. Walter Map, the indefatigable distorter of heretical opinions, gives a harsh portrait of what seemed to him Valdès's pretentions and the dangers that unauthorized lay preachers posed to clergy (no. 24). At the council Valdès made a formal profession of faith before the pope and council (no. 25). So far, Valdès and his followers remained well within the Church and its discipline.

Shortly after 1179, however, Valdès and his followers, and probably others who took Valdès's name, began to preach against clerical vices and urged people to reform their spiritual lives. In 1184 Pope Lucius III condemned "The Poor Men of Lyons," as Valdès's followers called themselves, among other heretics (below, no. 29), and from 1185 to 1205 the Waldensian movement became more severe in attacking clerical morals, insisting on the right of lay-people to preach, and spreading their doctrine into Italy and Languedoc, then into northeastern France and the Rhineland. Like the Cathars, the Waldensians recognized extensive religious rights for women, and like them wore distinctive, simple costumes that attracted public attention and elicited public sympathy. Caught between the orthodox Church and the Cathars, whom they bitterly opposed, the Waldensians soon developed a more radical approach. Antisacramentalism was added to antisacerdotalism, and many Waldensians rejected the Church and the clergy outright; they urged the universal priesthood of all believers, and they veered toward Donatism. In 1205 French Waldensians separated from Italian Waldensians, and in the two great years of preaching of 1206 and 1207, many Waldensians, notably Bernard Prim and Durand of Huesca, returned to the Church (below, no. 35). In spite of their veering into heresy, the increasing radicalization of their doctrines, and persecution from ecclesiastical and temporal authorities, the Waldensians survived in France, Italy, Germany, and in Piedmont, where Waldensian communities existed at the time of the sixteenth-century Reformation, and where some survive today.

Besides the Waldensians, other groups, such as the Humiliati, the Speronisti, and, on the side of orthodoxy, the Poor Catholics and the Franciscans, all pursued the ideal of evangelical poverty, and, on both sides of the line dividing orthodoxy from heterodoxy, lived similar styles of life. The durability and development of the Waldensian sects is illustrated by the remarks from a treatise attributed to David of Augsburg, written in Bavaria around 1270 (no. 26).

Several inquisitors produced handbooks of heretical beliefs during the thirteenth century, and from these some of our best information concerning them may be drawn. Sometimes, however, parts of these books were taken up by other writers, and sometimes later writings were attributed to earlier inquisitors. A good example is the immensely long work known as the Passau Anonymous, written by a cleric associated with the diocese of Passau in the 1260s, dealing with Jews and Moslems as well as with different kinds of heretics. This work was shortened by another author in the 1270s, and to the shortened version was attached the name "Pseudo-Reinerius," attributing it perhaps to the earlier inquisitor and former Cathar heresiarch Rainier Sacconi. Although Sacconi did write a short work on the beliefs of the Cathars and Waldensians (above, no. 21), his text on the Waldensians was very brief:

Concerning the heresy of the Leonists, or the Poor Men of Lyons

That which has been said above is sufficient concerning the heresy of the Cathars. Now we must speak of the heresy of the Leonists, or the Poor Men of Lyons. This heresy is divided into two groups. The first group is called the Ultramontane Poor, and the second [group] the Poor of Lombardy, and the latter derive from the former. The first group, that is the Ultramontane Poor, maintains that all oaths and swearing are forbidden by the New Testament and are mortal sins. And they say, concerning temporal justice, that kings, princes, and officials are not permitted to punish malefactors.

They also say that a simple layman may consecrate the body of the Lord. And I believe they say even that a woman may do this, since they have never denied this to me.

They also say that the Roman Church is not the Church of Christ.

Concerning the Poor of Lombardy

The Poor of Lombardy agree with [the statements above] concerning swearing oaths and temporal justice. Concerning the body of the Lord, however, they believe even worse things than the other group, saying that it may be consecrated by any person as long as he is without mortal sin.

They also say that the Roman Church is the church of the wicked, and of the beast and the whore, of whom may be read in the Apocalypse. And they say that it is no sin to eat meat in Lent or on ferial days against the precept of the Church, although it must be done without giving scandal to others.

They also say that the church of Christ endured in the bishops and other prelates up to the time of the blessed Sylvester, and by him was [perverted] until they themselves have restored it. They say however that [during all this time between Sylvester and themselves] there were nevertheless some who feared God and were saved.

They also say that infants may be saved without baptism.

Somehow, the text on Waldensianism of the Passau Anonymous, included in selections here (no. 27), became attributed to "Reinerius" in the shortened Passau text and is often referred to as Rainier Sacconi's own text. It is, however, the work of the Passau Anonymous himself, and provides a useful example from mid-thirteenth-century Germany of authorities' views of the Waldensians.

The text of the Passau Anonymous printed here is a literal translation of the selections printed by Patschovsky and Selge, up to the subsection, "On the sacraments of the Church." After that selection, the translation is abridged. It is important to get some flavor of the wealth of biblical citations in this remarkable tract, and of the combative character of the author, who answers the heretics' views himself in the course of his description of them. Sometimes it is difficult to know of whom he is speaking. One of the most remarkable features of the treatise is the author's acute awareness of the kinds of ecclesiastical abuses which he thinks lie behind the heretics' beliefs. He always introduces these with the term *Occasio*, which I have translated as "They say this because," or "This is occasioned." These short parts of the treatise provide a wealth of information on thirteenth-century popular religion and church practices, and the Anonymous pulls no punches when describing abuses.

LITERATURE

Wakefield and Evans, *Heresies of the High Middle Ages*, pp. 200-42, 257-58, 278-89, 346-51, 373-446; Moore, *Birth of Popular Heresy*, pp. 111-12, 132-54; Moore, *Origins of European Dissent*, pp. 228-31; Lambert, *Medieval Heresy*, pp. 67-94, 151-64. Latin texts in Fearns, *Ketzer und Ketzerbekämpfung*, pp. 38-51; Alexander Patchovsky, and K.V. Selge, *Quellen zur Geschichte der Waldenser*, Texte sur Kirchen- und Theologiegeschichte, vol. 18 (Gütersloh, 1973); Kurt-Victor Selge, *Die Ersten Waldenser*, 2 vols. (Berlin, 1967); G. Gonnet, *Enchiridion Fontium Valdensium* (Torre Pellice, 1958). On Waldensian history, see particularly G. Gonnet and A. Molnar, *Les Vaudois au moyen âge* (Turin, 1974); Christine Thouzellier, *Catharisme et Valdéisme en Langue-doc* (Paris, 1960); Lester K. Little, *Religious Poverty and the Profit Economy in Medieval Europe* (Ithaca, N.Y., 1978), pp. 120-28.

On the interesting career of Sacconi, see Franjo Sanjek, O.P., "Raynerius Sacconi, O. P., *Summa de Catharis*," *Archivum Fratrum Praedicatorum* 44 (1974): 31-60. The best study of the Passau Anonymous is that of Alexander Patschovsky, *Der Passauer Anonymous* (Stuttgart, 1968). For the "Pseudo-Reinerius" shortened version of the Anonymous, see Margaret Nickson, "The 'Pseudo-Reinerius' Treatise, the Final Stage of a Thirteenth-Century Work on Heresy from the Diocese of Passau," *Archives d'histoire doctrinale et littéraire du moyen age* 34 (1967): 255-314. Later work in Germany is described in Richard Kieckhefer, *Repression of Heresy in Medieval Germany (Philadelphia, 1979).*

23   Etienne de Bourbon: The Waldensians and Vernacular Scripture

A certain rich man of the city [Lyons], called Waldo, was curious when he heard the gospel read, since he was not much lettered, to know what was said. Wherefore he made a pact with certain priests, the one, that he should translate to him the Bible, the other, that he should write as the first dictated. Which they did; and in like manner many books of the Bible, and many authorities of the saints, which they called *Sentences*. Which when the said citizen had often read and learned by heart, he proposed to observe evangelical perfection as the apostles observed it; and he sold all his goods, and despising the world, he gave all his money to the poor, and usurped the apostolic office by preaching the gospel, and those things which he had learned by heart, in the villages and open places, and by calling to him many men and women to do the same thing, and teaching them the gospel by heart, . . . who indeed, being simple and illiterate men and women, wandered through villages and entered houses and preached in open places, and even in churches, and provoked others to the same course.

24   Walter Map: On the Waldensians, 1179

I saw in the council at Rome under the celebrated Alexander, third pope of the name, Waldenses, illiterate laymen, called from their founder Waldes (Waldo), a citizen of Lyons on the Rhone. These presented to His Holiness a book written in the French tongue, containing the text and gloss of the Psalter and of very many books of both Old and New Testaments. They besought him with great importunity to confirm the license of their preaching, because they seemed to themselves experts, although they were mere smatterers.

From Margaret Deanesly, *The Lollard Bible and Other Medieval Biblical Versions* (Cambridge: Cambridge University Press, 1920). p. 26. Reprinted with the permission of the publisher.

For it usually happeneth that birds which do not see the subtle snares or nets believe that there is free passage everywhere. Do not those persons who are occupied all their days with sophistries—men who can ensnare and yet can scarce be snared, and who are ever delvers in the deep abyss—do not those men, in fear of disfavor, profess with reverence to bring forth all things from God, whose dignity is so lofty that no praises or no merits of preachments can attain to that height, unless sovereign mercy hath borne them aloft? On every dot of the divine page, noble thoughts are wafted on so many wings, and such wealth of wisdom is amassed that he alone to whom God hath given something [to draw with] may drink from the full [well]. Shall, therefore, in any wise pearls be cast before swine, and the word given to laymen who, as we know, receive it foolishly, to say nothing of their giving what they have received? No more of this, and let it be rooted out! "Let the precious ointment run down from the head upon the beard and thence upon the clothing"; "let clean waters be drawn from the fountain, not muddy from the marketplace." I, the least of the many thousand who were called to the council, derided them, because their petition produced so much higgling and hesitation, and when I was summoned by a certain great bishop, to whom that mightiest of popes had entrusted the charge of confessions, I sat down, "a mark for their arrows." After many masters of the law and men of learning had been admitted, there were brought before me two Waldenses who seemed the chief of their sect, eager to argue with me about the faith, not for the love of seeking the truth, but that by convicting me of error they might stop my mouth as of "one speaking lies." I sat full of fear— I confess—lest under pressure of my sins the power of speech in so great a council should be denied me. The bishop ordered me, who was making ready to reply, to try my eloquence against them. At the outset I suggested the easiest questions, which anybody should be able to answer, for I knew that when an ass is eating thistles, its lips disdain lettuce: "Do you believe in God the Father?" They answered, "We believe." "And in the Son?" They replied, "We believe." "And in the Holy Spirit?" Their reply still was, "We believe." I kept on, "In the Mother of Christ?" And they again, "We believe." Amid the derisive shouts of all, they withdrew in discomfiture, which was richly deserved, because they were ruled by none, and sought to be made rulers, like Phaethon who "did not know the names of his horses."

These have nowhere a fixed abode, but wander about by two and two, barefooted, clad in sheepskins, possessing nothing, "having all things in common" like the apostles, naked following the naked Christ. Now their beginnings are lowly because they can find no entrance anywhere, for, should we let them in, we should be driven out. Let him who doth not believe hear what hath already been said of like sort. In these times of ours which we condemn and deride, there are doubtless those who wish to keep faith, and should they be put to the test, they would, as in times gone by, lay down their lives for their shepherd, Lord Jesus, but because we have been led astray or lured away by a strange sort of zeal, our times have grown as base as though of iron. Ancient days pleased as though they shone with gold. We possess histories handed down from the beginning to our times, we read old fables, and we have understanding of the mystic meaning from which cometh the pleasure we should find in them. Bear in mind the envious Cain, the citizens of Sodom and Gomorrah—not one man, say I, but all men wallowing in a sea of lust—Joseph, sold by his brethren, Pharaoh punished by many plagues, a people showing themselves, by their worship of the golden calf, rebellious to God and to him who was chosen by God through the clearest of signs in the desert, the pride of Dathan, the impudence of Zimri, the perjury of Achitophel, the avarice of Nabal, and innumerable prodigies of lust, in unbroken series from the beginning to our times, and therefore do not shrink back with too great pride from things of our day like unto these or perhaps even less base. But because endurance of evils is more severe than mere hearsay, we are silent over what we hear and we wail over what we suffer. Thus, bearing in mind that there have been worse things, let us show restraint in those things that are lighter. Indeed warning fables set before us Atreus and Thyestes and Pelops and Lycaon and many others like these that we may shun their fates. The judgments of histories also are not without their value, for both kinds of narratives have the same practice and design. For history, which is based on truth, and fable, which weaveth a tissue of fancy, both bless the good with a happy end so that virtue may be loved, and damn the bad with a foul ending, wishing to render wickedness hateful. In narratives adversity succeedeth in turn to prosperity and vice versa, with frequent change of fortune, in order that, both being always kept before our eyes, no forgetfulness of either may arise on account of the other, but that each may be kept in due bounds by proper infusion of its opposite. Thus exaltation or destruction will never pass the mean; that is to say, by the contemplation of things to come, meditation will neither be empty of hope nor free from fear—I mean, of temporal things to come, because that "perfect charity" which is heavenly "casteth out fear."

25   Valdès's Profession of Faith

In the name of the Father and of the Son and of the Holy
Spirit and of the most blessed and ever Virgin Mary. Be it known to all
the faithful that I, Valdès, and my brothers, the holy gospels having
been set before us, believe in our hearts, understand by our faith,
confess by our mouths, and affirm by means of simple words that the
Father, Son, and Holy Spirit are three persons, one God, and the whole
Trinity of the Godhead coessential, and consubstantial and coeternal,
and coomnipotent, and are single persons in a Trinity full God, and all
three persons one God, as [the creeds] *"credo in deum"* [the Apostles'
Creed], and *"credo in unum deum"* [the Nicene Creed, above, no. 5],
and *"quicumque vult"* [the "Athanasian" Creed] state.

We believe by heart and confess by mouth that the Father, the Son,
and the Holy Spirit, One God of whom we speak, is the creator and
maker and ruler, and at the proper place and time, disposer of all
things visible and invisible, in the heavens and the air, in the waters
and on the earth.

We believe one and the same God to be the author of the New and
the Old Testaments, that is of the laws of Moses and of the prophets
and the apostles, who, in a trinity, as it has been said, created all
things. John the Baptist, sent by God, was holy and just, and in his
mother's womb was full of the Holy Spirit.

We believe in our heart and confess by our mouth that the
Incarnation of the Divinity was made not in the Father nor in the Holy
Spirit, but in the Son only.

We believe in our heart and confess by our mouth that he who was
in his divinity the Son of God the Father, true God from the Father,
was also a true man by his mother, having true flesh from his mother's
womb and a human rational soul; that there were in him both natures,
that is, God and man, one person, one Son, one Christ, one God with
the Father and the Holy Spirit, the ruler and creator of all things, born
of the Virgin Mary by a true parturition of the flesh; that he ate and
drank and slept, that he grew tired and rested from his journey, that he
suffered a true passion in his flesh and died a true death of his body
and resurrected a true resurrection of his flesh and a true resumption

of his soul, in which afterwards he ate and drank, ascended into heaven, sits at the right hand of the Father, and in him will come to judge the living and the dead.

We believe in One Holy Catholic Church, apostolic and immaculate, outside of which no one can be saved. We reject in no way the sacraments which are celebrated [in the Church] by virtue of the inestimable and invisible virtue of the Holy Spirit, even though they may be administered by a sinful priest, as long as the Church accepts him; nor do we withdraw from the ecclesiastical offices or benedictions celebrated by him; but with a loving spirit [we] embrace them as if [they had been offered] by the most righteous [of priests]. We approve, therefore, of the baptism of infants; if they should die after baptism before they have committed sin, we confess that they may be saved. Truly in baptism all sins, both that sin originally contracted and those committed voluntarily, we believe are forgiven. We allow that confirmation performed by a bishop, by the laying-on of hands, is to be accepted as holy and venerable. We firmly believe and simply affirm that the Sacrifice [of the Mass], that is of the bread and wine, after consecration are the body and blood of Jesus Christ, in which nothing more may be achieved by a good priest, and nothing less may be achieved by a bad priest. We concede that sinners and penitents of heart, confessing by mouth, and [performing] works of satisfaction according to the scriptures, may be able to obtain God's pardon, and we most freely communicate with them. We do not deny that marriages of the flesh are contracted according to the [instructions of the] Apostle, and we prohibit the breaking of marriages contracted truly and ordinarily, nor do we denounce second marriages. We venerate the anointing of the sick with consecrated oil. We humbly praise and faithfully venerate ecclesiastical orders, that is, the episcopacy and the priesthood and others above and below, and all which is recited or sung ordinarily in the Church. We believe that the devil was made, not by condition [of God's creation], but by [the devil's] evil will. We do not condemn the eating of meat. We believe in our heart and confess by our mouth the resurrection of this our body, and not any other. We firmly believe and affirm that at the Last Judgment individuals will receive either rewards or punishments for what they have done while in this flesh. We do not doubt that almsgiving and sacrifices and certain other good deeds of the faithful may benefit the dead. And since faith, according to the apostle James, "without works is dead," we renounce the world, and what we used to have, according to God's counsel, we have given to the poor and have become paupers ourselves, so that we may not be solicitous for the morrow, and we are able to accept neither gold nor silver, nor anything except for daily food and clothing from anyone. We propose to live according to these counsels as if they were precepts of the gospel. Others, however, remaining in the world, and possessing their own, making charities and other good deeds out of their own possessions, and following God's precepts, we also believe and hold that these too may be saved. We assert that according to your discretion, that if it should happen that any people should ever come before you, claiming to be our representatives, if they have not this faith [i.e., the faith sworn to in this document], know for certain that they are not from us.

26 David of Augsburg:
On the Waldensians of Bavaria, 1270

The New Orders of mendicant preachers, the Dominicans and Franciscans, produced clergy specifically trained to observe, describe, and combat the heretical movements of the thirteenth century. David of Augsburg was a member of the south German Province of the Franciscan order, a preacher of great skill, and briefly, an inquisitor. His description suggests the persistence of the problems of heretics and scripture down to the end of the thirteenth century.

And because they presumed to interpret the words of the gospel in a sense of their own, not perceiving that there were any others, they said that the gospel ought to be obeyed altogether according to the letter: and they boasted that they wished to do this, and that they only were the true imitators of Christ. . . . This was their first heresy, contempt of the power of the Church. . . . They give all their seal to lead many others astray with them: they teach even little girls the words of the Gospels and Epistles, so that they may be trained in error from their childhood. . . . They do not receive the Old

From Margaret Deanesly, *The Lollard Bible and Other Medieval Biblical Versions* (Cambridge: Cambridge University Press, 1920), p. 63. Reprinted with the permission of the publisher.

Testament as of faith, but they learn only certain passages from it, in order to attack us and defend themselves, saying that, when the gospel came, all the old things passed away. And similarly they pick out the words of Sts. Augustine, Jerome, Gregory, Ambrose, John Chrysostom, Isidore, and short passages from their books, in order to prove their illusions and to resist us. And they very easily lead simple people astray, by dressing up their sacrilegious doctrine with fair passages from the saints; but they pass over in silence those passages of the saints which seem to contradict them, and by which their error is refuted. They teach their docile and fluent disciples to repeat the words of the Gospels and the sayings of the apostles and other saints by heart, in the vulgar tongue, so that they may know how to teach others and lead the faithful astray. . . . All their boasting is about their singularity; for they seem to be more learned than other men, because they have learnt to say by heart certain words of the Gospels and Epistles in the vulgar tongue. For this reason they esteem themselves superior to our people, and not only to lay people, but even to literate people; for they are fools, and do not understand that a schoolboy of twelve years old often knows more than a heretical teacher of seventy; for the latter knows only what he has learnt by heart, while the former, having learnt the art of grammar, can read a thousand Latin books, and to some extent understand their literal meaning.

27   The Passau Anonymous: On the Origins of Heresy and the Sect of the Waldensians

ON THE CAUSES OF THE HERESY

There are six causes of heresy. The first is vainglory. Since [heretics] see learned men honored in the Church, they wish to be honored for learning themselves.

The second cause is that men and women, great and lesser, day and night, do not cease to learn and teach; the workman who labors all day teaches or learns at night. They pray little, on account of their studies. They teach and learn without books. They even teach in the houses of lepers. For an introduction, they teach that it is necessary to avoid the seven mortal sins and three other things, that is, lying, slandering, and swearing. These they prove by many authorities and call the ten commandments. When someone has been a student [of theirs for as little as] seven days, he seeks someone else to teach, as one curtain draws another. Whoever excuses himself, saying that he is not able to learn, they say to him, "Learn but one word each day, and after a year you will know three hundred, and you will progress." I heard from the mouth of a believer in their doctrine that a certain heretic—whom I knew—for this purpose, that he might turn him away from our faith and pervert him to his own, swam to him at night in winter across the River Ibbs. The negligence of the doctors of the faith shames us who do not show so much zeal for the truth of the Catholic faith as a perfidious Lyonist shows for the error of infidelity.

The third cause is that they have translated the Old and New Testaments into the vulgar tongue, and thus teach and learn them. I have seen and heard a certain unlearned, illiterate rustic who could recite the Book of Job word for word, and many others, who knew the entire New Testament perfectly. And since they were illiterate lay-people, they expounded scripture falsely and corruptly, as in the Epistle of John [1:11] "His own received Him not," translating "His own" as "pigs," mistaking *sui* for *sues*. And in the Psalm [67:31] "Rebuke the wild beasts of the reeds," they say, "Rebuke the animals of the swallows," mistaking *harundinis* for *hirundinis*. They also give titles to Psalms: *Eructavit* [Psalm 44], they call "The Maid Psalm." *Exsurgat* [Psalm 67] they call the "Revenge Psalm." *De profundis* [Psalm 129] they call "The Calling Psalm," and so with others. They teach and learn at hidden times and places, nor do they admit anyone who is not a believer of theirs. When they assemble in a place, they first say, "Beware, lest there be a curved stick among us," that is, lest there be a stranger present. They order their teaching to be concealed from the clergy, so that some of them speak by signs which no one knows but themselves, and thus they transform words themselves which no one knows but themselves: they call a church a "stonehouse," clerics "scribes," religious "Pharisees," and the same with many other things. They never answer directly.

The fourth cause is the bad example given by some persons. Whence, when they see anyone living badly, they say, "The apostles did not live this way, nor do we, who are imitators of the apostles."

The fifth cause is the insufficient learning of some people who preach sometimes what is frivolous and sometimes what is false.

Therefore, whatever a doctor of the Church teaches that he cannot prove by the text of the New Testament, they consider to be a complete fable.

The sixth cause is irreverence, which certain ministers of the Church exhibit toward the sacraments.

The seventh cause is the hatred that they have toward the Church. I have heard from the mouth of heretics that they intend to reduce clerics and religious to the status of ditchdiggers by abolishing their tithes and possessions and by the power and number of their believers and sympathizers. When a certain heresiarch named Hainricus, a glovemaker from Thewin, was led to execution, he stated before all, "It is right that you should condemn us in this matter, for, if we were not a minority among you, the sentence of death which you exercise against us in this manner we would exercise against your clergy and religious and laypeople."

In all the cities of Lombardy and the province of Provence, and in other kingdoms and lands, there are more schools of the heretics than of theologians, and they have more hearers; they debated publicly, and they convoked the people to solemn disputations in fields and forums, and they preached in houses, nor was there anyone who dared to stop them, on account of the power and number of their sympathizers. I myself have frequently been present at the inquisition and examination of heretics, and there are calculated to be in the diocese of Passau forty churches that have been infected with heresy. And in the parish of Kemenaten alone there are ten schools of heretics, and the priest of this parish was killed by heretics, and no judgment [against them] followed.

THAT THE SECT OF THE POOR OF LYONS IS WORSE THAN
CERTAIN OTHER SECTS

Among all those sects which exist or have existed, none is more dangerous to the Church of God than that of the Lyonists [Waldensians], and there are three causes for this. First, because it is older. Some say that it existed from the time of [Pope] Sylvester [I, (314-35)]; others say that it existed from the time of the apostles. Second, because it is more widespread. For there is hardly a place in which this sect does not slither. Third, because when other sects generate horror in their audience by the awfulness of their blasphemies about God, these Lyonists have a great appearance of holiness—before men they live justly and believe properly everything concerning God and all articles that are in the creed—they blaspheme only the Roman Church and clergy, which it is easy to make laypeople to believe.

How Heretics Are to Be Recognized

Heretics are to be recognized by their morals and their words. In moral behavior they are composed and modest. They take no pride in their clothing, which is neither too rich nor too abject. They do not undertake any business because they seek to avoid lying and oaths and fraud, but they often make their living by the work of their hands, as craftsmen; their learned men are weavers and textile workers. They do not increase their riches, but are satisfied with necessities. They go neither to taverns, nor to shows, nor to any such vanities. They avoid anger. They are always working, teaching, or learning, and therefore they pray little. They go to church deceptively, and they offer, and confess, and take communion, and are present at sermons—but they accept preaching verbally only.

They may also be recognized by their words, which are precise and modest. They avoid detraction, scurrility, and lightness of expression, as well as lying and taking oaths. They never say "truly," or "certainly," or the like, because they think that this would be an oath. They rarely respond directly to questions, so that if you ask them, "Do you know the Gospels and the Epistles?" they respond, "What might these things teach me?" Or they will say, "They ought to learn this, who are great or profound of intellect, or who are leisured and suitable," as if to say, "yes, yes, no, no this is permitted to you to say, as Christ commanded."

How the Waldensians Recruit [New Followers]

They seek to become shrewd, whereby they may insinuate themselves as familiars of nobles and great people. And they do this in the following manner: They freely display rings and jewels to lords and ladies, and those to whom these are sold often ask, "Have you any more for sale?" They answer, "I have more precious gems than these here, and these I would give to you, if only you will give me a pledge of security and promise not to go to the clergy." When the necessary promises have been received, they say, "I have a jewel of such brightness that through it man may know God, and another that shines so brightly that the love of God rises up in the heart of him who has it." And they speak like this metaphorically of other jewels. Then they recite to them some devotional text, such as Luke [1:26], "The angel of the Lord, Gabriel, is sent . . ." or a sermon of the Lord, such as John [13:1], "Before the festival day . . ." or a moral chapter of the Apostle [Paul, (Rom. 12:1)], "I beseech you by the mercy of God . . ." When these begin to interest the hearer, they then recite the chapter of Matthew [23:2] "Upon a throne . . ." [and Luke 11:52 and 20:47], "Woe unto you that bear the keys of knowledge, you do not enter, and you prevent others from entering," and "Woe to you, who devour the houses of widows," and "Woe," which follows. When asked by their hearers how these curses are to be understood, they answer, "They refer to the clergy and religious."

Then the heretic makes a comparison between the state of the Roman Church and his own state, saying, "The doctors of the Roman Church are luxurious in their garments and in their morals, as in Matthew [23:7], they like to have places of honor at feasts and be addressed as 'Rabbi' by men. We however, seek none of that. They are incontinent, whereas each one of us has a wife and lives with her chastely. They are wealthy and avaricious, of whom it is said [Luke 6:25] 'Woe unto you wealthy for you have your reward here.' We truly have enough food and enough to clothe us, and we are content with these. They are voluptuaries, of whom it is written [Matt. 23:14; Luke 20:47] 'Woe to you, who devour the houses of widows'; we, however, sustain ourselves as you see. They fight, and wage war, and order killing and burning of the poor, of whom it is said [Matt. 26:52] 'Everyone who takes up the sword will perish by the sword.' We truly suffer persecution and death for the sake of justice. They eat the bread of idleness [Prov. 31:27], working at nothing. We, however, work with our hands. They alone wish to be called 'doctors,' of whom it is said [Matt. 23:13; Luke 11:52] 'Woe unto you who bear the key of knowledge,' and so forth. Among us, however, women teach as much as men, and the student of seven days may already begin to teach another. The doctor is rare among them who knows literally by heart three successive chapters of the New Testament. Among us, however, the man or woman is rare who does not know how to recite that text in the vulgar tongue. Wherefore they [the Catholic clergy] are the blind leading the blind. And since we have the true faith of Christ and a holy life and we teach our doctrines to all, the scribes and Pharisees freely persecute us unto death, like Christ.

"Beyond this, they say more and do nothing, and they say there are heavy burdens on the shoulders of men, but they do not move a finger.

We, however, do everything that we teach. They think that the traditions of men, rather than those of God, are to be observed, such as fasting and feast days and going to church and other things, which have been instituted only by men. We, however, urge people to follow the doctrine of Christ and the apostles. They burden penitents with great penances but do not move a finger. We, however, teach the example of Christ to the sinner [John 8:11]: 'Go, and sin no more,' and we release them from sin by the imposition of hands. And we send souls directly to heaven. They, however, send all souls to purgatory." These and other things the heretics say: "Think, which status is preferable, and which faith—ours, or that of the Roman Church?" And they choose theirs. And thus they turn others from the Catholic faith and subvert them to error, and make believers of them, and receivers, and sympathizers, and defenders, and for many months they hide in their houses, teaching about their sect.

THE PASSAU ANONYMOUS'S TRACTATE CONCERNING
THE WALDENSIANS

In this little work, first, the error of the heretics will be laid out; second, the heretical authority or explanation; third, the solution of the error; fourth, the authority or explanation of the Catholics; fifth, the cause or occasion of the error of the first sect of heretics, that is, the Poor of Lyons.

On the Roman Church

The first error of the Lyonists and Runkarii is that the Church of Rome is not the church of Jesus Christ, but the church of the wicked and of the whore in the Apocalypse [17:3] "who sits upon a great beast" and which failed with [Pope] Sylvester [I] when it was infused with the venom of temporal wealth. That they themselves are the church of Jesus Christ, because they themselves observe the doctrine of the Gospels and of the apostles by words and deeds. They hold all statutes of the Church in contempt, claiming that they are not proved by authorities and good reasons; Leviticus [10:1]: "Now Nadab and Arihu took their firepans and got fire from foreigners, which they had not been told to do, and fire devoured them." Gloss: "Fire from foreigners" signifies those who teach and observe foreign traditions against the laws of God. But these are the traditions of the Church, and so forth. Solution: "Traditions of foreigners," that is, contrary to the gospel. In like manner, Deuteronomy [4:2; 12:32]: "Neither add anything to, nor take anything away from the word." Solution: "Neither add anything to" means anything that will corrupt the meaning of the text. And in like manner Exodus [31:11]: "Whatever I command you, go and do that." Solution: We should do whatever God commands us by himself, as in the Gospels; certain things are commanded by ministers, as in the Apostolic Epistles. Matthew [5:17]: "I did not come to take away the law, but to fulfill it." They say that evangelical and apostolic doctrine suffices for salvation, and that the canons and statutes of the Church are [merely] the traditions of the Pharisees. Matthew [15:3]: "Why do you transgress the command of God by your own traditions?" Against: If it was permitted to Moses and to the Prophets to add to and change the law in ways that were not contrary to the law of God, such as in the case of fighting on the Sabbath; and if it was permitted to the apostles to add to the doctrine of Christ; therefore the successors of the apostles, that is the doctors of the Church, may also add things which are useful and honest. Christ commanded, "They are to be baptized in the name of the Father and of the Son and of the Holy Spirit"; the apostles, however, in the name of Christ, against the form of Christ [1 Cor. 17:12]: "I, I say, and not the Lord." The Eucharist, which they took once before they ate, the Apostle orders to be eaten by those fasting. The Apostle ordained the rule against anyone in orders having two wives and the practice of excommunicaton. [The apostle] James instituted confession and extreme unction. If it is permitted to heretics to make prayers and benedictions and new expositions and to make and have new constitutions, which the apostles did not have, therefore and for the same reason should it be permitted to the Church. Matthew [23:2]: "Upon a throne, etc., everything, which they tell you, do, etc." Deuteronomy [17:2]: "Whoever, swelling with pride, refuses to obey the priests, he will die." From this it is shown that we are obliged to obey the institutions of the Church and of prelates. In the same book [Deut. 21:5]: "All enterprise hangs upon the word of the priest." Luke [10:16]: "Whoever hears you, hears Me." Romans [13:11]: "For every spirit is subjected to the highest powers." Hebrews [13:17]: "Obey those set above you, etc." On the occasion of this error they say that the statutes of the Church are grave and numerous, while those of Christ are light and few. Acts [15:10]: "Why do you provoke God by laying upon the shoulders of these novices a yoke which neither our fathers nor ourselves are able to bear?" They say that certain statutes of the Church are contrary to the laws of God, such as that concerning the possessions of the Church, Deuteronomy [18:1]: "The priest will not have a part with the people." The statutes of Christ, they say, are universal, while those of the Church are local, such as that concerning tithes. Deuteronomy [12:5; 14:22]. The church of the East does not care for the laws [of the Church of the West?]. Those who make laws do not observe them; Matthew [23:4]: "They make up heavy loads and pile them on men's shoulders, but will not lift a finger to lift the load themselves." The statutes of the Church are frequently changed, such as the grades of consanguinity, but the laws of Christ are never changed; Luke [11:33]: "For my words will not pass away." The Church makes laws which favor itself, such as those pertaining to ecclesiastical liberties. The laws of Christ are finite, but the laws of the Church seem to be infinite.

On the pope and the clergy

The pope, they say, is the head of all errors, and they call prelates scribes and religious Pharisees. They say it is a sin that clergy perform no labor. They also say that the clergy are full of avarice, envy, and pride. Concerning pride: [Matt. 23:6]: "They want first place at banquets and to be called 'Rabbi' by all men." Avarice: because they do all on account of greed; Jeremiah [6:13]: "All avaricious people strive to move from the lesser to the greater place." Envy: because they alone wish to be teachers; Matthew [23:13]: "Woe unto you, you scribes who hold the key of knowledge, and close up the kingdom of heaven before all men." From which they claim that all men, and even women, are allowed to preach. Numbers [11:29]: "Moses said: That it should happen, that all should be prophets." Corinthians [1 Cor. 14:5]: "I wish you all to speak by tongues, etc." [1 Cor. 14:31]: "Each of you may prophesy individually, so that all may learn." Matthew [Luke 19:40]: "If these remain silent, the very stones will cry out." Apocalypse [22:17]: "He who hears, let him speak: Come." The apostles when they preached were laypeople. If it is permitted to a layperson to preach on account of need, how much more on account of God? Against this, is Romans [10:15] "How shall they preach, unless they are sent?" To this they reply that they are sent by divine inspiration. The order of doctors is particular to the Church of God; Eph. [4:11]: "And he gave some of them to be doctors, and others to be pastors." Corinthians [1 Cor. 14:34]: "Women should keep silence in Church, for it is not permitted for them to speak." Heretics are better preachers than Catholic preachers, since they claim that anything that a preacher says that is not proved by the New or the Old Testaments is a lie. They say that they should obey God alone, and not the pope or the prelates.

Acts [5:29]: "It is better to obey God than man." They say that when the Church offers occasion in preaching to say that the pope is God on earth, greater than men and equal to the angels, and that he cannot sin, that this is idolatry. So they criticize us, that we call the pope a father, and an abbot of monks. Matthew [23:9]: "Call no man father on earth." They also deny that some say that prelates are to be obeyed, no matter what they command; they hold in contempt those genuflexions offered to priests; Apocalypse [19:10]: "And I fell at the feet of the angel, and he said, 'Behold, do not do that.' "

On the sacraments of the Church

They condemn all the sacraments of the Church. It is an occasion of irreverence for them when the priests administer the sacraments, and because of the evil lives of many of the ministers, they say that they are venal sacraments. They say that the pope and all bishops are murderers, because of the wars they wage against Christians, pagans, and heretics. And they condemn those who preach [the Crusade], for Prussians and pagans are not to be brought to the faith by the sword, but by the preaching of preachers. Against this Exodus [32:27]: "Moses said, 'Arm yourselves, each of you, with a sword . . . . Each of you kill his brother.' " And Acts [5:1-5], where Peter cursed Ananias and Ananias died.

On baptism

Concerning baptism some people err when they say that by baptism little ones cannot be saved. Matthew [Mark 16:16]: "Whoever believes and is baptized, will be saved." But an infant cannot believe, and therefore cannot be saved. Solution: infants are baptized in the faith of their parents. Some of [the heretics] rebaptize, others baptize by the hand. They criticize that the godfather does not understand the question of the priest. Against this is Matthew [19:14] "Suffer the little children to come unto me."

They reject chrism. Against this is Luke [Mark 6:13]: "The Apostles anointed with oil."

On confirmation

They care nothing for confirmation. Few receive this sacrament, even fifty-year-olds, who are remote from bishops. They condemn bishops for reserving to themselves this sacrament [and not letting priests perform it], who are more worthy to make the body of God. Solution: Only the Apostles may impose hands, as in Matthew and Acts.

On the body of the Lord

They say that the sacrament of the Eucharist may not be conferred by a priest in the state of mortal sin; Kings [2 Sam. 6:6-8]: "Oza was struck dead, for he had touched the ark." And John did not dare to touch the crown of the Lord's head. They say that a good layman, and even a woman, may consecrate the Eucharist, if they know the words. They say that transubstantiation is in the mouth of him who takes the host worthily, and not in the hand conferring it; Psalm [10:17]: "For the Lord heard the desires of the poor." They say that the Levites administered the body of the Lord, such as Lawrence and Tarsicius the Acolyte who suffered at Rome.

[The Anonymous lists the different forms in which the Eucharist had been made historically, concluding with the example of Eucharistic service in Bavaria.]

They say that the body of the Lord is handled and taken by unworthy people and sinners, while worthy and holy virgins and widows are not allowed to be given it, except in Holy Week. . . .

On the mass

They say that the mass is nothing, since neither Christ nor the apostles sang. They say that Christ was sacrificed a single time, but priests sacrifice Him repeatedly in one day. They say that masses are sung for alms; Matthew [23:14; Mark 12:40]: "Woe unto thee, who devour the houses of widows all for prolix and superfluous prayers." They do not sing after matins or vigils. They say that it is a sin to sell masses. They say that the first mass of a new priest is less efficacious than the hundredth. . . . They say that the chant of the Church is merely an infernal jangling. . . . They hold the canonical hours in contempt. . . . They say that one Pater Noster is worth more than the sound of the bells from ten churches.

o   o   o

On the sacrament of penance

Concerning the sacrament of penance, they say that a cleric bound by mortal sin cannot absolve the sins of others, but that a good layperson can. . . . They say that it is better to confess to a good layperson than to a wicked priest. . . . Bohemian priests hear the confessions of Germans, and neither understands the other. . . . Some say that without the offering of a gift, confession is worth nothing. Therefore the poor often neglect to confess; this is to Judaize. They claim that one of the signs of piety is to recognize guilt where there is no guilt. Mothers who do not see the spirit leave the bodies of their sick children are forced by priests to undertake public penance, a thing which is customarily imposed only for the most serious crimes. . . .

On the sacrament of marriage

They condemn the sacrament of marriage, saying that husband and wife sin mortally if they have sexual intercourse without hope of having children. . . . Some of them repute matrimony to be mere fornication. . . and that therefore those who are married may not be saved. . . .

o   o   o

On the sacrament of orders

They say that the sacrament of [Holy] Orders is nothing, because the apostles were laypeople. They say that Christ did not give the apostles stoles, or albs, or rings, or anything else. . . . They deride clerical tonsure, which the apostles did not have. . . . They say that the Church greatly errs by forbidding priests to marry, because the Old and New Testaments permitted it and it greatly dissuades them from fornication. . . .

On excommunication

They condemn excommunication, claiming that the excommunicator is cursed. . . . If anyone curses anyone else, he himself is cursed. . . . They delight in times of Interdict, because then they are able to corrupt Christians and make them vilify the cult of God. They say that it is impious to punish the innocent by taking the sacraments away from them for the sins of others. They say that to do this is also to deprive God of praise. The Church commits a fraud when it says that souls suffer in purgatory. They say that by this the devotions of the living faithful are diminished, and that therefore no one need pay tithes. They are given occasion for this when excommunications are multiplied for trivial causes or when anyone does not come to church because of having failed to pay the due tithes. . . .

On tithes

They say that tithes are not to be paid, because the early Church did not pay them. They say that if tithes ought to be paid, then the Church, too, should pay them. If you say that the Jews paid tithes, they respond that we should then observe all the other legalia of the Old Testament. . . . They say that those who pay tithes are damned, as are laymen who receive tithes, since they spend them wickedly.

On possessions

They say that clerics ought to have no possessions or property.

On indulgences

They do not believe in indulgences. . . . They hold the absolutions of the Church as nothing. They care nothing for irregularity. They do not believe in ecclesiastical dispensations. This is occasioned by the multiplication of indulgences, and because all sins can be relaxed for money.

On holy days

They care nothing for holy days, for they say that one day is just like any other. Against this is God's command to keep holy the Sabbath day. To this they respond that if we are to observe the decalogue, then we must also be circumcised. . . .

o   o   o

On church buildings

They hold walled churches to be a horror, and they call them "stonehouses" in the vernacular. . . . They say that prayers count no more in churches than in any other house. . . . The occasion for this criticism is the performance of lewd spectacles in churches, and the pomp of ceremonies, and the grandeur of the buildings. . . .

o   o   o

On church decoration

They say that it is a sin to decorate churches, and that it is better to clothe paupers than priests. . . . They reject thurification. . . . They say that pictures are idolatries. Their occasion for this attitude is that distorted pictures or lewd pictures in churches inspire horror rather than devotion. . . . They condemn the chant of the Church, saying that power is in the word, not in music. Their occasion for this is protracted and superfluous chant, verse piled upon verse. . . . They condemn processions, for the fooleries that happen in them.

On saints

They do not believe in saints, except the apostles and those who are mentioned in the Gospels or in Acts. . . . They invoke no saints, unless perhaps the Virgin Mary or God alone. Their occasion for this is that there are in fact false saints, such as Iwan, and certain others, of whom neither the names nor the merits are known. Sometimes fountains are venerated, as in Dross, where a priest baptizes a crucifix in the fountain and the people offer to the fountain. And there are holy trees, such as St. Christopher, and shrines in fields. . . . When someone mentions St. Nicholas, they all sigh, but when Jesus Christ is named, they stay silent. They do not believe in the legends or passions of the saints. The occasion for this is the legend of the baptism of Constantine and other incredible legends, as in the legends of Margaret and Juliana and the Seven Sleepers.

On miracles

They do not believe in the miracles of the saints. The reason for this is the number of false miracles, the oil, blood, and tears [coming from] images, and celestial lights. Also the presence of hypocrites called Stercer, who pretend to have different kinds of illnesses and then pretend to be cured.

On relics

They do not believe in the relics of the saints. . . . This is because of the proliferation of false relics which certain people carry through villages and display playfully in taverns. . . such as the milk of the Virgin Mary. . . and relics of the angels. . . and different churches wage lawsuits over the bodies of the saints which they claim to have, such as the case of the body of St. Mark, St. Dionysius, St. Vitus, and others.

On the Holy Cross

They are horrified at the Holy Cross, because of the suffering Christ experienced upon it.

o   o   o

On purgatory

They deny purgatory, claiming that there are only two ways, one for the elect to heaven, and the other for the damned to hell. . . . They say that masses and offerings and other acts for the benefit of the soul produce nothing, and that weekly observance and anniversaries are made only for the sake of alms. . . . They say that the prayers of a good layman are worth more than those of a wicked priest, and that one Pater Noster is more efficacious than many masses. . . . They say that laypeople get no benefit from prayers said in Latin.

On temporal judgment

They condemn judges and princes and claim that malefactors are not condemned. Their occasion for this is that princes and judges are tyrants. . . and that justice is venal in the tribunals of laity and clergy alike.

On oaths

They say that taking oaths is a mortal sin. . . . Their occasion for this is the frequency of oaths, and the eagerness to take oaths for trivial causes, since these lead to perjury. The heretics, who never take oaths, are like the devil, of whom it is written that he never swore.

V
THE WAY OF *CARITAS*: PREACHING, PENITENCE, AND PASTORALISM

A modern historian has characterized the twelfth and early thirteenth centuries as "a period of considerable flexibility and real experiment in dealing with dissident movements." In tracing the history of ecclesiastical response to religious dissent, historians have often neglected the way of *caritas* in their haste to get on to the way of *potestas*—the Albigensian Crusade, the Inquisition, and the other forms, such as the doctrine of legal infamy, by means of which the Church's powers of coercion were so dramatically and spectacularly displayed. Yet the way of *caritas* marked much of the history of the first century and a half of religious dissidence, and, although violence was certainly exercised against heretics and dissidents (and occasional energetic reformers) during this period, it was more often than not exercised by laypeople, usually by mob action. Individual bishops, lacking a reliable guide in law, inquired of their colleagues, or of Rome, what they should do; and in the early period expulsion from the diocese or excommunication were generally the strongest punishments they meted out. Twelfth-century conciliar legislation urged various forms of ecclesiastical discipline, but none stronger than excommunication (no. 28). Some churchmen urged toleration. Even the first papal decree against heretics everywhere in Europe, Pope Lucius III's *Ad Abolendam* of 1184 (no. 29), did not deal with the doctrinal problems of heresy as much as it established the category of contumacy for practicing heretics. Ecclesiastical discipline varied from time to time and from place to place, often from bishop to bishop. Within this period, the Church looked hard at itself, explored ways of persuading dissidents to return to obedience, and launched a great pastoral effort designed to teach religion effectively.

In the light of the later turn toward *coercitio*, toward the use of power and force in the Crusades and the Inquisition, it is easy to neglect this early phase of charity; but undoubtedly this phase was very effective, if not in Languedoc or against the Cathars or Waldensians, then elsewhere and against other groups. One reason for this flexibility was that learned churchmen knew perfectly well that many of the clergy were emminently deserving of the criticism they received. Pope Innocent III once said of the bishops of Narbonne that "they are dumb dogs, unable to bark," that is, ignorant pastors and teachers, whose lives and whose teaching did not suffice to care for their congregations. High churchmen knew of many groups in the twelfth century whose attempts to follow what they called "the apostolic life" might make them appear dissident when in fact their motives were the highest and their lives beyond reproach. The early history of papal dealings with the Waldensians illustrates the general tone of prelatic concern; it was chiefly with unauthorized preaching and reading unauthorized translations of scripture— that is, with matters of ecclesiastical obedience rather than with doctrine—that the popes were concerned in the case of Valdès and his followers. Missions to Languedoc, such as that of St. Bernard in 1145 and Henry of Clairvaux in 1178, were instructed to offer examples of Christian life and teaching, not force, and the legacy of these early Cistercian missions was the founding of the two Mendicant orders, the Order of Friars Minor, or Franciscans, in 1210, and the Order of Preachers, or Dominicans, in 1216. Throughout their early years, both orders were enjoined to live exemplary lives and preach proper doctrine. Discussions, often open, were held between heretics and orthodox Christians throughout the twelfth and into the thirteenth century. Often, these debates showed up the higher clergy for the incompetents they were; more often, prelates themselves acknowledged the difficulty of teaching and preaching among their other duties and showed exemplary concern for the spiritual well-being of the heretics, as well as the orthodox, in their diocese. The popes' willingness to hear appeals from convicted heretics underlines papal awareness of the poor quality of some higher churchmen.

Although papal steps against heretics became progressively harsher in the late twelfth century (nos. 30-31), even Pope Innocent III (1198-1216) worked to establish the New Orders and see that heretics were converted if conversion was possible. Two examples of Innocent's success here are the conversions of Durand of Huesca, a Waldensian, in 1208 (no. 35), and Bernard Prim in 1210.

Absolution following penitence remained widely available in the early thirteenth century, and although small-scale inquiries (*inquisitiones*) and probing
confessional techniques were also developed at this time, they more often than
not ended in penance rather than punishment.

The early zeal of the New Orders, whose story has recently been well told by
Rosalind Brooke in *The Coming of the Friars*, struck favorable responses
among dissidents and orthodox alike. Burchard of Ursperg (no. 32) reflects this
early impact, and St. Antony's Sermon to the Fish (no. 33) gives something of
the popular and dramatic flavor that their work produced. The zeal and
originality of St. Francis of Assisi and St. Dominic are perhaps the most striking
examples of the flexibility of ecclesiastical response into the second decade of
the thirteenth century.

The accretion of theological definitions that characterized the work of
theologians, teachers, and church councils in the twelfth century, however,
gradually assembled a coherent, consistent body of doctrine that was expressed
in conciliar legislation in the Fourth Lateran Council of 1215 (no. 30) and in
the work of systematic thinkers such as St. Thomas Aquinas later in the
thirteenth century (no. 34). The systematization of dogma made orthodox
teaching easier, but it also made the line between heresy and orthodoxy
sharper. The twin movements of dogmatic definition and the papal juridical
approach to heretics (no. 31) slowly increased ecclesiastical resistance to heresy
and dissent. By the early thirteenth century, Robert Grosseteste, bishop of
Lincoln and first chancellor of Oxford, gave what became the standard
definition of heresy, and the inclusiveness of his definition reflects the broad
spectrum of variety in the Church's experience of heresy and dissent in the
century and a half preceding 1200: "Heresy is an opinion chosen by human
faculties, contrary to sacred scripture, openly held, and pertinaciously defended. *Hairesis* in Greek, *choice* in Latin." With the definition of these four
elements, a theological and legal concept of heresy came into existence. First,
heresy had to be an opinion that human faculties (not delusion or coercion by
demons) had reached (thus placing the responsibility squarely upon the heretic
personally); second, that opinion had to be contrary to sacred scripture (this
should be understood in terms of the Church's teaching on scripture as well).
Third, the opinion had to be openly held or taught (secret, private heresy
posed another problem for Grosseteste and later theologians and canon
lawyers) and pertinaciously defended—that is, the heretic had to be visible
and had to refuse to listen to reason, persuasion, or charitable injunctions.

Finally, although preaching developed during the thirteenth century into the great medium of communications that it remained until the twentieth, pastoral sermons were not the only ones preached. Although such stories as those told by Caesarius of Heisterbach (below, no. 36) preached no violence toward heretics, the violence of the language and imagery of this literature undoubtedly stirred and kept stirred popular hostility. In spite of large-scale reconciliation and reconversion, heresy remained a favorite target of preachers for centuries.

LITERATURE

Moore, *Origins of European Dissent*, pp. 244-61; Lambert, *Medieval Heresy*, pp. 95-107; Wakefield and Evans, *Heresies of the High Middle Ages*, pp. 189-94, 210-29; Brenda Bolton, "Tradition and Temerity: Papal Attitudes toward Deviants, 1159-1216," in D. Baker, ed., *Schism, Heresy, and Religious Protest*, Studies in Church History, vol. 9 (Cambridge, 1972), pp. 79-91; Rosalind B. Brooke, *The Coming of the Friars* (London, 1975). See also Elizabeth Kennan, "Innocent III and the First Political Crusade," *Traditio* 27 (1971): 231-50, and John Mundy, *Europe in the High Middle Ages, 1150-1309* (New York, 1973), pp. 515-600. See also Herbert Grundmann, *Religiöse Bewegungen im Mittel-alter*, 2d ed. (Hildesheim, 1961); M.-D. Chenu, *Nature, Man and Society in the Twelfth Century*, translated by Jerome Taylor and Lester Little (Chicago, 1968); Christopher Brooke, *Medieval Church and Society* (New York, 1972); R. W. Southern, *Western Society and the Church in the Middle Ages* (Baltimore, 1970); Lester K. Little, *Religious Poverty and the Profit Economy in Medieval Europe* (Ithaca, N.Y., 1978).

28   The Third Lateran Council, 1179: Heretics Are Anathema

CANON 27

Summary

Heretics and all who defend and receive them are excommunicated. If they die in their sin, they shall be denied Christian burial and are not to be prayed for.

Text

Though ecclesiastical discipline contents itself with spiritual judgment and does not inflict bloody punishments, it is, however, aided by the ordinances of Catholic princes, for men often seek a salutary remedy for their souls only when they fear that some severe corporal punishment will be imposed upon them. Wherefore, since in Gascogne, in the territory of Albi, in Toulouse and its neighborhood, and in other places, the perversity of the heretics, whom some call Cathari, others Patarini, and others again Publicani [Pauliciani?], has assumed such proportions that they practice their wickedness no longer in secret as some do, but preach their error publicly and thus mislead the simple and the weak, we decree that they and all who defend and receive them are anathematized, and under penalty of anathema we forbid everyone to give them shelter, to admit them to his land, or to transact business with them. If anyone should fail herein, and die in that sin, not under pretext of privileges granted him by us nor by any other subterfuge, shall an offering be made for him nor shall he receive Christian burial.

With regard to the Brabantians, Aragonians, Basques, Navarese, and others who practice such cruelty toward the Christians that they respect neither churches nor monasteries, spare neither widows nor orphans, age nor sex, but after the manner of pagans destroy and lay waste everything, we decree likewise that those who hire or patronize them throughout the regions in which they rave so madly, shall be publicly denounced in the churches on Sundays and on solemn festivals and shall be regarded as subject to the same punishment as the aforesaid heretics; nor shall they be restored to the communion of the Church till they have abjured that pestiferous society and its heresy. Those who are bound to them by any agreement and are hereby released from the obligation of fealty, deference, and all service so long as they [the heretics] continue in their iniquity. These and all the faithful we command in remission of their sins that they vigorously oppose such pests and defend with arms the Christian people. Let their possessions be confiscated and let the princes be allowed to reduce to slavery men of this kind. Those who may in conflict with these heretics die in true repentance, let them not doubt that they will receive the remission of their sins and the fruit of eternal reward. Trusting in the mercy of God and in the authority of the Apostles Peter and Paul, we also grant to the faithful who take up arms against them and at the advice of the bishops or other prelates undertake to conquer them, a

From H. J. Schroeder, *Disciplinary Decrees of the General Councils* (St. Louis: B. Herder, 1937), pp. 234-35.

remission of two years' penance; or if they are engaged there for a longer period, we leave it to the discretion of the bishops, to whom the care of this matter has been committed, to grant further remission in accordance with the character of the labor performed. Those who refuse obedience to the admonition of the bishops in this matter, are to be denied the reception of the body and blood of the Lord. In the meantime we place under the protection of the Church, as we do the crusaders to the Holy Land, those who in the ardor of faith take up this work of conquering them, and we decree that they remain secure from all disturbances in their possessions as well as in their persons. If anyone shall presume to molest them, let him be excommunicated by the bishop of the locality and let the sentence be observed by all till the things taken from them be returned and a suitable satisfaction made for the loss incurred. Bishops and priests who do not vigorously resist the aforesaid evils shall be deprived of their office till they have obtained the mercy of the Apostolic See.

29   Pope Lucius III: The Decretal *Ad Abolendum*, 1184

In order to put an end to the evil of various heresies which has begun to break forth in modern times [*modernis coepit temporibus pullulare*] in most parts of the world, the power of the Church ought to be aroused; when, indeed, with the sanction of imperial power, both the insolence of heretics, in their attempts to promote falsehood, may be put down, and the truth of Catholic unity, shining forth in the Holy Church, may display her, free from all charge of false doctrine.

We, therefore, supported by the power, and presence, of our most dear son Frederick, the illustrious emperor of the Romans, semper Augustus, with the common consent of our brethren, and of other patriarchs, archbishops, and many princes, who have assembled from various parts of the world, have, with the general sanction of this present decree, risen up against those heretics, to whom divers names have ascribed the profession of various errors, and, by the tenor of this constitution, with apostolical authority, we condemn all heresy, howsoever it may be named.

In the first place, therefore, we lay under a perpetual anathema the Cathari, Patarini, and those who falsely call themselves Humiliati, or Poor Men of Lyons, Passagini, Josepini, and Arnaldistae; and since some, having a form of godliness, but, as the apostle has said, denying the power of it, have assumed to themselves the office of preaching— though the same apostle says, "How shall they preach, except they be sent?"—we include, in the same perpetual anathema, all who shall have presumed to preach, either publicly or privately, either being forbidden, or not sent, or not having the authority of the Apostolic See, or of the bishop of the diocese; and also all who presume to think, or to teach, concerning the sacrament of the body and blood of our Lord Jesus Christ, or of baptism, or of the remission of sins, or of matrimony, or of the other sacraments of the Church, otherwise than as the Holy Roman Church teaches and observes; and, generally, all persons whom the said Roman Church, or the individual bishops in their dioceses, with the concurrence of their clergy, or the clergy themselves if the see be vacant, with the consent, if need be, of the neighboring bishops, shall have adjudged to be heretics.

And we decree that their receivers and defenders, and, in like manner, all who show any countenance, or favor, to the aforesaid heretics, to encourage them in their heretical pravity—whether they be *consolati*, or *credentes*, or *perfecti*, or by whatever superstitious names they may be called—shall be subjected to a similar sentence.

Since, however, it sometimes happens that the severity of ecclesiastical discipline which is required by offences may be condemned by those who do not understand its benefits, we further decree by this present ordinance that whosoever shall be manifestly convicted of the errors aforesaid, if he be a clerk, or in any pretended holy orders, shall be stripped of all the prerogatives of the ecclesiastical order; and being thus deprived of all ecclesiastical office, as well as privilege, he shall be left to the discretion of the secular power to receive due punishment; unless, immediately after the detection of his error, he shall consent voluntarily to return to the unity of the Catholic faith, and publicly to abjure his error, as the bishop of the diocese shall direct, and shall make such satisfaction as shall be fitting. A layman, however, to whom the guilt of the aforesaid pests shall either publicly or privately attach (unless, as before said, he immediately returns to the orthodox faith, abjuring his heresy, and making satisfaction) shall be left to the discretion of the secular judge, to receive due punishment according to the nature of his offense.

Those who shall be found to be only suspected by the Church shall be subjected to a like sentence, unless they shall demonstrate their innocence by a sufficient proof, at the discretion of the bishop, according to the nature of the suspicion and the quality of the person. Those, however, who, after the abjuration of error, or after they have (as we have said) cleared themselves under the examination of their own bishop, shall be convicted of having relapsed into their abjured heresy, we decree to be left to the secular judgment, without any further hearing; and that the goods of the condemned persons shall be applied to the service of those churches to which they belong, under proper regulations.

Moreover, we decree that the aforesaid excommunication, under which we desire that all heretics should lie, shall be renewed by all patriarchs, archbishops, and bishops, on the principal festivals, and as often as public solemnities, or any other occasion, shall offer, for the glory of God and the rebuke of heresy; ordaining, by apostolical authority, that if any member of the episcopal order shall be found negligent or slothful in this matter, he shall be considered as suspended from his episcopal dignity and ministry for the space of three years.

To these things we add, with the concurrence of the bishops, and by the suggestion of the emperor and his princes, that every archbishop or bishop, by himself, or his archdeacon, or by other trustworthy and fit persons, shall twice, or once, in the year go round any parish in which it shall have been reported that heretics reside; and there call upon three or more persons of good credit, or, if it seem expedient, on the whole neighborhood, to take an oath that if anyone shall know that there are heretics in the place or any persons holding secret conventicles or differing in life and manners from the common conversation of the faithful, he will make it his business to point them out to the bishop or archdeacon. Moreover, the bishop or archdeacon shall cite the accused to appear before him, who, unless they shall clear themselves from the charges brought against them to their satisfaction, according to the custom of the country—or if, after such clearance, they shall relapse into their error—they shall be punished by the judgment of the bishop. If, however, any of them, through damnable superstition, denying the lawfulness of oaths, shall refuse to swear, they are from that very circumstance to be adjudged heretics, and to be subjected to the punishment aforesaid.

Moreover, we ordain that counts, barons, rectors, consuls of cities and other places, being called upon by the archbishops and bishops, shall bind themselves with an oath that in all the matters aforesaid, they will stoutly and effectually aid the Church against heretics, and their associates, when they shall be called upon so to do; and will, bona fide, endeavor, according to their office and power, to put in execution the ecclesiastical and, at the same time, imperial statutes of which we have spoken. If, however, they fail to observe this, let them be deprived of that honor which they possess and on no account be raised to any other, their persons being bound by excommunication, and their lands subjected to an interdict. Also, let any city which shall think fit to resist these decretal ordinances, or which, when called upon by the bishop, shall neglect to punish those who do so, be cut off from intercourse with other cities, and understand that it is deprived of its episcopal dignity.

We also decree that all favorers of heretics, as being condemned to perpetual infamy, are not to be admitted as advocates and witnesses, or to other public offices. If, however, there should be any who, being exempt from the control of diocesan jurisdiction, are subject only to the authority of the Apostolic See, let them, with regard to all matters hereinbefore ordained respecting heretics, submit to the judgments of the archbishops and bishops, and obey them on this behalf, as legates of the Roman See, notwithstanding their privileges of exemption.

30 The Fourth Lateran Council, 1215: Credo and Confession, Canons 1, 3, 21

1. We firmly believe and openly confess that there is only one true God, eternal and immense, omnipotent, unchangeable, incomprehensible, and ineffable, Father, Son, and Holy Ghost; three Persons indeed but one essence, substance, or nature absolutely simple; the Father [proceeding] from no one, but the Son from the Father only, and the Holy Ghost equally from both, always without beginning and end. The Father begetting, the Son begotten, and the Holy Ghost proceeding; consubstantial and coequal, coomnipotent and coeternal, the one principle of the universe, Creator of all things invisible and visible, spiritual and corporeal, who from the beginning of time and by his omnipotent power made from nothing creatures both spiritual and

From H. J. Schroeder, *Disciplinary Decrees of the General Councils* (St. Louis: B. Herder, 1937), pp. 237-39, 242-44, 259-60.

corporeal; angelic, namely, and mundane, and then human, as it were, common, composed of spirit and body. The devil and the other demons were indeed created by God good by nature but they became bad through themselves; man, however, sinned at the suggestion of the devil. This Holy Trinity in its common essence undivided and in personal properties divided, through Moses, the holy prophets, and other servants gave to the human race at the most opportune intervals of time the doctrine of salvation.

And finally, Jesus Christ, the only begotten Son of God made flesh by the entire Trinity, conceived with the cooperation of the Holy Ghost of Mary ever Virgin, made true man, composed of a rational soul and human flesh, one Person in two natures, pointed out more clearly the way of life. Who according to his divinity is immortal and impassable, according to his humanity was made passable and mortal, suffered on the cross for the salvation of the human race, and being dead descended into hell, rose from the dead, and ascended into heaven. But he descended in soul, arose in flesh, and ascended equally in both; He will come at the end of the world to judge the living and the dead and will render to the reprobate and to the elect according to their works. Who all shall rise with their bodies which they have that they may receive according to their merits, whether good or bad, the latter eternal punishment with the devil, the former eternal glory with Christ.

There is one Universal Church of the faithful, outside of which there is absolutely no salvation. In which there is the same priest and sacrifice, Jesus Christ, whose body and blood are truly contained in the sacrament of the altar under the forms of bread and wine; the bread being changed [transubstantiatio] by divine power into the body, and the wine into the blood, so that to realize the mystery of unity we may receive of him what he has received of us. And this sacrament no one can effect except the priest who has been duly ordained in accordance with the keys of the Church, which Jesus Christ himself gave to the apostles and their successors.

But the sacrament of baptism, which by the invocation of each Person of the Trinity, namely, of the Father, the Son and Holy Ghost, is effected in water, duly conferred on children and adults in the form prescribed by the Church by anyone whatsoever, leads to salvation. And should anyone after the reception of baptism have fallen into sin, by true repentance he can always be restored. Not only virgins and those practicing chastity, but also those united in marriage, through the right faith and through works pleasing to God, can merit eternal salvation. . . .

3. We excommunicate and anathematize every heresy that raises itself against the holy, orthodox, and Catholic faith which we have above explained; condemning all heretics under whatever names they may be known, for while they have different faces, they are nevertheless bound to each other by their tails, since in all of them vanity is a common element. Those condemned, being handed over to the secular rulers or their bailiffs, let them be abandoned, to be punished with due justice, clerics being first degraded from their orders. As to the property of the condemned, if they are laymen, let it be confiscated; if clerics, let it be applied to the churches from which they received revenues. But those who are only suspected, due consideration being given to the nature of the suspicion and the character of the person, unless they prove their innocence by a proper defense, let them be anathematized and avoided by all until they have made suitable satisfaction; but if they have been under excommunication for one year, then let them be condemned as heretics. Secular authorities, whatever office they may hold, shall be admonished and induced and if necessary compelled by ecclesiastical censure, that as they wish to be esteemed and numbered among the faithful, so for the defense of the faith they ought publicly to take an oath that they will strive in good faith and to the best of their ability to exterminate in the territories subject to their jurisdiction all heretics pointed out by the Church; so that whenever anyone shall have assumed authority, whether spiritual or temporal, let him be bound to confirm this decree by oath. But if a temporal ruler, after having been requested and admonished by the Church, should neglect to cleanse his territory of this heretical foulness, let him be excommunicated by the metropolitan and the other bishops of the province. If he refuses to make satisfaction within a year, let the matter be made known to the supreme pontiff, that he may declare the ruler's vassals absolved from their allegiance and may offer the territory to be ruled by Catholics, who on the extermination of the heretics may possess it without hindrance and preserve it in the purity of faith; the right, however, of the chief ruler is to be respected so long as he offers no obstacle in this matter and permits freedom of action. The same law is to be observed in regard to those who have no chief rulers (that is, are independent). Catholics who have girded themselves with the cross for the extermination of the heretics, shall enjoy the indulgences and privileges granted to those who go in defense of the Holy Land.

We decree that those who give credence to the teachings of the heretics, as well as those who receive, defend, and patronize them, are excommunicated; and we firmly declare that after any one of them has been branded with excommunication, if he has deliberately failed to make satisfaction within a year, let him incur *ipso jure* the stigma of infamy and let him not be admitted to public offices or deliberations, and let him not take part in the election of others to such offices or use his right to give testimony in a court of law. Let him also be intestable, that he may not have the free exercise of making a will, and let him be deprived of the right of inheritance. Let no one be urged to give an account to him in any matter, but let him be urged to give an account to others. If perchance he be a judge, let his decisions have no force, nor let any cause be brought to his attention. If he be an advocate, let his assistance by no means be sought. If a notary, let the instruments drawn up by him be considered worthless, for, the author being condemned, let them enjoy a similar fate. In all similar cases we command that the same be observed. If, however, he be a cleric, let him be deposed from every office and benefice, that the greater the fault the graver may be the punishment inflicted.

If any refuse to avoid such after they have been ostracized by the Church, let them be excommunicated till they have made suitable satisfaction. Clerics shall not give the sacraments of the Church to such pestilential people, nor shall they presume to give them Christian burial, or to receive their alms or offerings; otherwise they shall be deprived of their office, to which they may not be restored without a special indult of the Apostolic See. Similarly, all regulars, on whom this punishment may be imposed, let their privileges be nullified in that diocese in which they have presumed to perpetrate such excesses.

But since some, under the "appearance of godliness, but denying the power thereof," as the apostle says, arrogate to themselves the authority to preach, as the same apostle says: "How shall they preach unless they be sent?"—all those prohibited or not sent, who, without the authority of the Apostolic See or of the Catholic bishop of the locality, shall presume to usurp the office of preaching either publicly or privately, shall be excommunicated and unless they amend, and the sooner the better, they shall be visited with a further suitable penalty. We add, moreover, that every archbishop or bishop should himself or through his archdeacon or some other suitable persons, twice or at least once a year make the rounds of his diocese in which report has it that heretics dwell, and there compel three or more men of good character or, if it should be deemed advisable, the entire neighborhood, to swear that if anyone know of the presence there of heretics or others holding secret assemblies, or differing from the common way of the faithful in faith and morals, they will make them known to the bishop. The latter shall then call together before him those accused, who, if they do not purge themselves of the matter of which they are accused, or if after the rejection of their error they lapse into their former wickedness, shall be canonically punished. But if any of them by damnable obstinacy should disapprove of the oath and should perchance be unwilling to swear, from this very fact let them be regarded as heretics.

We wish, therefore, and in virtue of obedience strictly command, that to carry out these instructions effectively the bishops exercise throughout their dioceses a scrupulous vigilance if they wish to escape canonical punishment. If from sufficient evidence it is apparent that a bishop is negligent or remiss in cleansing his diocese of the ferment of heretical wickedness, let him be deposed from the episcopal office and let another, who will and can confound heretical depravity, be substituted.

21. All the faithful of both sexes shall after they have reached the age of discretion faithfully confess all their sins at least once a year to their own [parish] priest and perform to the best of their ability the penance imposed, receiving reverently at least at Easter the sacrament of the Eucharist, unless perchance at the advice of their own priest they may for a good reason abstain for a time from its reception; otherwise they shall be cut off from the Church [excommunicated] during life and deprived of Christian burial in death. Wherefore, let this salutary decree be published frequently in the churches, that no one may find in the plea of ignorance a shadow of excuse. But if anyone for a good reason should wish to confess his sins to another priest, let him first seek and obtain permission from his own [parish] priest, since otherwise he [the other priest] cannot loose or bind him.

Let the priest be discreet and cautious that he may pour wine and oil into the wounds of the one injured after the manner of a skillful physician, carefully inquiring into the circumstances of the sinner and the sin, from the nature of which he may understand what kind of advice to give and what remedy to apply, making use of different experiments to heal the sick one. But let him exercise the greatest precaution that he does in any degree by word, sign, or any other manner make known the sinner, but should he need more prudent counsel, let him seek it cautiously without any mention of the person.

He who dares to reveal a sin confided to him in the tribunal of penance, we decree that he be not only deposed from the sacerdotal office but also relegated to a monastery of strict observance for the remainder of his life. . . .

31   Pope Innocent III: The Decretal *Cum ex officii nostri*, 1207

In order altogether to remove from the patrimony of St. Peter the defilement of heretics, we decree, as a perpetual law, that whatsoever heretic, especially if he be a Patarene, shall be found therein, shall immediately be taken and delivered to the secular court to be punished according to law. All his goods also shall be sold, so that he who took him shall receive one part, another shall go to the court which convicted him, and the third shall be applied to the building of prisons in the country wherein he was taken. The house, however, in which a heretic had been received shall be altogether destroyed; nor shall anyone presume to rebuild it; but let that which was a den of iniquity become a receptacle of filth. Moreover, their believers and defenders and favorers shall be fined one fourth part of their goods, which shall be applied to the service of the public.

32   Burchard of Ursperg: On the New Orders

There arose two monastic orders in the church, whose youth was renewed like the Eagle's and which were confirmed by the Apostolic See—namely those of the Franciscans and the Dominicans— and which were approved of, perhaps, on this account; because two sects which still exist had arisen in Italy, one of which called itself the Humiliati, and the other the Poor Men of Lyons, whom Pope Lucius formerly placed among the heretics because some superstitious doctrines and rites were found among them. Moreover, in their private discourses, which they generally made in secret places, they spoke disrespectfully of the Church of God, and of the priesthood. I saw, at that time, some of their number, who were called Poor Men of Lyons as the Apostolic See, with a certain leader of theirs, I think Bernard; and they were trying to get their sect confirmed and privileged by the Apostolic See. They went about through the towns, and villages, saying, forsooth, that they lived the life of the apostles, not desiring to have any possessions, or any fixed dwelling-place. The Lord Pope, however, disapproved of some superstitious points in their way of life— namely that they cut off the upper part of their shoes, and walked apparently barefoot. Besides, though they wore a kind of hood, as if they belonged to some monastic order, they did not cut their hair otherwise than as laymen. This also appeared scandalous respecting them—that men and women went travelling about together, and commonly lived in the same house, and (it was said) sometimes lay in the same bed. All which things, however, they asserted to have come down from the apostles. The Lord Pope therefore, instead of them, confirmed some others who rose up in their place, who called them-selves Poor Minors [*Pauperes Minores*] and who rejected the before-mentioned superstitious and scandalous matters, but went really barefoot both in summer and winter, and received neither money nor anything else but food, unless it happened that someone might of his own accord offer them some necessary garment, but they did not ask anything from anybody. These, however, afterwards considering that sometimes too much talk of humility becomes boasting, and that the name of poverty, falsely assumed by so many, was vainglorious in the sight of God, chose rather to be called Minor Friars [*Minores Fratres*] than Poor Minors, being in all things obedient to the Apostolic Sse. The others, namely the Dominicans, are supposed to have come in the place of the Humiliati. For the Humiliati, having no authority or license from the prelates, but thrusting their sickle into the harvest of others, preached to the people and took upon them generally to regulate their lives, to hear their confessions, and to bring into discredit the ministry of the priests. The pope, wishing to correct these things, instituted and confirmed the Order of Preachers [or Dominicans], for the former were uneducated and illiterate, and employed in manual labor, and preached, obtaining what was necessary for their support from their followers; but these latter, constantly occupied in study, and in reading the sacred scriptures, had no other occupation than that of writing books, and most diligently hearing them from their superiors, so that they could go forth with the arrows and the bow, and all the armor of the mighty, and stand for the defense of the Holy Mother Church, and go up against them and place themselves as a wall for the house of Israel. While they confirm faith and instruct in virtue, they teach and commend the statutes of the Church, and reprove and correct the sins and vices of men, being nevertheless obedient in all things to the Apostolic See, from which they derive their chief authority."

33   St. Antony's Sermon to the Fish

Christ the blessed was pleased to show forth the great sanctity of his most faithful servant St. Antony, and how men ought devoutly to listen to his preaching, by means of creatures without reason. On one occasion, amongst others, He made use of fishes to reprove the folly of faithless heretics, just as we read in the Old Testament how, in ancient times, he reproved the ignorance of Balaam by the mouth of an ass.

St. Antony, being at one time at Rimini, where there were a great number of heretics, and wishing to lead them by the light of faith into the way of truth, preached to them, for several days, and reasoned with them on the faith of Christ and on the holy scriptures. They not only resisted his words, but were hardened and obstinate, and refused to listen to him. At last St. Antony, inspired by God, went down to the seashore, where the river runs into the sea, and, having placed himself on a bank between the river and the sea, he began to speak to the fishes as if the Lord had sent him to preach to them, and said, "Listen to the word of God, O you fishes of the sea and river, as the faithless heretics refuse to do so."

No sooner had he spoken these words than suddenly a great multitude of fishes, both small and great, approached the bank on which he stood, and never before had so many been seen in the sea or in the river; all kept their heads out of the water and seemed to be attentively looking on St. Antony's face; all were arranged in perfect order and most peacefully, the smaller ones in front near the bank, after them came those a little bigger, and last of all, where the water was deeper, the large ones.

When they had placed themselves in this order, St. Antony began to preach to them most solemnly, saying: "My brothers the fishes, you are bound as much as it is in your power to return thanks to your Creator, who has given you such a noble element for your dwelling; for you have at your choice sweet water and salt water; you have many places of refuge from the tempest; you have likewise a pure and transparent element for your nourishment. God, your bountiful and kind Creator, when he made you, ordered you to increase and multiply, and gave you his blessing. In the universal deluge all other creatures perished; you alone did God preserve from all harm. He has given you fins to enable you to go where you will. To you was it granted, according to the commandment of God, to keep the prophet Jonas, and after three days to throw him safe and sound on dry land. You it was who gave the tribute-money to our Savior Jesus Christ when, through his poverty, he had nothing to pay. By a singular mystery you were the nourishment of the eternal King, Jesus Christ, before and after his resurrection. Because of all these things you are bound to praise and bless the Lord who has given you so many and so much greater blessings than to other creatures."

At these words the fishes began to open their mouths and bow their heads, and endeavored, as much as was in their power, to express their reverence and show forth their praise. St. Antony, seeing the reverence of the fishes towards their Creator, rejoiced greatly in spirit, and said, with a loud voice, "Blessed be eternal God, for the fishes of the sea honor him more than men without faith, and animals without reason listen to his word with greater attention than sinful heretics." And whilst St. Antony was preaching the number of the fishes increased, and none of them left the place he had chosen.

And the people of the city, hearing of the miracle, made haste to go and witness it. With them came the heretics of whom we have spoken above, who, seeing such a wonderful and manifest miracle, were touched in their hearts, and all threw themselves at the feet of St. Antony to hear his words. The saint then began to expound to them the Catholic faith. He preached so eloquently that all those heretics were converted and returned to the true faith of Christ; the faithful were filled with joy and greatly comforted and strengthened in the faith. After this St. Antony sent away the fishes with the blessing of God; and they all departed rejoicing as they went, and the people returned to the city. St. Antony remained at Rimini for several days, preaching and reaping much spiritual fruit in the souls of his hearers.

34   St. Thomas Aquinas: Whether Heretics Should Be Tolerated

II-II, Q. 11, ART. 3

We proceed thus to the Third Article:

Objection 1. It seems that heretics ought to be tolerated. For the Apostle says [2 Tim. 2:24-25]: "The servant of the Lord must not wrangle . . . with modesty admonishing them that resist the truth, if peradventure God may give them repentance to know the truth, and they may recover themselves from the snares of the devil." Now if heretics are not tolerated but put to death, they lose the opportunity of repentance. Therefore it seems contrary to the Apostle's command.

Obj. 2. Further, whatever is necessary in the Church should be tolerated. Now heresies are necessary in the Church, since the Apostle says [1 Cor. 11:19]: "There must be . . . heresies, that they who are reproved may be manifest among you." Therefore it seems that heretics should be tolerated.

Obj. 3. Further, the Master commanded his servants [Matt. 13:30] "to suffer the cockle to grow until the harvest," i.e., the end of the world, as a gloss explains it. Now holy men explain that the cockle denotes heretics. Therefore heretics should be tolerated.

On the contrary, the Apostle says [Titus 3:10-11]: "A man that is a heretic, after the first and second admonition, avoid: knowing that he, that is such an one, is subverted."

I answer that with regard to heretics two points must be observed: one, on their own side; the other, on the side of the Church. On their own side there is the sin, whereby they deserve not only to be separated from the Church by excommunication, but also to be severed from the world by death. For it is a much graver matter to corrupt the faith which quickens the soul than to forge money, which supports temporal life. Wherefore if forgers of money and other evildoers are forthwith condemned to death by the secular authority, much more reason is there for heretics, as soon as they are convicted of heresy, to be not only excommunicated but even put to death.

On the part of the Church, however, there is mercy which looks to the conversion of the wanderer, wherefore she condemns not at once, but "after the first and second admonition," as the Apostle directs; after that, if he is yet stubborn, the Church no longer hoping for his conversion, looks to the salvation of others, by excommunicating him and separating him from the Church, and furthermore delivers him to the secular tribunal to be exterminated thereby from the world by death. For Jerome commenting on Gal. 5:9, "A little leaven," says: "Cut off the decayed flesh, expel the mangy sheep from the fold, lest the whole house, the whole paste, the whole body, the whole flock, burn, perish, rot, die. Arius was but one spark in Alexandria, but as that spark was not at once put out, the whole earth was laid waste by its flame."

Reply Obj. 1. This very modesty demands that the heretic should be admonished a first and second time; and if he be unwilling to retract, he must be reckoned as already "subverted," as we may gather from the words of the Apostle quoted above.

Reply Obj. 2. The profit that ensues from heresy is beside the intention of heretics, for it consists in the constancy of the faithful being put to the test, and "makes us shake off our sluggishness, and search the scriptures more carefully," as Augustine states [*De Gen. cont. Manich.* 1:1]. What they really intend is the corruption of the faith, which is to inflict very great harm indeed. Consequently we should consider what they directly intend, and expel them, rather than what is beside their intention, and so tolerate them.

Reply Obj. 3. According to *Decret.* xxiv. [qu. 3, can *Notandum*], "To be excommunicated is not to be uprooted." A man is excommunicated, as the Apostle says [1 Cor. 5:5], that his "spirit may be saved in the day of Our Lord." Yet if heretics be altogether uprooted by death, this is not contrary to Our Lord's command, which is to be understood as referring to the case when the cockle cannot be plucked up without plucking up the wheat, as we explained above [Q. 10, A. 8, *ad* 1], when treating of unbelievers in general.

35   Pope Innocent III and Durand of Huesca, 1210

To the archbishop and suffragans of the Church of Tarragona. In imitation of Him who is the God, not of discord but of peace, who desires that all men shall be saved and come to the knowledge of truth, we received with fatherly kindness our beloved sons Durand of Huesca and his companions when they came to the Apostolic See and we have acquired full understanding of the matters which they charged them- selves to explain to us on their own behalf as well as for their brethren. We know, therefore, from the things which they said to us about the articles of faith and the sacraments of the Church when they were carefully examined, that they are versed in the orthodox faith and that they build upon Catholic truth. Moreover, for greater assurance, bringing forth the gospels and placing the text of their confession thereon, we received this oath from them:

"I (it begins), Durand of Huesca, in your consecrated hands, Most High Pontiff, Lord Innocent, invoke God as my soul's witness that I absolutely and truly believe what is contained in this document in all things, and I will never believe the contrary; but I will resist with all my might those who do believe contrary to this. To you, truly, as successor to the Blessed Apostle Peter, to archbishops, bishops, and other prelates in whose dioceses or parishes I may dwell, I tender obedience and reverence, as deserved as it is devout."

The text of the confession follows:

"Let it be known to all the faithful that I, Durand of Huesca, and J., and E., and B., and all our brethren, believe in heart, perceive through faith, confess in speech, and in unequivocal words affirm that the Father, the Son, and the Holy Spirit are three persons, one God, the whole Trinity, the same in essence and substance, coeternal and omnipotent, and that each person of the Trinity is fully God, as is expressed in the creeds, the Apostle's Creed, the Nicene Creed, and the Athanasian Creed. We believe in heart and confess in words that the Father, the Son, and the Holy Spirit of whom we testify, is creator,

From Walter Wakefield and A. P. Evans, *Heresies of the High Middle Ages* (New York: Columbia University Press, 1969), pp. 222-26. Reprinted with the permission of the publisher.

maker, governor, and disposer of all things, corporeal and spiritual, visible and invisible. We believe that the author of the New and Old Testaments is one and the same God who, existing in the Trinity, as we have said, created everything out of nothing. We believe that John the Baptist, holy and righteous, was sent by him and was filled with the Holy Spirit in his mother's womb.

"We believe in heart and confess in words that the incarnation of divinity came to pass not in the Father or in the Holy Spirit but only in the Son, so that he who in divinity was the Son of God the Father, true God from the Father, was in humanity the son of man, true man from his mother, having true flesh from the womb of his mother and a rational human soul, of both natures at one and the same time, that is, God and man, one person, one son, one Christ, one God with the Father and the Holy Spirit, author and ruler of all. Born of the Virgin Mary by true birth of the flesh, he ate and drank, slept and rested when wearied by travel, suffered with true suffering of his flesh, died in a true death of his body, and rose again with true resurrection of his flesh and true restoration of his soul to the body; in that flesh He afterward ate and drank, ascended into heaven, sits at the right hand of the Father, and in it shall come to judge the quick and the dead.

"We believe in heart and confess by mouth that there is one Church, not that of heretics, but holy, Roman, catholic, and apostolic, outside of which, we believe, no one can be saved. We do not in any way reject the sacraments which are celebrated in it with the aid of the inestimable and invisible power of the Holy Spirit, even though they be ministered by a sinful priest, as long as the Church accepts him. Nor do we disparage the ecclesiastical offices or benedictions celebrated by such a one, but with devout mind we embrace them as if performed by the most righteous; for the wickedness of a bishop or of a priest has no harmful effect upon the baptism of children, nor on the celebration of the Eucharist, nor on the performance of other ecclesiastical offices for those in their charge. We approve, therefore, of the baptism of infants, whom we confess and believe to be saved if they shall die after baptism before they commit sin. We believe that in baptism all sins are remitted, that original inherited sin as well as those which are committed by one's own will. We hold that confirmation performed by a bishop, that is, by the imposition of hands, is holy and worthy of reverent acceptance. We firmly and indisputably with pure heart believe and affirm in unequivocal, faithful words that the sacrifice, that is, the bread and wine, is, after consecration, the true body and true blood of our Lord Jesus Christ; in this, we believe, nothing more is accomplished by a good priest, nothing less by an evil one, for it is effected not by the merit of the consecrant but by the word of the Creator and in the power of the Holy Spirit. Hence, we firmly believe and confess that no one, however worthy, religious, holy, and prudent he may be, can or ought to consecrate the Eucharist or perform the sacrifice of the altar unless he is a priest regularly ordained by a visible and tangible bishop. To this office there are, we believe, three things necessary: a certain person, the priest himself, duly established in that office by a bishop, as we have already said; those solemn words which are set forth by the holy fathers in the canon; and the faithful purpose of him who offers them. And consequently, we firmly believe and confess that whosoever believes and expresses himself as qualified to perform the sacrament of the Eucharist without the preceding episcopal ordination, as we have said, is a heretic, a participant and partner in the damnation of Korah and his accomplices and ought to be cut off from the whole Holy Roman Church.

"We believe that forgiveness is granted by God to truly penitent sinners and most willingly will we consort with them. We venerate the anointing of the sick with consecrated oil. We do not deny that carnal marriage may be contracted as the Apostle says; we utterly forbid that those united in lawful fashion shall separate. We believe and confess that a man united with his wife may be saved and we do not even condemn a second or later marriage. We put no reproach at all upon the eating of meat.

"We believe preaching to be necessary and most praiseworthy, but we believe it is to be exercised by the authority or license of the highest pontiff or by permission of prelates. In all places, indeed, where manifest heretics abide, where they forsake and blaspheme God and the faith of the Holy Roman Church, we believe that we should confound them by disputation and exhortation in all ways according to God, as adversaries of Christ and the Church, and with bold countenance oppose them with the word of the Lord, even unto death. We humbly praise and faithfully venerate the ecclesiastical orders and all that is appointed to be read or sung as holy in the Holy Roman Church. We believe that the devil was made evil not by nature but by his will. We believe in heart and confess in words the resurrection of this flesh which we bear and no other. We firmly believe and affirm that the judgment by Jesus Christ is still to come, and that each person will receive either punishment or reward for those things committed in this flesh which we bear. We believe that alms, the Mass, and other good works can benefit the faithful who have died. We believe and confess that persons remaining in the world and owning their own goods, giving alms and doing other good works out of their own, and observing the commandments of the Lord may be saved. We believe that by the Lord's command clerics ought to receive tithes, first fruits, and oblations."

Verily, since not only true faith but good performance is requisite for salvation, for even as it is impossible to please God without faith, so faith without works is dead, we have caused a record to be made in these pages of the proposal for their way of life, the content of which follows.

"To the honor of God and his Catholic Church and for the salvation of our souls we have resolved to believe in heart and confess in words the Catholic faith, whole and inviolate in its entirety, maintaining ourselves under the direction and governance of the Roman pontiff. We have renounced the world; whatever we may come to have we shall bestow upon the poor according to the Lord's commandment. We have resolved to be poor in such fashion that we shall take no thought for the morrow, nor shall we accept gold or silver, or anything of that sort from anyone, beyond food and clothing sufficient for the day. Our resolve is to follow the precepts of the gospel as commands, devoting ourselves to prayer according to the seven canonical hours, saying the Lord's Prayer fifteen times, followed by the Apostle's Creed, the Miserere, and other prayers. Inasmuch as most of us are clerics and almost all are educated, we are resolved to devote ourselves to study, exhortation, teaching, and disputation against all sects of error. Disputations, however, are to be conducted by the more learned brethren, proved in the Catholic faith and instructed in the law of the Lord, so that enemies of the Catholic and apostolic faith are confounded."

VI
THE WAY OF *POTESTAS*: CRUSADE AND CRIMINAL SANCTIONS

As early as the eleventh century, heretics, dissidents, and reformers had been physically persecuted and killed, but the first stirrings of violence against dissidents were usually the result of popular resentment. Although Roman law contained severe strictures against heretics and schismatics, it was not consistently known or applied during the eleventh and early twelfth centuries, nor was there a universally used reference work of ecclesiastical law before 1140. A text from Caesarius of Heisterbach's handbook for the teaching of Cistercian novices, the *Dialogue on Miracles* (no. 36) illustrates popular violence against heretics. Technically, the responsibility for dealing with heresy belonged to bishops, and bishops had always had the right (although they appear rarely to have made use of it) to use the legal procedure known as *inquisitio* (in this early sense, simply a form of inquest) to discover it. As the texts in chapters II through V above make clear, neither of these methods seemed particularly successful, and until the late twelfth century the Church relied more on warnings, injunctions to prelates and clergy, preaching missions led by Cistercians, and penitential discipline of an irregular character to curb the growth of heresy and dissent.

From the late twelfth century on, however, the Church began to turn to the way of *potestas*, force, at first in those cases where nothing else seemed to work, and later routinely. In 1184, Pope Lucius III issued the decretal *Ad Abolendam* (above, no. 29), which formally instituted the episcopal inquisition throughout Latin Christendom and condemned heresy in universal terms as contumacy toward ecclesiastical authority. The Fourth Lateran Council in

1215 (above, no. 30) reiterated early statements on the excommunication of heretics, and by the time of the council the legal punishment known as infamy, which entailed severe legal restrictions, was inflicted on heretics, as is reflected in both canon and Roman law. Other firm steps were taken against heretics in general in the last years of the twelfth and first years of the thirteenth century. In 1199 Pope Innocent III issued his decretal *Vergentis in senium,* which stated that the heretics were to be considered comparable to traitors in Roman law, thus opening up a broad legal avenue for further juridical actions.

In 1208 the murder of Innocent's legate, Peter of Castelnau, in Languedoc led to Innocent's launching of a crusade against heretics in southern France, long known as the Albigensian Crusade. At the same time, Innocent developed the doctrine that temporal rulers were obliged to drive heresy from their lands or risk their lands being declared open to Christians who would do so. The invocation of the "secular arm" of temporal society had dramatic results. Between 1220 and 1231 Emperor Frederick II enacted a series of laws for Germany and Sicily (no. 41) that were the harshest temporal laws yet against heretics. The punishments in these decrees ranged from legal incapacitation, exile, confiscation of goods, and disinheritance of offspring to death itself. In 1231 Pope Gregory IX issued the decretal *Excommunicamus,* which was an extension of *Ad Abolendam* and inflicted further disabilities on those convicted of heresy or those guilty of supporting or sympathizing with heretics:

> We excommunicate and anathematize all heretics, Cathars, Patarines, the Poor of Lyons, the Passagians, the Josephites, Arnoldists, Speronists, and others under whatever name they may be included, for although they may have different appearances, they are bound together the same at the tail, since by vanity they take pleasure in this. Those condemned by the Church will be relaxed to the secular arm where they will be punished by the debt of hatred; clerks are to be degraded from their orders first. If any of those mentioned above, after they have been condemned, wish to return to the Church and perform appropriate penance, they are to be perpetually imprisoned. Those who believe in heretical errors we adjudge to the same process.
>
> Receivers, defenders, and aiders of heretics we submit to the sentence of excommunication, most firmly decreeing that if afterward such a one is marked for excommunication, the presumption [of heresy] shall not cease, and they shall be by this act itself declared infamous, nor shall they be fit for public office or public advice, nor shall they be elected to any office nor admitted to testimony. They shall be intestate, so that, having no testament, they shall accede to no inheritance. They may not commence any negotiation themselves,

but they may be compelled by others to negotiate. They may never obtain judgment in a case, and the cases of others will be preferred to theirs.

In the same year Gregory issued the decretal *Ille humani generis*, written to the prior of the Dominican convent in Regensburg (no. 38), charging him with the organization of an inquisitorial tribunal, with authority derived directly from the pope. This momentous act, the creation of a tribunal outside the normal procedure of the local bishop, was the birth of the papal Inquisition.   ✓ 1231

In addition to the founding of the papal Inquisition, conciliar legislation of the early thirteenth century called for harsher penalties against heretics. The Council of Toulouse in 1229 (no. 37) and that of Tarragona in 1242 (no. 39) issued extreme condemnations of heresy. The success of the Dominican inquisition under papal authority led to the creation of a separate profession, virtually, of inquisitor, and a specialized literature based upon inquisitorial archives, reflecting a sharp awareness of the content of heretical beliefs, and listing step by step the process by which a heretic was to be brought to confess or to die (no. 40). The genre of inquisitors' handbooks grew in the period between the thirteenth and the sixteenth centuries, so that these books, in spite of their repetition and frequent plagiarism, are some of our best sources for heretical beliefs.

The success of the papal inquisition and the Albigensian Crusade inspired other rulers besides Frederick II to issue laws dealing with heretics. In Germany, the *Schwabenspiegel* of 1235 (no. 42), several French ordinances of the thirteenth century (no. 43), and the early fifteenth-century English statute *De haeretico comburendo* of 1401 (no. 44) trace this development. By the end of the thirteenth century, the full force of spiritual and temporal power had been invoked against heretics, their supporters and sympathizers. The crystallization of ecclesiastical authority and the willingness of temporal authorities to follow it led to the extraordinarily ferocious techniques that have characterized the Inquisition in later historiography: torture, the testimony of secret witnesses, the deprivation of the accused of a defense, and the *animadversio debita*, the burning by the secular arm.

LITERATURE

There has been a large literature on the history of spiritual coercion from the fourth through the twentieth centuries. For our period, the complexities of the Church's response to heresy are effectively summed up in Moore, *Origins of*

European Dissent, pp. 243-84, and Lambert, *Medieval Heresy*, pp. 95-181. Both these works provide ample bibliographical references. For the procedure of the Inquisition, see the 1963 abridgment of Henry C. Lea's *History of the Inquisition of the Middle Ages* (New York, 1887), one of the monuments of American medieval scholarship. In the 1963 volume, which extracts the most durable of Lea's conclusions, see especially the introduction by Walter Ullmann. Henri Maisonneuve, *Études sur les origines de l'Inquisition* (Paris, 1960), is the most recent general study. On the Albigensian Crusade, see the works of Walter Wakefield and Jonathan Sumption cited in the introduction to chapter IV. On the use of torture, see E. Peters, *The Magician, the Witch and the Law* (Philadelphia, 1978), appendix 1, *"Res fragilis:* Torture in Early European Law,"* pp. 183-95, with full bibliography. Several articles deal extensively with papal attitudes toward heretics: Brenda Bolton, "Tradition and Temerity: Papal Attitudes to Deviants, 1159-1216," in D. Baker, ed., *Schism, Heresy, and Religious Protest*, Studies in Church History, vol. 9 (Cambridge, 1972), pp. 79-91; more thorough is Helmut G. Walther, "Häresie und päpstliche Politik: Ketzerbegriff und Ketzergesetzgebung in der Übergangsphase von der Dekretistik zur Dekretalistik," in W. Lourdaux and D. Verhelst, eds., *The Concept of Heresy in the Middle Ages (11th-13th Centuries)* (Louvain-The Hague, 1976), pp. 104-43, as is, in the same anthology of studies, O. Hageneder, "Der Häresiebegriff bei den Juristen des 12. und 13. Jahrhunderts," pp. 42-103. On the transition toward coercion, see the interesting article by Raoul Manselli, "De la *'persuasio'* à la *'coercitio,'*" *Cahiers de Fanjeaux* 6 (1971), 175-97, with extensive bibliographical references.

On particular topics mentioned in this introduction see the following. For the Crusade, Elizabeth Kennan, "Innocent III and the First Political Crusade," *Traditio* 27 (1971): 231-50; on the importance of Innocent III's *Vergentis*, see Walter Ullmann, "The Significance of Innocent III's Decretal *Vergentis*," in *Études d'histoire du droit canonique dediées à Gabriel Le Bras* (Paris, 1965), vol. 1, pp. 729-42, and O. Hageneder, "Studien zur Dekretale *Vergentis* (X. 5. 7. 10)," *Zeitschrift der Savigny-Stiftung für Rechtsgeschichte, Kanonistische Abteilung* 49 (1963): 138-73, and Maisonneuve, *Études sur les origines de l'inquisition*, pp. 156-80.

There are extensive Latin texts in Kurt-Victor Selge, ed., *Texte zur Inquisition*, Texte zur Kirchen- und Theologiegeschichte, vol. 4 (Gütersloh, 1967), and Fearns, *Ketzer und Ketzerbekämpfung*, pp. 52-77. See also G. G. Coulton, *The Death Penalty for Heresy from 1184 to 1921* (London, 1924); A. C.

Shannon, *The Popes and Heresy in the Thirteenth Century* (Villanova, 1949); Richard W. Emery, *Heresy and Inquisition in Narbonne* (reprint ed., New York, 1967). On inquisitors' handbooks, see the references in Edward Peters, "Editing Inquisitors' Handbooks in the Sixteenth Century: Francisco Peña and the *Directorium Inquisitorum* of Nicholas Eymeric," in *The Library Chronicle* 40 (1975); *Bibliographical Studies in Honor of Rudolf Hirsch*, pp. 95-107; and Walter L. Wakefield, "Notes on Some Antiheretical Writings of the Thirteenth Century," *Franciscan Studies* 27 (1967): 285-321.

In addition to the extensive works of Lea and Grundmann, see also E. van der Vekené, *Bibliographie der Inquisition* (Hildesheim, 1963).

A recent study explores some of the consequences of the doctrine of infamy when it was applied to heretics and to their children: Kenneth Pennington, "*Pro Peccatis Patrum Puniri*: A Moral and Legal Problem of the Inquisition," *Church History* 47 (1978): 137-54.

36   Caesarius of Heisterbach: The Stake

About the same time several heretics were arrested at Cologne under Archbishop Rheinbold, and after being examined and convicted by learned men, were condemned by the secular tribunal. Sentence was passed, and they were about to be led out to the stake, when one of them, by name Arnold, whom the rest acknowledged as their leader, begged, as was said by those present, that he might be given some bread and a bowl of water. Some thought that this request should be granted, but others who were wiser dissuaded them, saying that with these some diabolical charm might be wrought which would be a stumbling block and perhaps ruin for the weak.

Novice—I cannot think what he can have wished to do with bread and water.

Monk—From the words of another heretic, who was arrested and burnt three years ago by the king of Spain, I think that he wished to use them for a sacrilegious communion, which would be a viaticum for his disciples to eternal damnation. For a Spanish abbot of our order, who had been one of the bishops and prelates of the Church who had condemned the errors of this heretic, told us, when passing our way, that part of his teaching was that any rustic could make the Body of Christ at his own table out of the bread that he was eating; this accursed heretic was a blacksmith.

Novice—How then did it fare with the heretics of Cologne?

Monk—They were taken outside the town, and were together put into the fire near the Jewish cemetery. After the flames had taken strong hold of them, in the sight and hearing of a great crowd, Arnold placed his hand on the heads of his dying disciples, and exhorted them, "Stand fast in your faith, for this day you shall be with Laurence," and yet they were very far from the faith of Laurence. There was a maiden among them, beautiful though a heretic, and she was drawn from the fire by the compassion of some who promised that they would provide her with a husband, or if it seemed better, would place her in a nunnery. She consented to this in words, but when the heretics were now dead, she said to those who had charge of her, "Tell me, where does that seducer lie?" and when they pointed out to her where Master Arnold lay, she slipped from their hands, veiled her face with her robe, and threw herself upon the body of the dead man, and with him went down to burn for ever in hell.

37   The Council of Toulouse, 1229

Canon 1. We appoint, therefore, that the archbishops and bishops shall swear in one priest, and two or three laymen of good report, or more if they think fit, in every parish, both in and out of cities, who shall diligently, faithfully, and frequently seek out the heretics in those parishes, by searching all houses and subterranean chambers which lie under any suspicion. And looking out for appendages or outbuildings, in the roofs themselves, or any other kind of hiding places, all which we direct to be destroyed.

Canon 6. Directs that the house in which any heretic shall be found shall be destroyed.

Canon 10. Also we decree that if any *hæretici vestiti*, having voluntarily abandoned their heresy, shall return to the Catholic faith, acknowledging their error, they shall not remain in the town in which they previously dwelt, if that town be suspected of heresy; but shall be placed in a Catholic town, which lies under no suspicion of heresy. Moreover, in detestation of their ancient error, they shall thenceforth wear two conspicuous crosses, of a different color from their garments; nor shall any such person be allowed to discontinue these crosses without letters testimonial of his reconciliation from his bishop. Nor in future shall any public office be entrusted to any such persons, nor shall they be admitted in any matters of law unless they shall have been restored to unity, with a sufficient penance by the Lord Pope or by his legate *a latere*.

Canon 11. Heretics, however, who through fear of death or from any other cause, so that it be not done voluntarily, shall return to Catholic unity, are to be imprisoned by the bishop of the place, to perform penance, with proper caution, to prevent their having the power of corrupting others; they are to be supported, as the bishop shall direct, by those who shall obtain their property; or, if they had no property, the bishop shall provide for them.

Canons 12. and 13. require an oath against heresy, and regular confession to a priest three times in the year, from all persons who have arrived at years of discretion.

Canon 14. We prohibit also that the laity should be permitted to have the books of the Old or the New Testament; unless anyone from motives of devotion should wish to have the Psalter or the Breviary for divine offices or the hours of the blessed Virgin; but we most strictly forbid their having any translation of these books.

Canon 15. We decree, also, that whosoever shall be considered as a heretic or be marked with suspicion shall not henceforth exercise the profession of a physician; and when any sick person shall have received the holy communion from the hand of his priest, let him be vigilantly looked after until his death or recovery; lest any heretic or person suspected of heresy should get access to him; for we have understood that wicked and abominable things have often occurred from the access of such persons.

Canon 16. When also any one shall wish to make a will, let it be witnessed by his priest, or by some other ecclesiastic if his own priest cannot be had, together with such men of good credit as he shall choose to call in; and wills otherwise made shall be invalid and of no force.

38   Pope Gregory IX:
The Decretal *Ille humani generis*, 1231

Gregory bishop, servant of the servants of God, to his beloved sons. . . Prior Burchard and Theoderic, brothers of the Order of Preachers in Regensburg, greetings and apostolic benediction.

That inveterate enemy of the human race, the instigator of all evils, whom his own pride drew down from the highest to the lowest state, [is] not content that by his wicked deceptions he led mankind to the Fall and to the labors of wretchedness. He craftily tries to ensnare mankind in his pestilential nets, artfully contriving against them that they may not reascend to obtain once again that height from which they once fell.

In these recent times, perfidiously attempting to deprave the faith by his ministers, the workers of iniquity, he has spread deadly poison, scheming seditiously that enemies who appeared familiar [to mankind] might be efficacious at doing mankind injury. Exuding pleasant appearances, these sting with their tails like scorpions, and they would infuse their pestilential poison even into the golden chalice of Babylon.

Although the heretics have lain concealed for a long time, scuttling about in hiding like crabs and, like little foxes, attempting to destroy the vineyard of the Lord of Hosts, now, however, their sins leading them on, they rise up in the open, like horses ready for battle, and manifestly presume to rise up against [the Church] publicly, preaching in certain places, seeking food in the simple, and victims in those without learning. Wishing to entrap some of the faithful in their wiles, they have made themselves teachers of error, who once were students of truth.

Wherefore it is fitting that we rise up against them manfully, so that the faith of Christ may flourish and this heresy of theirs be confounded, and that a crown should be the reward of those who resist temptation. Since, therefore, the faith has recently shone forth in Germany, and by it we desire to do battle with these poisonous animals, lest perhaps the simple be seduced by their artful deceptions, and the learned be deceived dangerously and led to the depth of evils by their depraved artifices, because these also attack the foundations of faith, we, who are as a father constituted by the gospels, come into the vineyard of the Lord at the eleventh hour among the workers, or, rather more truly, above the workers, warned by the voice of the bridegroom to catch the little foxes who seek to destroy the vineyard of the Lord, stricken by grief of heart, unable to sustain such contempt of the Creator, and seeking to wipe out the danger of these beasts.

We seek, urge, and exhort your wisdom, by apostolic letters sent to you under the apostolic seal, that you be sent as judges into different districts to preach where it seems useful to you to the clergy and people assembled together, using for this purpose other discreet people known to you, and to seek out diligently those who are heretics or are infamed of heresy. If you should discover heretics or people infamed of heresy, unless they should be willing, upon examination, to obey the commands of the Church, you are to proceed against them according to our statutes against heresy recently promulgated, as well as against the receivers, defenders, and helpers of heretics as the statutes state. If any heretic, having abjured, wishes to return to the unity of the Church, you may receive him according to the Church's formula of absolution, and lay upon him the burden that it is customary to lay upon such people, paying very close attention to the possibility that someone may appear to revert [to orthodoxy] and under the appearance of piety may commit impiety, and that the angel of Satan may transform himself into an angel of light, on account of which it has been ordained (as I have made to be promulgated by Brother Hugo, sent as preacher of the word of God in Germany) that you must investigate them thoroughly and the nature of their beliefs by the discretion given you by God.

You may exercise the office thus given to you freely and efficaciously, concerning this and all of the things which we have mentioned above, and all in particular places who are swayed by your preaching [may be accepted thus back into the Church] within twenty days. We release from their penitence for three years by the power and mercy of Almighty God and the blessed apostles Peter and Paul those who offer you help, advice, or favor against heretics, or their helpers, receivers, or defenders in fortified places, castles, or other places against the rebels against the Church. And if any of these die in the active prosecution of this work, we grant them full forgiveness for all the sins for which they have been contrite in heart and confessed orally. And lest anyone be reluctant to aid you in the business mentioned above, in offering censure against those contradictors and rebels against the Church which we wield through your priesthood, we concede to them the free faculty of wielding the sword against the enemies of the faith.

We give you the permission to restrain those preachers and seekers of alms whose interest is chiefly charitable from the office of preacher of this business, which is none of their affair, so that if you are not able to interest all in involving themselves in the pursuit of this affair, the two of you may pursue it.

Given at Rieti, 10 kalends of December, in the fifth year of our pontificate.

39   The Council of Tarragona, 1242

In the first place, it is inquired, who are to be called *heretics?* who *suspected?* who *believers?* who *favorers?* who *receivers?* who *defenders?* and who *relapsed?* and this is explained in the following manner:

Heretics are those who persist in their error, like the Inzabbatati, who say that we ought in no case to swear—that obedience is not due to the ecclesiastical or secular powers—and that corporal punishment is not to be inflicted on anyone, and the like.

Believers in the said heresies are, in like manner, to be called heretics.

He may be called *suspected* of heresy who hears the preaching or reading of the Inzabbatati, or who has knelt in prayer with them, or who has kissed them, or who believes those Inzabbatati to be good men, or other things which may probably induce suspicion. And he may be said to be *simply suspected* who has even once prayed or done any of the aforesaid things with them. If, however, he has frequently heard their preaching and reading, or has prayed, or has done any of the aforesaid things with them, he may be said to be *vehemently suspected.* But, if he has done *all* the aforesaid things, especially if it be *frequently,* he may be said to be *most vehemently suspected.* We state the matter in this way, in order that a discreet judge may increase or diminish the required proof of innocence, as may appear expedient.

Concealers [*celatores*] we understand to mean those who have seen Inzabbatati in the street, or in a house, or in any other place, and knew that they were Inzabbatati, and did not inform against them when they had the opportunity of discovering them to the Church, or to the magistrate, or to others who might apprehend them.

By *Hiders* [*occultatores*] we understand those who have entered into an agreement not to discover the heretics, or Inzabbatati, or who have otherwise prevented their being discovered.

Receivers are those who have twice or more received heretics, or Inzabbatati, knowing them to be such, i n their house or in any other place belonging to them. A *receptacle* we understand to be a house or inn, where heretics or Inzabbatati have twice or more assembled for preaching or reading; or even where heretics, or Inzabbatati, have been frequently entertained.

Defenders we understand to be those who knowingly defend heretics, or Inzabbatati, by word, or deed, or any other device in their lands or elsewhere, so that the Church may be the less able to perform its duty of extirpating heretical pravity.

Favorers we understand to mean all the foregoing classes in a greater or less degree; and even those who otherwise, in any manner, have given them counsel, help, or favor. And all favorers we consider to be so far suspected that they ought to clear themselves, and to abjure heresy, and all favoring, and ought to be reconciled to the Holy Mother Church.

The *relapsed* are those who, after having abjured and renounced heresy, return to their former belief of it. In like manner we say that those have relapsed into the favoring of heresy, who, after having abjured heresy, or the favoring of it, do good to the heretics, or conceal them; and all the persons aforesaid in case they shall be found, except those who are suspected without favoring, we anathematize with the greater excommunication.

A doubt also arises with some whether those who have relapsed into belief, and heretics who are teachers, if after apprehension they desire to repent, should be delivered to the secular judgment? And it appears to us that they should not, but that in every case such persons should be sentenced to imprisonment.

40   A Manual for Inquisitors at Carcasonne, 1248-49

LETTER OF COMMISSION

To the pious and discreet men, beloved in Christ, Friars William Raymond and Peter Durand of the Order of Preachers, Pons, a friar of the same order in the province of Provence, a servant of little use and unworthy, sends greetings and the spirit of charity.

With full confidence in your discretion and devotion, in virtue of the authority of the Lord Pope which is entrusted to us in this region, we have decided to send you, for remission of your sins, to make inquisition of heretics and their believers, fautors, receivers, and defenders, and also of persons who are defamed, in the province of Narbonne, with the exception of the archdeaconries of Villelongue and Villemur of the diocese of Toulouse and in the dioceses of Albi, Rodez, Mende, and Le Puy; by that same authority directing you to proceed vigorously and prudently in this business, pursuant to the mandate and decree of the Apostolic See. If both of you are unable to be present to carry out this commission, one of you nevertheless may accomplish it.

Given at Narbonne, 21 October 1244.

THE PROCEDURE OF THE INQUISITION

This is the procedure. Within the limits of inquisition entrusted to and defined for us by the prior of the province under the authority stated above, we choose a place which seems to be well suited to the purpose, from which or in which we make inquisition of other localities. Calling the clergy and people together there, we deliver a general sermon, in which we read aloud the letters of both the Lord Pope and the prior of the province concerning the form and the authorization of the Inquisition, and we make what explanation is necessary; thereafter, we issue a general summons, either orally to those present or by letter to those who are absent, in the following form:

From Walter L. Wakefield, *Heresy, Crusade and Inquisition in Southern France* (Berkeley and Los Angeles: University of California Press, 1974; London: George Allen & Unwin, 1974), pp. 250-57. Reprinted with the permission of the publishers.

Method of citation

The inquisitors of heretical depravity [send] greetings in the Lord to so and so, parish priest. We enjoin and strictly instruct you, in virtue of the authority we wield, to summon in our name and by our authority all the parishioners of such and such church or inhabitants of such and such place, men from the age of fourteen, women from the age of twelve, or younger if perchance they shall have been guilty of an offense, to appear before us on such a day at such a place to answer for acts which they may have committed against the faith and to abjure heresy. And if no previous inquisition has been made in that place, we will grant indulgence from imprisonment to all from that place who have not been cited by name or who have not yet earned the indulgence, if, within a specified time, they come voluntarily as penitents to tell the exact and full truth about themselves and about others.

This we call the period of grace or of indulgence.

Method of abjuration and the form of the oath

We require each and every person who presents himself for confession to abjure all heresy and to take oath that he will tell the full and exact truth about himself and about others, living and dead, in the matter of the fact or crime of heresy or Waldensianism; that he will preserve and defend the Catholic faith; that he will neither harbor nor defend heretics of any sect whatever nor befriend them nor believe in them, but rather that he will in good faith pursue and seize them and their agents or, at least, will disclose them to the Church or to princes and their *baillis* who are eager and able to seize them; and that he will not obstruct the Inquisition, but rather will set himself against those who impede it.

Formula for the interrogatory

Thereafter, the person is diligently questioned about whether he saw a heretic or Waldensian, where and when, how often and with whom, and about others who were present; whether he listened to their preaching or exhortation and whether he gave them lodging or arranged shelter for them; whether he conducted them from place to place or otherwise consorted with them or arranged for them to be guided or escorted; whether he ate or drank with them or ate bread blessed by them; whether he gave or sent anything to them; whether he acted as their financial agent or messenger or assistant; whether he held any deposit or anything else of theirs; whether he received the

Peace from their book, mouth, shoulder, or elbow; whether he adored a heretic or bowed his head or genuflected and said "Bless us" before heretics or whether he was present at their baptisms or confessions; whether he was present at a Waldensian Lord's Supper, confessed his sins to them, accepted penance or learned anything from them; whether he was otherwise on familiar terms with or associated with heretics or Waldenses in any way; whether he made an agreement, heeded requests, or received gifts in return for not telling the truth about himself or others; whether he advised or persuaded anyone or caused anyone to be persuaded to do any of the foregoing; whether he knows any other man or woman to have done any of the foregoing; whether he believed in the heretics or Waldenses or their errors.

Finally, after that which he has confessed about himself or testified about other persons on all of these matters—and sometimes on others about which he was questioned, but not without good reason—has been written down, in the presence of one or both of us, with at least two other persons qualified for careful discharge of this task associated with us, he verifies everything which he caused to be recorded. In this way we authenticate the records of the Inquisition as to confessions and depositions, whether they are prepared by the notary or by another scribe.

And when a region is widely infected we make general inquisition of all persons in the manner just described, entering the names of all of them in the record, even of those who insist that they know n othing about others and have themselves committed no crime, so that if they have lied or if subsequently they commit an offense, as is often found true of a number of persons, it is on record that they have abjured and have been interrogated in detail.

The method of summoning individuals

Moreover, when we summon anyone individually we write in this form:

> In our name and by our authority, you [the priest] are to issue a summary citation to so and so, once and for all, to appear on such a day at such a place to answer for his faith (or for such and such an offense or to receive sentence of imprisonment or, more simply, penance for acts committed or to defend a deceased parent or to hear sentence in his own case or in the case of a deceased person whose heir he is).
>
> In individual as well as multiple summons, after describing the authority by which we issue them, which is on record for the region,

we list in order of rank and locality the names of persons; we state the
reasons for the summons; we assign safe places and the limit of delay
without contempt. To no one do we deny a legitimate defense, nor
do we deviate from established legal procedure, except that we do
not make public the names of witnesses, because of the decree of the
Apostolic See, wisely made by Lord Gregory [IX] and afterward
renewed by our most blessed pope, Innocent [IV], as a prerogative
and absolute necessity of the faith, on which point we have letters of
confirmation from several cardinals. In this matter, we proceed
according to the holy counsel of prelates, with all necessary prudence
and are, as well in the case of those against whom inquisition is made
as in the case of those who are witnesses.

We use this form in imposing penances and issuing condemnations:
We require those who wish to return to ecclesiastical unity for that
reason to abjure heresy again, and we solemnly bind them by official
affidavits to observance and defense of the faith, to the pursuit of
heretics, and to active assistance in inquisitions, as stated above, and
to acceptance and fulfillment of penance imposed at our discretion.
Thereafter, having granted the boon of absolution according to the
usage of the Church, we impose on the penitent the penance of
imprisonment with this formula:

Method and form of reconciling and punishing those who
return to ecclesiastical unity

In the name of our Lord Jesus Christ. We, inquisitors of heretical
depravity, etc. Through the inquisition which by apostolic mandate
we make of heretics and persons who are defamed, we find that you
(so and so) as you have confessed in legal proceedings before us, have
adored numerous heretics, harbored them, visited them, and believed
in their errors. Having on that account been taken into custody, you
nevertheless declare that you desire to return to ecclesiastical unity
and to recant sincerely and unfeignedly, as recorded above; you
subjugate yourself of your own will to the penalty for heretics if you
act to the contrary; you recognize that you are absolved from the
excommunication by which you were bound for previous acts, under
the condition and reservation that if you are found to have suppressed
the truth, either about yourself or about others, or if you do not carry
out and fulfill the penance and commands which we lay upon you,
the aforesaid absolution has no effect thereafter and you will be
adjudged to be entirely noncompliant. With the cooperation and
assistance of such and such prelates and men learned in law, by their
counsel and that of others, in accordance with apostolic command,
and by virtue of the oath you have taken, we direct you to do penance
for the acts stated above, by which you have shamefully offended

God and the Church, and to betake yourself without delay to the decent and humane prison prepared for you in (such and such) a city, there to make your salutary and permanent abode. If, indeed, you refuse to carry out our command, either by delaying to enter or, perchance, by leaving after you have done so or by doing anything else in contradiction to what you abjured or swore or promised, whatever the time you came before us, thus revealing your fictitious confession [and your deceit] in manifesting repentance we hold you guilty thenceforward as impenitent and bound by worse sins; and, pursuant to the authority we wield, we bind by the chains of excommunication as fautors, receivers, and defenders of heretics all who knowingly either harbor or defend you or in any way lend counsel and aid to your refusal to comply; and we decree that the reconciliation and mercy granted to you can have no further effect, at the same time, in full justice, relinquishing you as a heretic to the secular arm from that moment on.

Letters concerning the performance of penances

In respect of the penances which we give to those who are not to be imprisoned, we issue letters in the following form:

To all faithful Christians who shall inspect the present letter, (so and so), inquisitors, etc. Since (so and so), the bearer sinned by the crime of heretical morbidity, as revealed by his own confession made in proceedings before us, and of his own will returns humbly to the bosom of Holy Church, at the same time abjuring heretical morbidity, and now has been absolved from the chains of excommunication according to the usages of the Church, we decree for him that in detestation of his error he shall wear two crosses, one on the breast and one on the shoulders, yellow in color, two palms in height, two in breadth, each arm three fingers in width. The clothing on which he wears the crosses shall never be yellow in color. As long as he lives he shall attend mass and vespers on Sundays and feast days, as well as a general sermon if one is delivered in the village where he shall follow processions for (so many) years, bearing large branches in his hand, walking between the clergy and the people, in each procession in which he appears displaying himself in such aspect that he reveals to the people that he is doing penance there because of acts he committed against the faith. He shall visit over (so many) years such and such sanctuaries, and in each of these pilgrimages just stated he is required to present our letter, which we wish him to have and carry to the prelate of the church he is visiting, and to bring back to us a letter from him attesting that the pilgrimage was accomplished in proper form. Therefore, dearly beloved, we request that you in no way molest or allow others to molest (so and so), who is carrying our letter and wearing crosses and fulfilling the things we have enjoined for him by reason of the acts stated above which he committed against the faith, when you find him deporting himself in all respects as a Catholic. If, however, you see him behaving otherwise or attempting to do so, you should hold him to be a perjurer and excommunicate and bound by even worse sins. And from that time on we decree that the reconciliation and mercy granted to him can have no further effect, and not only do we, pursuant to the authority we wield, bind him by the chain of excommunication as a heretic, but we do the same, as fautors, receivers, or defenders of heretics, for all who knowingly harbor or defend him or in any other way lend him aid, counsel, or favor.

Form of sentence for release to the secular arm

We condemn by sentences, such as the following, heretics and their believers, having first stated and exposed their crimes and errors and other matters, as is customary in procedures of this kind:

We, the inquisitors aforesaid, having heard and carefully weighed the crimes and defaults of (so and so), named above, and especially those circumstances which ought most significantly to influence us in the work of extirpating heretical morbidity and planting the faith, either by punishment or forgiveness, with the reverend fathers (so and so) associated and acting with us, by definitive sentence adjudge (so and so), named above, to be a heretic, because he believed in the errors of heretics and is proved still to believe them and because, when examined or when convicted and confessing, he flatly refused to be recalled and to give full obedience to the mandates of the Church. We relinquish him now to secular judgment and, by the authority which we wield, we not only condemn him as a heretic but also we bind with the chain of excommunication as fautors, receivers, and defenders of heretics all persons who knowingly henceforth either harbor or defend him or lend him counsel, aid, or favor.

Form of sentence for those who died as heretics

Likewise, we condemn deceased heretics and believers, having set forth their errors, crimes, and other matters in this way:

We, inquisitors, etc., having seen and carefully reviewed and considered the sins and defaults of (so and so), named above, and the defense offered in his behalf, and the circumstances which must be taken into account and evaluated in respect of the persons and the words of the witnesses, and other matters, with (so and so) associated and acting with us, adjudge (so and so) by definitive verdict to have died as a heretic and, condemning him and his memory with equal severity, we decree that his bones be exhumed from the cemetery, if they can be distinguished from others, and burned in detestation of so heinous an offense.

We issue and impose the condemnations and sentences here described solemnly and deliberately before a convocation of clergy and people, there requiring those on whom we impose the penances described here to abjure and to take an oath, as noted above; and an official record of the condemnations and of the penances of imprisonment is made, attested by our seals and the witness of others who are present.

The substance of letters in respect of the other penances which are imposed is entered in the records.

We do not proceed to the condemnation of anyone without clear and evident proof or without his own confession, nor, God permitting, will we do so. And all the major condemnations and penances which we have issued and do issue, we pronounce with not only the general but also the specific signed counsel of prelates.

We do various other things, indeed, in procedure and in other matters which cannot easily be reduced to writing, holding in all things to the letter of the law or to specific apostolic ordinances. We cause the goods of heretics, the condemned and the imprisoned as well, to be confiscated, and we insist that this be done, as we are duty bound to do. It is in this way that heretics and believers are particularly confounded. And if justice is well done in respect of the condemned and those who relapse, if their property is surely confiscated, and if prisoners are adequately provided with necessities, the Lord will gloriously and wonderfully be made manifest in the fruit of the Inquisition.

41 The *Liber Augustalis*
of Frederick II, 1231

Title I
About Heretics and Patarine

Heretics try to tear the seamless robe of our God. As slaves to the vice of a word that means division, they strive to introduce division into the unity of the indivisible faith and to separate the flock from the care of Peter, the shepherd to whom the Good Shepherd entrusted it. Inside they are violent wolves, but they pretend the tameness of sheep until they can get inside the sheepfold of the Lord. They are the most evil angels. They are sons of depravity from the father of wickedness and the author of evil, who are resolved to deceive simple souls. They are snakes who deceive doves. They are serpents who seem to creep in secretly and, under the sweetness of honey, spew out poison. While they pretend to administer the food of life, they strike from their tails. They mix up a potion of death as a certain very deadly poison. These sects have not been marked by their ancient names lest they stand out in public, or, what is perhaps worse, not content to be called Arians from Arius or Nestorians from Nestorius or something of the like from the same kinds of fellows, they call themselves Patarines like those who have been exposed to suffering, in example of the martyrs who underwent martyrdom for the Catholic faith. Indeed, these miserable Patarines, who do not possess the holy faith of the Eternal Trinity, offend at the same time three persons under one cover of wickedness: God, their neighbors, and themselves. They offend God because they do not know the faith of God, and they do not know his son. They deceive their neighbors insofar as they administer the delights of heretical wickedness to them under the guise of spiritual nourishment. They rage against themselves even more cruelly insofar as, besides risking their souls, these sectaries, lavish of life and improvident with death, also expose their bodies to the enticements of cruel death which they could avoid by true knowledge and the steadfastness of true faith.

From James M. Powell, *The Liber Augustalis* (Syracuse: Syracuse University Press, 1971), pp. 7-10. Reprinted with permission of the publisher.

What is even worse, the survivors are not frightened by the example. We cannot contain our emotions against such men so hostile to God, to themselves, and to mankind. Therefore, we draw the sword of righteous vengeance against them, and we pursue them more urgently insofar as they are known to practice the crimes of their superstition within the Roman Church herself, which is considered the head of all the other churches, to the more evident injury of the Christian faith. Now they divert the little streams of their perfidy from the boundaries of Italy, especially from the region of Lombardy in which we know for certain that their wickedness is widespread, even into our Kingdom of Sicily. Because we consider this so repulsive, we have decided in the first place that the crime of heresy and these condemned sects should be numbered among the public crimes as it was promulgated in the ancient laws wherever there are those judged by their name to be sectaries. Indeed, the crime of treason against us should be adjudged more horrible because it is recognized that someone has attempted injury to the divine majesty, though in the force of judgment one should not exceed the other. For just as the crime of high treason deprives the persons and goods of those condemned and, after their death, condemns even the memory of the dead, we also desire that the same penalty should be observed in the aforesaid crime for which the Patarines are known. In order to expose the wickedness of those who because they do not follow God walk in darkness, even if no one reports it, we desire that the perpetrators of these crimes should be investigated diligently and should be sought after by our officials like other criminals. We order that those who become known by an inquisition, even if they are touched by the evidence of a slight suspicion, should be examined by ecclesiastics and prelates. If they should be found by them to deviate from the Catholic faith in the least wise, and if, after they have been admonished by them in a pastoral way, they should be unwilling to relinquish the insidious darkness of the devil and to recognize the God of Light, but they persist in the constancy of conceived error, we order by the promulgation of our present law that these Patarines should be condemned to suffer the death for which they strive. Committed to the judgment of the flames, they should be burned alive in the sight of the people. We do not grieve that in this we satisfy their desire, from which they obtain punishment alone and no other fruit of their error. No one should presume to intervene with us in behalf of such persons. But if anyone does, we shall turn against him the deserved stings of our indignation.

TITLE II
ABOUT THE SHELTERERS, BELIEVERS, ACCOMPLICES,
AND SUPPORTERS OF PATARINES

We order that the shelterers, believers, accomplices of Patarines, and those who support them in any way at all, who give no heed to fear for themselves so that they can protect others from punishment, should be sent into perpetual exile and all their goods confiscated. Their sons should not be presented for any honors but should labor under the disgrace of perpetual infamy. They should not be admitted at all as witnesses in cases from which the infamous are barred. However, if one of the sons of those who shelter or support Patarines exposes someone whose perfidy is proved openly, he will obtain as a reward of the faith he has acknowledged the benefit of full restitution of his original reputation from the imperial clemency.

42 The *Schwabenspiegel:* Concerning Heretics, 1235

Where persons are believed to be heretics, they shall be accused before the spiritual court, for they should in the first place be tried by ecclesiastics. When they are convicted they shall be taken in hand by the secular court, which shall sentence them as is right; that is to say, they shall be burned at the stake. If, however, the judge protects them, or makes any illegal concessions and does not sentence them, he shall be excommunicated, and that in the most severe form. This shall be done by a bishop. The delinquent judge shall, moreover, be judged by his superior temporal judge, if he have one, as he himself should have judged the heretic. In case a feudal prince does not bring heretics to judgment, but protects them, the ecclesiastical court shall excommunicate him. If such prince does not yield within the space of a year, his bishop, who excommunicated him, shall report his evil deeds to the pope and the length of time he has remained excommunicated for the same. Then shall he [the pope] with propriety deprive him of his princely office and of all his dignities. The pope shall bring his sentence to the notice of his king and his other judges. These shall substantiate the sentence of the pope with their sentence. The offender shall be deprived of all his goods, his fiefs and all his worldly honors. Thus shall lords and poor men be judged. The fitness of this is thus shown.

There was once a pope at Rome called Zacharias. In his time there was a king of France called Lescandus who protected the heretics unlawfully. He was king before King Pippin, King Charles's father. Him the pope deposed from his kingship and from all his honors, and Pippin became king in his stead during his natural life. We read, too, that Pope Innocent deposed King Otto of the Roman Empire on account of his ill deeds. This the popes have a right to do, as God spake to Jeremiah, saying, "I have set thee over all the nations and over all the kingdoms to judge."

43   Thirteenth-Century French Royal Legislation Against Heretics

A.

Moreover, since the keys of the Church are often despised in that country [Languedoc], we command that excommunicated persons shall be avoided according to the canonical provisions, and that if any one shall contumaciously remain in a state of excommunication for a year, he shall be forced by material means to return to the unity of the Church, in order that those who are not induced to leave their evil way by the law of God, may be brought back by temporal penalties. We therefore order that our bailiffs shall, after one year, seize all the property, both real and personal, of all such excommunicated persons. And on no account shall such property be in any way returned to such persons until they have been absolved and have rendered satisfaction to the Church, and then only by our special order.

B.

If any one be suspected of heresy, the magistrate shall lay hold of him and send him before the bishop. If he be convicted, he shall be burned, and all his personal property shall revert to his lord.

C.

We, °°°°, a Seneschal and a *Vicarius* of Toulouse, and, °°°°, a judge in ordinary (and so with other officials then present) swear by these holy gospels of God, that we will hold to the faith of our Lord Jesus Christ and the Holy Roman Church, and will cause it to be held, and will defend it with all our power against every one. We will likewise pursue, and take, and cause to be taken, wherever we can, all heretics with their adherents, aiders, abettors, helpers, and defenders, as well as all fugitives on account of heresy. These aforesaid, if we know where they are to be found, or where any one of them is to be found, we will accuse and denounce to the Church and to the inquisitors. Moreover, we swear that we will not commit any bailliage, judicature, administrative or other public office, to any one of the pestiferous persons, nor will we permit any one to use or hold any public office who is suspected or defamed for heresy, or any one sentenced for the crime of heresy or otherwise precluded by the inquisitors, or by law, from holding a public office. We will not receive anything from the aforesaid, nor have them in our family, or society, or service, or knowingly take council with them. If the contrary should result from ignorance, we will expel the aforesaid straightway, so soon as the matter shall be brought to our notice by the inquisitors of heresy, or others worthy of faith. In these things, and in all others which relate to the office of the inquisition for heresy, we will be obedient to God, the Roman Church, and the inquisitors of this same heresy. So help us God and these, his holy gospels.

From James M. Powell, *The Liber Augustalis* (Syracuse: Syracuse University Press), pp. 7-10. Reprinted with permission of the publisher.

44 The English Statute
De haeretico comburendo, 1401

Whereas it is showed to our sovereign lord the king on behalf of the prelates and clergy of his realm of England in this present Parliament, that although the Catholic faith, founded upon Christ, and by his apostles and the Holy Church sufficiently determined, declared, and approved, has been hitherto by good and holy and most noble progenitors of our sovereign lord the king in the said realm, amongst all the realms of the world, most devoutly observed, and the English Church by his said most noble progenitors and ancestors, to the honor of God and of the whole realm aforesaid, laudably endowed, and in her rights and liberties sustained, without that the same faith or the said Church was hurt or grievously oppressed, or else disturbed by any perverse doctrine or wicked, heretical, or erroneous opinions:

Yet nevertheless divers false and perverse people of a certain new sect, damnably thinking of the faith of the sacraments of the Church and the authority of the same, and, against the law of God and of the Church, usurping the office of preaching, do perversely and maliciously, in divers places within the said realm, under the color of dissembled holiness, preach and teach in these days, openly and privily, divers new doctrines and wicked, heretical, and erroneous opinions, contrary to the same faith and blessed determinations of the Holy Church.

And of such sect and wicked doctrine and opinions, they make unlawful conventicles and confederacies, they hold and exercise schools, they make and write books, they do wickedly instruct and inform people, and, as much as they may, excite and stir them to sedition and insurrection, and make great strife and division among the people, and do daily perpetrate and commit other enormities horrible to be heard, in subversion of the said Catholic faith and doctrine of the Holy Church, in diminution of God's honor, and also in destruction of the estate, rights, and liberties of the said English Church; by which sect and wicked and false preachings, doctrines, and opinions of the said false and perverse people, not only the greatest peril of souls, but also many more other hurts, slanders, and perils, which God forbid, might come to this realm, unless it be the more plentifully and speedily helped by the king's majesty in this behalf, namely:

Whereas the diocesans of the said realm cannot by their jurisdiction spiritual, without aid of the said royal majesty, sufficiently correct the said false and perverse people, nor refrain their malice, because the said false and perverse people go from diocese to diocese, and will not appear before the said diocesans, but the same diocesans and their jurisdiction spiritual, and the keys of the church, with the censures of the same, do utterly disregard and despise, and so they continue and exercise their wicked preachings and doctrines, from day to day, to the utter destruction of all order and rule of right and reason.

Upon which novelties and excesses above rehearsed, the prelates and clergy aforesaid, and also the Commons of the said realm being in the same Parliament, have prayed our sovereign lord the king, that his royal highness would vouchsafe in the said Parliament to provide a convenient remedy: the same our sovereign lord the king—graciously considering the premises, and also the laudable steps of his said most noble progenitors and ancestors, for the conservation of the said Catholic faith, and sustentation of God's honor, and also the safeguard of the estate, rights, and liberties of the said English Church, to the praise of God, and merit of our said sovereign lord the king, and prosperity and honor of all his said realm, and for the eschewing of such dissensions, divisions, hurts, slanders, and perils, in time to come, and that this wicked sect, preachings, doctrines, and opinions should from henceforth cease and be utterly destroyed—by the assent of the estates and other discreet men of the realm, being in the said Parliament, has granted, stablished, and ordained from henceforth firmly to be observed: That none within the said realm, or any other dominions subject to his royal majesty presume to preach, openly or privily, without the license of the diocesan of the same place first required and obtained—curates in their own churches, and persons hitherto privileged, and others of the canon law granted, only except. And that none, from henceforth, preach, hold, teach, or instruct anything, openly or privily, or make or write any book contrary to the Catholic faith or determination of the Holy Church, nor that any of such sect and wicked doctrines and opinions shall make any conventicles, or in any wise hold or exercise schools. And also that none from henceforth in any wise favor such preacher, or maker of any such and the like conventicles, or holding or exercising schools, or making or writing such books, or so teaching, informing, or exciting the people, nor them, nor any of them, maintain or in any wise sustain.

And that all and singular having such books or any writings of such wicked doctrine and opinions, shall really, with effect, deliver, or cause to be delivered, all such books and writings to the diocesan of the same place within forty days from the time of the proclamation of this ordinance and statute. And if any person or persons, of whatsoever kind, estate, or condition he or they be, from henceforth do or attempt against the royal ordinance and statute aforesaid, in the premises or in any of them, or such books, in form aforesaid, do not deliver, then the diocesan of the same place, in his diocese, such person or persons, in this behalf defamed or evidently suspected, and every of them, may, by the authority of the said ordinance and statute, cause to be arrested, and under safe custody in his prisons to be detained, till he or they, of the articles laid to him or them in this behalf, canonically purge him or themselves, or else such wicked sect, preachings, doctrines, and heretical and erroneous opinions abjure, according as the laws of the Church do require; so that the said diocesan, by himself or his commissaries, do openly and judicially proceed against such persons so arrested and remaining under his safe custody to all effect of the law, and determine that same business, according to the canonical decrees, within three months after the said arrest, any lawful impediment ceasing.

And if any person, in any case above expressed, be, before the diocesan of the place, or his commissaries, canonically convicted, then the same diocesan may cause to be kept in his prison the said person so convicted according to the manner of his default, and after the quality of the offense, according and as long as to his discretion shall seem expedient, and moreover put the same person to pay a pecuniary fine to the lord the king, except in cases where he, according to the canonical decree, ought to be left to the secular court, according as the same fine shall seem competent to the diocesan, for the manner and quality of the offense, in which case the same diocesan shall be bound to certify the king of the same fine in his exchequer by his letters patent sealed with his seal to the effect that such fine, by the king's authority, may be required and levied to his use of the goods of the same person so convicted.

And if any person within the said realm and dominions, upon the said wicked preachings, doctrines, opinions, schools, and heretical and erroneous informations, or any of them, be, before the diocesan of the same place, or his commissaries, convicted by sentence, and the same wicked sect, preachings, doctrines and opinions, schools and informations, do refuse duly to abjure, or by the diocesan of the same place, or his commissaries, after abjuration made by the same person, be pronounced relapsed, so that according to the holy canons he ought to be left to the secular court, whereupon credence shall be given to the diocesan of the same place, or to his commissaries in this behalf—then the sheriff of the county of the same place, and the mayor and sheriff or sheriffs, or mayor and bailiffs of the city, town, or borough of the same county nearest to the same diocesan or the said commissaries, shall be personally present in preferring of such sentences, when they, by the same diocesan or his commissaries, shall be required: and they shall receive the same persons and every of them, after such sentence promulgated, and them, before the people, in a high place [*eminenti*] cause to be burnt, that such punishment may strike fear to the minds of others, whereby no such wicked doctrine and heretical and erroneous opinions, nor their authors and favorers in the said realm and dominions, against the Catholic faith, Christian law, and determination of the Holy Church be sustained (which God forbid), or in any wise suffered. In which all and singular the premises concerning the said ordinance and statute, the sheriffs, mayors, and bailiffs of the said counties, cities, boroughs, and towns shall be attending, aiding, and supporting, to the said diocesan and his commissaries.

VII
INTELLECTUAL POSITIONS CONDEMNED IN THE THIRTEENTH AND FOURTEENTH CENTURIES

The monastic heresies of the ninth century—Adoptionism (above, no. 8), Gottschalk's concern with predestination, and others—and such cases as that of Berengar of Tours in the eleventh century and Peter Abelard in the early twelfth (above, nos. 13-14) were the result of disputes at the most learned and least popular levels of society. Even the well-known case of Abelard had few popular followers. From the age of Abelard on, however, several movements brought intellectual heresy into greater prominence. First, the rapid growth of the schools and the foundation of universities in the late twelfth and early thirteenth centuries widened the scope of intellectual debate by qualifying more people to participate in it. Second, the science of theology was greatly influenced, by the discipline of logic, and by the infusion of Arabic and Greek thought after the middle of the twelfth century. Third, the very medium of teaching and study raised the question of secret teaching and study, one that was raised in Abelard's case and echoed down through the thirteenth century. Fourth, a number of older works that appeared increasingly to be of doubtful orthodoxy circulated in greater numbers in the late twelfth century. One of these was the work of John the Scot, a ninth-century philosopher whose reputation grew in the late twelfth and early thirteenth centuries. Finally, there was the general resistance to the new universities on the part of the monastic institutions and some prelates, and the ensuing criticism of university learning. The charge of wasting time on frivolous study is not new in the twentieth century.

Among the most important centers of university and intellectual life was the University of Paris, "the mother of the sciences," as Pope Gregory IX called it, and the most prominent center of theological studies in Europe. It is not surprising that so many of the following documents illustrate Parisian statements and problems, for the theology faculty of Paris became immensely influential during the thirteenth century, and its statements weighed heavily with popes and kings alike. One of the earliest encounters of Paris theologians with heretics in the rarefied atmosphere of university life was the case of the disciples of Amalric of Bene. Amalric's reading of John the Scot and others led him to a doctrine of modified pantheism, and some of his less mentally adept followers produced a debasement of his doctrine in the early years of the thirteenth century. The leader and the doctrine were condemned in 1210, and they are described in Caesarius of Heisterbach's *Dialogue on Miracles*, written around 1235.

Amalric of Bene was not the only scholar condemned in 1210. Joachim of Flora, a Calabrian Cistercian abbot whose commentaries on the Apocalypse were regarded as erroneous, had his writings condemned in that year, although posthumously, and David of Dinant, another pantheist, was also condemned in the same year. Condemnation in the university circle, however, did not at first mean quite the same thing as condemnation in a spiritual or temporal court. Frequently the epithet "heretic" was hurled by one academic critic at a colleague, and the disputes between representatives of the New Orders and the older faculty of universities produced some extremely heated disputes. In spite of the acrimony and charges of heresy that often surrounded these exchanges, the masters of the universities were generally strong enough corporately to withstand outside interference, whether from bishops or inquisitors, most of the time.

Occasionally, however, the pull of one heterodox doctrine or another proved too great, and the university itself acted to condemn the teaching or reading of certain books. The most striking instance of this is the condemnation of the reading of Aristotle's works on natural philosophy early in 1210 and again in 1277. Throughout the thirteenth century, the University of Paris issued several lists of condemned propositions. In 1240 it condemned a list of "errors" drawn from various propositions concerning the afterlife, Trinitarianism, and predestination. In 1270 a list of propositions condemned by Stephen Tempier, bishop of Paris (no. 45) included the first signs of Averroism, the doctrine of the great

Arabic commentator on Aristotle that the human intellect is single and collective. A document of 1272 (no. 46) illustrates the concerns of the university on the eve of the great condemnations of 1277 (no. 47).

Latin Averroism did not end with the condemnation of 1270, and the mingling of Aristotelianism with theology, especially over questions on the collective intellect and the eternity (uncreatedness) of the universe lasted into the fifteenth century. Petrarch, the great humanist of Avignon and Florence, depicted an encounter with an Averroist around the middle of the fourteenth century (no. 49).

Besides the problems arising from the Aristotelianism of Arabic commentators and enthusiastic Latin scholars, other dissenting intellectual movements also troubled the late thirteenth- and fourteenth-century world. Political philosophy, too, borrowed from Aristotle, and some writers used it to attack the authority of the pope and clergy. Like most intellectuals, fourteenth-century thinkers were reluctant to bow their heads before men whom they considered their intellectual inferiors, and sometimes, as in the case of the political philosophers Marsiglio of Padua and John of Jandun, their propositions dealt chiefly with political problems (no. 48). By the fourteenth century academic protection, although still in place and largely effective, could not save the most outspoken dissidents from active persecution. One result of this new danger in university circles was the increasing intellectual conservatism of universities in the late fourteenth and fifteenth centuries. With the exception of the careers of John Wyclif at Oxford (below, nos. 56-59) and the intellectual and social turmoil at the University of Prague in the late fourteenth century (below, nos. 61-63), universities emerged in the early fifteenth century as bastions against heresy and treated even intellectual dissent among their members very roughly.

LITERATURE

For the period 1200-1500 the best general work is that of Gordon Leff, *Heresy in the Later Middle Ages* (New York, 1967), 2 vols. For the Amalrician condemnation see Wakefield and Evans, *Heresies of the High Middle Ages*, pp. 258-64, and Lambert, *Medieval Heresy*, pp. 101-2. For the Parisian condemnations, see the discussion and bibliography in Gordon Leff, *Paris and Oxford Universities in the Thirteenth and Fourteenth Centuries* (New York, 1968), especially pp. 185-270; Lynn Thorndike, *History of Magic and Experimental Science*, 8 vols. (New York, 1923-58); idem, *University Records and*

Life in the Middle Ages (reprint ed., New York, 1975); Mary Martin McLaughlin, *Intellectual Freedom and Its Limitations in the University of Paris in the Thirteenth and Fourteenth Centuries* (New York, 1977); Etienne Gilson, *A History of Christian Philosophy in the Middle Ages* (New York, 1955), especially chapter 5; John F. Wippel, "The Condemnations of 1270 and 1277 at Paris," *The Journal of Medieval and Renaissance Studies* 7 (1977): 169-202. On Latin Averroism in fourteenth-century Italy, see John Herman Randall, "The Development of Scientific Method in the School of Padua," *Journal of the History of Ideas* (1940); there are other Petrarchan texts on Averroism translated in Ernst Cassirer, Paul Oskar Kristeller, and John Herman Randall, Jr., *The Renaissance Philosophy of Man* (reprint ed., Chicago, 1967), pp. 140-43. For Ockham generally, see Paul Vignaux, *Philosophy in the Middle Ages: An Introduction* (New York, 1959); Gordon Leff, *The Dissolution of the Medieval Outlook* (New York, 1976); idem, *Medieval Thought: St. Augustine to Ockham* (reprint ed., Baltimore, 1962).

45   Errors Condemned at the University of Paris, 1270

Etienne Tempier, bishop of Paris (1268-80) and a former master of theology, condemned thirteen doctrines in 1270 which were all drawn from the work of Aristotle and Averroes and probably taught in the arts faculty. Although these propositions may have been simply topics for debate and academic exposition, they touched upon theological error sufficiently, in the bishop's eyes, to warrant their condemnation. These condemnations evidently failed to take hold, because in 1277 Tempier issued the great condemnation of 219 propositions in much more detailed form, and with direr consequences.

These are the errors condemned and excommunicated with all who taught or asserted them knowingly by Stephen, bishop of Paris, in the year of the Lord 1270, the Wednesday after the feast of the blessed Nicholas in the winter.

From Lynn Thorndike, *University Records and Life in the Middle Ages* (New York: Columbia University Press, 1944), pp. 80-81. Reprinted with the permission of the publisher.

The first article is: That the intellect of all men is one and the same in number.

2. That this is false or inappropriate: Man understands.

3. That the will of man wills or chooses from necessity.

4. That all things which are done here below depend upon the necessity of the celestial bodies.

5. That the world is eternal.

6. That there never was a first man.

7. That the soul, which is the form of man as a human being, is corrupted when the body is corrupted.

8. That the soul separated after death does not suffer from corporal fire.

9. That free will is a passive power, not active; and that it is moved necessarily by appetite.

10. That God does not know things in particular.

11. That God does not know other things than himself.

12. That human actions are not ruled by divine Providence.

13. That God cannot give immortality or incorruptibility to a corruptible or mortal thing.

46   Faith and Philosophy in the Arts Faculty of Paris, 1272

Etienne Tempier's condemnations of 1270 and 1277 were directed against the unrestricted use of Aristotle and Averroes by the arts faculty, and in 1272 that faculty itself issued a statute "against artists treating theological questions and that no one shall dare to determine [argue] against the faith questions which touch the faith as well as philosophy."

To each and all of the sons of Holy Mother Church who now and in the future shall see the present page, the masters of logical science or professors of natural science at Paris, each and all, who hold

From Lynn Thorndike, *University Records and Life in the Middle Ages* (New York: Columbia University Press, 1944), pp. 85-88. Reprinted with the permission of the publisher.

and observe the statute and ordinance of the venerable father Symon by divine permission cardinal priest of the title of St. Cecilia, legate of of the Apostolic See, made after separate deliberation of the nations, and who adhere expressly and entirely to the opinion of the seven judges appointed by the same legate in the same statute, greeting in the Saviour of all. All should know that we masters, each and all, from the preceding abundant and considered advice and deliberation of good men concerning this, wishing with all our power to avoid present and future dangers which by occasion of this sort might in the future befall our faculty, by common consent, no one of us contradicting, on the Friday preceding the Sunday on which is sung "Rejoice Jerusalem," the masters one and all being convoked for this purpose in the church of Ste. Geneviève at Paris, decree and ordain that no master or bachelor of our faculty should presume to determine or even to dispute any purely theological question, as concerning the Trinity and incarnation and similar matters, since this would be transgressing the limits assigned him, for the Philosopher says that it is utterly improper for a nongeometer to dispute with a geometer.

But if anyone shall have so presumed, unless within three days after he has been warned or required by us he shall have been willing to revoke publicly his presumption in the classes or public disputation where he first disputed the said question, henceforth he shall be forever deprived of our society. We decree further and ordain that if anyone shall have disputed at Paris any question which seems to touch both faith, and philosophy, if he shall have determined it contrary to the faith, henceforth he shall forever be deprived of our society as a heretic, unless he shall have been at pains humbly and devoutly to revoke his error and his heresy, within three days after our warning, in full congregation or elsewhere where it shall seem to us expedient. Adding further that, if any master or bachelor of our faculty reads or disputes any difficult passages or any questions which seem to undermine the faith, he shall refute the arguments or text so far as they are against the faith or concede that they are absolutely false and entirely erroneous, and he shall not presume to dispute or lecture further upon this sort of difficulties, either in the text or in authorities, but shall pass over them entirely as erroneous. But if anyone shall be rebellious in this, he shall be punished by a penalty which in the judgment of our faculty suits his fault and is due. Moreover, in order that all these may be inviolably observed, we masters, one and all, have sworn on our personal security in the hand of the rector of our faculty and we all have spontaneously agreed to be so bound. In memory of which we have caused this same statute to be inscribed and so ordered in the register of our faculty in the same words. Moreover, every rector henceforth to be created in the faculty shall swear that he will cause all the bachelors about to incept in our faculty to bind themselves to this same thing, swearing on their personal security in his hand. Given at Paris the year of the Lord 1271, the first day of April.

47 The Condemnation of 219 Propositions at Paris, 1277

On 18 January 1277, Pope John XXI wrote to Stephen Tempier, bishop of Paris, requesting a report from the bishop concerning certain errors of faith which were said to be taught at the university:

> A story we have heard lately has troubled our ears and made bitter our spirit. It states that in Paris, where the living fountain of wisdom and salvation has until now generously bubbled out, bearing along its limpid, clear banks an understandable catholic faith all the way to the ends of the earth, certain errors injurious to that faith are said recently to have arisen again. We wish and command, therefore, that by the present authority vested in you, you diligently make inspection and inquiry concerning by which persons and in which places these errors mentioned above are written, and when you find this out, do not neglect to send the information to us by your messenger.

The bishop did far more than the pope requested. Taking advantage of the long-standing rivalry between the secular masters of theology and the school of Dominicans at Paris, Tempier enlisted the aid of some of the seculars, including the well-known Henry of Ghent, and produced not a report to the pope, but a list of 219 propositions drawn from various sources alleged to be in use among the Dominicans (including the teachings of the theologians Siger of Brabant and Thomas Aquinas), which Tempier condemned on 7 March 1277. In effect, the bishop of Paris and his team of secular masters of theology assembled in about one month a massive attack on Dominican theologians on the grounds that their teachings included the theological errors of Aristotle and Averroes, Aristotle's great Arabic commentator.

Although Tempier's condemnations did not fulfill the pope's request, and although they ran only within Tempier's jurisdiction, the diocese of Paris, they contributed to a new temper at the university, one that grew guarded and moved away from the direction Aquinas had set. Moreover, they influenced other condemnations that followed quickly in England. Eleven days after Tempier's condemnations were published, Robert Kilwardby, a Dominican enemy of Aquinas, published a shorter list modeled on Tempier's that ran within the archdiocese of Canterbury, of which Kilwardby was archbishop, and included Oxford University. Although the English list contained only thirty propositions, they drew more directly on positions attributed to Aquinas. Kilwardby's successor, the Franciscan John Peckham, reissued the condemnations in 1284 and 1286. Thus, within nine years, the position of Aquinas was attacked several times at the two most influential centers of the study of theology and philosophy in western Europe.

The text of Kilwardby's condemnations may be found in H. Denifle and A. Chatelain, eds., *Chartularium Universitatis Parisiensis* (Paris, 1889), 1:558-59. The condemnations of Tempier, translated in part here, are from the same volume, pp. 543-58. In his long study of the philosopher Siger of Brabant, Pierre Mandonnet also edited the 219 propositions (Pierre Mandonnet, *Siger de Brabant et l'averroïsme latin au XIIIe siècle* (Louvain, 1908), 2:175-91. The differences between the two editions are worth noting. Denifle and Chatelain printed the list of errors in the order in which they appear in the manuscript, which is haphazard, inconsistent, and shows obvious signs of haste. Mandonnet printed the propositions in a different order, grouping them into coherent categories, and producing an analytical text that is easier for the modern reader to follow but misleading in its appearance of orderliness and consistency. The selection given here is a translation of part of the Denifle-Chatelain list in the original sequence, prefaced by a short discussion of Mandonnet's list.

Mandonnet's list, in outline, considers the categories of errors analytically:

I. Errors in Philosophy (1-179)
   On the Nature of Philosophy (1-7)
   On the Knowability of God (8-10)
   On the Nature of God (11-12)
   On Divine Wisdom (13-15)
   On Divine Will and Power (16-26)
   On the Causation of the World (27-32)
   On the Nature of the Intelligences (33-55)

A complete English translation according to Mandonnet's order and categories may be found in Ralph Lerner and Muhsin Mahdi, eds., *Medieval Political Philosophy: A Sourcebook* (New York, 1963), pp. 335-54, and in J. Katz and R. Weingartner, eds., *Philosophy in the West* (New York, 1965), pp. 532-42.

In the following selections, numbers in brackets following the translations refer to the Mandonnet arrangement. The condemnations begin with a letter from Tempier describing the dangers of erroneous doctrines. At the end of the letter, Tempier lists several other works that he condemns, including the popular *Art of Courtly Love*, written by Andreas Capellanus late in the twelfth century, and certain books of magic and necromancy. For Andreas, see John J. Parry, trans., *The Art of Courtly Love*, by Andreas Capellanus (reprint ed., New York, 1969) and A. J. Denomy, "The *De Amore* of Andreas Capellanus and the Condemnation of 1277," *Medieval Studies* 8 (1946):107-49. For the importance of the condemnation of the magic books, see my own work, *The Magician, the Witch, and the Law* (Philadelphia, 1978), chap. 4.

Stephen, by divine favor the unworthy servant of the church of Paris, sends greetings in the name of the son of the glorious Virgin to all who read this letter. Reports from great and serious persons, moved by zeal for the faith, state that some students in the arts at Paris, exceeding the proper boundaries of their disciplines, presume to treat in the schools and dispute certain manifest and execrable errors, or rather certain vanities and false madness which are listed in the roll attached to this letter. They do not listen to the saying of [Pope]

Gregory [I, (590-604)]: "Let him who wishes to speak wisely exercise great care, so that by his speech he does not disrupt the unity of those who hear him," especially when they take the above errors from the writings of pagans, which—for shame!—through their inexperience they say are so pertinent that the students do not know how to respond to them. So that they do not appear to assert [directly] that which they insinuate, they conceal their answers, and, wishing to avoid Scylla, they fall into Charybdis. They say that these things are true according to philosophy, but not according to the Catholic faith, as if there [could be] two contrary truths, and as if against the truth of sacred scripture there [might be] another truth in the words of pagans who have been damned, [pagans] of whom it is written: "I condemn the wisdom of the wise," since true wisdom condemns false wisdom. Such [students] should listen to the advice of the wise man, when he says: "If you are wise, respond to your neighbor['s questions]; but if [you are not wise], put your hand over your mouth, lest you be caught [uttering] an unlearned word, and confounded." So that such unguarded speech does not lead the ignorant into error, we, having taken the advice of doctors of sacred scripture, as well as other prudent men, strictly prohibit these things and others like them, and we utterly condemn them, excommunicating all those who dogmatize these errors or any of them [individually], or who defend them, or presume to uphold them in any way whatsoever, as well as those who listen to them, unless within seven days they reveal themselves to us personally or to the chancellor of Paris. We shall also proceed against them according to the character of their guilt by other punishments, as the law dictates.

By the same sentence, we also condemn the book *De Amore* [*The Art of Courtly Love*], or *The God of Love*, which begins with the words: "I am greatly impelled," and which ends with the words: "Beware, therefore, Walter, of practicing the commands of love . . . etc."; the book of Geomancy which begins with the words: "The Indians think . . ." and ends with the words: "You will find, therefore, that to think about these things . . ."; and also books, rolls, and necromantical booklets, whether these contain experiments of sorcery, methods of invoking the demons, or conjurations that put the soul in peril, or those which treat in these ways or others orthodox faith and good morals in a plainly adversary fashion. We excommunicate all those who teach and hear things from those books, rolls, or booklets, unless within seven days they come before us or before the chancellor of Paris in the manner specified above, and in addition we will inflict other penalties as the occasion requires.

Given in the year of our Lord one thousand two hundred seventy-six, on the Sunday on which *Laetare Jerusalem* is chanted at the court of Paris.

Here ends the letter. There follow the errors noted in the roll.

1. That God is not three and one because trinity is not in accord with the highest simplicity. Where there is indeed real plurality, there is necessarily addition and composition. An example of this is a pile of stones. [185]

2. That God is not able to generate things like Himself because anything that is generated has a beginning based on something else, from which it depends. And for God to generate would not be a sign of perfection. [186]

3. That God does not know things other than himself. [13]

4. That nothing can be eternal in terms of the end to which it is directed if it is not eternal in terms of its beginning. [87]

5. That all things that are separated are coeternal with the first principle. [39]

6. That when all the heavenly bodies return to the same point, which is in thirty-six thousand years, the same effects as now will return. [92]

7. That the intellect is not the form of the body, except in the same sense as the navigator is the form of the ship, and that it is not an essential perfection of man. [123]

[One can see from Mandonnet's rearrangement of just the first seven of Tempier's condemned errors that the list must have been compiled in haste, without an effort to classify the propositions according to any principle of organization.]

16. That one should not worry about the faith if something is said to be heretical because it is against the faith. [201]

21. That nothing occurs by chance, but instead everything comes from necessity, and that everything that occurs in the future will come from necessity. That which will not occur is impossible. Nothing occurs contingently if all causes are considered.—This is an error because the concurrence of causes is part of the definition of chance, as Boethius says in *The Consolation of Philosophy*. [102]

31. That the human intellect is eternal, since it comes from a cause that is always the same, and since it is not material, by means of which it exists in potency before it exists in act. [130]

32. That the [human] intellect is one [and the same] for all men, since although it may be separated from a particular [human] body, it cannot be separated from humanity collectively. [117]

33. That raptures and visions do not occur, unless in nature. [177]

34. That the first cause cannot create a plurality of worlds. [27]

36. That we may know God in essence while in this mortal life. [9]

40. That there is no more excellent condition than that of being a philosopher. [1]

42. That the first cause does not have knowledge of future contingencies. The first reason is that future contingencies are not beings. The second is that future contingencies are particulars. God, however, knows [only] by means of an intellectual power which cannot know particulars. Whence, if there were not [also] senses, the intellect might not be able to distinguish between Socrates and Plato, although it could distinguish a man from a jackass. The third reason is the relation of causes to effects; divine foreknowledge is the necessary cause of those things which are foreknown. The fourth reason is the relation of knowledge to things known; for although knowledge is not the cause of that which is known, it is confined to one or another part of contradiction by that which is known, and this is much more true of divine knowledge than of ours. [15]

48. That God cannot be the cause of new creation, nor can he be the cause of anything new. [22]

56. That God may not know contingencies immediately, unless by their particular and proximate causes. [14]

66. That there are many first movers. [99]

72. That separate substances, since they are not material, by which they would first exist in potency rather than in action, and since they are from a cause that always exists in the same way, are therefore eternal. [41]

80. That everything that is not composed of material is eternal, since, because it is not made by the transmutation of material, it could not have existed previously; therefore, it is eternal. [40]

87. That the world is eternal in regard to all the species contained in it, and that time is eternal, as are motion, material, agent, and recipient. And because these derive from the infinite power of God, it is impossible that there can be something new in the effect without there being something new in the cause. [85]

91. That the reason of [Aristotle] proving that the movement of the heavens is eternal is not [merely] sophistical, and that it is to be wondered at, that wise men do not perceive this. [80]

95. That there are three principles in the heavens; the subject of eternal motion, the spirit of the celestial body, and the first mover as desired.—The error is in regard to the first two [of these]. [31]

96. That God cannot multiply individuals of the same species without matter. [42]

98. That the world is eternal, because that which has a nature by which it is able to exist in the whole future has a nature by which it has been able to exist in the whole past. [84]

99. That the world, although it was made out of nothing, was not made newly, and although it passed from nonbeing to being, nonbeing did not precede being except in nature. [83]

105. That the form of man does not come from something extrinsic, but is educed from the potency of matter, for otherwise generation would not be univocal. [120]

109. That the substance of the soul is eternal, and that acting and possible intelligences are eternal. [129]

111. That no form deriving from something extrinsic may make a single whole with matter, for that which is incorruptible cannot form a whole with that which is corruptible. [121]

116. That the soul is inseparable from the body, and that which tends to corrupt the harmony of the body [must also therefore] corrupt the soul. [133]

140. That to make an accident exist without a subject has the character of an impossibility, implying a contradiction. [196]

147. That what is simply impossible may not be done by God, nor by another agent.—Error, if "impossible" is understood according to nature. [17]

154. That the wise men of this world are the philosophers. [2]

175. That the Christian law impedes learning. [180]

179. That there is no reason to go to confession, except to keep up appearances. [203]

180. That there is no need to pray. [202]

183. That simple fornication, that is, between an unmarried man and an unmarried woman, is not a sin. [205]

184. That creation is not possible, although to hold the opposite [doctrine] accords with faith. [189]

185. That it is not true that something could come from nothing, nor that anything was made at the first creation. [188]

197. That some things may occur by chance in respect to first causes, and that it is false [to say that] everything is ordained by the first cause, since then it would happen by necessity. [93]

211. That the human intellect in its natural character can attain to a knowledge of the first cause.—This sounds very wicked, and it is an error if it pertains to the question of immediate cognition. [8]

215. That nothing can be known about God, except that he is, or that he exists. [10]

218. That an intelligence, whether an angel or a separate soul, is nowhere. [53]

219. That separate substances are nowhere, according to their substance.—Error, if by this is understood that substance is not in any place. If, however, it is to be understood that by substance is meant the reason of being in a place, it is true that they are nowhere according to substance. [54]

This is the end of the roll of errors containing two hundred and ten and nine articles condemned at Paris by Stephen, faithful servant and bishop, in the year of the Lord one thousand two hundred and seventy-six, on the Sunday on which *Laetare Jerusalem* is sung at the court of Paris.

48   The Condemnation of Marsiglio of Padua and John of Jandun, 1327

The comprehensive condemnations of 1270 and 1277 set the tone for later thirteenth- and early fourteenth-century condemnations of other philo-sophical and doctrinal errors. One of the most famous of these occasions was Pope John XXII's condemnation of the doctrines said to be found in the political treatises of two of the most articulate philosophers of the period, Marsiglio of Padua and John of Jandun, opponents of John XXII and supporters of the antipapal emperor Louis of Bavaria.

1. That what we read about Christ in the Gospel of St. Matthew, that he himself paid tribute to Caesar, when he ordered the stater which had been taken from the mouth of the fish [cf. Matt.

From H.J.D. Denzinger, *The Sources of Catholic Dogma*, translated by Roy J. Deferrari (St. Louis: B. Herder, 1965), pp. 194-95.

17:26] to be given to those who sought a drachma, he did this not with condescension out of liberality or piety, but forced by necessity.

[Thence according to the Bull they concluded]:

That all temporal affairs of the Church are subject to the emperor and he can accept these things as his own.

2. That blessed Peter the Apostle had no more authority than the other apostles had nor was he the head of the other apostles. Likewise that God did not send forth any head of the Church, nor did he make anyone his vicar.

3. That it pertains to the emperor to correct, to appoint, to depose, and to punish the pope.

4. That all priests, whether the pope or archbishop or a simple priest, are by the institution of Christ equal in authority and jurisdiction.

5. That the whole Church joined together can punish no man by forced punishment, unless the emperor permits this.

We declare by sentence the above mentioned articles . . . to be *contrary to Sacred Scripture* and *enemies of the Catholic faith, heretics,* or *heretical and erroneous,* and also that the above mentioned Marsilius and John, will be heretics—rather they will be manifest and notorious archheretics.

49   Petrarch: On Some Fourteenth-Century Latin Averroists, 1364

In spite of Tempier's condemnations of 1270 and 1277, Latin Averroism survived and flourished in Italy in the fourteenth century. Francesco Petrarca was one of the most vigorous opponents of Averroism, calling the philosopher Averroes "that frantic dog . . . who is prompted by an undescribable fury to bark at his Lord and Master Jesus Christ and the Catholic faith." The translation here is that of James Harvey Robinson, *The Pre-Reformation Period,* Translations and Reprints from the Original Sources of European History, vol. 3 (Philadelphia, 1902), pp. 17-18.

How are we to deal with another monstrous kind of pedant who wears a religious garb, but is most profane in heart and conduct, he who would have us believe that Ambrose, Augustine, and Jerome were ignoramuses, for all their wordy treatises? I do not know the origin of these new theologians, who do not spare the great teachers and will soon cease to respect the apostles and the gospel itself. They will soon turn their impudent tongues even against Christ, unless He whose cause is at stake interferes to curb the raging beasts. For it has already become a well-established habit with these fellows to express their scorn by a mute gesture or by some impious observation whenever revered names or sacred subjects are mentioned. "Augustine," they will say for example, "saw much, but understood little." Nor do they speak less insultingly of other great men.

Recently one of these philosophers of the modern stamp happened to be in my library. He did not, it is true, wear the habit of a churchman, but, as we know, the real Christian is known by his belief. He was one of those who think that they live in vain unless they are constantly snarling at Christ or his divine teachings. When I cited some passage or other from the holy scriptures, he exploded with wrath, and with his face, naturally ugly, still further disfigured by anger and contempt, he exclaimed, "You are welcome to your two-penny church fathers; as for me, I know the man for me to follow, for 'I know him whom I have believed.' " "But," I replied, "you use the words of the Apostle; would that you would take them to heart!" "Your Apostle," he answered, "was a sower of words and a lunatic." "You reply like a good philosopher," I said. "The first accusation was brought against him by other philosophers and the second to his face, by Festus, governor of Syria. He did indeed sow the word with such success that, cultivated by the beneficent plow of his successors and watered by the holy blood of the martyrs, it has borne such an abundant harvest of faith as all may behold." At this he burst forth into a sickening roar of laughter. "Well, be a good Christian! As for me I put no faith in that stuff. Your Paul and your Augustine and all the rest of the crowd you preach about, were a set of babblers. If you could but digest Averroes you would quickly see how far superior he was to these empty-headed fellows." I was very angry, I must confess, and could scarcely keep from striking his filthy, blasphemous mouth. "It is the old feud between me and the heretics of your class. You may go," I cried, " — you and your heresy, never to return." With this I plucked him by the gown and, with a want of ceremony less in consonance with my habits than his own, hurried him out of the house.

There are thousands of instances of this kind where nothing will prevail—neither the majesty of the Christian name, nor the reverence for Christ himself, whom the angels fall down and worship, though weak and depraved mortals may insult him; not even the fear of punishment or the armed inquisitors of heresy. Prison and stake are alike impotent to restrain the impudence of ignorance and the audacity of heresy.

Such are the times, my friend, upon which we have fallen; such is the period in which we live and are already growing old. Such are the judges against whom I have so often inveighed, who are innocent of knowledge or virtue, and yet harbor the most exalted opinion of themselves. Not content with losing the works of the ancients, they must attack their ability and their ashes. They rejoice in their ignorance, as if what they did not know were not worth knowing. They give full reign to their unlicensed and conceited spirits and freely introduce among us new authors and outlandish teachings.

VIII
THE SPIRITUAL
FRANCISCANS AND
VOLUNTARY POVERTY

The devotional movements of the early thirteenth century are particularly striking in their variety and in their tendency to exist always on the margins of ecclesiastical approval. Some dissenting groups remained outside the pale of orthodoxy, while others—the *Humiliati* for instance—managed to stay just inside the boundaries the legitimacy, at least as those boundaries were defined by ecclesiastical authorities. One of the most distinctive features of the thirteenth and fourteenth centuries, as the last chapter may have suggested, is the increasingly systematic character of ecclesiastical authority, which was not always careful in defining the difference between the varieties of search for an authentic spiritual life and the point at which that search either became heterodox or disobedient. Often it was the changing definitions of ecclesiastical authorities, rather than the changing character or beliefs of religious groups, that moved the boundary between legitimate membership in the Church and heterodox belief. Perhaps the most dramatic episode in thirteenth- and fourteenth-century Church history in this respect was the growth and persecution of the Spiritual Franciscan movement, the subject of this chapter. But to see that movement in a clearer light, it is necessary to examine briefly other devotional movements of the thirteenth and fourteenth centuries that encountered similar, if less drastic, resistance from authority.

One of the most vigorous movements of the search for apostolic life in the twelfth century was that of lay women who began, in Flanders and France, to establish religious communities belonging to no order and to live there collectively, earning their livings by labor. There were several of these groups, one of the most notable of which congregated around Mary of Oignies at Liège early in the thirteenth century. Jacques de Vitry, the great preacher and historian, became an advocate of such groups as Mary's, and praised them and circulated his praises widely:

> For you have seen and rejoiced, in the lily gardens of the Lord, many bands of holy virgins in different places who, spurning carnal pleasures for the sake of Christ and condemning the riches of the world for desire of the Kingdom of Heaven, cleave to the heavenly bridegroom in poverty and humility and seek their slender fare by the work of their hands, although their families have abundance.

The Beguines' renunciation of family wealth and marriage, their active laboring to support themselves, and the devotional strength of their communities attracted the praise of others besides Jacques de Vitry in the late twelfth and early thirteenth centuries. Primarily an urban phenomenon, the Beguines,

> who are unable to find monasteries which will receive them, live together in a single house . . . under the discipline of one who excels the others in integrity and foresight. They are instructed in manners and letters, in vigils and prayers, in fasts and various torments, in manual work and poverty, in self-effacement and humility. . . . [They] live in profound poverty, having naught else but what they can acquire by spinning and working with their hands, content with shabby clothes and modest food.

The independence of the Beguines and the general ecclesiastical concern over varieties of individual devotion and their propensity to turn into heresy generated objections to their way of life among both clergy and laity. Even Jacques de Vitry had to defend them against some of these accusations early in the thirteenth century. Later in the century they suffered from some of the opprobrium that had begun to attach to the Mendicant Orders, being denounced as hypocrites and secret sinners. In fact, in Provence, members of the spiritualist movement in the Franciscan Order were called Beguins. They fell under stricter censures for their lack of affiliation with any recognized order. The Council of Vienne in 1312 issued stringent criticisms of such ways of life, and the decretal *Cum de quibusdam mulieribus* banned their activities outright, although it left an escape clause that many Beguines and female members of the Franciscan Order took advantage of. The decretal caused considerable disruption in the Beguines' religious communities. One of the best examples of invective against Beguines is contained in the biography of the German mystic Ruysbroeck in an account of the doctrines of a Beguine named "Bloemardinne" of Brussels. Throughout the fourteenth and fifteenth centuries, pious communal groups of laypeople were the targets of frequent ecclesiastical and lay criticism. And charges of heresy were consistently brought against them.

In addition, fourteenth-century inquisitors, misunderstanding the language of mystical devotion that some Beguines used, believed that the Beguines and others were devotees of a "Heresy of the Free Spirit," which promulgated heretical doctrines about union with God, and lived licentiously, believing themselves exempt from all laws. Robert Lerner has shown conclusively that there existed no such widespread heresy or group, but the name of the "Heresy of the Free Spirit" remained attached to several groups, especially Beguines, for a long time and complicated their and others' efforts to find a viable form of Christian life in the face of widespread suspicion and hostility.

For the Beguines, religious life outside of the recognized orders proved to be very difficult. But in the fouteenth century, religious life inside the Franciscan Order proved even more violently troubled. The controversy over the Spiritual Franciscans dominated the turn of the thirteenth and fourteenth centuries and lasted into the fifteenth, touching most corners of Europe. St. Francis himself and his first companions had lived a life of strict poverty, modeling their lives after those of Christ and the apostles. Francis left strict but characteristically vague injunctions in both his Rule for the order and his will, prohibiting the ownership of any form of property. After St. Francis died in 1226, the question of the constitution of the order remained in doubt. Pope Honorius III had issued a papally approved Rule for the order in 1223, but in 1230 Pope Gregory IX issued the decretal *Quo elongati*, which institutionalized and modified Franciscan poverty and explained vague provisions in the Rule and the saint's last instructions. Gregory's constitution for the order permitted *usus moderatus* (moderate use) of goods, but not *dominium* or *proprietas* (outright ownership). The decretal also recognized certain classes of helpers called *custodes* or *nuntii*, who would manage property and affairs for the order so that the saint's intentions and the order's needs would both be met.

Several strands of thirteenth-century thought and emotion troubled the order particularly. Some friars felt that as the order grew and undertook more work in Christian society some of the earlier strictures ought to be relaxed for the sake of increased efficiency. This view met opposition from other friars, who insisted on a rigorous interpretation of poverty, or the *usus pauper*. This conflict was exacerbated by the order's struggle with the secular clergy and by the introduction of new forms of thought, but it was kept within bounds by the long and energetic leadership of St. Bonaventure, minister-general of the order from 1257 to 1274. After Bonaventure's death, a crisis in the leadership of the order permitted stronger tensions to develop and hostilities inside and outside the order to flourish virtually unchecked. Among St. Bonaventure's many works was his *Apologia pauperum* (The Defense of the Mendicants), which sharply distinguished between *dominium* and *usus* (no. 50) and influenced the legislation of Pope Nicholas III, whose decretal *Exiit qui seminat* of 1279 incorporated most of Bonaventure's views, insisted on moderate use of goods, and permitted the friars the wherewithal for study as well as the necessities for life. In addition to these developing views of the order's constitution and the problem of *usus pauper*, other strains of thought also entered the order and later became linked to the problem of apostolic poverty. The most significant of these was Joachimism, the development of the beliefs of Joachim of Flora, Calabrian Cistercian abbot who had died in 1198. Some of Joachim's views were condemned at the Fourth Lateran Council in 1215, but his immensely influential views on the nature of history and prophecy found willing listeners, particularly within the Franciscan order. In 1254 Gerardo da Borgo San Donnino published a work in which he identified the Franciscans with Joachim's prophesied new age of the Holy Spirit, bringing down upon himself considerable opposition from inside and outside the order. The Joachite strain in Franciscan thought touched many thinkers, and its apocalyptic tone appealed to those friars who felt that what they called "the carnal Church" was opposing the true spirituality of St. Francis and his genuine followers. Although it is improper to speak of hard and firm parties in the order in the late thirteenth century, several groups and individuals stand out as indicating a movement which drew certain doctrines of poverty and certain Joachite ideas together.

In Provence, the names of Hugues de Digne and later Peter Olivi stand out as expert theologians strongly concerned with the spiritual life of the order and strains of Joachite thought. After a long career of persecution, Olivi ended his life in 1298, after publishing his *Commentary on the Apocalypse*, a powerful, learned, and strongly Joachite work. In Tuscany, many friars grouped themselves around Ubertino da Casale, a gifted writer and polemicist, who was an acute observer of Franciscan faults (no. 51). Perhaps the most vehement segment of the order were the brothers of the Marches, led by Conrad of Offida and later Angelo da Clareno, whose *History of the Seven Tribulations* provided a retrospective view of the thirteenth century to justify the four-teenth-century spiritual wing of the order. From 1289 to 1294 under the leadership of Raymond Gauffridi and the brief papacy of Celestine V, the spiritual groups within the order appeared to prosper, and the divisions between them and the modernizers, later called the Conventuals, grew wider. From 1294 on, however, the internal affairs of the order were the primary concerns of the minister-general Michael of Cesena and several popes, most importantly, of John XXII (1316-34). Under pressure from both the minister-general and the pope, the groups of Spirituals (the name by which the defenders of strict apostolic poverty were known) were pressured to stop criticizing the modified doctrine of *usus pauper* and obey the orders of their superiors. In 1318 four friars at Avignon were burnt as heretics on the ground that to refuse to obey a papal order was *ipso facto* heretical. As superior forces moved to restrict criticism within the order, the Spirituals—Zelanti, or Fraticelli, as some of them were later called—grew more antagonistic.

In 1321 the dispute was carried further when a friar at Narbonne preached that Christ and the apostles had possessed nothing and that the Spirituals were simply following Christ's example and the *apostolica vita* by opposing any relaxation of St. Francis's original intentions. Pope John XXII countered with three remarkable decretals. The decretal *Gloriosam ecclesiam* of 1318 (no. 52) defined the theological errors of the Fraticelli, and stated that their direct attacks on the legitimacy of ecclesiastical authority were themselves heretical. *Quia nonumquam* of 1322 modified the regulations of *Exiit qui seminat* and other earlier papal decretals ordering the moderate *usus pauper*, while at the same time enunciating the principle that it was licit for one pope to alter decrees made by his predecessors, a step that generated in its turn the Spirituals' doctrines of papal infallibility—to protect themselves from just such changes. In 1323 the decretal *Cum inter nonullas* (no. 53) declared heretical the view that Christ and the apostles had no property. The force of John XXII's opposition drove many Spirituals into outright disobedience, some of them— including the minister-general Michael of Cesena—into the camp of John's opponent, the emperor Louis of Bavaria. The Church's hostility to the Spirituals persisted, and many were hunted down and several executed in the fourteenth and fifteenth centuries. The attack of such later writers as James of the March (no. 54) suggests the nature of the dispute in the middle of the fifteenth century.

LITERATURE

In general, see Leff, *Heresy in the Later Middle Ages*, a survey that requires correction in a number of places, especially in its treatment of Beguines and the "Free Spirit" problem. For the Beguines, see Brenda Bolton, "*Mulieres Sanctae*," *Studies in Church History* 10 (1973): 77-95, reprinted in Susan Mosher Stuard, ed., *Women in Medieval Society* (Philadelphia, 1976), pp. 141-58, and especially Robert E. Lerner, *The Heresy of the Free Spirit in the Later Middle Ages* (Berkeley and Los Angeles, 1972); also Lambert, *Medieval Heresy*, pp. 173-81.

On the problem of the Spiritual Franciscans, see Decima L. Douie, *The Nature and the Effect of the Heresy of the Fraticelli* (1932; reprint ed., New York, 1978); M. D. Lambert, *Franciscan Poverty* (London, 1961); David Burr, *The Persecution of Peter Olivi* (Philadelphia, 1976). For the influence of Joachimism, see M. E. Reeves, *The Influence of Prophecy in the Later Middle Ages: A Study in Joachimism* (Oxford, 1969); Lambert, *Medieval Heresy*, pp. 182-206.

50   St. Bonaventure: On *dominium* and *usus*

St. Francis of Assisi had lived a strict life of poverty, and the ideal of Franciscan poverty continued to exert a great influence in the order after St. Francis's death in 1226. The Rule of 1223 stated explicitly that "the brothers shall appropriate to themselves neither a house, nor any land, nor any thing." In the decretal *Quo elongati* of 1230, Pope Gregory IX explained this part of the Rule:

> We say that the brothers ought not to have *proprietas* [proprietorship] either individually or in common, but only may have the *usus* [use] of the things and books and movable goods which they are permitted to have, and the brothers, as the minister-general and the provincial may order, may use them, leaving the *dominium* of their communities and houses to those to whom it is known to pertain.

Further disputes followed the somewhat complex ways by which the possession of goods and money was handled by the order and its benefactors, and in 1269, St. Bonaventure, who was minister-general of the order from 1257 until his death in 1274, wrote his *Defense of the Mendicants (Apologia Pauperum)*.

Bonaventure's treatise firmly upholds the doctrine of poverty, tries to make precise what St. Francis and Gregory IX had left vague, and greatly influenced Pope Nicholas III's attitude toward poverty in the order.

Jesus Christ, the Origin of all good, the Foundation and Founder of the New Jerusalem, who "appeared to this end, that he might destroy the works of the devil," embraced with great eagerness the very opposite of such covetousness, advocating poverty by his example and preaching it by his word. Because the vice of covetousness and its disorder find their root in a disposition of the mind and their occasion and fuel in things possessed externally, extirpation of it must apply to both in order that the damaging passion of greed and alluring possession of earthly wealth may be given up both spiritually and materially. Commenting on this passage from Matthew: "Peter addressed Him, saying 'Behold, we have left all,' " Bernard says: "This is excellent and should not be imputed to you as being unwise. For 'the world with its lusts is passing away,' and it is better to abandon such things than to be abandoned by them. And the best reason to avoid wealth is that it is impossible, or almost impossible, to have it without being attached to it."

If this twofold abdication, of the world and of its lusts, also called poverty of the spirit, is the means by which the root of all evil is perfectly cut off and the foundation of Babylon destroyed, we may conclude reasonably and certainly that this same poverty of the spirit, because of the analogy and closeness it has to what was said, is the root and foundation of that evangelical perfection by which we are conformed to Christ and planted with him, and through which we become his dwelling place. For this reason, Christ himself, when he explained perfection to his disciples on the Mount, placing "upon the holy mountain," that is, in the mind of the apostles, the foundations of the "New Jerusalem, coming down out of heaven," that is, the luminaries of evangelical perfection, and exalting the other virtues, began with the excellence of holy poverty when he said: "Blessed are the poor in spirit, for theirs is the kingdom of heaven." Later, when advising on how to be perfect, He insisted first on the practice of poverty as he lived it, for he said: "If thou wilt be perfect, go, sell what thou hast,

From St. Bonaventure, *Defense of the Mendicants*, Vol. 4 of *The Works of St. Bonaventure*, translated by José de Vinck (Patterson, N.J.: The St. Anthony's Guild Press, 1966), pp. 126-29. Reprinted with the permission of St Anthony's Guild.

and give to the poor . . . ; and come, follow me." Jerome, commenting on this same passage, writes to Demetriades: "It is an act of apostolic perfection and of perfect virtue to sell all one has and to give to the poor—thus becoming weightless and unimpeded and flying up with Christ toward heavenly delights."

There are two aspects to the possession of temporal goods: ownership and use. Since the use of temporal goods is a necessary condition of the present life, evangelical poverty consists in renouncing the ownership and property of earthly things, but not their use, which must be limited, however, in the spirit of the Apostle's advice to Timothy: "Having food and sufficient clothing, with these let us be content."

Hence, the nature of evangelical perfection may be seen: it is the virtue which renounces temporal goods and by which a man lacking private property is sustained with things he does not own. Since the dominion over temporal goods may be given up in two ways, there are two ways of being sustained with what is not one's own. Correspondingly, there is a double mode and perfection in evangelical poverty. Since the dominion over things is twofold, that is, it may consist either in private or in common ownership, the one relating things to a person and the other to a group, and since it is possible to disclaim the former while retaining the latter, it is also possible to disclaim the latter together with the former. Hence, in parallel with this twofold mode of poverty, there will be two kinds of perfect profession of poverty. In the one, a man renounces all private and personal dominion over temporal goods and is sustained by things he does not own, things that are not his but are shared with a community. In the other, a man renounces all dominion over temporal goods, both private and common, and is sustained by things that are not his but someone else's: his sustenance is kindly and justly provided by an outsider.

The first form of poverty prevailed among the company of the faithful of which it is said in the Acts: "The multitude of the believers were of one heart and one soul, and not one of them said that anything he possessed was his own, but they had all things in common." Commenting on this passage from the scriptures, Jerome writes to Demetriades: "In the Acts of the Apostles, at the time when the blood of our Lord Jesus Christ was still warm and a faith still new was burning in the faithful, they used to sell whatever they owned, 'and bring the price of what they sold, and lay it at the feet of the apostles,' in order to show that money was to be trodden underfoot, 'and distribution was made to each, according as anyone had need.' " Bede has a gloss on the same passage, concerning how the form of monastic or cenobitic life was handed down: "Those who lived in such a way that all things were common to them in the Lord were called cenobites. And this manner of life is all the happier since it is an imitation of the life of the future, when all things will belong to all."

But the exemplar and form of the second mode of poverty appeared even before the apostles, for it is Christ the Master of Perfection who instituted it for them when He sent them out to preach, as said in Matthew: "Do not keep gold, or silver, or money in your girdles, nor wallet for your journey, nor two tunics, nor sandals, nor staff; for the laborer deserves his living." And the gloss says here: "He almost takes away the things indispensable for life lest those who teach that all things are in God's power be overconcerned with the morrow. Hence, they take with them not even what they need nor any supply of food nor the slightest thing besides their clothes."

Thus does the Lord impose upon the apostles and preachers of truth a form of extreme and rigorous poverty to be observed by renouncing not only material possessions, but even money and other things by which a community's life is generally sustained and held together. Being poor men established in a state of supreme renouncement to ownership, they could take with them no money or food, they had to wear simple clothing and walk without shoes. Hence, in their deeds and their manner of life they would lift before them holy poverty as a standard of perfection. Christ observed in himself this same perfect norm of poverty as a special prerogative which he established for the apostles to observe, and which he counseled to those who wished to follow in their footsteps.

51 Ubertino da Casale: Violations of *dominium* and *usus*

In 1223 Pope Honorius III issued the decretal *Solet annuere*, which contained the papally approved Rule of the Order of Friars Minor. This rule became the basis of later commentary and dispute. In 1312, Ubertino da Casale provided a commentary on the Rule for the Council of Vienne, emphasizing the role of apostolic poverty in it. The text is printed in F. Ehrle, "Zur Vorgeschichte des Concils von Vienne," *Archiv für Literatur- und Kirchengeschichte des Mittelalters* 3 (1887): 1-195. The selection given here is from pp. 104-7.

THE RULE (FROM THE DECRETAL *SOLET ANNUERE* OF HONORIUS III)

I firmly ordain to all friars that in no manner may they receive money for themselves or through the mediation of another person.

UBERTINO'S EXPLICATION

Concerning this article let it be noted that our fathers and masters from the beginning, and chapters general agree that it has been decreed that the term *denarios* is to be understood literally as money, and the term *pecuniam* as any kind of goods which are received so that they may be sold and in place of the price converted into other objects of value. There have been many offenses against this article [of the Rule], and so great is the indifference to it that as many as are able have their own accounts and agents and spend as they like on books, food, drink, delicate clothing, and other amenities of life in the manner of prelates. Note that they do so indifferently, those who have possessions, having always with them bursars as their personal servants, who spend the property of the brothers in such a way that these brothers appear by all signs to be the lords, not only of their goods, but of the expenditures of their servants. And the brothers carry with them wallets in which money is contained, and if perchance some boys carry the friars' wallets, they are often ignorant of what they contain, since the brothers themselves carry the keys on their own persons. And although these sometimes [technically] have the name of agents, in that they purport to be the agents of those people who give goods to the friars, they are in fact neither servants nor agents, for that money has no other master than the friars themselves.

Note that in the church of St. Francis in Assisi and in St. Mary of the Portiuncula, where the order was born, money is continually received in the name of offerings, and has been received for many years, even before this privilege. Under the protection of a privilege given by Pope Nicholas [IV], both of these convents live by means of money against the Rule. And even though this privilege is in some ways destroying the Rule, not only ought it not to have been asked for, but its privileges ought to be spurned by the brothers; however, which is worse, these privileges are not even observed with moderation.

Another offense has taken root in their convents in other places and other provinces, that money is received in the churches of the friars in the name of offerings for new masses and other things, a thing which is not to be excused, when the friars themselves are the receivers of this money which the offerers intend to be given to the Church or its ministers and our churches have neither ministers nor brothers. Yet another offense consists in placing closed receptacles in churches and putting money in them, which the brothers collect at an opportune time. Yet another offense consists in placing candles from the sacristy in a dish in the church, and when men and women wish to light the candles, they offer money and place it on the dish, and a servant of the brothers is the custodian of the dish and keeps track of the money, thereby selling the candle ten times over. And thus it is wrong to communicate with those whom Jesus expelled from the Temple.

52   Pope John XXII: The Decretal *Gloriosam ecclesiam*, 1318, on the Errors of the Fraticelli

As a report worthy of faith holds, the sons of the above-mentioned rashness and impiety have been driven to this weakness of mind, that they think impiously in opposition to the most renowned and salutary truth of the Christian faith; they condemn the sacraments of the Church which should be venerated, and in an attack of blind fury they who should be crushed by it, press against the glorious primacy of the Roman Church, saying that it ought to be overthrown by all nations.

1. Thus, the first error which breaks forth from their dark workshop invents two churches, the one carnal, packed with riches, overflowing with riches [others, luxuries], stained with crimes which they declare

From H. J. D. Denzinger, *The Sources of Catholic Dogma*, translated by Roy J. Deferrari (St. Louis: B. Herder, 1965), pp. 191-92.

the Roman prefect and other inferior prelates dominate; the other spiritual, cleansed by frugality, beautiful in virtue, bound by poverty, in which they only and their companions are held, and which they, because of the merit of their spiritual life, if any faith should be applied to lies, rule.

2. The second error, by which the conscience of the above-mentioned insolent is stained, cries out that the venerable priests of the Church and other ministers of jurisdiction and order are so devoid of authority that they cannot pass sentences, nor perform the sacraments nor instruct nor teach the subject people, imagining that these have been deprived of all ecclesiastical power, whom they see are free of their own heresy; because only in themselves (as they themselves vainly think), just as the sanctity of a spiritual life, so authority remains; and in this matter they are following the error of the Donatists. . . .

3. The third error of these men conspires with the error of the Waldensians, since both declare that an oath was to be taken in no case, propounding that who happen to be bound by the sacredness of an oath are defiled by the contagion of mortal sin and are bound by punishment.

4. The fourth blasphemy of such wicked men, breaking forth from the poisoned fount of the Waldensian teachings pretends that priests rightly and even legitimately ordained according to the form of the Church, yet weighed down by any sins cannot consecrate or confer the ecclesiastical sacraments. . . .

5. The fifth error so blinds the minds of these that they declare that the gospel of Christ has been fulfilled in them alone at this time, because up to now (as they foolishly think) it has been concealed or indeed entirely extinct. . . .

There are many other things which these very presumptuous men are said to babble against the venerable sacrament of matrimony; many things which they foolishly believe concerning the course of time and the end of time; many things which they propagate with lamentable vanity concerning the coming of the Antichrist, which they declare even now to be close at hand. All these things, because we recognize them as partly heretical, partly senseless, partly fabulous, we decree must be condemned together with their authors rather than pursued or refuted with a pen. . . .

53 Pope John XXII: The Decretal *Cum inter nonullas,* 1323

Since it often happens among learned men that doubt is raised as to whether the persistent assertion that our Redeemer and Lord Jesus Christ and his apostles did not possess any goods or other property, either privately or in common, should be designated heretical, since different people hold differing and even contradictory opinions on the subject, we, desiring to put an end to this controversy and agreeing with the advice of our brothers, declare by this everlasting edict that a persistent assertion of this kind shall henceforth be designated as erroneous and heretical, since it expressly contradicts holy scripture, which expressly states in some places that they [Christ and the Apostles] did possess some things. [This persistent assertion] suggests that holy scripture itself, from which the articles of orthodox faith draw their legitimacy, contains the beginnings of falsehood, and, in this case, it makes the Catholic faith doubtful and uncertain by undermining the authority of scripture.

In the future, persistently to assert that our Redeemer and his apostles had no right to use these same goods that scripture says that they had, and that they did not have the right to sell or donate them, or to obtain other goods by exchanging them (when holy scripture states that they did so or could have done so), since such an assertion implies that the practices of [Christ and the Apostles] would have been unjust (which, in the case of use, actions, or possessions on the part of our Redeemer, the Son of God, is impious, contrary to sacred scripture, and inimical to Catholic doctrine), we declare, agreeing with the advice of our brothers, that this persistent assertion shall properly be designated erroneous and heretical.

54   James of the March: Against the Spirituals, ca. 1450

James of the March was a Franciscan preacher who made himself the persecutor of the surviving Spirituals in the first half of the fifteenth century. These remarks on popes and heresy and the heresy of the Spirituals are contained in a letter James wrote in answer to Spirituals' charges.

And again I say unto thee, [O heretic], that albeit certain supreme pontiffs have died in unfaith, yet thou shalt ever find that, when one pope died in heresy, a Catholic pope immediately succeeded him. Wherefore it cannot be found, in the whole series of the list of supreme pontiffs, that any two popes were successively and immediately heretics; and thus it is not said that faith hath failed without qualification in the order of popes; since, when our Lord said to Peter, "I have prayed for thee, that thy faith fail not," he said it not only for him but for the whole Church. But ye shortsighted Michaelists hold as heretics all the popes who have succeeded the aforesaid John [XXII] and all who favor, believe in, or adhere to him; wherefore ye deceive yourselves and have become heretics. . . . Yet, supposing that a pope were heretical, and not publicly condemned, still bearing his office; supposing that a simple person, not a public person, enquired of that Lord Pope concerning the unity of the faith, and the pope then instructed him in that heresy which he himself held for a truth; then the man thus instructed, if he be not made conscious [of his error] from some other quarter, is not to be adjudged an heretic, seeing that he believeth himself to be instructed in the Catholic faith. If therefore the simple brethren, and the rest of the clergy and laity who hear Pope John [XXII] proclaiming his own decrees [concerning the poverty of Christ] as Catholic,—even supposing that they were heretical—if these men, I say, have believed in them, they are not to be condemned as heretics, especially since they are considered by all to be in the majority; thou therefore, being a Michaelist, art thou not an heretic? For in a matter so weighty the Michaelists ought to have looked to the

Reprinted from *Life in the Middle Ages* by G. G. Coulton (Cambridge: Cambridge University Press, 1928) by permission of Cambridge University Press.

determination of the Holy Church, and more especially of the Roman Court, to which it specially pertaineth to decide such points as concern the essentials of faith; but these [Fraticelli], with the rashness habitual to heretics, refer to themselves and to their own knowledge, thus plunging into heresy and apostasy.

o   o   o

But I desire thee to be won over to thine own salvation; wherefore know for certain that it is a property of the Catholic faith, which was in St. Peter, to grow under persecution and oppression, and to wax more worthy. But the sect of Michaelists faileth and groweth more debased under persecution. For all Catholic doctors attribute to the true faith that it waxeth ever in tribulation and oppression, as is clear from the times of the martyrs, when a hundredfold more were converted than those who were slain; and the more the Church was oppressed, the more glorious she rose up again; wherefore that most excellent Doctor Hilary saith: "This is proper to the Church, that she conquereth when she is hurt; when she is rebuked, then she understandeth; when she hath abandoned, then doth she obtain." And Cassiodorus: "The Church of God hath this quality in especial, to flourish under persecution, to grow in oppression, to conquer under injury, and to stand all the firmer when men deem her overcome." So also Augustine [*De Civ. Dei*, cap. 71] and Gregory [*Moralia*, xviii, 13]. Moreover it is yet more marvelous, as the aforenamed doctors assert, that the Church unresisting subdueth her persecutors, and prevaileth more without resistance than when she withstandeth her adversaries; but this sect of Michaelists had at first most mighty and powerful defenders; yet now it hath but gross boors. Especially mayest thou see how all other rites which do and did exist have taken their source and origin from St. Peter and his successors, but with the lapse of time they have grown in riches by the dignity, wisdom, virtue, and multitude of their adherents; while all other rites which were not [founded] in St. Peter and his Catholic successors have so dwindled that no man is left in them who knew his own rite and could defend it and was able even to expound it. . . . Therefore the Greeks, and all other sects which have departed from the faith of Peter, have dwindled in wisdom, honor, and power; and all other heretical sects (which up to St. Augustine's time numbered two hundred, as he himself saith in his *Book of Heresies*) have failed, and have all ended in lechery. . . . Moreover, in God's Church there are always holy men through whom God worketh many miracles; for ever [apparent lacuna in text] even as now at this present time God hath raised twenty-three dead men through St. Bernardino of the Friars Observant of our Order, as approved by the commissaries deputed by the supreme pontiffs of the Holy Roman Church; thrice, at three different times, hath the Holy Roman Church inquired into the miracles aforesaid, and innumerable others which God worketh through His servant Brother Bernardino, as they have been received and approved by the Holy Roman Church, and as I have seen with mine own eyes; as appeareth also by the [votive] images of gold and silver that hang in testimony of his miracles within the church of St. Francis of Aquila; so also of many other saints who have been since John XXII, but whom ye condemn together with the whole Church. And it is marvellous indeed that in the case of all heretics and schismatics, since they have withdrawn from the Church, God hath wrought no miracles among them (for miracles, as Riccardus and Scotus say, are wrought by God for confirmation of faith in Him); but it is never found of you who make a church of your own, nor hath it ever been heard of that any of you have wrought any miracle, except that in burning they stink like putrid flesh. Whereof ye have an example in Fabriano, while Pope Nicholas V was there; some of these heretics were burned, and the whole city stank for three days long; and this I know because I smelt the stench of them for those three days even in my convent; and—whereas I had persuaded them all to come back to the faith, all of whom returned and confessed and communicated, and wept tears of compunction, and were thus justified even though they had relapsed—yet one who was called Chiuso of Fabriano, the treasurer of those heretics, would never return. I testify before God that he never called upon God to help him, or the Virgin, or any saint; nor did he pray that God would forgive his sins; but as one desperate and withered he continued saying: "The fire cannot burn me!" and I bear witness before God that he burned for three days long, while men brought fresh wood again and again! [The saint goes on to accuse the Fraticelli of the same crimes which they themselves laid to the charge of the orthodox clergy.]

IX

PEASANT CATHARS IN THE ARIÈGE IN THE EARLY FOURTEENTH CENTURY

Between 1318 and 1325 Jacques Fournier, Cistercian monk, former abbot of Fontfroide, bishop of Pamiers (and later Pope Benedict XII), conducted an inquisition in his diocese, located at the foot of the Pyrenees. Pamiers had been erected into a diocese by Pope Boniface VIII in 1295 particularly to check the lively surviving Catharism in the area. Fournier's inquisition was extremely thorough, and it kept superb records, which Fournier later in life had copied out and left in the papal library at Avignon after his papacy. Fournier's inquisitorial register was edited in 1965 by Jean Duvernoy and made an important contribution to our knowledge of late Catharism in the peasant communities of the diocese of Pamiers. It has been the subject of much scholarly research, but the greatest work to come from it is Emmanuel LeRoy Ladurie's brilliant analysis of one community among the several that Fournier visited, *Montaillou, village occitan de 1294 à 1324* (Paris, 1975), which quickly became a best-seller in France and has been translated into English by Barbara Bray as *Montaillou: The Promised Land of Error* (New York, 1979).

The question of the character of the religious culture of rural Europe has long been a matter of debate among historians and sociologists, and LeRoy Ladurie's work has contributed immensely to part of that debate. Had all of rural Europe become Christianized, or were the beliefs of parts of it an amalgam of residual paganism, half-understood Christian dogmas, and strains of contemporary heretical doctrines? The question has engaged not only historians of the late Middle Ages, but students of the seventeenth and eighteenth centuries as well, and, as some of the materials printed here suggest, heresy records may be among the best kinds of sources for illuminating the vexing question of peasant beliefs. Besides the beliefs recorded in this chapter, the reader should also refer to the descriptions of popular customs recorded by the Passau Anonymous (above, no. 27) and some of the selections in chapter II, which, although they are highly literary, may catch something of popular activity.

Although the texts from Fournier's register translated here are not as broad as those used by LeRoy Ladurie, they conveniently reflect some of the major tenets of late Cathar belief. The chapter is divided into sections of testimony dealing with the soul and the afterlife, criticism of orthodox beliefs—in the creation, prayers for the dead, indulgences, the Virgin's power to intervene in human life, and the eucharist—and disregard for the mass.

LITERATURE

The texts here have been translated by Mr. Steven Sargent, of the University of Pennsylvania, from Jean Duvernoy, ed., *Le Régistre d'Inquisition de Jacques Fournier (Benoît XII), évêque de Pamiers (1318-1325)*, 3 vols. (Paris, 1965), with volume and page numbers following each text in Roman and Arabic numerals, respectively. See Emmanuel LeRoy Ladurie, *Montaillou: The Promised Land of Error*, trans. Barbara Bray (New York, 1979), a slightly abridged version of LeRoy Ladurie, *Montaillou, village occitan de 1294 à 1324* (Paris, 1975). The *Journal of Peasant Studies* occasionally has contributions on medieval peasant life, and a general introduction may be found in Georges Duby, *Rural Economy and Country Life in the Medieval West*, trans. Cynthia Postan (Columbia, S.C., 1968). For a slightly later period, see Keith Thomas, *Religion and the Decline of Magic* (New York, 1971), and Jean Delumeau, *Catholicism between Luther and Voltaire* (London and Philadelphia, 1977), esp. pp. 129-231.

55 The Inquisitorial Register of Jacques Fournier

THE SOUL AND THE AFTERLIFE

Testimony of Raimond de l'Aire, of Tignac

An older man told him that a mule has a soul as good as a man's; "and from this belief he had by himself deduced that his own soul and those of other men are nothing but blood, because when a person's blood is taken away, he dies. He also believed that a dead person's soul and body both die, and that after death nothing human remains, because he didn't see anything leave the mouth of a person when he dies. From this he believed that the human soul after death has neither good nor evil, and that there is no hell or paradise in another world where human souls are rewarded or punished" (II:129-30).

Testimony of Guillemette Benet, of Ornolac

"She confessed that three years earlier she was at the market place in the village of Ornolac, and she fell from a wall to the ground and injured her nose so that the blood ran from it. . . . When she saw the blood going out from her nose she said, 'Soul, soul, and soul is nothing but blood!' " (I:263-64).

On another occasion she watched a child as it died in her arms to see if its soul would leave its mouth. "When she saw nothing except breath go out of his mouth she said, 'Take notice: when a person dies, one sees nothing leave his mouth except air. If I saw something else come out, I would believe that the soul is something. But now because only air has come out, I do not believe that the soul is anything' " (I:264).

She also noticed that a decapitated chicken "made a commotion as long as the blood ran from its body. It happens the same way for men and women: they live as long as they have blood" (I:260).

Testimony of Raimond Sicre, of Ascou

Raimond and others were talking about the unusual weather in the village square of Ascou, a village close to Ax. It was 9 May and snowing, and everyone feared that the snow would weigh down the grain and destroy it.

A witness reported that Raimond said, "We certainly need a good grain harvest because when there is no bread in the stomach, there is no soul" (II:357, also 359). Raimond's belief rested on his observation that "if a person goes eight days without eating, or even four days, his body and soul deteriorate and disappear. Asked what he meant by this deterioration and disappearance of the soul if a person doesn't eat, he answered that he didn't intend this in a bad way or in bad faith" (II:362-63). Stated succinctly, Raimond believed that "a man doesn't have any other soul or sustenance in his body except food" (II:370).

Raimond asserted that one of his friends said to him, "On account of a few words that you said this year you have been harassed, and you didn't believe that you were saying these things with the evil meaning that has been imputed to them" (II:368). Raimond himself told the man who denounced him that "he didn't believe that he had said these words with the intention the witness had read into them" (II:357). The witness who denounced Raimond, a resident of the town of Ax, said that he had heard that some unnamed people of the village of Ascou, where Raimond lived, had cursed him for revealing Raimond's words and had wished bad fortune on him (II:357).

Testimony of Jacotte Corot, of Ax

"There will never be any other world but this one, nor will dead men and women ever be resurrected" (I:151).

Testimony of Arnaud de Savinhan, of Tarascon, a stonecutter

He believed that "there was no other world except this present one" (I:166). For this and other unorthodox beliefs he was imprisoned for sixteen months and thereafter had to wear crosses. He did not perform this latter penance and was arrested again. He complained of the severity of his earlier punishment, since "he felt that he was without blame . . . because he had not seen [Albigensian] heretics" (II:436). He endured five and a half more years of strict imprisonment as punishment for his failure to perform his earlier penance, and after his release he had to wear crosses.

Testimony of Guillaume Austatz, of Ornolac, a farmhand

"He said that he believed that if each soul had its own body, then the world would hardly be able to contain so many souls, because although they are small quantities, nevertheless since there were so many of them they would fill up the world. From this he appeared to believe that souls are corporeal, having hands, feet, and the other members, and he was asked if he believed this. He answered that at the time he was talking about he believed that human souls had the corporeal form of men and women and members just like the members of the human body" (I:211).

On another occasion Guillaume was talking to other men in the village square in Ornolac about the place where dead souls go. Guillaume said that paradise "was as big as if the area from Toulouse up to Merens were made into one house that would occupy the whole area, and may souls can fit into it" (I:202).

Testimony of Peter Maury, of Montaillou

"Asked if he had heard from heretics or believed that the human soul has members separate from the body, as well as a form and figure and flesh and bones just like the human body, he responded that he had not heard this from heretics but that he nevertheless believed that the human soul separated from the body has all these attributes and is like a person. He had always believed this from the time when he had gained the use of reason, although he was amazed at how this could be; for if the soul of a human going out of his body is in the figure of a man, how could it be that no one sees it leaving the body in human figure and form?" (III:243).

Testimony of Guillaume Fort, of Montaillou

"He said that she [a woman who 'goes with the dead souls of men and women'] had seen souls having flesh and bones and all members, like the head, feet, and hands and other members" (I:448).

Testimony of Arnaud Gelis, of Pamiers

He said "he believed that the souls of all men and women, both while they are in the body and after they have left the body, have all members like eyes, ears, noses, and all other members similar to the members of those bodies in which they were living or had lived; and he had believed this the whole time of his memory" (I:137).

Testimony of Jean Rocas, of le Salvetat [an impenitent monotheist]

"And he said that he had always believed that the person whom he called the Father was a man having flesh, bones, head, hands, soul, and all the other things any other person has" (II:241-42).

"He also said that he believes that Christ [sic] descended into hell but descended there in body and soul and not in soul alone, because the soul is not able to do anything without the body" (II:243).

Testimony of Jean Maury, of Montaillou

"Likewise he believed that although God was a good heavenly Father, he had never descended from heaven nor did he accept the body of a worldly human; nevertheless existing in himself in heaven, he has a heavenly rather than terrestrial body similar in form and figure to the terrestrial human body; and he has flesh and bones, although spiritual, not earthly, ones; and in the likeness and figure of his own celestial body he made Adam out of earth. And he believed likewise concerning all spirits that remained in heaven with the Father. . . . But he nevertheless did not believe that the Father of the spirits and the spirits that stayed with him ate anything or drank, but that they lived by the grace of God; and even less did he believe that they brought forth any wastes because he did not believe that there were any filthy things in heaven but rather that all things were beautiful there" (II:515-16)

Testimony of Arnaud Sicre, of Tarascon

"And once, he said, he heard Peter Maury and his brother Jean talking about human souls: where they might be able to be received, because so many men were living and so many had already died. And the priest [with whom they were talking] said that all human souls which exist are able to be received in the space of a single finger of a man's hand. And when the witness [Arnaud] and Peter and Jean Maury were amazed at this, the priest added that all souls are able to fit in the place of one button; and when they were even more amazed at this, the priest said, 'We others do not wish to say to you, who are beasts [heretics?], what the human soul is lest you err greatly' (II: 73-74).

Testimony of Guillaume Fort, of Montaillou

"He believed that the souls of good men go to heavenly paradise, but that the souls of bad men, both now and after the last judgment, will go among the cliffs and precipices and that demons will throw them down from the cliffs onto the rocks below.

"Asked who taught him these errors, he said that he himself had thought up the idea that after death human bodies do not revive and are not resurrected. He came to the conclusion that souls without bodies will appear at the last judgment and will be judged by Christ, but that the souls of evil men both now and after the judgment will wander among the cliffs and be thrown down from the heights. And he believed this and believes it still, informed, as he said, in this by the common talk in the lands of Aillon and Saltu [the area where

Montaillou lies] that Arnalda Riba of Bellicadro of the diocese of Electensis goes with the souls of dead men and women; and it is said that she sees the souls of evil people being led by the demons through the cliffs and rough places, and that the demons throw them down from the cliffs.

"He said that she had seen souls having flesh and bones and all members . . . and they are thrown down by the demons; and it hurts and afflicts them greatly, but nevertheless they are not able to die.

". . . A certain blacksmith of the place [i.e., Bellicadro] called Bernard den Alazaicis said to the rector that he himself had seen the souls going down among the cliffs and rough places, and that they were thrown down from the cliffs" [all four passages, I: 447-48].

Testimony of Arnaud Gelis, of Pamiers

Arnaud's beliefs (I:138-39)

1. The souls of dead people do not do any other penance except to wander from church to church, some faster, some slower according to their sinfulness.

2. After they are finished going around to churches through the streets, the souls go to the place of rest, which is on this earth. They stay there until the judgment day.

3. No soul of any man except the most saintly goes directly to heaven or the heavenly kingdom. Souls do this on the day of judgment.

4. Souls of children who died before baptism go to an obscure place until the judgment day. There they feel neither pain nor pleasure. After the judgment day they enter paradise.

Roman Catholic orthodoxy (I:140-41)

1. All souls of dead people go to purgatory, where they do the penance they had not completed on earth. And when this is done they go to the heavenly paradise where Christ, Mary, the angels, and the saints reside.

2. When their penance is done, the souls of the dead go to the joy of the celestial paradise, which is no place of rest on earth, but rather in heaven.

3. All souls of the dead, when their penance is done in purgatory (if they had need of it), enter the heavenly kingdom.

4. The souls of unbaptized children will never be saved or enter the kingdom of heaven.

5. No soul of a dead person, no matter how evil, has entered or will enter hell.

5. The souls of all evil persons—i.e., those who perpetrate great crimes that they do not confess or do penance for—go immediately after death to hell, where they stay and are punished for their sins.

6. At the last judgment God will have mercy on all who held the Christian faith and no one will be damned, no matter how evil he was.

6. All souls that held the Christian faith and accepted its sacraments and obeyed its commandments will be saved; but those who, even though holding the faith and accepting the sacraments, did not live according to the commandments will be damned.

7. Christ will have mercy on the souls of all heretics, Jews, and pagans; therefore none of them will be damned.

7. All souls of heretics, pagans, and Jews, who did not want to believe in Christ, will be damned. They will be punished eternally in hell.

8. Human souls, both before the body's death and after, have their own bodily form just like their external body. And the souls have distinct members like hands, eyes, feet, and the rest.

8. Human souls, both while in the body and after its death, because they are spirits, are not corporeal, nor do they have corporeal members, nor do they eat or drink, nor do they suffer such corporeal necessities.

9. Hell is a place only for demons.

9. Hell is a place for demons and for wicked people, where each is punished eternally as he deserves.

Some other beliefs imputed to Arnaud by witnesses:

10. The souls of the dead do not eat, but they do drink good wine and warm themselves at fires. The wine is not, however, diminished by their drinking it (I:551).

11. "Those who move their arms and hands from their sides when they walk along do great evil . . . [since] such moving arms throw down many souls of the dead to the earth" (I:545).

Disbelief in the survival of the soul after death: Testimony of Guillemette Benet

"She also said and confessed that during this year around Easter, Raymond Benet had a newborn son who was dying. Raymond called her as she was going to the grove for wood so that she might hold the dying boy. She held him from morning to night, observing him to see if anything went out of the boy's mouth when he died. When she saw nothing except exhalation to go out of his mouth, she said, 'Take notice: when a person dies, one sees nothing go out from his mouth except air. If I were to see that something else came out, I would believe that the soul is something; but now, because only air has come out, I do not believe that the soul is anything.'. . . .

"She remained two years in the belief that the human soul is nothing but blood while a person is living; and that the soul dies when the person, or the human body, dies. Asked if at the time when she believed that the human soul died with the body, she believed that there was a heaven and a hell, or that the soul after death would be punished or rewarded, she answered that at that time she did not believe that there was either a heaven or a hell, nor that there was any other world but the present one, nor that souls would be rewarded or punished in another world. Asked why she believed this, that the human soul is nothing but blood while the person lives, and dies with the body, she answered that she believed this, first, because she saw that when all the blood has left an animal, it dies; and, second, because she did not see anything leave the body of a dying person except air. . . .

"Asked if, since she believed that human souls died with the bodies, she also believed that men would be resurrected and would live again after death, she answered that she did not believe that the resurrecting of the human body would happen, since she believed that as the dead body was buried, the soul was buried with the body; and since she saw that the body putrefied, she believed that it would never be resurrected. . . .

"Asked if she believed that the soul of Jesus Christ, who died on the cross, had died with his body, she answered yes, because although God is not able to die, nevertheless Jesus Christ died and therefore, even though she believed that God always existed, nevertheless she did not believe that Christ's soul lived and existed. . . .

"Asked if she believed that Christ was resurrected, she said yes and that God had done this."

CRITICISM OF ORTHODOX BELIEFS

Disbelief in the creation: Testimony of Arnaud de Savinhan

"He said that as long as he could remember, which might be about thirty years since he was then about forty-five years old, he had believed completely that God had not made the world, namely heaven, earth, and the elements, but that it had always been existing in and of itself, and was not made by God nor by anyone else. Nevertheless he always had believed that Adam was the first man and that God had made him, and thereafter there had been human generation. But before God had made Adam, the world had lasted infinitely into the past; and he [the witness] did not believe that the world had had a beginning.

"He also said that he had believed for all that time up to the beginning of May in the present year that the world had never had a beginning, and thus that it would never end, and that the world would go on in the same way in the future as it did now; and that just as men were generated now and as they had been generated from Adam onward, there would always be in the future the generation of men, and of vines, and of the other plants, and of all animals; nor would that generation ever end. He believed that there was no other world except the present one . . . ." (I:166).

Uselessness of prayers for the dead: testimony of Guillelme Cornelhano

"He also said that in the same year at the feast of the Assumption of the Blessed Mary, the witness himself was in Alet at the house of Huguet Sornhano, and they were holding a big party there. . . . A certain poor man called Brother Ipitalis, who died sometime [afterwards] in Rega, arrived clothed in a blanket. Food was given to him; and when he began to eat, Huguet said to him to say the Ave Maria by singing [it]. And the man replied that he would rather say a Pater Noster and an Ave Maria for his soul and those of his dead parents. Huguet answered that he needn't say a Pater Noster and an Ave Maria for his soul or those of his parents because that which was done for the soul of the dead didn't do any good. And when it was said to Huguet by his father that he was saying bad things, Huguet answered that there had been a disputation in Carcassonne about this which he had attended, and there it had been determined that what was done for the dead had no value" (II:123).

Disbelief in indulgences: testimony of Guillelme Cornelhano

"He also said that about two years before around the feast of Pentecost . . . a seller of indulgences passed by [him and Guillelma Vilara, wife of Arnald Cuculli] who had with him many indulgences. And after he had left them, Guillelma said, "Do you believe that any man is able to indulge or absolve anyone of his sins? Don't believe it, because no one can absolve anyone except God." And when he himself said that the pope and all priests could absolve man from sins, Guillelma answered that it was not so, only God could [do that]" (II:121-22).

Belief and disbelief in Mary's power to intervene in a case of theft: testimony of Gualharda, wife of Bernard Ros of Ornolac

She said that "this year around the feast of the birth of John the Baptist, a certain quantity of money and other things were stolen from her; she had been keeping them in a box which had been broken into. She went to Guillelm, the bailiff of Ornolac, and requested him to perform his office and seek out the thief and make it so that she would get her things back. He turned a deaf ear to her request; so she, grieving and crying, went to the church of Blessed Mary of Montgauzy in order to obtain a miracle from her, namely the recovery of the money and goods. The better to obtain this [miracle], she fixed candles around the altar of Blessed Mary. And when she returned to Ornolac and again petitioned Guillelm about the theft and he refused to intervene, she reminded him that just as he had tracked down some grain stolen from himself that year, he was obligated to search for her stolen money and goods. Guillelm responded that he searched for the grain because he would know it when he found it, but that he would not recognize her money and goods. And Gualharda then said, 'I confided in the Blessed Mary of Montgauzy when I visited the church there, and I asked her to return to me the money and the goods stolen from me; and she will vindicate me against those who have stolen these things if she can not restore the goods.' Then Guillelm said . . . that Blessed Mary did not have the power to recover the money and goods of Gualharda; and when she replied that of course Mary had that power and that he was speaking evil things and that Mary would vindicate her, Guillelm answered that Blessed Mary did not kill men or perpetrate death" (I:192-93).

Hysteria accompanied by disbelief in the true presence:
testimony of Aude Faure

"On a certain day [soon after her marriage] she was going to the church of the Holy Cross to hear mass. She heard on the way from some women, whose names she forgets, that during the preceding night a certain woman [had given birth to] a daughter in [a house on] a street inside the fortress of Marveil, and that she [the woman] had not been able to reach the house. Having heard this, she [Aude] thought of the disgrace that women bring forth [*emittunt*—'give out,' literally; it can mean 'express'] in giving birth, and when she saw the body of the Lord being elevated at the altar, she had the thought that the body of the Lord had been stained [*infectum*] from that disgrace; and from this she fell into the error of believing that the body of the Lord Jesus Christ was not there" (II:94). . . .

"Before that disgraceful thought it had not seemed to her that the body of Christ was stained by that disgrace or any other; nevertheless that shameful thought occurred to her when the body of Christ was elevated, and she was not able to believe that the body of the Lord was there at the altar, nor was she able to call on him or to look at him, since this thought hung above her as did many other thoughts that occurred to her during the elevation" (II:94). . . .

"They both [Aude and her servant Aladaycis] went to the house of Guille Romundo, where Aladaycis received the body of Christ; that done, Aladaycis and Aude returned to Aude's house. And when they had stayed there some while, Aude began to be troubled and to shout. . . . Aladaycis and Guillelma, another of Aude's servants, believing that Aude was suffering from the falling sickness of Saint Paul, since Aude in a [recent] illness and earlier had been used to suffer that disease, said to Aude, 'Oh, Mistress, what do you have? Why are you so troubled?' And Aude said, 'What am I to do? For I have lost my sense and am delirious and cannot call on God or the Blessed Virgin Mary.' And Aladaycis and Guillelma fell to their knees and prayed and asked the Blessed Virgin Mary to help Aude" (II: 101:-2).

DISREGARD FOR THE MASS

Testimony of Peter Sabatier

"When questioned, Peter said and confessed willingly that about three years ago on a certain day in the village of Varillis . . . when he returned from the church [to his house], he said that whatever things the priests and clerics were chanting and singing in the church were lies and tricks; but he never doubted, rather always believed, that the sacraments of the church and its articles of faith were true."

He persisted in this belief "for about a year, and believed out of silliness that priests and clerics, in singing and chanting those things in the church while performing the divine offices, sang and chanted in order to have the contributions, and that there was no good effect wrought by those divine offices" (I: 146).

Disbelief in the efficacy of the mass: testimony of Raimund de l'Aire

"He also said that at that time he believed that what was done by the priests in the church during mass or in the other divine offices was without value."

Disregard of the sermons at mass: testimony of Arnaud de Savinhan

He says that "Although he went to masses, nevertheless he did not hear the sermons, being occupied with his business and his art of stone-cutting" (I: 167).

Irreverence: testimony of Peter Aces, farmhand, fifteen or sixteen years old

"And when they were there, they began to joke among themselves; and among other things he himself [Peter] said that what the priest elevated during the mass resembled a round slice of radish or turnip, and that the cup that the priest elevated resembled a glass jar, since it shone like a jar made of glass" (III: 462).

SUPERSTITION AND SORCERY

An incident of sorcery: testimony of Jacotte Corot

The witness "was questioned by the bishop about an act of sorcery or 'art of Saint George' that was said to have been perpetrated on the balcony of her house in Ax by Berenger Vascon, a notary of Taras-cona. . . ." She confessed that "about two years ago or earlier, around the feast of Saint Michael in September, Arnold Mondo of Ax, her son-in-law, had lost in the market at Foix two woolen cloths, which loss greatly disturbed him. And on a certain day he brought with him a clerk, who Arnold said would show him who had the cloths, because he knew how to 'make acts.' Arnold asked her to fetch the daughter of Arnold Pelicer of Ax, saying that they wished to put this girl 'in the art,' so that he could see who had the two cloths. She [Jacotte] went and got the girl, bringing her back with her, and led the girl into her house, climbing up to the balcony of the house with her. On the balcony were the clerk and Arnold Mondo, and she [Jacotte] left the girl there with them, because she did not wish to see the 'art' being done. Afterwards Arnold, her son-in-law, said to her that they had done the 'art' (I: 156-57).

[Editor's note: This sorcery, consisting of making a child look into a mirror in order to recover an object lost or stolen, appears to have been very much appreciated. If it was not tolerated, it remained only a venial offense.]

Practices performed on the dead to bring good fortune: testimony of Fabrissa Riba

"She also said that when Ponclus Clergue, father of the priest [of Montaillou], died, many people from Alliou came to the priest's house. The body was placed in the room called the *foganhu* [kitchen] and had not yet been wrapped in cloth. The priest [Pierre Clergue] made everyone leave the house except Alamainis Ademeria, and Bruna, wife of Guillelm Porcell and the natural daughter of Prades Tavernier, the heretic. They remained with the priest and the corpse. And she heard that the women along with the priest then took off the hair and [finger- and toe-] nails of the dead man; and they were said to have done this for this reason: so that good fortune would remain in that house" (I: 328).

Invocation of the devil: testimony of Arnaud Laufre

"He also said that Guillelme Carreria said to him that he had heard that Bor (Raimund de l'Aire) was plowing in a field in Bodiers . . . with two untamed oxen. When the oxen moved out of alignment, the yoke that was over their necks was brought down under the necks. Seeing this Raimund said, 'Devil, put back that yoke in its proper place!' And when this was said, the yoke was reversed up over the necks of the oxen" (II: 126).

X

THE AGE OF WYCLIF AND HUS

The last quarter of the fourteenth century and the first quarter of the fifteenth are dominated by two great critics of the Church, John Wyclif in England and John Hus in Bohemia. Both were university graduates in theology, Wyclif from Oxford and Hus from Prague, and both began their careers as scholars and teachers, developed points of view from which they criticized ecclesiastical abuses, and finally drew further and further away from orthodox doctrine, attracting large popular followings as they did so. Indeed, the linkage between learned heretics and popular followings in the cases of Wyclif and Hus is an important aspect of the late Middle Ages.

John Wyclif was born around 1330 and spent most of his life at Oxford. His intellectual formation was shaped early by the nominalism of William of Ockham, but Wyclif soon turned to a rigid theological Augustinianism and a biblical fundamentalism that led him to criticize ecclesiastical abuse harshly, as in his treatise on the increasingly popular doctrine of indulgences (no. 56) and further in his theological and political writings. In 1378 Pope Gregory XI wrote a letter to the masters and chancellor of Oxford University censuring some of Wyclif's opinions (no. 57), and Wyclif's reply to Gregory's successor, Urban VI (no. 58), suggests both his attitude and something of his sprightly style. Some of Wyclif's admirers spread his ideas through less learned ranks of English society and veered close to a kind of Waldensianism, and their work included the production of an English translation of the Bible. Academics, lower clergy, preachers, and pious lay people from the middle groups in society took over many of Wyclif's doctrines, and they and a group of men from the lower ranks of the nobility were collectively called Lollards. Between their anticlericalism, reflected in the Lollard Conclusions of 1394 (no. 60), and their increasing theological deviance, the Lollards became not only the most significant group of dissenters in England, but one of the most interesting movements in lay piety in the later Middle Ages.

Wyclif's doctrines appealed to other scholars as well, however, and even long after his death were regarded as sufficiently influential for them to be formerly condemned at the Council of Constance in 1415 (no. 59). Wyclif's ideas also traveled far beyond England, and some of them reached as far as Bohemia and elsewhere in the intellectually cosmopolitan university world of the late fourteenth century. The University of Prague had been founded in 1348 by the Emperor Charles IV, and by the end of the fourteenth century it had become a center for the reform of the Church in Bohemia. From the 1360s on, wandering preachers preached lay piety and anticlerical sentiments, in Czech, to sympathetic audiences. Matthias of Janov (d. 1394), a learned cleric, wrote treatises condemning the wealth and abuse of the Bohemian Church, laying out the principles of a revived spiritual life for lay people, expressing his fear of the coming of Antichrist, and urging frequent communion for the laity. Thus, the Bohemian reform movement, although originally independent of Wyclifism, came to espouse some of its strongest principles, particuarly after Wyclif's writings became known there. John Hus, who was ordained a priest in 1400, first encountered Wyclif's writings at the University of Prague, and when Hus turned his back on a conventional clerical career and became the resident preacher and pastor at the Bethlehem Chapel in Prague, he developed, under Wyclifite influence, his own unique vision of a Christian people and a reformed Church. Ecclesiastical opposition drove Hus into exile in 1412, when he sharpened his doctrinal ideas. His denunciations of clerical abuses (no. 61) and his treatise on the Church of 1413 brought him to the attention of the Council of Constance (1415-18). The council formally condemned Wyclif's doctrines (no. 62), called Hus before it, and examined, condemned, and burned him as a heretic (no. 63). Hus's execution launched a ferocious civil war in Bohemia, and gave the Czech master the character of a martyr.

Hussitism and Wyclifism were the last great medieval heresies before the Reformation, and they swept along large numbers of popular followers. For the first time, learned heresy appealed to a popular audience, indicating a linkage that had profound results over the next two centuries. Wyclif, Occam, Marsiglio, and Hus were not, however, the only thinkers concerned with the Church and its abuses. Orthodox thinkers as well sought means of reform, as did temporal authorities, councils and popes. The treatise of John of Brevicoxa, a Paris theologian, late in the fourteenth century (no. 64), reveals the other side of the coin of Wyclif and Hus, and a mind no less sensitive and troubled by the dilemmas of his own age. Brevicoxa's treatise *On the Church and Heresy* from the end of the fourteenth century is an appropriate document with which to end this collection, since it takes up, fifteen centuries later, the same problems that had troubled St. Paul and Tertullian, but in a very different way and in a very different world.

LITERATURE

For Wyclif and English Lollardy, see K.B. MacFarlane, *The Origins of Religious Dissent in England* (New York, 1966); Margaret Deanesley, *The Lollard Bible* (Cambridge, 1920); Norman P. Tanner, ed., *Heresy Trials in the Diocese of Norwich, 1428-1431*, Camden Society Fourth Series, vol. 20 (London, 1977); Lambert, *Medieval Heresy*, 217-71; J. A. Robson, *Wyclif and the Oxford Schools* (Cambridge, 1966); Anne Hudson, *Selections from English Wycliffite Writings* (Cambridge, 1978); and Derek Baker, ed., *Medieval Women* (Oxford, 1978). On Hus and Bohemian Hussitism, see Lambert, *Medieval Heresy*, pp. 272-334; Howard Kaminsky, *A History of the Hussite Revolution* (Berkeley and Los Angeles, 1969); Matthew Spinka, *John Hus: A Biography* (Princeton, 1968). Superb annotated collections of documents in translation for this period are C. M. D. Crowder, *Unity, Heresy and Reform, 1378-1460* (New York, 1977), and Heiko A. Oberman, *Forerunners of the Reformation* (New York, 1966). On the temper of the period in England, see Jeanne Krochalis and Edward Peters, ed. and trans., *The World of Piers Plowman* (Philadelphia, 1975).

56 John Wyclif: On Indulgences

Alithia. We have here touched on the subject of indulgences; and as the granting of these appears to me quite in accordance with this blasphemous presumption of the friars, I could wish that you would say something on this topic.

Phronesis. As the pride of those who hate God ever tends upward, so although the fountain head of heresy and sin takes its rise in the very beginning of darkness, the rivulet of the friars strives unnaturally to raise itself above its source. I confess that the indulgences of the pope, if they are what they are said to be, are a manifest blasphemy, inasmuch as he claims a power to save men almost without limit, and not only to mitigate the penalties of those who have sinned, by granting them the aid of absolutions and indulgences, that they may never come to purgatory, but to give command to the holy angels, that when the soul is separated from the body, they may carry it without delay to its everlasting rest.

The friars give a color to this blasphemy by saying that Christ is omnipotent, and excels all his good angels, and that the pope is his plenary vicar on earth, and so possesses in everything the same power as Christ in his humanity. It is here that lawyers, in common with the friars, cry as wolves, and contradicting themselves, say that when they consider the power of this God upon earth they cannot lift up their face to heaven. Whence, to declare the power of the pope, the false brethren, according to the secrets of their faith, proceed as follows:

They suppose, in the first place, that there is an infinite number of supererogatory merits, belonging to the saints, laid up in heaven, and above all, the merit of our Lord Jesus Christ, which would be sufficient to save an infinite number of other worlds, and that, over all this treasure, Christ hath set the pope. Secondly, that it is his pleasure to distribute it, and, accordingly, he may distribute therefrom to an infinite extent, since the remainder will still be infinite. Against this rude blasphemy I have elsewhere inveighed. Neither the pope, nor the Lord Jesus Christ, can grant dispensations, or give indulgences to any man, except as the Deity has eternally determined by his just counsel. But we are not taught to believe that the pope, or any other man, can have any color of justice to adduce for so doing; therefore, we are not taught that the pope has any such power.

Again, I inquire, concerning these supererogatory eternal merits, what member of the Church is the subject of them? If in Christ and his members, it appears wonderful, on many accounts, that the pope should be able to subtract them from their proper subjects. First, because an accident cannot exist without a subject; secondly, because no one of them is in any need of it, their hour of probation being passed. In the third place, because he is rewarded fully, according to his own merit. How, therefore, can the pope, by such imaginary rapine, do both God and them an injury? Also, by a *reductio ad impossibile*, it is made plain that if any mortal shall be finally condemned during the time of any pope, the pope himself will be guilty of his destruction, because he has neglected to save him; for he has power enough to accomplish the salvation of such a man, nor is there any obstacle in the way of his so doing, except, perhaps, his own sloth; and accordingly for such sloth, he is to be blamed. But who can be equal to such a dispensation, except God alone? But since God may not recall the office, by reason of the absolute agreement which he has made therewith, it appears to unbelievers that as long as that office remains, the pope cannot err, or be condemned, inasmuch as his mind, like that of Christ, is not liable to sin. But where is there a greater blasphemy, than that by reason of the mere Caesarean power, which is contrary to the law of Christ, Antichrist should be possessed of such authority? Whence it appears to many, that of all the sufferings endured by Christ from the hand of man, this is one of the greatest— the suffering arising from the permission given to Antichrist to reign so long, and so widely to deceive the people!

Moreover, it appears that this doctrine is a manifold blasphemy against Christ, inasmuch as the pope is extolled above his humanity and deity, and so above all that is called God—pretensions which, according to the declarations of the apostle, agree with the character of Antichrist; for he possesses Caesarean power above Christ, who had nowhere to lay his head. In regard to spiritual power, so far as the humanity of Christ is concerned, it would seem that the pope is superior to our Lord Jesus Christ; for it behooved Christ to suffer the most bitter passion for the salvation of man; and we believe, that on the ground of the divine justice, men attain to whatever happiness may be theirs, by virtue of Christ's passion. But this renegade says that it is allowable that he should live as luxuriously as he may choose, and that, by the bare writing of one of his scribes, he can introduce wonders, without limit, into the Church Militant! Who, then, can deny his being extolled above the Lord Jesus Christ, in whose life we read not that Christ, or any one of his apostles, granted such absolutions or indulgences? Yet had such power been at their command, it is on many grounds probable that they would not have been absolutely idle in the use of it, especially when Christ condemns the slothful servant, for not trafficking with the talent entrusted to him; and he requires at the hand of the prelate the souls committed to his care, and lost through his negligence, as appears from the third chapter of Ezekiel. Which alternative, then, should we maintain—that Christ and his apostles possessed no such power, or that they were culpable in hoarding such treasure, in place of bringing it forth for the good of the Church? But what greater insanity than to adopt such a conclusion!

Similar in its folly is the doctrine which teaches that the pope dispenses these same merits of the saints, for the service of men, to any extent, according to his pleasure. For it behooves Christ to do more, both on his own part, to fulfill the claims of justice; and on that of the sinner, whom it becomes him to affect, imparting grace to him, that he may prove worthy of the divine assistance.

The same may be said concerning the fiction of the keys of Antichrist, for it is not necessary that the believer should insist on the foundation of this pretension, since the argument will be found to be one without sequence. Christ, they say, granted to Peter, the Apostle, in the nearest degree following his own example, such power over the keys, and therefore we ought, in the same manner, to concede to Antichrist, who, in word and deed, is still more preeminently his opposite, as great, or even greater, power in the Church! Christ gave to Peter, and to others possessing a knowledge of the law of God, the power of judging according to the law of that knowledge, both in binding and loosing, agreeably to the Church Triumphant. But, now, this renegade will not be regulated by the mind of the Church above, nor by any authority; but, as might be expected from Antichrist, he sets forth new laws, and insists, under pain of the heaviest censure, that the whole Church Militant shall believe in them; so that anything determined therein shall stand as though it were a part of the gospel of Jesus Christ.

In such infinite blasphemies is the infatuated church involved, especially by the means of the tail of this dragon—that is, the sects of the friars, who labor in the cause of this illusion, and of other Luciferian seductions of the church. But arise, O soldiers of Christ! Be wise to fling away these things, along with the other fictions of the prince of darkness, and put ye on the Lord Jesus Christ, and confide, undoubtedly, in your own weapons, and sever from the church such frauds of Antichrist, and teach the people that in Christ alone, and in his law, and in his members, they should trust; that in so doing, they may be saved through his goodness, and learn above all things honestly to detect the devices of Antichrist!

57 Pope Gregory XI to the Masters of Oxford: On Wyclif

Gregory, bishop, servant of the servants of God, to his beloved sons, the chancellor and university of Oxford, in the diocese of Lincoln, grace and apostolic benediction.

We are compelled to wonder and grieve that you, who, in consideration of the favors and privileges conceded to your university of Oxford by the Apostolic See, and on account of your familiarity with the scriptures, in whose sea you navigate, by the gift of God, with auspicious oar, you, who ought to be, as it were, warriors and champions of the orthodox faith, without which there is no salvation of souls—that you through a certain sloth and neglect allow tares to spring up amidst the pure wheat in the fields of your glorious university aforesaid; and what is still more pernicious, even continue to grow to maturity. And you are quite careless, as has been lately reported to us, as to the extirpation of these tares; with no little clouding of a bright name, danger to your souls, contempt of the Roman Church, and injury to the faith above-mentioned. And what pains us the more is that this increase of the tares aforesaid is known in Rome before the remedy of extirpation has been applied in England where they sprang up. By the insinuation of many, if they are indeed worthy of belief, deploring it deeply, it has come to our ears that John de Wyclif, rector of the church of Lutterworth, in the diocese of Lincoln, professor of the sacred scriptures (would that he were not also Master of Errors), has fallen into such a detestable madness that he does not hesitate to dogmatize and publicly preach, or rather vomit forth from the recesses of his breast certain propositions and conclusions which are erroneous and false. He has cast himself also into the depravity of preaching heretical dogmas which strive to subvert and weaken the state of the whole Church and even secular polity, some of which doctrines, in changed terms, it is true, seem to express the perverse opinions and unlearned learning of Marsiglio of Padua of cursed memory, and of John of Jandun, whose book is extant, rejected and cursed by our predecessor, Pope John XXII, of happy memory. This he has done in the kingdom of England, lately glorious in its power and in the abundance of its resources, but more glorious still in the glistening piety of its faith, and in the distinction of its sacred learning; producing also many men illustrious for their exact knowledge of the holy scriptures, mature in the gravity of their character, conspicuous in devotion, defenders of the Catholic Church. He has polluted certain of the faithful of Christ by besprinkling them with these doctrines, and led them away from the right paths of the aforesaid faith to the brink of perdition.

Wherefore, since we are not willing, nay, indeed, ought not to be willing, that so deadly a pestilence should continue to exist with our connivance, a pestilence which, if it is not opposed in its beginnings, and torn out by the roots in its entirety, will be reached too late by medicines when it has infected very many with its contagion; we command your university with strict admonition, by the apostolic authority, in virtue of your sacred obedience, and under penalty of the deprivation of all the favors, indulgences, and privileges granted to you and your university by the said See, for the future not to permit to be asserted or set forth to any extent whatever the opinions, conclusions, and propositions which are in variance with good morals and faith, even when those setting them forth strive to defend them under a certain fanciful wresting of words or of terms. Moreover, you are on our authority to arrest the said John, or cause him to be arrested and to send him under a trustworthy guard to our venerable brother, the archbishop of Canterbury, and the bishop of London, or to one of them.

Besides, if there should be, which God forbid, in your university, subject to your jurisdiction, opponents stained with these errors, and if they should obstinately persist in them, proceed vigorously and earnestly to a similar arrest and removal of them, and otherwise as shall seem good to you. Be vigilant to repair the negligence which you have hitherto shown in the premises, and so obtain our gratitude and favor, and that of the said See, besides the honor and reward of the divine recompense.

Given at Rome, at Santa Maria Maggiore, on 31 May, the sixth year of our pontificate.

58   Wyclif's Response to Pope Urban VI

I have joyfully to tell what I hold, to all true men that believe and especially to the pope; for I suppose that if my faith be rightful and given of God, the pope will gladly confirm it; and if my faith be error, the pope will wisely amend it.

I suppose over this that the gospel of Christ be heart of the corps of God's law; for I believe that Jesus Christ, that gave in his own person this gospel, is very God and very man, and by his heart passes all other laws.

I suppose over this that the pope be most obliged to the keeping of the gospel among all men that live here; for the pope is highest vicar that Christ has here in earth. For moreness of Christ's vicar is not measured by worldly moreness, but by this, that this vicar follows more Christ by virtuous living; for thus teacheth the gospel, that this is the sentence of Christ.

And of this gospel I take as belief that Christ for time that he walked here was most poor man of all, both in spirit and in having; for Christ says that he had nought for to rest his head on. And Paul says that he was made needy for our love. And more poor might no man be, neither bodily nor in spirit. And thus Christ put from him all manner of worldly lordship. For the gospel of John telleth that when they would have made Christ king, he fled and hid him from them, for he would have none such worldly highness.

And over this I take it as belief that no man should follow the pope, nor no saint that now is in heaven, but in as much as he follows Christ. For John and James erred when they coveted worldly highness; and Peter and Paul sinned also when they denied and blasphemed in Christ; but men should not follow them in this, for then they went from Jesus Christ. And this I take as wholesome counsel, that the pope leave his worldly lordship to worldly lords, as Christ gave them—and move speedily all his clerks to do so. For thus did Christ, and taught thus his disciples, till the fiend had blinded this world. And it seems to some men that clerks that dwell lastingly in this error against God's law, and flee to follow Christ in this, are open heretics, and their fautors are partners.

And if I err in this sentence, I will meekly be amended, yea, by the death, if it be skillful, for that I hope were good to me. And if I might travel in mine own person, I would with good will go to the pope. But God has needed me to the contrary, and taught me more obedience to God than to men. And I suppose of our pope that he will not be Antichrist, and reverse Christ in this working, to the contrary of Christ's will; for if he summon against reason, by him or by any of his, and pursue this unskillful summoning, he is an open Antichrist. And merciful intent excused not Peter, that Christ should not clepe him Satan; so blind intent and wicked counsel excuses not the pope here; but if he ask of true priests that they travel more than they may, he is not excused by reason of God, that he should not be Antichrist. For our belief teaches us that our blessed God suffers us not to be tempted more than we may; how should a man ask such service? And therefore pray we to God for our pope Urban the sixth, that his old holy intent be not quenched by his enemies. And Christ, that may not lie, says that the enemies of a man are especially his home family; and this is sooth of men and fiends.

59   The Council of Constance, 1415: The Condemnation of Wyclifism

1. In the sacrament of the altar the material substance of bread and likewise the material substance of wine remain.

2. In the same sacrament the accidents of the bread do not remain without a subject.

3. In the same sacrament Christ is not identically and really with His own bodily presence.

4. If a bishop or priest is living in mortal sin, he does not ordain, nor consecrate, nor perform, nor baptize.

5. It is not established in the gospel that Christ arranged the mass.

6. God ought to obey the devil.

7. If man is duly contrite, every exterior confession on his part is superfluous and useless.

From H. J. D. Denzinger, *The Sources of Catholic Dogma*, translated by Roy J. Deferrari (St. Louis: B. Herder, 1965), pp. 208-11.

8. If the pope is foreknown and evil, and consequently a member of the devil, he does not have power over the faithful given to him by anyone, unless perchance by Caesar.

9. After Urban VI no one should be received as pope, unless he live according to the customs of the Greeks under their laws.

10. It is contrary to sacred scripture that ecclesiastical men have possessions.

11. No prelate should excommunicate anyone, unless first he knows that he has been excommunicated by God; and he who so excommunicates becomes, as a result of this, a heretic or excommunicated.

12. A prelate excommunicating a cleric who has appealed to the king, or to a council of the kingdom, by that very act is a traitor of the king and the kingdom.

13. Those who cease to preach or to hear the word of God because of the excommunication of men, are themselves excommunicated, and in the judgment of God they will be considered traitors of Christ.

14. It is permissible for any deacon or priest to preach the word of God without the authority of the Apostolic See or a Catholic bishop.

15. No one is a civil master, no one a prelate, no one a bishop, as long as he is in mortal sin.

16. Temporal rulers can at their will take away temporal goods from the Church, when those who have possessions habitually offend, that is, offend by habit, not only by an act.

17. People can at their will correct masters who offend.

18. The tithes are pure alms and parishioners can take these away at will because of the sins of their prelates.

19. Special prayers applied to one person by prelates or religious are not of more benefit to that person than general (prayers), all other things being equal.

20. One bringing alms to the Brothers is excommunicated by that very thing.

21. If anyone enters any private religious community of any kind, of those having possessions or of the mendicants, he is rendered unfit and unsuited for the observance of the laws of God.

22. Saints, instituting private religious communities, have sinned by instituting them.

23. Religious living in private religious communities are not of the Christian religion.

24. Brothers are bound to acquire their food by the labor of hands and not by begging.

25. All are simoniacs who oblige themselves to pray for others who assist them in temporal matters.

26. The prayer for the foreknown is of avail to no one.

27. All things happen from absolute necessity.

28. The confirmation of youths, ordination of clerics, and consecration of places are reserved to the pope and bishops on account of their desire for temporal gain and honor.

29. Universities, studies, colleges, graduations, and offices of instruction in the same have been introduced by a vain paganism; they are of as much value to the Church as the devil.

30. The excommunication of the pope or of any prelate whatsoever is not to be feared, because it is the censure of the Antichrist.

31. Those who found cloisters sin and those who enter (them) are diabolical men.

32. To enrich the clergy is contrary to the rule of Christ.

33. Sylvester, the pope, and Constantine, the Emperor, erred in enriching the Church.

34. All of the order of mendicants are heretics, and those who give alms to them are excommunicated.

35. Those entering religion or any order, by that very fact are unsuited to observe divine precepts, and consequently to enter the kingdom of heaven, unless they apostasize from these.

36. The pope with all his clergy who have possessions are heretics, because they have possessions; and all in agreement with these, namely all secular masters and other laity.

37. The Roman Church is a synagogue of Satan, and the pope is not the next and immediate vicar of Christ and His apostles.

38. The decretal letters are apocryphal and they seduce from the faith of Christ, and the clergy who study them are foolish.

39. The emperor and secular masters have been seduced by the devil to enrich the Church with temporal goods.

40. The election of the pope by cardinals was introduced by the devil.

41. It is not necessary for salvation to believe that the Roman Church is supreme among other churches.

42. It is foolish to believe in the indulgences of the pope and bishops.

43. Oaths are illicit which are made to corroborate human contracts and civil commerce.

44. Augustine, Benedict, and Bernard have been damned, unless

they repented about this, that they had possessions and instituted and entered religious communities; and thus from the pope to the last religious, all are heretics.

45. All religious communities without distinction have been introduced by the devil.

60   The Lollard Conclusions, 1394

Wyclif's followers were called Lollards, a name derived perhaps from the Dutch term *lollaerd*, meaning someone who muttered or mumbled (here, possibly, muttering prayers), and associated with the Latin term *lolia*, "tares" or "cockle" (see above, no. 10). Wyclifism was driven from Oxford University by 1382, but some lower clergy and devout lay people, including some landed gentry, circulated Wyclif's teachings vigorously, including the famous "Lollard Conclusions" of 1394, a document that bitterly attacked the Church in England and inspired first considerable resistance and then the formidable statute *De haeretico comburendo* (above, no. 44).

1. That when the Church of England began to go mad after temporalities, like its great stepmother the Roman Church, and churches were authorized by appropriation in divers places, faith, hope, and charity began to flee from our Church, because pride, with its doleful progeny of mortal sins, claimed this under title of truth. This conclusion is general, and proved by experience, custom, and manner or fashion, as you shall afterwards hear.

2. That our usual priesthood which began in Rome, pretended to be of power more lofty than the angels, is not that priesthood which Christ ordained for his apostles. This conclusion is proved because the Roman priesthood is bestowed with signs, rites, and pontifical blessings, of small virtue, nowhere exemplified in holy scripture, because the bishop's ordinal and the New Testament scarcely agree, and we cannot see that the Holy Spirit, by reason of any such signs, confers the gift, for he and all his excellent gifts cannot consist in any one with mortal sin. A corollary to this is that it is a grievous play for wise men

to see bishops trifle with the Holy Spirit in the bestowal of orders, because they give the tonsure in outward appearance in the place of white hearts; and this is the unrestrained introduction of antichrist into the Church to give color to idleness.

3. That the law of continence enjoined on priests, which was first ordained to the prejudice of women, brings sodomy into all the Holy Church, but we excuse ourselves by the Bible because the decree says that we should not mention it, though suspected. Reason and experience prove this conclusion: reason, because the good living of ecclesiastics must have a natural outlet or worse; experience, because the secret proof of such men is that they find delight in women, and when thou hast proved such a man mark him well, because he is one of them. A corollary to this is that private religions and the originators or beginning of this sin would be specially worthy of being checked, but God of his power with regard to secret sin sends open vengeance in his Church.

4. That the pretended miracle of the sacrament of bread drives all men but a few to idolatry, because they think that the Body of Christ which is never away from heaven could by power of the priest's word be enclosed essentially in a little bread which they show the people; but God grant that they might be willing to believe what the evangelical doctor says in his Trialogus (4:7), that the bread of the altar is habitually the Body of Christ, for we take it that in this way any faithful man and woman can by God's law perform the sacrament of that bread without any such miracle. A final corollary is that although the Body of Christ has been granted eternal joy, the service of Corpus Christi, instituted by Brother Thomas [Aquinas], is not true but is fictitious and full of false miracles. It is no wonder; because Brother Thomas, at that time holding with the pope, would have been willing to perform a miracle with a hen's egg; and we know well that any falsehood openly preached turns to the disgrace of Him who is always true and without any defect.

5. That exorcisms and blessings performed over wine, bread, water and oil, salt, wax, and incense, the stones of the altar, and church walls, over clothing, mitre, cross, and pilgrims' staves, are the genuine performance of necromancy rather than of sacred theology. This conclusion is proved as follows, because by such exorcisms creatures are honored as being of higher virtue than they are in their own nature, and we do not see any changes in any creature which is so exorcized, save by false faith which is the principal characteristic of the devil's art. A corollary: that if the book of exorcizing holy water, read in

church, were entirely trustworthy we think truly that the holy water used in church would be the best medicine for all kinds of illnesses— sores, for instance; whereas we experience the contrary day by day.

6. That king and bishop in one person, prelate and judge in temporal causes, curate and officer in secular office, puts any kingdom beyond good rule. This conclusion is clearly proved because the temporal and spiritual are two halves of the entire Holy Church. And so he who has applied himself to one should not meddle with the other, for no one can serve two masters. It seems that hermaphrodite or ambidexter would be good names for such men of double estate. A corollary is that we, the procurators of God in this behalf, do petition before Parliament that all curates, as well superior as inferior, be fully excused and should occupy themselves with their own charge and no other.

7. That special prayers for the souls of the dead offered in our Church, preferring one before another in name, are a false foundation of alms, and for that reason all houses of alms in England have been wrongly founded. This conclusion is proved by two reasons: the one is that meritorious prayer, and of any effect, ought to be a work proceeding from deep charity, and perfect charity leaves out no one, for "Thou shalt love thy neighbor as thyself." And so it is clear to us that the gift of temporal good bestowed on the priesthood and houses of alms is a special incentive to private prayer which is not far from simony. For another reason is that special prayer made for men condemned is very displeasing to God. And although it be doubtful, it is probable to faithful Christian people that founders of a house of alms have for their poisonous endowment passed over for the most part to the broad road. The corollary is: effectual prayer springing from perfect love would in general embrace all whom God would have saved, and would do away with that well-worn way or merchandise in special prayers made for the possessionary mendicants and other hired priests, who are a people of great burden to the whole realm, kept in idleness: for it has been proved in one book, which the king had, that a hundred houses of alms would suffice in all the realm, and from this would rather accrue possible profit to the temporal estate.

8. That pilgrimages, prayers, and offerings made to blind crosses or roods, and to deaf images of wood or stone, are pretty well akin to idolatry and far from alms, and although these be forbidden and imaginary, a book of error to the lay folk, still the customary image of the Trinity is specially abominable. This conclusion God clearly proves, bidding alms to be done to the needy man because they are the image

of God, and more like than wood or stone; for God did not say, "let us make wood or stone in our likeness and image," but man; because the supreme honor which clerks call *latria* appertains to the Godhead only; and the lower honor which clerks call *dulia* appertains to man and angel and to no inferior creature. A corollary is that the service of the cross, performed twice in any year in our church, is full of idolatry, for if that should, so might the nails and lance be so highly honored; then would the lips of Judas be relics indeed if any were able to possess them. But we ask you, pilgrim, to tell us when you offer to the bones of saints placed in a shrine in any spot, whether you relieve the saint who is in joy, or that almshouse which is so well-endowed and for which men have been canonized, God knows how. And to speak more plainly, a faithful Christian supposes that the wounds of that noble man, whom men call St. Thomas, were not a case of martyrdom.

9. That auricular confession which is said to be so necessary to the salvation of a man, with its pretended power of absolution, exalts the arrogance of priests and gives them opportunity of other secret colloquies which we will not speak of; for both lords and ladies attest that, for fear of their confessors, they dare not speak the truth. And at the time of confession there is a ready occasion for assignation, that is for "wooing," and other secret understandings leading to mortal sins. They themselves say that they are God's representatives to judge of every sin, to pardon and cleanse whomsoever they please. They say that they have the keys of heaven and of hell, and can excommunicate and bless, bind and loose, at their will, so much so that for a drink, or twelve pence, they will sell the blessing of heaven with charter and close warrant sealed with the common seal. This conclusion is so notorious that it needs not any proof. It is a corollary that the pope of Rome, who has given himself out as treasurer of the whole Church, having in charge that worthy jewel of Christ's passion together with the merits of all saints in heaven, whereby he grants pretended indulgence from penalty and guilt, is a treasurer almost devoid of charity, in that he can set free all that are prisoners in hell at his will, and cause that they should never come to that place. But in this any Christian can well see there is much secret falsehood hidden away in our Church.

10. That manslaughter in war, or by pretended law of justice for a temporal cause, without spiritual revelation, is expressly contrary to the New Testament, which indeed is the law of grace and full of mercies. This conclusion is openly proved by the examples of Christ's preaching here on earth, for he specially taught a man to love his enemies, and to show them pity, and not to slay them. The reason is

this, that for the most part, when men fight, after the first blow, charity is broken. And whoever dies without charity goes the straight road to hell. And beyond this we know well that no clergyman can by scripture or lawful reason remit the punishment of death for one mortal sin and not for another; but the law of mercy, which is the New Testament, prohibits all manner of manslaughter, for in the gospel: "It was said unto them of old time, Thou shalt not kill." The corollary is that it is indeed robbery of poor folk when lords get indulgences from punishment and guilt for those who aid their army to kill a Christian people in distant lands for temporal gain, just as we too have seen soldiers who run into heathendom to get them a name for the slaughter of men; much more do they deserve ill thanks from the King of Peace, for by our humility and patience was the faith multiplied, and Christ Jesus hates and threatens men who fight and kill, when He says: "He who smites with the sword shall perish by the sword."

11. That the vow of continence made in our Church by women who are frail and imperfect in nature is the cause of bringing in the gravest horrible sins possible to human nature, because, although the killing of abortive children before they are baptized and the destruction of nature by drugs are vile sins, yet connection with themselves or brute beasts or any creature not having life surpasses them in foulness to such an extent as that they should be punished with the pains of hell. The corollary is that widows and such as take the veil and the ring, being delicately fed, we could wish that they were given in marriage, because we cannot excuse them from secret sins.

12. That the abundance of unnecessary arts practiced in our realm nourishes much sin in waste, profusion, and disguise. This, experience and reason prove in some measure, because nature is sufficient for a man's necessity with few arts. The corollary is that since St. Paul says, "having food and raiment, let us be therewith content," it seems to us that goldsmiths and armorers and all kinds of arts not necessary for a man, according to the apostle, should be destroyed for the increase of virtue; because although these two said arts were exceedingly necessary in the old law, the New Testament abolishes them and many others.

This is our embassy, which Christ has bidden us fulfill, very necessary for this time for several reasons. And although these matters are briefly noted here they are however set forth at large in another book, and many others besides, at length in our own language, and we wish that these were accessible to all Christian people. We ask God then of his supreme goodness to reform our Church, as being entirely out of joint, to the perfectness of its first beginning.

61   John Hus: On Simony

A large amount of Hus's work has been translated into English. The whole of Hus's *On Simony* may be found in Matthew Spinka, ed., *Advocates of Reform: From Wyclif to Erasmus* (Philadelphia, 1953). Hus's treatise *On Simony* is indicative of the strong resentment of ecclesiastical abuses which is paralleled in Wyclif's condemnation of indulgences and characterizes much of the temper of fourteenth- and fifteenth-century dissent. Wyclif's doctrines were finally formally condemned at the Council of Constance in 1415 (no. 59), and the council's identification of Hus with Wyclifism laid the groundwork for the trial, condemnation, and burning of Hus himself (nos. 62-63). Hus's eloquent correspondence before his death may be read in Matthew Spinka, *The Letters of John Hus* (Manchester, 1972). Hus's treatise *On the Church* has been translated by David Schaff, *The Church, by John Hus* (New York, 1915). C.M.D. Crowder, *Unity, Heresy and Reform 1378-1460* is excellent on Hus, and the council in its wider setting is described in sources translated in Louise Ropes Loomis, *The Council of Constance*, ed. K.M. Woody and J.H. Mundy (New York, 1961), and in Matthew Spinka, ed. and trans., *John Hus at the Council of Constance* (New York, 1965).

Simony is an evil consent to an exchange of spiritual goods for nonspiritual, about which more will be said. But know that these three heresies are not entirely independent of each other, but are connected with each other. Nevertheless, they are differentiated from each other so that apostasy is the rejection of the law of God; blasphemy is the defamation of the divine faith; and simony is the heresy of overthrowing the divine order. Thus with these three heresies the entire Holy Trinity is contemned: God the Father is contemned by apostasy, for he rules mightily by a pure and immaculate law; he also has provided a bride of Christ which is the congregation of all the elect; God the Son, who is the Wisdom of God, is contemned by the second heresy—blasphemy; and God the Holy Spirit, who in his supreme goodness

From Matthew Spinka, ed., *Advocates of Reform: From Wyclif to Erasmus*, The Library of Christian Classics, Vol. XIV. Published simultaneously in Great Britain and the U.S.A. by the S.C.M. Press, Ltd., London, and the Westminster Press, Philadelphia. Used by permission.

wisely and humbly governs God's house, is contemned by the accursed simony which is contrary to his order. For the simoniac opposes the Holy Spirit, intending to derange his good order, and thus also peace. And since in accordance with the testimony of Christ the sin against the Holy Spirit is unforgivable both in this world and the next, I will write about this sin. For simony is a spiritual leprosy which is difficult to be driven out from the soul save by God's special miracle. Moreover, since this leprosy spreads from one to another, so that one simoniac infects many others, faithful Christians should diligently guard against it. But because a man cannot easily guard against an evil he does not know, simony must therefore be made known.

Simony, as the word signifies, is trafficking in holy things. And since both he who buys and he who sells is a merchant, a simoniac is both he who buys and he who sells holy things. *Consequently, simony comprises both buying and selling of holy things.* But since there can be blameless buying and selling of a holy thing, for a man may buy himself the Kingdom of Heaven, not every buying or selling is simony. For, as has been said above, simony is an evil consent to an exchange of a spiritual for a nonspiritual thing. For that a man may worthily buy the Kingdom of Heaven, which is blessedness, the Lord affirms through the prophet Isaiah, "Come and buy without silver." And the Saviour affirms that the Kingdom of Heaven is like unto a merchant seeking goodly pearls, who, having found one pearl of great price, went and sold all that he had and bought it. Thus it behooves a man to buy the holy thing, for unless he purchase it he shall not attain to heavenly joy. Likewise a preacher or teacher may properly exchange his learning for temporal necessities. As Saint Paul says, "For if we give you spiritual things, is it a great matter if we receive of you carnal things?" Therefore, in order that you may know that simony has its source and nest in the evil will, it is defined as an evil consent to such an exchange. Accordingly, you perceive that one commits simony not only when the transaction is completed or when a tacit exchange of the spiritual for the material thing takes place, but even when one's corrupt will consents to such an exchange. For fornication is first a mortal sin in the soul, and afterward in deed.

Nevertheless, a difficulty presents itself in regard to what a spiritual thing is. For every man who commits a mortal sin is a simoniac, since he sells his soul and his human dignity—which are spiritual things—to the devil. Therefore, understand that simony in a particular sense designates an improper exchange among men dealing with the spiritual offices of the house of God.

The simple-minded imagine that there is no simony except that a priest haggle about the body of God, saying, "What will you give me for the body of God?"; or, "How much will you take for that altar, or that church, or other benefice?" But the saints who know the scriptures regard [as simony] the evil will whereby a man demands for a spiritual thing a material recompense, favor, or praise. Accordingly, Saint Gregory says: "There are many who do not take money payments for ordination, but yet grant the ordination for human favor, and from this human praise seek their sole reward. Thus the gift which they had freely received they do not freely give, because they expect in exchange for the granting of the holy office the payment of favor. Thus the prophet has well said in describing a righteous man, 'Blessed is he who withdraws his hand from every gift.' Excellently he says 'from every gift'; for some gifts consist of service, others are transmitted by hand, others by the tongue. The gift consisting of service is the appointment of an unworthy candidate; the gift transmitted by the hand, that is, anything which may be purchased, is money; the gift conveyed by the tongue is praise or improper promise. Hence in conferring consecration, he withdraws his hand from every recompense when in exchange for the sacred things he not only asks no money but likewise no human praise" . . . .

Thereby Saint Gregory means that whenever anyone confers a spiritual gift improperly, either himself or through another, either openly or covertly, either in consideration of service, of material gift, or human favor, he thereby commits simony, contrary to the scriptures and Christ's command, "Freely have ye received, freely give." The apostles received freely, without bribery, without unworthy subservience, or material favor; therefore, they likewise gave freely, without such bribery. But since now clergy do not receive freely, they likewise do not give freely, neither absolution, nor ordination, nor extreme unction, nor other spiritual things.

From this exposition, as well as from the customs which we plainly observe among clerics, we may learn that there are but few priests who have secured their ordination or their benefices without simony, so they on the one hand and their bishops on the other have fallen into simony. And since simony is heresy, if anyone observe carefully he must perceive that many are heretics. Nor is there any difference among them, except that among those who occupy higher ecclesiastical offices they are more numerous, more persistent, and fatter simoniacs, and accordingly heretics . . . .. Pope Paschal says that "manifest simoniacs should be rejected by the faithful as the first and pre-eminent heretics; and if after admonition they refuse to desist, they should be suppressed by the secular power. For all other sins in comparison with the heresy of simony are as if of no account". . . .

Furthermore, Saint Gregory writes: "To you, priests, I say this with weeping, that we have found that many of you ordain for money, selling spiritual gifts, and from these sinful evils you heap up material profit. Why do you not call to mind what the voice of God says: 'Freely have ye received, freely give'? Why do ye not bring before your eyes how the Savior, having entered the Temple, had overthrown the tables of the sellers of doves and had scattered the money of the money-changers? And who are the sellers of doves in God's temple today but those in Christendom who accept money for laying on of hands? For the Holy Spirit from heaven is given by laying on of hands. Accordingly, a dove is sold when the gift of the Holy Spirit is sold for money. But our Redeemer overturns the tables of the dove sellers, for he destroys the priesthood of such traffickers. Therefore the holy canons condemn the heresy of simony and order the degradation of such from priesthood". . . . And, knowing that priests employ much cunning in excusing themselves, he immediately adds: "The day will surely come and is not far off, when the Pastor of pastors shall appear and shall make public the deeds of every man; and he who now punishes the sins of the inferiors through their superiors shall then condemn the sins of the superiors themselves. For that reason having entered the Temple, he made a whip of cords and expelled from the house of God the wicked traffickers and overturned the tables of the dove sellers. For he chastises the transgressions of the subjects through the pastors, but the wickedness of the pastors he himself shall punish. This judge shall surely come, and before him no one shall hide in silence, nor shall anyone deceive him by denials". . . .

Saint Remigius, commenting on the same passsage as Saint Gregory, writes as follows: "Hear and apprehend this, priests of the Holy Church, that is, of the Christian communion, and beware lest ye convert the house of God into a den of robbers. For he is a robber who seeks [material] reward from the law and is diligent in the sacramental service for sake of gain. Hence they should fear that they be not cast out of the spiritual temple, as the others [the dove sellers] were cast out of the temporal temple; for the Lord visits his Father's house [i.e., the Holy Church] every day and casts out those who busy themselves with unrighteous gain, accounting as guilty of the same sin both the buyers and the sellers. For the sellers are those who bestow ordination for remuneration; and buyers those who pay money for the truth [i.e., the holy office], and, having paid money to the sellers, buy sin for themselves."

Let us notice that the passage says, "He overturned the tables of the money-changers, as well as of the sellers of doves." What else can be understood by the tables of the money-changers but the altars which are converted by the covetousness of the priests into the tables of money-changers? And what else can be meant by the tables of the dove sellers but the dignity of masters in the Holy Church, which dignity, if it be used for gain, shall be emptied? And what can be signified by doves but the Holy Spirit, who appeared above the Lord in the likeness of a dove? And who are the dove sellers but those who, by the laying on of hands, sell the Holy Spirit for a consideration? . . . For whenever a bishop sells the gift of the Holy Spirit, even though he dazzles men by his episcopal robes, in the eyes of God he is already deprived of his priesthood. Accordingly, the holy canons condemn the heresy of simony, and ordain that those who demand money for the gift of the Holy Spirit be deprived of priesthood. . . .

62   The Council of Constance, 1415: The Condemnation of Hus's Errors

1. One and only is the holy universal Church which is the aggregate of the predestined.

2. Paul never was a member of the devil, although he did certain acts similar to the acts of those who malign the Church.

3. The foreknown are not parts of the Church, since no part of it finally will fall away from it, because the charity of predestination which binds it will not fall away.

4. Two natures, divinity and humanity, are one Christ.

5. The foreknown, although at one time he is in grace according to the present justice, yet is never a part of the holy Church; and the predestined always remains a member of the Church, although at times he may fall away from additional grace, but not from the grace of predestination.

From H. J. D. Denzinger, *The Sources of Catholic Dogma*, translated by Roy J. Deferrari (St. Louis: B. Herder, 1965), pp. 212-15.

6. Assuming the Church as the convocation of the predestined, whether they were in grace or not according to the present justice, in that way the Church is an article of faith.

7. Peter is not nor ever was the head of the Holy Catholic Church.

8. Priests living criminally in any manner whatsoever defile the power of the priesthood, and as unfaithful sons they think unfaithfully regarding the seven sacraments of the Church, the keys, the duties, the censures, customs, ceremonies, and sacred affairs of the Church, its veneration of relics, indulgences, and orders.

9. The papal dignity has sprung up from Caesar, and the perfection and institution of the pope have emanated from the power of Caesar.

10. No one without revelation would have asserted reasonably regarding himself or anyone else that he was the head of a particular church, nor is the Roman Pontiff the head of a particular Roman Church.

11. It is not necessary to believe that the one whosoever is the Roman Pontiff, is the head of any particular church, unless God has predestined him.

12. No one takes the place of Christ or of Peter unless he follows him in character, since no other succession is more important, and not otherwise does he receive from God the procuratorial power, because for that office of vicar are required both conformity in character and the authority of Him who institutes it.

13. The pope is not the true and manifest successor of Peter, the first of the apostles, if he lives in a manner contrary to Peter; and if he be avaricious, then he is the vicar of Judas Iscariot. And with like evidence the cardinals are not the true and manifest successors of the college of the apostles of Christ, unless they live in the manner of the apostles, keeping the commandments and counsels of our Lord Jesus Christ.

14. Doctors holding that anyone to be emended by ecclesiastical censure, if he is unwilling to be corrected, must be handed over to secular judgment, certainly are following in this the priests, scribes, and Pharisees, who, saying that "it is not permissible for us to kill anyone" [John 18:31], handed over to secular judgment Christ himself, who did not wish to be obedient to them in all things, and such are homicides worse than Pilate.

15. Ecclesiastical obedience is obedience according to the invention of the priest of the Church, without the expressed authority of scripture.

16. The immediate division of human works is: that they are either

virtuous or vicious, because, if a man is vicious and does anything, then he acts viciously; because as vice, which is called a crime or mortal sin, renders the acts of man universally vicious, so virtue vivifies all the acts of the virtuous man.

17. Priests of Christ, living according to his law and having a knowledge of scripture and a desire to instruct the people, ought to preach without the impediment of a pretended excommunication. But if the pope or some other prelate orders a priest so disposed not to preach, the subject is not obliged to obey.

18. Anyone who approaches the priesthood receives the duty of a preacher by command, and that command he must execute, without the impediment of a pretended excommunication.

19. By ecclesiastical censures of excommunication, suspension, and interdict, the clergy for its own exaltation supplies for itself the lay populace, it multiplies avarice, protects wickedness, and prepares the way for the Antichrist. Moreover, the sign is evident that from the Antichrist such censures proceed, which in their processes they call fulminations, by which the clergy principally proceed against those who uncover the wickedness of the Antichrist, who will make use of the clergy especially for himself.

20. If the pope is wicked and especially if he is foreknown, then as Judas, the Apostle, he is of the devil, a thief, and a son of perdition, and he is not the head of the holy militant Church, since he is not a member of it.

21. The grace of predestination is a chain by which the body of the Church and any member of it are joined insolubly to Christ the Head.

22. The pope or prelate, wicked and foreknown, is equivocally pastor and truly a thief and robber.

23. The pope should not be called "most holy" even according to his office, because otherwise the king ought also to be called "most holy" according to his office, and torturers and heralds should be called holy, indeed even the devil ought to be called holy, since he is an official of God.

24. If the pope lives in a manner contrary to Christ, even if he should ascend through legal and legitimate election according to the common human constitution, yet he would ascend from another place than through Christ, even though it be granted that he entered by an election made principally by God; for Judas Iscariot rightly and legitimately was elected by God, Jesus Christ, to the episcopacy, and yet he ascended from another place to the sheepfold of the sheep.

25. The condemnation of the forty-five articles of John Wyclif made by the doctors is irrational and wicked and badly made; the cause alleged by them has been feigned, namely, for the reason that "no one of them is a Catholic but anyone of them is either heretical, erroneous, or scandalous."

26. Not for this reason, that the electors, or a greater part of them, agreed by acclamation according to the observance of men upon some person, is that person legitimately elected; nor for this reason is he the true and manifest successor or vicar of the Apostle Peter, or in the ecclesiastical office of another apostle. Therefore, whether electors have chosen well or badly, we ought to believe in the works of one elected; for, by the very reason that anyone who operates for the advancement of the Church in a manner more fully meritorious, has from God more fully the facility for this.

27. For there is not a spark of evidence that there should be one head ruling the Church in spiritual affairs, which head always lives and is preserved with the Church militant herself.

28. Christ through His true disciples scattered through the world would rule his Church better without such monstrous heads.

29. The apostles and faithful priests of the Lord strenuously in necessities ruled the Church unto salvation, before the office of the pope was introduced; thus they would be doing even to the day of judgment, were the pope utterly lacking.

30. No one is a civil master, no one is a prelate, no one is a bishop while he is in mortal sin.

63   Peter of Mladonovice: The Examination and Execution of Hus

Similarly on Friday, on the already mentioned 7 June, an hour after an almost total eclipse of the sun, they again brought Master John [i.e., Hus] to a hearing in the said refectory, which was surrounded

From Matthew Spinka, ed. and trans., *John Hus at the Council of Constance* (New York: Columbia University Press, 1965), pp. 167-80, 224-34. Reprinted with the permission of the publisher.

during each hearing by many city guards armed with swords, cross-bows, axes, and spears. In the meantime the king arrived and brought with him Lords Wenceslas and John along with Peter the bachelor. At this hearing were read the articles about which at Prague witnesses had testified before the vicar of the archbishop of Prague and also in Constance, to some of which he responded separately. Among them, when the said lords and Peter arrived, this article was in effect being ascribed to him.

It is also stated that the above-named Master John Hus in the month of June of the year of the Lord 1410, as well as before and after, preaching to the people congregated in a certain chapel of Bethlehem and in various other places of the city of Prague, at various times contrived, taught, and disputed about many errors and heresies both from the books of the late John Wyclif and from his own impudence and craftiness, defending them as far as he was able. Above all, he held the error hereafter stated, that after the consecration the host on the altar remains material bread. To that charge they produced as witnesses doctors, prelates, pastors, etc., as it is stated in the said testimony.

Then he, calling God and his conscience to witness, replied that he had not said or stated it; in reality, when the archbishop of Prague had commanded that the term "bread" be not even mentioned, he [Hus] rose to oppose it on the ground that even Christ in the sixth chapter of John eleven times called Himself "the angelic bread" and "giving life to the world," and "descending from heaven," and was so called by others. Therefore, he [Hus] did not want to contradict that gospel. He replied, moreover, that he had never spoken concerning the material bread. Then the cardinal of Cambrai, taking a paper that, he said, had come into his hands late the evening before, and holding it in his hand, questioned Master John if he regarded universals as real apart from the thing itself. And he responded that he did, since both St. Anselm and others had so regarded them. Thereupon the cardinal argued, "It follows that after the consecration there remains the substance of the material bread." And he advanced proof of it as follows: that in the act of consecration, while the bread is being changed and transubstan-tiated into the body of Christ—as you have already said—either there did or did not remain the most common substance of the material bread. If it did, the proposition was proved; if not, it follows that with the cessation of the particular there also ceased the universal substance of itself. He [Hus] replied that it ceased to exist in the substance of that particular material bread when it was changed or passed into the body of Christ, or was transubstantiated; but despite that, in other particulars it remains the same. Then a certain Englishman wished to prove by an exposition of the material that was the subject of discussion that material bread remained there. The Master said: "That is a puerile argument that schoolboys study"—and acquitted himself thereby. Then again a certain Englishman, standing beside Master John, wished to prove that after the consecration there remained the form of the substance of the material bread and the primal matter, while that bread was not annihilated. The Master responded that it was not annihilated, but that the particular substance ceased in that instance by being transubstantiated into the body of Christ. Again another Englishman—known as Master William—rose and said: "Wait, he speaks evasively, just as Wyclif did. For he [Wyclif] conceded all these things that this man concedes, yet nevertheless he holds that the material bread remains in the sacrament of the altar after consecration. In fact, he has adduced the whole chapter 'We believe firmly' in confirmation of that erroneous opinion of his." And he [Hus]: "I do not speak evasively but, God is my witness, sincerely and out of my heart." "But, I ask you, Master John, whether the body of Christ is there totally, really, and manifoldly?" And Master John responded that truly, really, and totally that same body of Christ that had been born of the Virgin Mary, had suffered, died, and had been resurrected, and that is seated at the right hand of the Father, was in the sacrament of the altar. And many irrelevancies on the subject of universals were mixed with the debate. That Englishman who had insisted on the primal matter said: "Why are irrelevancies that have nothing to do with the subject of faith mixed with it? He judges rightly about the sacrament of the altar, as he here confesses." But the Englishman Stokes said, "I saw in Prague a certain treatise ascribed to this Hus in which it was expressly stated that the material bread remains in the sacrament after consecration." The Master said: "With all respect to your reverence, it is not true."

Again for the confirmaton of that article they brought forth witnesses—masters, doctors, and pastors of Prague who deposed that at the table in the parsonage of a certain Prague pastor he [Hus] had defended his assertion concerning the remanence of the material bread. . . .

When these altercations ceased, the cardinal of Florence said: "Master John, you know that it is written that 'in the mouth of two or three witnesses stands every word' And look! here are well-nigh twenty witnesses against you—prelates, doctors, and other great and notable men, some of whom depose from common hearsay, others however from knowledge, adducing reasonable proofs of their knowlege. What, then, do you still oppose against them all?" And he replied: "If the Lord God and my conscience are my witnesses that I have neither preached nor taught those things they depose against me, nor have they ever entered my heart—even if all my adversaries deposed them against me, what can I do? Nor does this in the end hurt me."

The cardinal of Cambrai said: "We cannot judge according to your conscience, but according to what has been proved and deduced here against you and some things that you have confessed. And you would perhaps wish to call all who out of their knowledge deposed against you, adducing reasonable evidence of their knowledge, your enemies and adversaries? We, on the other hand, must believe them. You have said that you suspected Master Stephen Pàleč, who has certainly dealt humanely and very kindly with these books and articles, abstracting them even more leniently than they are contained in the book. And similarly all the other doctors. In fact, you were saying that you suspect the chancellor of Paris, than whom surely no more renowned doctor could be found in all Christendom."

Further it is stated that the said John Hus obstinately preached and defended the erroneous articles of Wyclif in schools and in public sermons in the city of Prague. He replied that he had neither preached nor wished to follow the erroneous doctrine of Wyclif or of anyone else, as Wyclif was neither his father nor a Czech. And if Wyclif had disseminated some errors, let the English see to that.

When they objected to him that he had resisted the condemnation of the forty-five articles of Wyclif, he replied that when the doctors had condemned his [Wyclif's] forty-five articles for the reason that none of them was Catholic, but that every one of them was either heretical, erroneous, or scandalous, he dared not consent to their condemnation because it was an offense to his conscience. And particularly of this: "Pope Sylvester and Constantine erred in endowing the Church." Also this: "If the pope or a priest is in mortal sin, then he neither transubstantiates, nor consecrates, nor baptizes"; but he qualified it that he does not do so worthily, but unworthily, for he was at the time an unworthy minister of God's sacraments. And they said: "It is stated unqualifiedly in your book." He replied, "I am willing to be burned if it is not stated as I have qualified it." Afterward they found it so qualified in the treatise Contra Paletz at the beginning of chapter two. . . .

He also said that he did not assent to the said condemnation [of the forty-five articles] for the reason that the judgment of the doctors was a copulative syllogism, the second part not being provable in relation to the other parts of the articles: that is, that any one of them was heretical, erroneous, or scandalous. Then Pàleč stood up and said, "Let the contrary of that syllogism be held as valid: some one of them is Catholic, that is neither heretical nor erroneous nor scandalous; which one is it?" The Master said, "Prove that concerning any part of your syllogism and you will prove the argument." However, despite that he declared specifically that he had not obstinately asserted any of those articles, but that he had resisted their condemnation along with other masters and had not consented to it, because he had wished to hear scriptural [proofs] or adequate reasons from those doctors which contended for the condemnation of the articles.

It was also stated that the said John Hus in order to seduce the people and the simple-minded dared with temerity to say that in England many monks and other masters convened in a certain church of St. Paul's against Master John Wyclif but could not convict him; for immediately thunder and lightning descended on them from heaven and smashed the door of the church, so that those masters and monks scarcely escaped into the city of London. This he said for the confirmation of the statements of John Wyclif, thereupon breaking out at people with the words "Would that my soul were where the soul of Wyclif is!"

He replied that it was true that, twelve years ago, before his [Wyclif's] theological books had been [available] in Bohemia, and his books dealing with liberal arts had pleased him [Hus] much, and he had known nothing but what was good of his life, he said: "I know not where the soul of that John W[yclif] is; but I hope that he is saved, but fear lest he be damned. Nevertheless, I would desire in hope that my soul were where the soul of John W[yclif] is!" And when he said that in the council, they laughed at him a great deal, shaking their heads. . . .

Before he was led away, the cardinal of Cambrai said to him: "Master John, you said not long ago in the tower that you would wish humbly to submit to the judgment of the council. I counsel you, therefore, not to involve yourself in these errors, but to submit to the correction and instruction of the council; and the council will deal mercifully with you."

The king likewise said: "Listen, John Hus! Some have said that I first gave you the safe-conduct fifteen days after your arrest. I say, however, that it is not true; I am willing to prove by princes and very many others that I gave you safe-conduct even before you had left

Prague. I commanded Lords Wenceslas and John that they bring you and guard you in order that having freely come to Constance, you would not be constrained, but be given a public hearing so that you could answer concerning your faith. They [the members of the council] have done so and have given you a public, peaceable, and honest hearing here. And I thank them, although some may say that I could not grant a safe-conduct to a heretic or one suspected of heresy. For that reason, as here the lord cardinal has counseled you, I likewise counsel you to hold nothing obstinately, but in those things that were here proved against you and that you confessed, to offer yourself wholly to the mercy of the sacred council. And they, for your sake and our honor and for [the sake of] our brother and of the kingdom of Bohemia, will grant you some mercy, and you will do penance for your guilt. . . ."

o   o   o

In like manner in that year of the Lord 1415, on July 5, the Friday after St. Procopius, the noble lords Wenceslas of Dubá and John of Chlum were sent by Sigismund, king of the Romans and of Hungary, along with four bishops, to the prison of the Brothers Minor in Constance to hear the final decision of Master John Hus: if he would hold the above-mentioned articles which had been, as has already been said, abstracted from his books, as well as those that had been produced against him during the course of the trial and by the depositions of the witnesses; or if he would, according to the exhortation of the council, abjure and recant them, as has been said. When he was brought out of the prison, Lord John of Chlum said to him: "Look, Master John! we are laymen and know not how to advise you; therefore see if you feel yourself guilty in anything of that which is charged against you. Do not fear to be instructed therein and to recant. But if, indeed, you do not feel guilty of those things that are charged against you, follow the dictates of your conscience. Under no circumstances do anything against your conscience or lie in the sight of God: but rather be steadfast until death in what you know to be the truth." And he, Master John Hus, weeping, replied with humility: "Lord John, be sure that if I knew that I had written or preached anything erroneous against the law and against the holy mother Church, I would desire humbly to recant it—God is my witness! I have ever desired to be shown better and more relevant scripture than those that I have written and taught. And if they were shown me, I am ready most willingly to recant." To those words one of the bishops present replied to Master

John, "Do you wish to be wiser than the whole council?" The Master said to him, "I do not wish to be wiser than the whole council; but, I pray, give me the least one of the council who would instruct me by better and more relevant scripture, and I am ready instantly to recant!" To these words the bishops responded, "See, how obstinate he is in his heresy!" And with these words they ordered him to be taken back to the prison and went away. . . .

[On the following day, 6 July, Hus was brought into the cathedral. The articles of which he was accused were rehearsed against him for the last time and he was condemned.]

When therefore all the articles offered against him were completed and read, a certain old and bald auditor, a prelate of the Italian nation commissioned thereto, read the definitive sentence upon Master John Hus. And he, Master John responded, replying to certain points in the sentence, although they forbade it. And particularly when he was declared to be obstinate in his error and heresy, he replied in a loud voice: "I have never been obstinate, and am not now. But I have ever desired, and to this day I desire, more relevant instruction from the scriptures. And today I declare that if even with one word I could destroy and uproot all errors, I would most gladly do so!" And when all his books, either in Latin written by himself or translated into whatever other language, likewise in that sentence condemned as suspect of heresy, were for that reason condemned to be burned—of which some were burned later, particularly the book *De ecclesia* and *Contra Paletz*, as it was called, and *Contra Stanislaum*—he, Master John, responded: "Why do you condemn my books, when I have ever desired and demanded better scriptural proofs against what I said and set forth in them, and even today I so desire? But you have so far neither adduced any more relevant scripture in opposition, nor have shown one erroneous word in them. Indeed, how can you condemn the books in the vernacular Czech or those translated into another language when you have never even seen them?" While the rest of the sentence was being read, he heard it kneeling and praying, looking up to heaven. When the sentence was concluded, as has already been mentioned, in each of its particular points, Master John Hus again knelt and in a loud voice prayed for all his enemies and said: "Lord Jesus Christ, I implore Thee, forgive all my enemies for Thy great mercy's sake; and Thou knowest that they have falsely accused me and have produced false witnesses and have concocted false articles against me! Forgive them for Thy boundless mercy's sake!" And when he said this, many, especially the principal clergy, looked indignantly and jeered at him. . . .

[Peter recounts the formal degradation of Hus from the priesthood. He was then crowned with a paper hat proclaiming that he was a heresiarch, of the devil's brood, and led away to be burnt.]

And having come to the place of execution, bending his knees and stretching his hands and turning his eyes toward heaven, he most devoutly sang psalms, and particularly, "Have mercy on me, God," and "In Thee, Lord, have I trusted," repeating the verse "In Thy hand, Lord," His own [friends] who stood about then heard him praying joyfully and with a glad countenance. The place of execution was among gardens in a certain meadow as one goes from Constance towards the fortress of Gottlieben, between the gates and the moats of the suburbs of the said city. . . .

[Hus said his last prayers; made a last profession of his orthodoxy to the bystanders; was chained to the stake amidst the faggots, two cartloads of which were piled about him, while a third was held in reserve; and rejected a final offer of the chance to abjure.]

When the executioners at once lit [the fire], the Master immediately began to sing in a loud voice, at first "Christ, Thou son of the living God, have mercy upon us," and secondly, "Christ, Thou son of the living god, have mercy upon me," and in the third place, "Thou Who are born of Mary the Virgin." And when he began to sing the third time, the wind blew the flame into his face. And thus praying within himself and moving his lips and the head, he expired in the Lord. While he was silent, he seemed to move before he actually died for about the time one can quickly recite "Our Father" two or at most three times.

When the wood of those bundles and the ropes were consumed, but the remains of the body still stood in those chains, hanging by the neck, the executioners pulled the charred body, along with the stake, down to the ground and burned them further by adding wood from the third wagon to the fire. And walking, they broke the bones with clubs so that they would be incinerated more quickly. And finding the head, they broke it to pieces with the clubs and again threw it into the fire. And when they found his heart among the intestines, they sharpened a club like a spit, and, impaling it on its end, they took particular [care] to roast and consume it, piercing it with spears until finally the whole mass was turned into ashes. And at the order of the said Clem and the marshal, the executioners threw the clothing into the fire along with the shoes, saying: "So that the Czechs would not regard it as relics; we will pay you money for it." Which they did. So they loaded all the smouldering ashes in a cart and threw it into the river Rhine flowing nearby.

Thus I have described, briefly but very clearly the sequence of the death and agony of the celebrated Master John Hus, the eminent preacher of the evangelical truth, so that in the course of time his memory might be vividly recollected. My principle has been not to dress up the account in a mass of highly embellished diction lacking the kernel of fact and deed, wherewith to tickle the itching ears desirous to feast thereon; but rather to speak of the marrow of the substance of the trial proceedings mentioned above, of what I have clearly learned from what I myself have seen and heard. He who knows all things is my witness that I lie not. I would rather suffer the blame of having used inept and awkward words so that it may be recognized that I have brought forth testimony to the truth, that the memory of the Master, its most steadfast champion, may thus live in the future!

64 John of Brevicoxa: On the Church and Heresy

John of Brevicoxa became a doctor of theology at the University of Paris in 1388. His treatise *De fide et ecclesia* was written in 1375, and in it John defended the thesis that many things necessary for salvation were not contained in scripture and could not be deduced by the unaided study of scripture. The *ecclesia* required tradition, the writings of the Fathers, and the statements of councils and popes for the full exposition of the faith. Thus, John stands in the tradition upholding the Church's *magisterium* in teaching, maintaining among academics what others were maintaining among local clergy and preachers. Twenty-five years before John's treatise, Jacopo Passavanti, a Florentine Dominican who died in 1357, wrote a manual called *The*

Mirror of True Repentance, as a guide for simple clergy and lay people. Passavanti realizes the need for educating the laity, not only in scripture, but in the broader traditions of the Church as well:

> Each Christian is bound to have some knowledge of holy scripture, and each according to the state and condition and rank that he holds; for in one manner should the priest and guide of souls know it, and in another manner the master and doctor and preacher, those who ought to step down into the deep sea of scripture, and know and understand the hidden mysteries, so as to be ready for the instruction of others, and to be prepared to render a reason, as the apostle says, for the things of the faith and of scripture, to whoever shall ask it. And in yet another manner the laity and unlettered parish priests are bound to have it, to whom it is sufficient to know in general the ten commandments, the articles of the faith, the sacraments of the Church, the sins, and ecclesiastical ordinances, the doctrine of the holy gospel, as far as is necessary to their salvation, and as much as they hear from their rectors and the preachers of the scriptures and the faith, not searching them subtly, nor putting the foot down too deeply into the sea of scripture, which not all people can do, nor ought they to wish to scan it, because very often one slips and drowns oneself in incautious and curious and vain researches. But each one ought to know, as much as befits his office, and the status which he holds.

Thus, across a broad spectrum of society and culture, fourteenth-century churchmen still faced the problem of authority and dissent, orthodoxy and heresy, but, as in the case of John of Brevicoxa, they could speak and write about these topics from wide and long experience. Fourteenth-century ecclesiology reflects the agony of the spiritual experience of the preceding three centuries and contrasts sharply with the genial uncertainty of the apostolic and post-apostolic periods.

On John, see now Francis Oakley, "The *Tractatus De Fide et Ecclesia, Romano Pontifice et Concilio Generale* of John Breviscoxe," *Annuarium Historiae Conciliorum* 10 (1978): 99-130, and R. N. Swanson, *Universities, Academics and the Great Schism* (Cambridge, 1979).

I. WHAT IS CATHOLIC TRUTH?

As to the first question, our task is to investigate Catholic truth. Provisionally, Catholic truth might be described as follows: "Catholic truth is that truth which any pilgrim, of sound mind and having been sufficiently instructed in the Law of Christ, is required to believe either explicitly or implicitly as a condition for salvation." The word "pilgrim" is used to distinguish the Church Militant from the Church Triumphant, that is, those in heaven who perceive many truths by unmediated vision. Hence they do not need to believe in things unseen. "In sound mind" is included so as to eliminate children, of whom nothing is required, and those who are mad and demented, of whom likewise nothing is required, as long as they are in that condition. The reference to sufficient instruction in the "Law of Christ" is for the sake of those who immediately after they were baptized were reared without any contact with Christians and were never instructed in the faith (if, indeed, there be any such persons). "Explicitly or implicitly" is included because no pilgrim is required to know all Catholic truths explicitly, as no one is required to know the entire Bible explicitly, even though all biblical truths are Catholic truths. "Required as a condition for salvation" is stated to rule out truths that are not Catholic, such as those of philosophy or geometry. No pilgrim is required to know these or believe these truths as a condition for salvation.

V. WHAT IS HERESY?

Now that we have seen what Catholic truth is, the next question related to this subject is: What is heresy or heretical falsehood? The answer is that heresy is false dogma, dogma contrary to the orthodox faith. Many have defined heresy in this fashion and therefore I do not want to give any other definition, as this one appears to be sufficient and good. No matter what other valid definition might be given, it would be consonant with this definition. For that heresy is false dogma is asserted by Jerome.

Schism is also heretically perverted dogma, contrary to the orthodox faith. These definitions of heresy and schism make clear that errors in

From *Forerunners of the Reformation*, edited and with an introduction by Heiko A. Oberman. Translations by Paul L. Nyhus. Illustrations by Key Documents. Copyright © 1966 by Heiko A. Oberman. Reprinted by permission of Holt, Rinehart and Winston, Publishers.

the fields of physics or geometry are not heretical errors. Against this definition it is argued thus: Many new heresies have arisen that have not yet begun to be false dogmas, contrary to the Catholic faith, and *this* defintion would allow that there was at one time false teaching not contrary to Catholic faith but part of Catholic faith. Therefore, the given definition is not satisfactory. The premise that many new heresies arise is proved by the following evidence: "Pope Urban excommunicated Pelagius and Coelestius because they introduced a new law into the church." And Gratian said, "Every heretic either follows a heresy already damned or frames a new one." Since, in fact, new heresies *are* framed, our premise holds.

VI. CAN NEW HERESIES AND NEW TRUTHS BE ESTABLISHED?

In order to solve this problem the following question can reasonably be asked. Is it the case that every assertion ought to be called heretical which in some way contradicts holy scripture, while every truth ought to be called Catholic which is consonant with scripture or with assertions deducible from scripture? Various opinions are held in regard to this question.

VII. HOW MANY CATEGORIES OF HERESY ARE THERE?

It should be noted that opinions vary as much about heresy as they do about Catholic truth. Regarding Catholic truth some have said that only those truths are Catholic which are found explicitly or implictly in scripture. Others say there are many other Catholic truths beyond those found in the canon. So also regarding heresies, there are diverse opinions.

Heresy contra scripture

Some say that the only propositions that are heretical are those which contradict scripture. They distinguish three types of heresy.

1. First are those assertions which are not merely in some fashion at cross purposes with scripture but are indeed verbal contradictions of scriptural assertions. An example of this type would be: "The Word did not become flesh."

2. Second are those assertions which to all intelligent and enlightened people are clearly incompatible with that which is contained in scripture. An example would be: "Christ was not born for our salvation."

3. Third are those assertions which are found to be in conflict with scripture, but, in this case, the conflict may not be evident to everyone but only to whose who are wise, steeped in holy scripture, and skilled in subtle considerations. An example of this type would be: "As far as His humanity is concerned Christ is not something."

Heresy contra scripture and tradition

Others posit five types of heresy or error, paralleling the five categories of Catholic truth.

1. The first type of heresy or error consists of those assertions which contradict things taught by scripture only. This type includes several kinds of error, which should properly be called heresies.

2. The second type of error consists of those which in any manner contradict the teaching of the apostles or of scripture. This type can be divided into many kinds, just as the first.

3. The third type consists of those which in any way oppose anything revealed to or any inspiration of the Church in the post-apostolic age.

4. The fourth type includes those which are contrary to chronicles or to the records of events or to apostolic histories.

5. The fifth type consists of those assertions which are shown to be incompatible with holy scripture, or with apostolic doctrine not found in scripture, or with truths inspired by or revealed to the Church, together with other truths which one cannot rationally deny. The incompatibility need not be evident from the wording of the proposition.

An example of this type is the assertion "The faith Augustine held was not true." Now it is granted that this assertion is not strictly and properly heresy, nevertheless it savors of manifest heresy. And from this kind of assertion, together with certain other half truths, manifest heresy clearly issues.

Thus it is clear that just as there are five categories of Catholic truth, so, according to the same pattern, there are five categories of heresy or error.

VIII. Is every heresy condemned?

After the aforesaid, one may ask whether every heresy is condemned. The answer to this question is yes. Our first evidence comes from the General Council convoked by Innocent III, where it was said in the text dealing with excommunication, "We excommunicate and anathematize every heresy which flaunts the holy Catholic and orthodox faith." Whence it follows that every heresy is condemned, just as every biblical truth is approved. Now it might be objected that in this chapter only that heresy which flaunts the faith specifically set forth by the General Council is condemned. It is answered that even if such were the case, the thesis can be established by the following argument: Since the entire Catholic faith has been approved in the aforesaid chapter, every heresy has been damned and excommunicated by the General Council. The premise is proved by the following: The Council gave its express approval to the assertion that at the chosen time the Holy Trinity imparted saving doctrine to mankind through Moses and the prophets and other servants. Therefore, the doctrine which the Trinity now imparts to the faithful, whether through its servants or through itself, is saving doctrine. From this it follows that in the aforesaid chapter the whole Catholic faith is approved.

Our second evidence comes from the gloss on canon law. "Every heretic has been excommunicated, however misled he may be." From this it follows that every heresy has been condemned. No one is condemned, that is, excommunicated, as a heretic unless his heresy has been established first. Only learned writers sometimes make this distinction between a heresy which has been condemned and one which has not been condemned. Gratian, as earlier alleged, seemed to approve this distinction when he said, "Every heretic either follows a heresy already condemned or frames a new one." In order to understand Gratian and others who made the same distinction it should be noted that some heresies are condemned explicitly and others are only condemned implicitly. Gratian and these others meant by heresies those explicitly condemned, so that what is *really* said is, "Every heretic either follows a heresy already explicitly condemned or else thinks up a new one." And by a new heresy he means one not explicitly condemned. And this is perfectly consonant with the fact that such a heresy is implicitly condemned.

IX. HOW MANY CATEGORIES OF HERESY ARE EXPLICITLY CONDEMNED?

Now the ninth question arises. What are the categories of heresy which have been explicitly condemned? The answer is that there are four categories of heresy explicitly condemned.

The first category consists of those that are condemned by a special condemnation which specifies the exact words of the heresy. The heresies of Arius, Macedonius, and many others are condemned in this way.

The second category consists of those heresies which contain statements contrary to the exact words asserted and approved by all the faithful of sound mind. Such a one is "God is not creator of all things visible and invisible."

The third category consists of those heresies which are verbatim contradictions of any volume, book, or treatise that has come to be regarded as equal in authority to canonical writing. All heresies which are verbatim contradictions of the biblical canon ought to be counted as heresies and explicitly condemned.

The fourth category explicitly condemned consists of those assertions from which a heresy so obviously follows that it is clear even to laymen of sound mind. These are the four categories of heresy that are explicitly condemned.

Now it may be asked what heresies are implicitly condemned. To this it is answered that there exist heresies which do not fall under any of the indicated categories but which are discovered only after detailed investigation by men steeped in holy scripture. They can determine to what extent canonical truth is contradicted or to what extent the content of scripture or the doctrine of the Universal Church is approved. Further they can show how less defined heresies follow from these heresies already explicitly condemned according to aforesaid categories. An example of such an implicit heresy was the questioning by the Greeks—before such a heresy was explicitly condemned by the Church—of the procession of the Holy Spirit from the Son.

X. WHAT IS A CATHOLIC?

From the aforesaid it is evident what is Catholic truth, what indeed is heresy, and what are the categories of heresy. Nothing, however, has been said to determine what characterizes a heretic and what characterizes a Catholic. These issues should be clarified.

First, then, what characterizes a Catholic? To answer this we should note that the term "Catholic" can be defined in three ways.

One definition of a Catholic is anyone, properly baptized, who does not persist in anything contrary to the law of Christ. In this definition are included both adults, who believe in the Law of Christ, and infants, who, although baptized, no more adhere to the Law of Christ than do Mohammedans.

Another definition of a Catholic is every adult of sound mind who preserves and obeys the Catholic faith complete and uncorrupted. To preserve the Catholic faith uncorrupted means to believe without doubt all things which pertain explicitly or implicitly to the orthodox Catholic faith.

The meaning of implicit faith was clarified earlier and, as was stated before, he who holds all things contained in scripture or taught by the Universal Church to be true and sane, and does not adhere stubbornly to anything contrary to Catholic truth, has a complete and uncorrupted faith and, according to this definition, ought to be counted as a Catholic.

When Catholic is understood in this sense, a man could be called a Catholic if he preserved the Catholic faith as previously described, even if he held the Law of Christ on rational grounds, yes, even when his very basis for adhering to the Law of Christ was suggestive arguments or indeed conclusive arguments.

The third way of defining a Catholic is one who preserves the Catholic faith as previously described and who accepts the Law of Christ, not on rational grounds but without rational proof. As we have said, the typical act of Catholic faith is an act caused by both a natural disposition and infused grace. Infused faith alone cannot cause this act without a natural disposition. Therefore, one is truly a Catholic who performs such acts as are typical of faith. And he who, on the basis of a natural disposition, taken together with infused faith, assents to this assertion, "the Law of Christ is true," or any equivalent assertion, and does not adhere stubbornly to anything contradictory, such a one is in the strict sense of the word a Catholic. With this distinction in mind it is clear what a Catholic is and in what ways a Catholic is defined.

XI. What is a Heretic?

There remains the task of clarifying what characterizes a heretic and whether the name heretic denotes one thing or several. To this question it is answered that the name heretic has several meanings.

The first way of understanding heretic is as one who has been excommunicated, as Pope Nicholas says.

A second interpretation says that a heretic is a corrupter of sacred things. Thus one who commits simony is called a heretic in a certain gloss, where it says, "Whoever acquires ordination through money is elevated not so much to the rank of prelate as to that of heretic."

The third way, much more exact, is to define heretics as those who reckon the Catholic faith to be false or contrived. Clearly, Jews and Saracens are heretics, but all doubters are also heretics, since actually they are unbelievers too.

The fourth way is to say heretics are those who now consider or have considered themselves to be Christians but who nonetheless hold stubbornly to views that are contrary to Catholic truth. "Who now consider or have considered" is included in this definition to account for those for those who were baptized by a rite which did not conform to the rite of the Church. They are not Christians, although they consider or have considered themselves Christians and yet continue to hold views contrary to Catholic truth. They should be punished differently from Saracens, although they are no less heretics than the Saracens.

The fifth way defines as heretics all who adhere stubbornly to any error which savors of heresy or of the perversions which accompany heresy. This way accords with the third and fourth ways because it includes as heretics Mohammedans and Jews as well as those properly baptized who err stubbornly against the faith. One might wish to consider the current definition which regards as a heretic him who has been convicted of heresy but will not recant and is, therefore, according to the usage of the Church, handed over to the secular court. When one refers in this fashion to a heretic one implies that the concept of heretic is limited to one who is baptized or conducts himself as if he has been baptized, but who stubbornly doubts or errs against the Christian faith. Jews and Mohammedans are excluded by the first part of the definition, as are those baptized in jest or baptized by a rite which does not conform to that approved by the Church. The second part of the definition includes those who imagine themselves baptized, and who live in Christian nations. The third part of the definition excludes those who, through lack of intelligence or ignorance but not through willfulness, doubt or err against the faith. It should now be clear that a heretic is one who, although informed of the truth, nevertheless persists in his doubt or error against the Catholic truth.

XII. HOW CAN WE DEFINE STUBBORNNESS?

We now go on to ask, "How can we define stubbornness?" To be stubborn is to persist in that which ought to be given up. That this definition is sound is confirmed thus: Perseverance and stubbornness are opposites; the persevering one persists in an error which he ought to give up. Now if we ask when is the erring one required to give up his error, it is answered that the erring one, regardless of how long he errs against the faith, is not to be reckoned stubborn or as a heretic if he is always ready to stand corrected, and to give up his error when he has been corrected according to accepted standards. Now what is correction according to accepted standards? Only that correction satisfies the accepted standards which points out clearly to the erring one that his position obviates Catholic truth. For example, if anyone should say, out of ignorance, that there are two persons in Christ, it should be pointed out to him from the decree of the Synod of Ephesus that this has been defined as the heresy of Nestorius and has been damned by the Synod. Therefore, he cannot deny that his position is contrary to Catholic truth. Such correction would be sufficient.

And thus, even though he might claim that it has not been clearly pointed out to him that his position obviates Catholic truth, if indeed it has been pointed out, he is forced to adhere to the judgment of the experts. For if the experts conclude that this had been sufficiently explained, he is, at that moment, immediately required to recant his position.

XIII. Is every doubter an unbeliever?

The text from canon law, "He who doubts the faith is an unbeliever," should be understood as follows: "He who doubts the faith," that is, who doubts the faith is true, "is an unbeliever," that is, has a weak faith. For the faithful ought to believe firmly the whole Catholic truth and, furthermore, must adhere firmly—that is, with steadfast faith—to any article in particular which is implicit. It is not required however, that everyone adhere to any particular Catholic truth explicitly. But he who doubts that the whole Christian faith is true is manifestly heretical and should be judged stubborn since he is not ready to be corrected, for no one is ready to be corrected by a doctrine which he believes to be false. That is to say, if someone doubts an axiom to an argument because he doubts one of the conclusions which he draws from the axiom, there is no reason to expect that one can ever convince him of the validity of the conclusions. But if one doubts only the conclusions, then we can expect that he can be led to accept them by reasoning from the axiom. Now, the axiom one should faithfully believe is that the Christian faith is true.

XIV. WHAT IS THE STRONGEST REASON FOR CONCLUDING THAT
ONE IS REQUIRED TO KNOW PARTICULAR ARTICLES OF FAITH?

From all we have said above it is evident that any Catholic of sound mind is required to know certain particular articles of faith in addition to the axiom, "The Christian faith is true." Therefore, it might be asked what is the strongest reason for concluding that any believer, as for example Socrates, is required to know one particular article rather than another, for example that the Holy Spirit proceeds from the Father and the Son.

To this question it is answered that the strongest reason for this conclusion is that such an article or such a truth is held to be Catholic by all the believers and Catholics with whom Socrates lives. Furthermore, such a truth is promulgated and preached publicly and frequently by preachers of the Word of God. Finally, a truth should be believed because it can be clearly deduced by enlightened Catholics from another truth which has been promulgated as Catholic in the aforesaid manner.

Whence it follows that there are many Catholic truths which no Catholic is required to believe explicitly even though believers of straighter mind are required to give explicit assent if these truths have been sufficiently promulgated and taught among all Catholics and believers.

A possible objection to this is that it would follow that those who preach the Word of God or teach Catholic truths bind the faithful to assent explicitly to certain truths. This seems untenable because before the proclamation of such truths the faithful were not required to give explicit assent to them, while after the proclamation of these truths the faithful were required to give faithful and explicit assent to them.

To this objection it may be answered that the preachers of the Word of God and teachers of Catholic truths do not bind Christians to believe these articles explicitly. God himself binds them to believe these articles explicitly through the agency of those who proclaim and preach. The answer to this question is evident, and this completes the discussion of the content of truth.

SOURCES AND ACKNOWLEDGMENTS

1. J.-P. Migne, *Patrologia Latina*, vol. 2, cols. 18-26.

2. Liguori G. Müller, *The "De Haeresibus" of St. Augustine* (Washington, D. C.: The Catholic University of America Press, 1956), pp. 85-97. Reprinted with the permission of the author and publisher.

3. Blomfield Jackson, trans., *The Ecclesiastical History, Dialogues and Letters of Theodoret* (New York: The Christian Literature Company, 1892), P. 34.

4. Ibid., pp. 41-42

5. H. J. D. Denzinger, *Enchiridion Symbolorum*, 30th ed. (Freiburg im Breisgau: Herder, 1950), pp. 29-30.

6. Excerpts from Clyde Pharr, *The Theodosian Code and Novels and the Sirmondian Constitutions* (copyright 1952 by Clyde Pharr), pp. 440-57. Reprinted with the permission of Princeton University Press.

7. W. M. Lindsay, ed., *Isidori Hispalensis Episcopi Etymologiarum sive Originum Libri XX* (Oxford: Clarendon Press, 1911), 7:14-8:5.

8. Migne, *Patrologia Latina*, vol. 101, cols. 87, 92, 99, 102, 120. Translated for this volume by Burton Van Name Edwards of the University of Pennsylvania.

9. R. I. Moore, *The Birth of Popular Heresy* (New York: St. Martin Press, 1975; London: Edward Arnold, 1975), pp. 10-15. Reprinted by permission of St. Martin's Press, Inc.

10. John F. Benton, ed. and trans., *Self and Society in Medieval France* (New York: Harper and Row, 1970), pp. 212-14. Reprinted by permission of Harper and Row, Inc.

11. Walter Wakefield and A. P. Evans, *Heresies of the High Middle Ages* (New York: Columbia University Press, 1969), pp. 115-17. Reprinted with permission.

12. C. C. Mierow, *The Deeds of Frederick Barbarossa by Otto of Freising* (New York: Columbia University Press, 1953), pp. 61-63, 142-44. Reprinted with permission.

13. Peter Abelard, *The Historia Calamitatum*, translated by Henry Adams Bellows (St. Paul: T.A. Boyd, 1922), pp. 83-87.

14. Samuel J. Eales, trans., *The Life and Works of Saint Bernard*, vol. 2 (London: John Hodges, 1889), pp. 543-48

15. S. R. Maitland, *Facts and Documents Illustrative of the . . . Albigenses and Waldenses* (London: C. J. G. and F. Rivington, 1832), pp. 344-50.

16. Samuel J. Eales, trans., *The Life and Works of Saint Bernard*, vol. 4, pp. 393-98.

17. Victor N. Sharenkoff, *A Study of Manichaeism in Bulgaria* (New York: Victor N. Sharenkoff, 1927), pp. 66-78.

18. S. R. Maitland, *Facts and Documents*, pp. 140-45.

19. Franjo Sanjek, O.P., "Le rassemblement hérétique de Saint-Félix-de-Caraman (1167) et les églises cathares au XIIe siècle," *Revue d'histoire écclésiastique* 67 (1972): 772-79.

20. S. R. Maitland, *Facts and Documents*, pp. 392-96.

21. Ibid., pp. 418-30.

22. Jeffrey Burton Russell, *Religious Dissent in the Middle Ages* (New York: John Wiley & Sons, 1971), pp. 71-76. Reprinted with permission.

23. Margaret Deanesly, *The Lollard Bible and Other Medieval Biblical Versions* (Cambridge: Cambridge University Press, 1920), p. 26. Reprinted by permission of the Cambridge University Press.

24. Frederick Tupper and Marbury B. Ogle, trans., *Master Walter Map's Book de Nugiis Curialium*, London: Chatto and Windus, 1924), pp.76-79.

25. A. Dondaine, "Aux origines du valdéisme: Une profession de foi de Valdès," *Archivum Fratrum Praedicatorum* 16 (1946): 191-235, at 231-32.

26. Margaret Deanesly, *The Lollard Bible and Other Medieval Biblical Versions* (Cambridge: Cambridge University Press, 1920), p. 63. Reprinted by permission of the Cambridge University Press.

27. Alexander Patschovsky and Kurt-Victor Selge, *Quellen zur Geschichte der Waldenser*, Texte zur Kirchen-und Theologiegeschichte, Heft 18 (Gütersloh: Gütersloher Verlagshaus Gerd Mohn, 1973), pp. 70-103.

28. H. J. Schroeder, *Disciplinary Decrees of the General Councils* (St. Louis: B. Herder Book Co., 1937), pp. 234-35.

29. S. R. Maitland, *Facts and Documents*, pp. 176-80.

30. H. J. Schroeder, *Disciplinary Decrees of the General Councils*, pp. 237-39; 242-44; 259-60.

31. S. R. Maitland, *Facts and Documents*, pp. 188-89

32. Ibid., pp. 398-400.

33. *The Little Flowers of Saint Francis* (London, 1899), pp. 122-25.

34. *Summa Theologica*, translated by Fathers of the English Dominican Province (London: Thomas Baker, 1917), 2: 153-55.

35. Walter Wakefield and A. P. Evans, *Heresies of the High Middle Ages* (New York: Columbia University Press, 1969), pp. 222-26. Reprinted with permission.

36. Caesarius of Heisterbach, *The Dialogue on Miracles*, translated by H. von E. Scott and C. C. Swinton Bland (London: George Routledge and Sons, 1929), 1: pp. 341-42.

37. S. R. Maitland, *Facts and Documents*, pp. 192-94.

38. Ibid., pp. 201-2.

39. Ibid., pp. 202-5.

40. Walter L. Wakefield, *Heresy, Crusade and Inquisition in Southern France 1100-1250* (Berkeley and Los Angeles: University of California Press, 1974; London: George Allen & Unwin, 1974), pp. 250-57. Reprinted with permission.

41. James M. Powell, ed. and trans., *The Liber Augustalis* (Syracuse: Syracuse University Press, 1971), pp. 7-10. Reprinted with permission.

42. James Harvey Robinson, *The Pre-Reformation Period*, Translations and Reprints from the Original Sources of European History, vol. 3 (Philadelphia: University of Pennsylvania Press, 1902), pp. 14-15.

43. Ibid., pp. 15-17.

44. H. Gee and W. J. Hardy, *Documents Illustrative of English Church History* (London, 1896), no. xlii.

45. Lynn Thorndike, *University Records and Life in the Middle Ages* (New York: Columbia University Press, 1944), pp. 80-81. Reprinted with permission.

46. Lynn Thorndike, *University Records and Life in the Middle Ages* (New York: Columbia University Press, 1944), pp. 85-88. Reprinted with permission.

47 H. Denifle and A. Chatelain, eds., *Chartularium Universitatis Parisiensis*, 1: 543-58.

48. H.J.D. Denzinger, *The Sources of Catholic Dogma*, trans. Roy J. Deferrari (St. Louis, Mo.: B. Herder Book Company, 1965), pp. 194-95.

49. James Harvey Robinson, *The Pre-Reformation Period*, pp. 2-33.

50. St. Bonaventure, *Defense of the Mendicants*, vol. 4 of *The Works of St. Bonaventure*, translated by José de Vinck (Patterson, N. J.: The St. Anthony's Guild Press, 1966), pp. 126-29. Reprinted by permission of St. Anthony's Guild.

51. F. Ehrle, "Zur Vorgeschichte des Conzils von Vienne," *Archiv für Literatur- und Kirchengeschichte des Mittelalters* 3 (1887): 104-7.

52. H.J.D. Denzinger, *The Sources of Catholic Dogma*, trans., Roy J. Deferrari (St. Louis, Mo.: B. Herder Book Company, 1965), pp. 191-92.

53. H.J.D. Denzinger, *Enchiridion Symbolorum*, 30th ed. (Freiburg im Breisgau: Herder, 1950), pp. 225-26.

54. Reprinted from G. G. Coulton, *Life in the Middle Ages I & II* (Cambridge: Cambridge University Press, 1967), pp. 235-38, by permission of The Cambridge University Press.

55. Translation by Steven Sargent, of the University of Pennsylvania, from J. Duvernoy, *Le Régistre d'Inquisition de Jacques Fournier (Benoit XII), évêque de Pamiers (1318-1325)*, 3 vols. (Paris, 1965).

56. Robert Vaughan, ed., *Tracts and Treatises of John de Wycliffe* (London: The Wycliffe Society, 1845), pp. 195-98.

57. E. P. Cheney, ed., *England in the Time of Wycliffe*, Translations and Reprints from the Original Sources of European History, vol. 2, no. 5 (Philadelphia: University of Pennsylvania, 1895), pp. 11-12.

58. Ibid., pp. 13-14.

59. H. J. D. Denzinger, *The Sources of Catholic Dogma*, trans. Roy J. Deferrari (St. Louis, Mo.: B. Herder Book Company, 1965), pp. 208-11.

60. H. Gee and W. J. Hardy, *Documents Illustrative of English Church History* (London, 1896), no. xli.

61. From *Advocates of Reform: From Wyclif to Erasmus*, The Library of Christian Classics, Volume XIV, edited by Matthew Spinka. Published simultaneously in Great Britain and the United States by the S. C. M. Press, Ltd., London, and the Westminster Press, Philadelphia, 1953. Used by permission.

62. H. J. D. Denzinger, *The Sources of Catholic Dogma*, trans. Roy J. Deferrari (St. Louis, Mo.: B. Herder Book Company, 1957), pp. 212-15.

63. Matthew Spinka, ed. and trans., *John Hus at the Council of Constance* (New York: Columbia University Press, 1965), pp. 167-80, 224-34. Reprinted with permission.

64. Heiko Augustinus Oberman, *Forerunners of the Reformation* (New York: Holt, Rinehart and Winston, 1966), pp. 68-69, 76-77, 80-87, 89-90. Reprinted with permission.

THE MIDDLE AGES
A Series Edited by Edward Peters

Heresy and Authority in Medieval Europe
Edward Peters, Editor

Throughout the Middle Ages and early modern Europe theological uniform
synonymous with social cohesion in societies that regarded themselves as
together at their most fundamental levels by a religion. To maintain a be
in opposition to the orthodox religion was to set oneself in opposition not
to church and state but to a whole culture in all of its manifestations. In
perception of dissent and in the steps taken to deal with it lies the history of
val heresy and the force it exerted on religious, social, and political commu
long after the Middle Ages.

By offering a series of original source materials in translation, Edward Pe
makes available the most compact, economical, and wide-ranging reader av
in English.

Popes, Lawyers, and Infidels
James Muldoon

This is the first complete study of consideration given by Christian Euro
to the legal status of the non-Christians they conquered. The central figure
development of these ideas was Pope Innocent IV, whose mission to the T
of Central Asia in the 13th century was the first attempt by a pope to conta
leaders of non-Christian society. Popes and lawyers adopted his argumen
justify the imposition of Christianity upon alien cultures throughout the ne
years.

The Magician, the Witch, and the Law
Edward Peters

Drawing a distinction between medieval "magic" and early modern "witch
Edward Peters argues that, in spite of scholarship to the contrary, early me
magic was considered a practical science, requiring study and skill. But a
European society became more articulate and self-conscious, the old trad
of magic as a science became associated with heresy and sorcery. Therea
the Middle Ages knew no safe, learned magic that was not subject to crimin
tion, then the magician, like the later witch, was punished for these offe

UNIVERSITY OF PENNSYLVANIA PRESS
3933 Walnut Street
Philadelphia, Pennsylvania 19104

DATE DUE

	FEB 17 2011		
	MAY 02 2011		
JUN 03 2013			
SEP 30 2013			
FEB 16 2013			
FEB 14 2020			